THE CHAIR OF SAINT PETER

THE CHAIR OF SAINT PETER

A History of the Papacy

WILLIAM J. LA DUE, J.C.D.

ORBIS BOOKS

Maryknoll, New York 10545

The Catholic Foreign Mission Society of America (Maryknoll) recruits and trains people for overseas missionary service. Through Orbis Books, Maryknoll aims to foster the international dialogue that is essential to mission. The books published, however, reflect the opinions of their authors and are not meant to represent the official position of the society. To obtain more information about Maryknoll or Orbis Books, please visit our website at www.maryknoll.org.

Library of Congress Cataloging-in-Publication Data

La Due, William J.
    The chair of Saint Peter: a history of the Papacy / William J. La Due.
        p.cm.
    ISBN 1-57075-335-0 (pbk.)
        1. Papacy—History. I. Title.

BX955.2 .L35 2000
262'.13'09—dc21

00-038494

Contents

Introductory Note

~

As a lifelong observer and student of Catholic Church organization and polity, I feel called upon to sort out my thoughts, impressions, and experiences, as well as a great deal of reading on these subjects over the years. It was especially the extremely fertile period of the 1960s—with the preparations for the council and with Vatican II itself—which brought about in me, and in many others, an immense shift in thinking regarding the nature and the mission, as well as the structure, of the Church. Through the four years of the council my mind-set as a canon lawyer took a whole new direction. The Church as a communion of many local churches became the primary point of reference, rather than the various organs of ecclesiastical government, Roman and local, and their respective functions and prerogatives. There was considerable hope that, as a result of the council, the Church would be able to reemphasize the significance of the local ecclesial communities, and to implement at as many levels as possible the newly resurrected principles of collegiality, regionalism, and subsidiarity. Priests' councils, parish and diocesan councils were established and have attained, in a good number of dioceses, a level of viability. However, the desired goal of expanded regional and collegial government throughout the Church has yet to be effectively realized.

As we experience the waning of the spirit and direction of Vatican II (1962-65) and anticipate the onset of the third millennium, many people— Catholics and non-Catholics, clergy, religious, and laity—are intrigued by what will come next. Will the tone of the papacy of John Paul II continue into the succeeding pontificate(s) or will the collegial, more dialogical spirit of the Vatican II years return? In my study of the papal office, I have tried to cut a swath between the biographical dictionaries of the popes which have been recently published on the one hand, and the more specialized studies of one pontificate or specific period of papal history on the other. My aim has been to begin with the reliable findings of current New Testament scholarship concerning the shape of the Christian churches in the first and early second centuries, and to trace what can be said with some assurance about the configuration of the church in Rome. The most authoritative research indicates that, unlike certain other sees such as Antioch in Syria, the Roman see did not possess a monarchical bishop until the mid-second century. Until that time the church in the capital of the empire was governed by a college of presbyters or presbyter-bishops. The next several centuries witnessed the gradual positioning of the papacy within the Roman and, later, the Byzantine Empire. Then, in the eighth century, we observe the popes' movement away from Byzantium and their concentration on the West. After 1100, we see a growing centralization of ecclesiastical government in the papal curia, and after 1250 or so, the excesses of papal centralization in terms of exorbitant taxation policies and an expanding papal monopoly on ecclesiastical appointments everywhere. Although the Council of Trent (1545-63) brought about a restoration of the power of local bishops in their respective dioceses, it also precipitated a remarkable augmentation of papal authority throughout the Church in the West. In the nineteenth and twentieth centuries we note the rise of what could be called papal absolutism, wherein the pope has become in many respects the single controlling authority within the Church.

This work attempts to follow the development of the papal office from the mid-second century up to the present time. It is clear that no one—even through the labor of a lifetime—can address this task exclusively through the use of primary sources. In fashioning this study, every effort has been made to bring the readers into direct contact with the most respected authors in the fields of ecclesiastical and papal history who are well received both within and outside the Catholic Church. My employment of original sources (e.g., works of the fathers of the Church and the acts of the ecumenical councils) has been deliberately limited to English versions which are available to readers who do not have the time or the opportunity to access the Greek and Latin texts.

Since the papal office is one of the more important functions in the development of Christian culture, it does not need a heated defense, nor does it deserve a negative polemic. My objective has been to trace the considerable evolution of the role, for better or for worse, throughout these intervening centuries. I am hopeful that this approach will counter the rather widely held, if not prevailing notion that the papacy has more or less always been what it has shown itself to be since the reign of Pius IX (1846-78). Inasmuch as this is clearly not the case, a broader view of the development of the papacy is highly desirable to serve as a more adequate foundation from which to look to the future.

CHAPTER 1

The Models of Church
in the New Testament

To trace the evolution of the papal office, one must go back to the first century A.D., to the very roots of the Christian experience. One must return to the origins of the Jesus movement which evolved out of the interaction of three forces. The primary force and the originator was, of course, Jesus of Nazareth, who provided the impetus through his engaging presence, his preaching, and his healing. The disciples, the second force, imitated their leader, proclaiming his good news of salvation and curing the sick as he had empowered them to do. And finally there were the enclaves of sympathizers or converts who remained behind in their native villages after he and his itinerant disciples had moved on.[1] These local people served as the base for the continuing operations of the evangelizers as they proceeded farther and farther into the hinterland. "After John had been arrested, Jesus came to Galilee proclaiming the gospel of God: 'This is the time of fulfillment. The Kingdom of God is at hand. Repent, and believe in the gospel' " (Mk 1:14-15). And, "He [Jesus] went around to the villages in the vicinity [of Nazareth] teaching" (Mk 6:6).

These rather plain verses introduce the public ministry of Jesus whose proclamation was almost always accompanied by healing. It was in this early period that he selected his disciples whom "he sent out to proclaim the kingdom of God and to heal the sick" (Lk 9:2). "He instructed them to take nothing for the journey but a walking stick—no food, no sack, no money in their belts. They were to wear sandals but not a second tunic" (Mk 6:8-9). The Twelve—and even the seventy-two in Luke—were instructed: "Whatever house you enter, stay there and leave from there. And as for those who do not welcome you, when you leave that town, shake the dust from your feet in testimony against them" (Lk 9:4-5). And then, "They set out and went from village to village proclaiming the good news and curing diseases everywhere" (Lk 9:6).

The saving, healing message of Jesus and his disciples penetrated into the villages and the countryside of Galilee and beyond. They stayed away, at least for the time that Jesus was with them, from the Hellenistic cities like Caesarea, Ptolemais, Tyre, and Sidon. He and they were not especially comfortable even

1

in Jerusalem, which was very conservative and closed to new ideas. For all intents and purposes, it lived off the temple, which had been in the process of a very elaborate reconstruction since about 20 B.C. Jerusalem was literally filled with construction workers and tradesmen, scribes, priests, students of the law, various and sundry temple employees, and merchants of every sort. The residents were very much committed to the status quo—perhaps like civil service employees anywhere.[2] They were not amenable to change of the dramatic variety advocated by the Zealots or even by the Jesus movement.

The country folk, on the other hand, were much more open to new ideas and to change. They were victims of all kinds of economic and social pressures—infertile land, frequently disappointing crop yields, heavy taxation by Rome and by the temple authorities, absentee landlords, and so forth. Jesus and his colleagues made more headway, therefore, in the country and in the villages. As they moved from place to place, they left followers, loyal friends in many of the hamlets where they labored. These people supported them, took care of them, providing them with food, comfort, and lodging which served as a base for their evangelizing activities. After the death and Resurrection of Jesus, this pattern of spreading the gospel naturally underwent significant changes. According to the Lucan account (Acts 1:4-5), the apostles and a group of faithful followers gathered in Jerusalem to await their baptism with the Holy Spirit which transformed them into men and women of exceptional courage and boldness. The original Jerusalem congregation was focused around the apostles as Acts relates:

> They devoted themselves to the teaching of the apostles, and to the communal life, to the breaking of the bread and to the prayers . . . many signs and wonders were done through the apostles . . . Every day they devoted themselves to meeting together in the temple area and to breaking bread in their homes . . . And every day the Lord added to their number those who were being saved. (Acts 2:42-47)

> With great power the apostles bore witness to the resurrection of the Lord Jesus, and great favor was accorded to them all. (Acts 4:33)

After the martyrdom of Stephen (Acts 7:54-60), a sizeable persecution broke out in Jerusalem, directed most probably against the Jewish Christians whose mother tongue was Greek. Stephen's speech had enraged the Sanhedrin and many of the conservative Jerusalem Jews inasmuch as he condemned them and their ancestors for paying little attention to the words of Moses and the prophets, and for exalting beyond due measure the importance of the temple and temple worship. The Christians who fled from Jerusalem scattered throughout the countryside of Judea and Samaria and engaged themselves in the preaching of the word (Acts 8:11-15). Philip, one of the Greek-speaking disciples who fled from Jerusalem, is described as traveling from Jerusalem to the city of Samaria (Sebaste) in Acts 8:5, and then later to Azotus west of Jerusalem. "Philip came to Azotus and went about proclaiming the good news to all the towns until he reached Caesarea" (Acts 8:40).

At the time of Paul's conversion (33-36 A.D.), the city of Damascus already had Christian disciples who welcomed him. "He stayed some days with the disciples in Damascus, and began at once to proclaim Jesus in the synagogues, that he is the Son of God" (Acts 9:19-20).

We encounter Peter in Chapter 9 of Acts moving about as a missionary. "As Peter was passing through every region, he went down to the holy ones living at Lydda" (Acts 9:32). Then at the invitation of some disciples, he made his way to Joppa (Jaffa), about forty miles northwest of Jerusalem on the Mediterranean. "And he stayed a long time in Joppa with Simon, a tanner" (Acts 9:43).

At the behest of a certain Cornelius, Peter journeyed to Caesarea, a Hellenistic city which served as the headquarters of the Roman procurators. There he baptized the gentile centurion, Cornelius, and his family after they had received the Holy Spirit (Acts 10:44-48). Peter then returned to Jerusalem to explain to the apostles and the followers what had happened and what he had done. "When they heard this, they stopped objecting and glorified God saying, 'God has then granted life-giving repentance to the gentiles too' " (Acts 11:18).

At the time of the persecution instigated by King Herod Agrippa (41-44 A.D.), probably toward the end of his reign, Peter was imprisoned and in all likelihood would have suffered the same end as James, the son of Zebedee (Acts 12:2). However, he miraculously escaped and shortly thereafter we read that "he left and went to another place" (Acts 12:17). Peter reappears at the time of the Council of Jerusalem (ca. 49 A.D.), acting as the principal spokesman for the apostles and the elders regarding the issue of circumcision for gentile converts. After the council, Peter disappears from the scene in Acts, surfacing a while later in Antioch (Gal 2:11), where a rather bitter dispute arises between him and Paul over Peter's refusal to eat with gentile Christians in the presence of James' people from Jerusalem. Concerning that confrontation, Paul later commented, "I opposed him to his face because he clearly was wrong" (Gal 2:11). Peter apparently remained in Antioch for some time, because he left a very deep and lasting impression upon the traditions of the church there. After this, there is little direct and undisputed information concerning the personal missionary endeavors of Simon Peter.

When last observed, Paul was preaching with great enthusiasm in Damascus. "After a long time had passed, the Jews conspired to kill him" (Acts 9:23). He quickly left Damascus, making his way to Jerusalem where Barnabas took him under his wing, introducing him to the apostles who accepted him as one of their own. "He [Paul] moved freely about Jerusalem, and spoke out boldly in the name of the Lord" (Acts 9:28). Encountering problems with conservative Jews who conspired to kill him—as they had killed Stephen—the disciples took him to Caesarea and dispatched him off to Tarsus (Acts 9:30).

The dispersion of the Jerusalem Christians after the martyrdom of Stephen resulted in the development of Christian enclaves as far away as Phoenicia, Cyprus, Antioch, Damascus, and perhaps Cyrenaica in northern Africa. At first the Christians at Antioch evangelized only Jews, but a change in policy took place through the efforts of several gentile converts from Cyprus and Cyrene. This change prompted the church in Jerusalem to dispatch Barnabas to Antioch to survey the situation. What Barnabas witnessed pleased him very much.

> He then went to Tarsus to look for Saul, and when he found him, he brought him to Antioch. For a whole year they met with the church and taught a large number of people, and it was at Antioch that the disciples were first called Christians. (Acts 11:25-26)

Shortly after the sharp encounter with Peter at Antioch, Paul must have departed on his second missionary journey. This effort must have taken him two or three years, because he seems to have traversed Asia Minor through the Roman provinces of Galatia and Asia (central and western Asia Minor), crossing over the Aegean Sea into the province of Macedonia and then southward to the province of Achaia. Paul's mission took him westward along the so-called "common route" from Antioch in Syria to the west coast of Asia Minor. In Macedonia he apparently made his way along the Via Egnatia, the major route between Greece and Rome.[3]

THE PAULINE MODEL

Paul's strategy, and the manner in which he set up his churches, differed from the missionary excursions of the disciples of Jesus' time, and even the missionary activity of Jesus himself. Paul made his way to the cities, especially those along the principal trade routes, such as Colossae, Laodicea, Philippi, Thessolonica, and Corinth. Although he normally traveled with a group of companions, their names and faces would change from time to time. Wayne Meeks points to a difference in the description of Paul's tactics between the narratives in Acts and in the Pauline letters. According to Acts, the apostle usually preferred public places for his preaching, such as the Areopagus in Athens. The letters, however, indicate a somewhat diverse approach.

> From the letters, although they by no means contradict all aspects of the Acts picture, we receive on the whole the impression of a less grand and

public mission, of communication more along the natural networks of relationship in each city and between cities. The families and houses of certain individuals seem to have been important.[4]

Also according to Acts, Paul and his retinue are described as going first to the synagogue or synagogues in the city they were visiting, while in the letters, Meeks attests to a different methodology.

Unfortunately we cannot simply accept the Acts picture of the mission as a direct, factual account. The pattern of always beginning in the synagogues accords ill with Paul's own declarations that he saw his mission as primarily or even exclusively to the gentiles . . . his policy seems to have been different from the way it is described in Acts.[5]

Paul's contacts as he moved from place to place were probably somewhat informal—relying for introductions on people he knew who had friends or relatives in the city to be visited. Also, his trade opened doors into the associations of tentmakers in various cities. These initial contacts could provide a place, i.e., a reasonably large private home or hall of some sort, for bringing interested people together. These groupings—of one or two dozen people who became converts—constituted the churches in the various locations. Larger cities, like Ephesus, could have several such churches. Rome—with a population in the first century A.D. of more than 500,000—and Antioch in Syria—the third largest city in the Empire next to Alexandria—could very well have had a dozen or more.[6]

   Stephanas of Corinth (I Cor 1:16); Priscilla and her husband, Aquila (Acts 18:1-3), who resided in Rome and later in Corinth and Ephesus; Gaius who seemingly lived in Corinth (Rom 16:23); and Philemon (Philem 1, 2) of Colossae are a few examples of converts to Christianity whose homes were used as meeting places for the new churches. As he traveled, Paul would maintain contact with these congregations—teaching, exhorting, encouraging, correcting, settling disputes—through his letters and through emissaries that he would dispatch from his retinue.

   This rather brief description of Paul's methods and missionary style can serve as a background for a discussion of the organizational structure that prevailed in the churches reflected in his undisputed letters, i.e., I Thessalonians, I and II Corinthians, Galatians, Romans, Philemon, and Philippians. The other organizational paradigms we shall examine from the New Testament are gleaned from Luke-Acts, Matthew, John, and the Pastorals. We will highlight points of similarity and difference among the five ecclesial models to the extent that this can be accomplished without twisting or distorting the evidence available. It is indeed surprising to discover the structural divergence as well as the differences in organizational emphasis from model to model within the major churches reflected in the New Testament. There are additional New Testament models, but these five are the most well documented and significant of the paradigms of church organization that surface in the canonical books of the New Testament.

A reading of the seven undisputed letters indicated above provides ample evidence that Paul is the one true authority figure in those communities. His influence is invariably respectful of the freedom and integrity of each congregation. Other than an occasional intervention, it is primarily the Holy Spirit who provides direction through the conferral of charisms on the individual members. These charisms (or gifts for the edification of the churches) were expected to furnish the groups with all the resources for their growing, developing communal life, except for outside assistance at certain times from Paul or one of his retinue. The administration of the communities was probably left in most cases to the hosts providing the house churches for the meetings and the worship of each group. There were, of course, prophets and teachers in the communities, but these were presumably provided by the Spirit, and the roles were not necessarily lifetime functions; the Spirit would confer the gifts as needed. In Corinth, there did not seem to be any fixed offices. The letter to the Romans makes no explicit mention of the church leaders there, nor does Galatians. Philippians—probably Paul's last letter—speaks in the introduction (Phil 1:1) of overseers and ministers (i.e., bishops and deacons), but these terms are more often interpreted today in this context as indefinite descriptions of functions of service to the congregations rather than as proper titles for specific offices.

One can explain this absence of offices and a legal system in Paul's churches to some extent because of his expectation of the imminent parousia, but this is very likely not the full explanation. The apostle's instinctive impulse was to respect the freedom and the charismatic gifts of the brothers and sisters; further, he was profoundly and unswervingly convinced that the Spirit would provide all that was needed. Paul's interference was to be exceptional and by no means continuous. That was the Spirit's role. It was the Spirit who was to provide the prophets (the voices of new revelation?), the teachers (those who would explain the Old Law and the Law of Christ?), and all the other gifts needed by the churches to make them grow and prosper. It was by no means a "top down" organizational concept that inspired Paul, but a "grassroots upward" notion that he refused to compromise. He, of course, was not unaware of the need to intervene when things became seriously unraveled, as was the case in I Corinthians 5:1-5 regarding the man living with his stepmother. The apostle ordered the congregation to expel the individual, but they were the ones who had to arrange for and effect the expulsion.

The heads of the various house churches appear to come closest to what could be termed "officials." However, they did not seem to have governing power over the group, and were apparently chosen because they had the resources to provide for meeting facilities and housing for visiting guests. Paul encouraged the brothers and sisters to pay proper respect to those "who are laboring among you and who are over you in the Lord and who admonish you" (I Thess 5:12). This is not generally understood to imply offices as such, but simply a diversity of (intermittent?) charismatic service functions within the church. Even the members of Paul's itinerant retinue—although they seem to share some of the apostle's authority—do not appear to have offices as such.

The Pauline paradigm reveals itself as a loosely structured, Spirit centered, grass-roots series of churches in which every believer was especially empowered to perform certain indispensable services needed by the others. The striking image of the body and the necessary coordination of all its parts (I Corinthians 12) reveal the very essence of the Pauline paradigm of church:

> There are different kinds of spiritual gifts but the same Spirit; there are different forms of service but the same Lord; there are different workings but the same God who produces all of them in everyone. To each individual the manifestation of the Spirit is given for some benefit . . . But one and the same Spirit produces all of these, distributing them individually to each person as he wishes. (I Cor 12:4-7, 11)

THE MODEL IN LUKE–ACTS

Whereas the seven undisputed letters of Paul were written between ca. 50 A.D. and his martyrdom in Rome in the 60s, the author of Luke-Acts—the source of the second New Testament church model—remains something of a mystery. He was certainly a gentile Christian, and it is commonly held that he wrote both the gospel and the Acts. That he was a gentile and was writing for gentile Christians are confirmed by the fact that he manifested no knowledge of the geography of Palestine, generally avoided semitic expressions, and omitted the traditions concerning Jesus' struggle against the pharisaic understanding of the law. It is not certain that Luke was the beloved physician mentioned in Philemon (24), Colossians (4:14), and II Timothy (4:11). The gospel's date of composition is commonly put between 70 and 90 A.D. Acts was written somewhat later—perhaps between 80 and 90 A.D.—although some scholars assign its composition to the last decade of the first century A.D. It is curious that although Luke esteemed Paul very highly, concentrating the second half of Acts on the apostle's endeavors, he does not reveal any knowledge of Paul's letters, which were probably collected toward the end of the first century. Luke, however, was certainly acquainted with one or several of Paul's churches, which explains his knowledge of Paul's travels, some of the apostle's materials, and his boundless appreciation for Paul's missionary efforts.

In the gospel, Luke frequently distinguishes between the twelve apostles and the disciples. In fact, he is the only one who describes the mission of the Twelve (9:1-6) and the mission of the seventy-two (10:1-12). The latter pericope may reflect the evangelizing experience of some of the churches of his own day. The terms "apostle" and "disciple" are not mutually exclusive in the gospel. Apostle rather consistently refers to the Twelve, but disciple is on occasion employed to identify them as well (22:11, 14). In the narrative relating Peter's confession of faith in Jesus as the Messiah (9:18-21), there is no special recognition of Peter, nor any reference to the conferral of the power of the keys, nor to any prerogative of binding and loosing. Few clues are given in the gospel as to the way in which the communities of believers were organized after the Resurrection, or how authority was exercised. The story line in the Lukan account moves from Galilee and Samaria to Jerusalem by means of an extensive travel narrative (9:51-19:28). All of the Resurrection appearances, including the Ascension, are located in the environs of Jerusalem. Acts then picks up the story in Jerusalem and moves it forward into Judea, Samaria, and eventually on to Rome. The term apostle in Acts has a very strict connotation. With but one exception (14:4)—where Paul and Barnabas are called apostles at Iconium in Asia Minor—the word refers exclusively to the Twelve who symbolize the New Israel. One of the first tasks the eleven undertook was the replacement of Judas. They were convinced that another had to be chosen to take his "office." The two essential qualifications were set by Peter:

> It is necessary that one of the men who accompanied us the whole time the Lord Jesus came and went among us, beginning from the baptism of John until the day on which he was taken up from us, become with us a witness to his resurrection. (Acts 1:21-22)

The twelfth place had to be filled by someone with that background. Out of the two proposed, Matthias was chosen by lot, which was their way of having the Holy Spirit decide.

The Jerusalem community of disciples was in the hands of the Twelve, whose main responsibility was preaching, giving witness to the Resurrection, prayer, and the healing of the sick. The duties of charitable administration were given over to seven reputable men who were selected by the body of disciples. These were presented to the apostles, "who prayed and laid hands upon them" (Acts 6:6). Although there is reference in Acts to the presence of presbyters or elders in Antioch early on (11:30), the first reference to that role in Jerusalem was on the occasion of the so-called Council of Jerusalem when Paul and Barnabas went to the Holy City to settle the question of the need for circumcision for gentile converts. They went up to deliberate with "the apostles and elders" regarding this issue (Acts 15:2). After the council (ca. 49 A.D.), the apostles disappear from the Jerusalem scene and the governance of the congregation is in the hands of James, the brother of the Lord, and the elders. The institution of elders no doubt originated in the predominantly Jewish Christian churches. For the Jews, elders were the professional guardians of the law. The role was probably taken over by Jewish Christians and adapted to their special needs.

> [The order of elders] . . . was adopted as something customary, something natural and by no means alien to the new community. The elders represented tradition, and were at the same time the natural leaders and the exponents of the idea of order in general . . . they now passed over into Judeo-Christianity.[7]

The institution of elders spread rapidly throughout the young Christian churches, although that institution apparently did not take hold in Paul's communities during his lifetime. Luke, however, assumes that presbyters were a part of the organizational fabric of all the churches. In Acts, he most likely overstates the case when he relates that Paul—even on his first missionary journey (i.e., prior to ca. 49 A.D.)—was in the habit of selecting elders in each of the churches he founded. "They [Paul and Barnabas] appointed presbyters for them in each church and, with prayer and fasting, commended them to the Lord in whom they had put their faith" (Acts 14:23).

The Lukan paradigm of church, especially in Acts, is quite different from Paul's. Luke takes pains to impose a sort of uniform pattern on all the churches about which he writes. He evidently gave Paul's congregations a presbyterial structure which they seemingly did not have, because he assumed that this was the way all the churches had been organized. Although in the Jerusalem community, James apparently possessed some authority over the presbyters, perhaps by virtue of his having been a brother of the Lord, the other circles of elders in the churches of Acts appear to be collegial bodies without a clearly designated monarchical leader. Paul's farewell speech at Miletus, addressed to the elders of Ephesus, reflects this collegial arrangement as Luke understood it (Acts 20:28-32). After the passing of the Twelve (60-70 A.D.?), the office of apostle ceases, leaving the elders as custodians of the apostolic witness and teaching. According to the available evidence, these leaders appear as the authoritative ruling body, with teaching and shepherding responsibilities within the congregations. As with the Pauline model, it does not seem that there are any persons permanently set aside to perform sacramental–liturgical functions. Apparently the liturgists in the communities described by Luke were selected as needed, either through the charismatic appointment of the Spirit or by the elders.

THE MATTHEAN MODEL

The third paradigm of church organization to be considered is that found in the gospel of Matthew, which has been traditionally called the gospel of the Church. The actual author of the work was most probably not the apostle Matthew, the customs officer (Mt 9:9-10) who was called Levi, the son of Alphaeus, in Mark (2:14), because the majority of scholars place the writing of this gospel within the time frame of 80-90 A.D., after the Twelve's passing. The author was most probably a Jewish Christian of the second generation who had received training as a rabbi and was a member of the congregation at Antioch. According to John Meier, "Matthew's gospel comes out of a lengthy Jewish Christian scribal tradition in Matthew's church."[8] The city of Antioch must have had a population of at least 100,000, perhaps much more, in the first century A.D., with Jews constituting no less than ten to fifteen percent of the total. There is strong evidence that the Christian church(es) at Antioch had broken all ties with the synagogue(s) by the time of the writing of the gospel (e.g., Mt 10:17; 13:54; 23:34). As a matter of fact, the synagogue was by this time considered by the Christians an alien and unfriendly institution.

One of the most frequently recurring themes in the first gospel is that of the kingdom. There are countless examples of what Jack Dean Kingsbury calls "kingdom language" in Matthew:

> In terms of Matthew's "kingdom language," it may be said of the church that here are the "sons of the kingdom" (5:45), to whom God has "given the kingdom" (21:43), who in Jesus Son of God share the "forgiveness" of the kingdom (26:28) and hear and understand "the word of the kingdom" (13:19), and who have been "instructed about the kingdom" (13:52) and hence know the "secrets of the kingdom" (13:11) . . . and have been entrusted with the "keys of the kingdom" (16:19), who pray fervently for the "coming of the kingdom" (6:10) . . . and who at the consummation of the age will "enter the kingdom" . . . (25:21, 23).[9]

The kingdom of God is not the Church, but the Church opens out to it. The kingdom is made up of the elect, while the Church has to deal with sin and division, hatred and lukewarmness. However, this constant, repeated interplay between the "now" and the "not yet," the state of the wayfarers and of the elect, places the gospel into an ecclesiastical milieu which constitutes one of its dominant themes.

A dramatic development can be seen in the evolution of the missionary thrust of the gospel, from 10:5-6 to 28:19. "Do not go into pagan territory or enter a Samaritan town. Go rather to the lost sheep of the house of Israel" (10:5-6). Go therefore and make disciples of all nations . . . teaching them to observe all that I have commanded you" (28:19-20).

The relational context as the gospel develops is unambiguously one of sons and daughters of God the Father, who have but one master, the Messiah.

> As for you, do not be called "Rabbi." You have but one teacher and you are all brothers. Call no one on earth your father; you have but one Father in heaven. Do not be called "Master"; you have but one master, the Messiah. The greatest among you must be your servant. Whoever exalts himself will be humbled; but whoever humbles himself will be exalted. (Mt 23:8-12)

The authority patterns within the congregation were very informal and familial, with the entire community responsible for ultimate decisions in terms of discipline. No local administration is referred to clearly (18:15-18). There were prophets (7:15-20) in the community (perhaps itinerant) and teachers or scribes who were experts in the interpretation of the law (23:6-12). The power to bind and loose of Matthew 16 (the right to declare licit or illicit?) and of Matthew 18 (the power to admit or to exclude?) did not seem to weigh heavily on anyone in Matthew's congregation, which in his day was without a monarchical head or even a discernible circle of elders or presbyters. However, it is possible that some type of shepherding function was present which might have been in the hands of the prophets and/or the teachers. The promises to Peter in Matthew 16 did not seem to serve as the ground for an authoritative leadership position for him either in Antioch or in Rome. There is no evidence of his having anything approaching monarchical authority in either church, although his role in Antioch might have been crucial in bringing the Jewish and gentile Christians together. He (or the tradition he left behind) may well have served a similar function in Rome.

The Matthean paradigm of ecclesiastical organization is structured "low to the ground," having an obviously familial tone. Honors, exalted titles, and appearances of domination are clearly out of the question. All believers are disciples, brothers and sisters in the Lord, sons and daughters of the Father in heaven. All are expected to work as members of the Father's family for the coming of the kingdom, which will ultimately embrace gentiles as well as Jews.

THE JOHANNINE MODEL

The fourth model of ecclesial organization in the New Testament to be considered is the church in John, including the gospel and the letters. Apparently the Beloved Disciple, who is the true hero of the Johannine writings, was an eye-witness to the key events in the life, death, and Resurrection of Jesus, but was not John, the son of Zebedee.[10] This Beloved Disciple was the source of the tradition behind the gospel, but was seemingly not the evangelist who composed the work ca. 90 A.D. Within the next five to ten years after that, a redactor modified the original gospel—possibly adding the prologue and the final chapter (21). According to this thesis of Raymond Brown, the three letters were written around 100 A.D. by someone in the Johannine circle identified as the presbyter, who was neither the evangelist nor the redactor of the gospel. Brown hypothesizes:

> It is for this group that I reserve the term "Johannine School" within the wide Johannine community. In particular I use it for those who felt so close to the Beloved Disciple that they sought to pass on his tradition through written interpretation. These include the evangelist, the redactor of the gospel (and any other writers involved in it), the author of the epistles and the tradition bearers with whom they associated themselves in their writing.[11]

There are two levels of history reflected in the gospel, i.e., the experience of Jesus and his disciples during his earthly sojourn, and the experience of the Johannine community prior to ca. 90 A.D. One of the constants throughout the first century was the persecution by the Jews—directed initially against Jesus and later against the community of the Beloved Disciple. This explains to a great extent the opposition to and dislike of the Jews reflected in the fourth gospel.

Brown alleges that one of the causes for the strong opposition of the synagogue to the Johannine Christians was the "high Christology" the community adopted rather early on.[12] As long as their belief in Jesus kept him somewhat subordinated to God the Father, there was no violent opposition from the synagogue. But as soon as their Christology developed themes suggesting Jesus' equality and oneness with the Father, violent opposition was forthcoming from the Jews (e.g., 5:17-18). It is conceivable that this high Christology (oneness with the Father, preexistence) which was not particularly common in the other Christian communities of the second and third generation, kept the Johannine church rather isolated, even from their fellow Christians in the other apostolic congregations. According to Brown, the community of the Beloved Disciple, after ca. 100 A.D., broke up, with the "secessionists" eventually spiralling off into docetism and gnosticism, while the "adherents" were eventually assimilated—along with their high Christology—into the Catholic Church of the second century.[13]

Opposition from the Jews and the lack of initial rapport with the other Christian groups precipitated something of a siege mentality within the community. This is evident in the negative reactions against the Jews (especially chapters 5-12) and also against the world (chapters 14-17) in the gospel, which also reveals a rather unstructured ecclesiology. John does not articulate any mandate to baptize, and in the story of the multiplication of the loaves (6:1-15) and the bread of life discourse (6:35-58), there is no reference to the allocating of responsibility for eucharistic ministry.[14] John does not even employ the term apostle. For him, discipleship is the controlling notion and, of course, the Beloved Disciple is the exemplar par excellence of intimacy with Christ. There is throughout the Johannine corpus an atmosphere of equality and fraternity among the disciples and believers which seems even to go beyond the relational climate of Matthew. In III John, there is a much discussed passage which seems to insinuate the beginnings of some kind of hierarchical organization, i.e., local house churches administered by a resident authority (Diotrephes) and the presence of the presbyter with a type of guardianship over a number of these communities. The information is apparently too sketchy to draw any firm conclusions regarding the role of Diotrephes, Gaius, the addressee of the letter, or the writer of the letter, the presbyter.

> The Presbyter to the beloved Gaius whom I love in truth . . . I wrote to the church, but Diotrephes, who loves to dominate, does not acknowledge us. Therefore if I come, I will draw attention to what he is doing, spreading evil nonsense about us, and not content with that, he will not receive the brothers, hindering those who wish to do so and expelling them from the church. (III Jn 1, 9-10)

Is this a reference to some sort of monarchical overseeing in the Johannine house churches? Does the presbyter exercise a type of overarching control over a number of these communities? There is really not much in the way of convincing evidence for either position. Apart from this piece of information from III John, little is known of the organizational fabric of the Johannine community. The Holy Spirit, however, played a dominant part:

> If you love me, you will keep my commandments. And I will ask the Father, and He will send you another Advocate to be with you always, the Spirit of truth, which the world cannot accept, because it neither sees nor knows it. But you know it because it remains with you, and will be in you. I will not leave you orphans. (Jn 14:15-18)

It was a Paraclete-centered church with little trace of offices or organizational structures (apart from III John). Actually, the truly critical issue remains the relationship of the individual believer, the disciple, to Jesus through the Spirit.

There is in the gospel a fascinating treatment of Peter, who is introduced to Jesus at the outset of his public life by Andrew, Peter's brother:

> Andrew, the brother of Simon Peter, was one of the two who heard John and followed Jesus. He first found his brother Simon and told him, "We

have found the Messiah" (which is translated Anointed). Then he brought
him to Jesus. Jesus looked at him and said, "You are Simon the son of John;
you will be called Kephas" (which is translated Peter). (Jn 1:40-42)

The relationship between Peter and the Beloved Disciple—in the estimate of
the Johannine community—is articulated in chapter 21 of the fourth gospel.
Although Peter, after his threefold confession of love for Jesus, is directed to
feed the lambs and the sheep, the role of the Beloved Disciple is given a place
of preeminence because of his unequaled love for the Master. This dramatically reveals the privileged position of the Beloved Disciple in the tradition of
the Johannine community.[15]

THE CHURCH IN THE PASTORALS

The fifth organizational model to be discussed is found in the Pastorals: I
and II Timothy and Titus. Since the nineteenth century the question of the
authorship of these letters has been debated. Are they the work of the apostle
Paul, or were they composed at a later date? The majority of biblicists currently hold the second position; i.e., that these three works were written after
Paul's death by one individual who was in the Pauline tradition and a strong
representative of his legacy, but little else is known about him. The dating of
the epistles varies widely as a result of the disputed question of authorship. If
one believes Paul is the author, they would most likely have been composed
toward the end of his life (ca. 65-66 A.D.). The greater probability, however, is
that they are pseudonymous, and can be situated anywhere from 80 A.D. to 125
A.D. A fair assumption would place the time of composition around the turn of
the first century A.D. They seem to have been directed to churches in Crete
(Titus) and the environs of Ephesus (I and II Timothy).

There are a number of differences between the Pastorals and the authentic
Pauline letters. For example, in the Pastorals there is no effort in the direction
of the development of the deposit of faith. One has the distinct impression
that doctrine has by this time been set in fixed formulas and handed down as
such. The period of evolving themes—observable in Galatians, Romans, and I
and II Corinthians—was past. The false teaching of the judaizing gnostics was
countered with the "correct teaching" that has been handed down and preserved. The admonition to hold fast to the teaching that has been handed
down is repeated again and again. We witness the distinction between the
teaching church (*ecclesia docens*) and the receiving church (*ecclesia discens*). This
is the type of climate that frowns on innovative notions and new, creative formulations of teachings. The second difference has to do with the expectation
of the parousia—which in Paul's authentic letters was considered imminent.
However, in the Pastorals the situation is quite different. The congregations

were making adjustments in anticipation of a long sojourn in the world. Other than the passage in II Timothy (3:1-9), one has the impression that Christians were reconciled to a normal life span in the world, and to the resolution of their problems and challenges over an extended period of time.

There is, in the judgment of the majority of biblical scholars, a considerable difference in regard to issues of church order between the authentic Pauline letters and the Pastorals. In I Timothy there is a discussion of the qualities desirable in the bishop (3:1-7) and in deacons (3:8-10). And later on, the author lays out a number of cautions regarding presbyters: "Presbyters who preside well deserve double honor, and especially those who toil in preaching and teaching" (5:17).

They should be compensated properly and the community should not precipitously give credence to accusations against them unless supported by trustworthy witnesses. It is not at all clear whether the bishop and the presbyters referred to here are indeed distinct offices. The fact that the bishop is spoken of in the singular, whereas the presbyters are addressed in the plural, does not seem to settle the issue. In Titus, it is, as a matter of fact, more generally agreed that the terms bishop and presbyter are interchangeable:

> For this reason I left you in Crete so that you may set right what remains to be done and appoint presbyters in every town, as I directed you, on condition that a man be blameless, married only once, with believing children who are not accused of licentiousness or rebellious. For a bishop as God's steward must be blameless, not arrogant, not irritable . . . holding fast to the true message as taught so that he will be able both to exhort with sound doctrine and to refute opponents. (Titus 1:5-9)

In the Pastorals there seems to be a merging of various traditions involving bishops and deacons on the one hand, and presbyters on the other. The virtues required of the candidates for the offices are really not charismatic qualities, but natural ones—those expected of a good husband and head of a household. Apparently ordination was required for some of the officeholders, as the admonition to Timothy reveals: "Do not neglect the gift you have, which was conferred upon you through the prophetic word and with the imposition of the hands of the presbyterate" (I Tim 4:14).

There is an abiding emphasis on correct teaching, especially in the wake of the damage being done by the judaizers and their primitive gnosticism. Extensive regulations and directives were issued by the author so that the churches would be able to remain faithful over the long haul. It is curious to note that obligations regarding cult did not seem to be touched on. The presbyter-bishops apparently did not have direct responsibility for the administration of baptism and the Eucharist.

Offices in the Pastorals have their origin in the Jewish tradition, and were in a formative, evolving stage when compared with the rather set arrangement of bishop, presbyters, and deacons—along with their respective roles—which presents itself in the letters of Ignatius of Antioch (ca. 110 A.D.). Nonetheless, Hans von Campenhausen notes:

> Canon law has arrived and, what is more, is regarded as entirely legitimate. The Pastoral Epistles do not bear witness to a canon law which is only beginning, but to one which is already fairly well developed; and they see that law as an integral part of the spiritual nature of the Church and its offices.[16]

CONCLUSIONS

The five models of church organization reviewed above are the most notable and the most frequently discussed. But there are other paradigms in the New Testament that reflect additional differences of emphasis and design. For example, the 1943 encyclical of Pius XII, *Mystici Corporis*, focused in a special way on the image of Church in the epistles to the Ephesians and Colossians. These pseudonymous letters of the Pauline tradition stress the unity and the holiness of the worldwide Church, the Church as the sum of all its individual communities existing everywhere. Ephesians particularly places much less emphasis on the local churches. Little is heard about church organization in Ephesians and Colossians, because this issue was not important to the writers compared with the lofty christological themes that formed the heart of the letters. This variety of forms and emphases continues throughout the New Testament, e.g., in I Peter, Hebrews, Revelation, and James. One would have to agree with Raymond Brown that there is "no evidence in those [New Testament] works that a consistent or uniform ecclesiology had emerged."[17]

It is difficult to determine how much the various churches were aware of the structural and theological differences which existed from congregation to congregation. However, in places like Ephesus and Antioch (and even Rome?), these differences must have been somewhat obvious since the several church traditions were living together in close proximity. Further, it must be recalled that a good many of these young congregations were located along the main trade routes. It is clear from Acts and from the Pauline corpus especially that Christians were traveling constantly from one end of the Roman world and back again. As they went from town to town, they frequently searched out fellow Christians who would offer them hospitality. They would fraternize, share their faith, and worship with them frequently as they moved from one place to another. But these differences of doctrinal emphasis and of church organization—except in rare cases such as the separation described in I John 2:19—apparently did not affect the communion (*communio*) which existed among them. "Of course, there were times when Peter, Paul and James differed among themselves; but these differences did not cause a break in *Koinonia* [communion] so far as anyone can prove."[18]

There is little doubt that the very same can be said regarding the churches in the Petrine, Pauline, and Jamesian traditions, to say nothing of the Johannine communities and those congregations reflected in the Pastorals. The diversity in organizational structure was truly considerable, and yet these differences—which must have been observed and perhaps even discussed—did not stand in the way of communion among the churches and their members. Unity and uniformity were not in any way synonymous in the Church of the first two, three, or four generations.

The journey from Paul's paradigm of church order, through Luke–Acts, Matthew, John and finally the Pastorals, leaves one with the impression of an irreconcilable mass of data. Paul's prophets and teachers were commissioned through the conferral of charisms by the Spirit. Those "laboring among the believers" (I Thess 5:12) appear to have been exercising charismatic service functions, perhaps of a temporary character. In Acts, elders appeared very early in Antioch and in Jerusalem. They seem to have been installed by appointment, without any type of ordination. With the death of the apostles, the apostolic office ceases, and what continued on was the apostolic witness which largely came from the elders who exercised teaching as well as shepherding roles. Luke's circle of presbyters apparently acted collegially. Matthew's church knew no elders. There were prophets (perhaps wandering) and teachers (or scribes), but no other local administration was referred to. In the famous ecclesial chapter (chapter 18), ultimate decision making apparently lay with the congregation. Believers were related to one another as brothers and sisters. There was an explicitly familial ambiance. Honors and titles of distinction of any sort were frowned on.

The Johannine community had some sect-like qualities which were not as apparent in other congregations. They were in serious conflict with the Jews and with the "world." The term "apostle" was not employed because discipleship was the controlling notion. As in Matthew's church, equality and fraternity were emphasized among the disciples. It seems that the community was quite unstructured apart from the inconclusive data in III John. The overriding emphasis was on the relationship of each individual believer with the risen Lord, through the Spirit. Peter's shepherding role, although significant, was relativized vis-à-vis that of the Beloved Disciple whose love of the Master was superior to all others. Finally, the Pastorals are located in a very different organizational field. There were offices and, in some cases, ordinations of officers (I Tim 4:14). There seemed to be a merging of the tradition of the presbyters with that of the bishops and deacons. The role of bishops and presbyters was not yet differentiated (Titus 1:5-7). Canon law has made its appearance, e.g., in the determination of the qualities for the various offices and in the repeated prescriptions for correct teaching. The church organization revealed in the letters of Ignatius of Antioch (110 A.D.) was drawing closer.

But what of all this diversity? Can all these varied organizational strains be reconciled? After studying Vatican II's Constitution on the Church, *Lumen Gentium*, David Bartlett affirms that such a reconciliation was presumed to be possible in the judgment of the framers of the document:

> The implication is that there is a uniform understanding of ministry in the New Testament and that every writer in the New Testament can be used to support the vision of every other writer. . . . *Lumen Gentium* assumes that bishops are the direct descendants of the apostles and what Scripture says about the apostles the Church can affirm about its bishops.[19]

A review of chapter III of the Constitution does incline one to agree, for the most part, with Bartlett regarding both assertions. In the light of the various paradigms of church polity that have been examined here, there appears to have been an attempt at reconciliation on the part of the council fathers which does not fully correspond to the diversity of the New Testament evidence, both in regard to the understanding of ministry and to the notion of the bishops as the direct and immediate descendants of the apostles.

James D.G. Dunn, after recapping the New Testament diversity regarding ministry and church order generally, states: "This means that out of the 'spaghetti junction' of first century Christianity only one road led toward the orthodox church order of Ignatius; others led in at least one other very different direction."[20]

That other different direction is described by Dunn:

> On the other we see what is best understood as a reaction against such institutionalizing trends, where in different ways, John, Hebrews and Revelation protest against the emergence of a church structured round office and intermediaries and insist on the immediacy of the individual believer's relation to God through Christ and on the corporate nature of priesthood and prophecy.[21]

Dunn then cites Ernst Käsemann's conclusion concerning New Testament diversity. Although Käsemann was looking at doctrinal differences rather than the variety of church order arrangements, the application of his statement to New Testament organizational diversity is warranted. After setting forth his premises, Käsemann observes: "the New Testament canon does not as such constitute the foundation of the unity of the Church. On the contrary, as such (that is, in its accessibility to the historian) it provides the basis for the multiplicity of confessions."[22]

Dunn's recapitulating observation is truly worth repeating:

This conclusion [re: the New Testament basis for the multiplicity of confessions] has not been sufficiently reckoned with in the twentieth century ecumenical movement, and its possible corollaries for modern denominational diversity need to be thought through with greater care and thoroughness.[23]

CHAPTER 2

Developments from *I Clement*
to Pope Stephen I

ca. 95 A.D. to 257

As we move beyond the writings of the New Testament, the first work of the apostolic fathers that focuses directly on church order is the letter of Clement to the church at Corinth. This epistle, most likely composed in the latter years of the reign of the Roman emperor Domitian (81-96 A.D.), enjoyed an extremely high reputation in the early Church from the second century on.[1] Apparently word came to Rome concerning the open conflict that had erupted in the Corinthian church over the removal from office of some or all of the appointed elders of the congregation. It seems that a "group of arrogant young men" had persuaded the majority of the church members that the presbyters had to be removed and stripped of their liturgical duties. Although the reason for the dispute is not clarified in the letter, the resulting chaos was evidently tearing the congregation apart. *I Clement* explains Rome's reason for addressing the Corinthians concerning this violent dispute:

> It is disgraceful, dear friends, yes, utterly disgraceful and unworthy of your conduct in Christ, that it should be reported that the well established and ancient church of the Corinthians, because of one or two persons, is rebelling against its presbyters.[2]

Although some have assumed that this intervention on the part of Rome represents the first exercise of a kind of Roman primacy, this action can be explained and justified in a much less dramatic fashion. The renowned patrologist, Berthold Altaner, offers this explanation:

> We cannot read into the whole letter a precise and directly authoritative intervention which would place the sister church under a juridical obligation. This proceeding of the Roman church—Clement himself plays nowhere an immediately active part—may partly be explained by the

primitive Christian vigilance and the concern of the churches for one another, also by the particularly close political and cultural relations between Corinth and Rome, since the former had been re-founded as a Roman colony (44 B.C.).[3]

The point of the letter is to persuade the Corinthian congregation to restore the appointed elders to their rightful offices. The assumption is that since the elders were blameless, they were unjustly removed (*I Clem* 44, 3). The underlying premise is that once the presbyters were duly appointed by their predecessors (and approved by the congregation), they were permanent and could not be removed except for malfeasance. This succession of ministers from the apostles themselves was divinely willed and could not be disrupted.

> Our apostles likewise knew through our Lord Jesus Christ, that there would be strife over the bishop's [i.e., the presbyter's] office. For this reason therefore, having received complete foreknowledge, they appointed the officials mentioned earlier and afterwards they gave the offices a permanent character; that is, if they should die, other approved men should succeed to their ministry. Those therefore who were appointed by them, or later on by reputable men with the consent of the whole church, and who have ministered to the flock of Christ blamelessly, humbly, peaceably and unselfishly, and for a long time have been well spoken of by all—these men we consider to have been unjustly removed from their ministry.[4]

I Clement considers the presbyterial system to be of apostolic origin, and the officeholders were to keep their positions—as long as they were blameless—for life. This was apparently the prevailing arrangement in Syria, Asia Minor, and in Rome, and it was considered in those locations to be of apostolic origin.[5] The presbyters were permanent cultic officials, separated clearly from the non-presbyterial members of the congregation. Although there is little New Testament evidence for this sharp separation, it is virtually canonized in *I Clement*, which had an enormous impact on the character of the Church as this separation deepened and became a constitutional dimension of the organization itself.

The terminology employed to distinguish officeholders is not uniform. At times *I Clement* refers to them as bishops (*episcopoi*) and at other times as presbyters (*presbyteroi*). The situation in Rome was no doubt similar. The Roman church was governed by a college of presbyters or presbyter-bishops until roughly the middle of the second century.[6] *I Clement* does not presume to force the Corinthian congregation to take a given course of action as a result of the intervention. It is assumed to be an independent community with the right to make its own decisions. There is no legal or juridical compulsion alluded to in the letter. The Romans were hoping to convince the Corinthians to restore the presbyters to their rightful offices; moral suasion was the only means employed. In the process, the principle of apostolic succession was enunciated, perhaps for the first time in the early Church. Christ appointed the apostles, the apostles appointed their successors, and so on. This arrangement could not be changed or tampered with because it was of divine origin. However, as was apparently the case in Corinth, there was no monarchical bishop in Rome at the end of the first century, nor can *I Clement* be cited as a clear indication, on the part of the Roman church, that it had a juridical right to intervene authoritatively in the affairs of the Corinthian congregation. The involvement of Rome was in all likelihood inspired by a familial concern for a sister church in chaos—a church that had been enriched at its foundation by the evangelizing efforts of the Roman "pillars," Peter and Paul (Gal 2:9).

The second of the apostolic fathers to deal with issues of early church order and the development of the church in Rome was Ignatius of Antioch. Ignatius was the bishop of the thriving church at Antioch in Syria—one of the largest Christian communities, if not the largest, at the turn of the first century. Whether he was the first or second monarchical bishop of that city is not certain. We recall that the early governance of the Antiochian congregation was in the hands of presbyters or presbyter-bishops. Sometime during the reign of the emperor Trajan (98-117), Ignatius was apprehended and transported from Syria to Rome, where he "became food for wild animals because of his testimony to Christ."[7] On his way to Rome—traveling as a prisoner under guard—he wrote seven letters to five churches in Asia Minor (Ephesus, Magnesia, Tralles, Philadelphia, and Smyrna), a letter to the Romans, and one to Polycarp, the bishop of Smyrna. Each letter makes special reference to the monarchical bishop of the congregation, except the one to the Romans, which is directed to the church which presides "in the place of the district of the Romans." This is a rather clear indication that the Roman congregation was presided over by elders or presbyters ca.110 A.D. The other five churches, which were situated in western Asia Minor, were all organized in a monarchical fashion. Around the bishop there was the council of presbyters who assisted the bishop in the governance of the church. The deacons were allotted the more ministerial tasks under the direction of the bishop and the elders. Only the bishop and his delegates were permitted to preside over public worship and dispense the sacraments (*Magn* 3, 1; *Trall* 12, 2). Marriages were to be conducted only with the bishop's consent (*Poly* 5, 2). Ignatius was aware that bishops had been appointed "throughout the whole world" (*Eph* 3, 2). He presumed this threefold hierarchical structure—bishop, presbyters, and deacons—to be the more usual arrangement. Church unity was defined by Ignatius in terms of the three-tiered ministry and the church people. This, in fact, was one of his predominant themes.

In the letter to the Romans, Ignatius makes no mention of the bishop, the presbyterate, or the deacons. He had to know that the Roman church was not presided over by a monarchical bishop, which was clearly the case in the other cities to which he had written. He made much of the fact that the Roman community was "worthy of praise, worthy of success, worthy of sanctification and presiding over love."[8] The last epithet, according to many scholars, reveals the widely acknowledged reputation for charity bestowed by other churches on the Roman congregation, even at that early date. The leadership of Rome in regard to the teaching function is pointed out in the letter. "You have never envied anyone; you taught others" (*Rom* 3, 1). Ignatius reminded the Romans that he did not presume to issue orders and directives to them. "I do not give you orders like Peter and Paul: they were apostles, I am a convict; they were free, but I am even now still a slave."[9] This statement attests dramatically to his awareness that Peter and Paul were the founders of the church in Rome.

The most valuable insight that can be gleaned from Ignatius is that although the monarchical episcopate was for him the more common, the more frequent form of church organization, he must have been aware that other types of ecclesiastical polity were to be found elsewhere, even in Rome. The absence of a monarchical bishop in Rome did not in any way color his admiration of, his affection for, or his communion with the congregation in the capital of the empire. Unity among the churches did not seem to be identified with structural uniformity. He had no trouble accepting other organizational arrangements as being consonant with the *communio* which tied all the Christian churches together.

A very different view, a sort of grassroots approach to church life in Rome, is revealed in the work called *The Shepherd of Hermas*, the first half of which was written ca. 100 A.D., while the last half was probably composed about 135-145 A.D. It is not an easy piece to read or to comprehend, but it does afford to those who take the time a precious glimpse into the life of the Roman congregation in the first half of the second century. The work was regarded as Sacred Scripture by Irenaeus, Tertullian, and Origen. Its genre is apocalyptic—which presupposes a divine revelation in the form of a vision or dream given through a mediator who interprets the vision. The theme of the vision deals with the possibility of and the conditions for reconciliation when one sins grievously after baptism.[10]

The author is a simple but genuinely pious man who was not a presbyter but a prophet. There is no discussion of liturgical functions in the piece, although it is heavily influenced by Jewish tradition. Hermas speaks of elders (*Vis* 3, 18), bishops, teachers, and deacons (*Vis* 3, 5, 1), and elsewhere he discusses true and false prophets (*Mand* 11, 1). There is absolutely no trace of a monarchical episcopate in the work. In fact, church officials are only infrequently mentioned. Since *The Shepherd of Hermas* was probably not completed until almost mid-century, this leads once again to the conclusion that the monarchical episcopate did not take root in Rome until ca. 140-150 A.D. The congregation must have been governed by the presbyters—which also seems to have been the case in *I Clement* and Ignatius. The sins and omissions of the presbyters are alluded to (*Para* 9, 31, 5), as well as the failings of deacons (*Para* 9, 26, 2) and prophets (*Para* 9, 27, 2). But those who teach well, shelter the needy, and care for the orphans and the widows will have their abundant reward.

The next figure who attracts our attention on the Roman scene is Justin the apologist, who was born in Palestine ca. 115 A.D. of a Greek family. As a youth, he traveled to Ephesus to study philosophy. Finding little solace in the teachings of several philosophical schools, he finally came upon a group of Platonists:

> In my helpless condition it occurred to me to have a meeting with the Platonists, for their fame was great. I thereupon spent as much of my time as possible with one who lately settled in our city—a sagacious man, holding a high position among the Platonists, and I progressed and made the greatest improvements daily.[11]

Justin, however, became frustrated because Platonism did not seem to allow him to "look upon God," which he thought to be the objective of Plato's philosophy. Coming upon an elderly man who gradually led him to the Sacred Scriptures, Justin became a Christian and dedicated himself to the task of being a Christian philosopher. He moved to Rome and set up a private philosophical school there. It was Justin who was the first to interpret Christianity in terms of Greek philosophy. Three of his works have survived: two apologies or defenses of the faith dedicated to the Roman emperor Antoninus Pius (138-161), and the *Dialogue with Trypho* which demonstrates the superiority of Christianity over Judaism. Justin was martyred in Rome along with six companions ca. 165, after confessing his Christian faith before the notorious city prefect, Rusticus Urbanus.

In chapter 65 of his *First Apology*, he has left us a precious description of a eucharistic celebration after a baptism, and in chapter 67 we are given a glimpse of a Sunday worship service in Rome in the middle of the second century.

> And on the day called Sunday, all who live in cities or in the country gather together in one place, and the memoirs of the apostles or the writings of the prophets are read, as long as time permits; then, when the reader has ceased, the president verbally instructs and exhorts to the imitation of these good things. Then we all rise together and pray, and as we before said, when our prayer is ended, bread and wine and water are brought, and the president in like manner offers prayers and thanksgivings, according to his ability, and the people assent, saying Amen; and there is a distribution to each, and a participation of that over which thanks have been given, and to those who are absent a portion is sent by the deacons.

And they who are well to do and willing, give what each thinks fit; and
what is collected is deposited with the president, who succors the orphans
and the widows, and those who through sickness or any other cause, are
in want . . . and in a word takes care of all who are in need.[12]

It is quite possible that this president who instructs, exhorts, and celebrates
the eucharistic worship and provides—presumably on an ongoing basis—for
the poor and the needy is the monarchical bishop of the Roman congregation.
However, Justin does not make that clear in this passage or elsewhere in his
writings. He was not concerned about the church order arrangements of his
day. Justin did, however, refer to the continuing existence of the prophetic gifts
in the Church. In his *Dialogue with Trypho* he says, "the prophetic gifts remain
with us, even to the present time. And thus you ought to understand that the
gifts formerly among your nation [i.e., the Jews] have been transferred to us."[13]
He seems to identify the prophetic with the teaching role and it is not clear
whether these are charismatic functions or duties related to an ecclesiastical
office. Justin spoke of the president of the assembly, the teachers and/or prophets,
and finally of deacons (whose work was largely ministerial). He does not seem
to reveal any reference to a wider role or responsibility for Rome vis-à-vis the
universal Church, although he clearly sees the Church as a reality composed of
a multitude of local churches. Addressing Trypho, the Jew, he said, "Now Leah
is your people and synagogue, but Rachel is our Church."[14]

THE MONARCHICAL EPISCOPATE IN ROME

Another scholar who visited Rome and made quite an impression there was
a man named Hegesippus. Since gnosticism was so rampant at that time, especially in the East, he decided to visit a number of the churches of apostolic
origin to gather information concerning the truly authentic Christian doctrine. This led him to Rome ca. 160 A.D., where he stayed a number of years,
from the pontificate of Anicetus (ca. 155-166) to that of Eleutherus (ca. 174-
189). He then returned to the East and wrote his memoirs, which Eusebius
quotes from several times in his fourth-century work, *The History of the Church*.
Hegesippus tried to demonstrate the existence of a historically continuous
tradition—in terms of an unbroken chain of bishops in the principal churches—
against the claims made by the gnostics that they alone possessed the more
important and valuable secret, saving message of Jesus. The gnostics traced
this message through their prophetic figures down to one or another apostle or
disciple of Jesus. By constructing a continuous list of bishops in the principal
churches which led back to the apostles themselves and therefore to Christ,
the assertion of the gnostics that they had a prior and more significant revelation could be contradicted. According to the reasoning of Hegesippus and

others, the unbroken chain of public witness going back to Jesus himself was far more critical than any alleged private, secret revelations claimed by the gnostics. Why, they reasoned, would Jesus have given more salvific private revelations to a few, rather than to all the apostles for the benefit of all true believers? It is felt that Hegesippus either constructed the list of Roman bishops from Peter to Anicetus, or found such a list and included it in his memoirs which have since been lost. Eusebius quotes from Hegesippus: "On arrival at Rome I pieced together the succession down to Anicetus, whose deacon was Eleutherus; Anicetus being succeeded by Soter and he by Eleutherus."[15]

Hegesippus apparently felt that by compiling a continuous list of bishops who handed the revelation of Jesus down—one to the other from generation to generation in each of the major apostolic churches—he could most effectively guarantee the authenticity of the Church's doctrine. The certification of this uninterrupted "handing down" of the authentic message of Jesus in the Roman church, the church of Peter and Paul, was certainly crucial, and this was apparently Hegesippus' contribution. Although the object of his efforts was praiseworthy, the historical validity of the Roman list is questionable because it is now quite generally accepted that the monarchical episcopate in Rome did not originate much before 140-150 A.D. The notion of apostolic succession, however, was clearly shifting from emphasis on the authentic teaching, which was handed down from generation to generation, to the list of teachers—one succeeding the other in an unbroken chain. The names prior to Anicetus that Hegesippus enumerated—people such as Linus, Clement, Evaristus, Telesphorus, etc.—were in all probability historical figures who were in one way or another prominent presbyters or presbyter-bishops in the Roman congregation. However, to position them in a continuous line of monarchical heads from Peter to Anicetus is not historically justifiable.

It was Irenaeus of Lyons who perfected Hegesippus' argument in book III, chapter 3 of his most important work, *Against Heresies*, where he says:

> It is within the power of all, therefore, in every church, who may wish to see the truth, to contemplate clearly the tradition of the apostles manifested throughout the world; and we are in a position to reckon up those who were by the apostles instituted bishops in the churches, and (to demonstrate) the succession of these men to our own times; those who neither taught nor knew of anything like what these (heretics) rave about. For if the apostles had known hidden mysteries, which they were in the habit of imparting to the "perfect" apart and privily from the rest, they would have delivered them to those to whom they were also committing the churches themselves.[16]

Irenaeus was born in Asia Minor, probably growing up in the city of Smyrna where, he says, he listened to the sermons of the bishop, Polycarp, in his youth

(*Against Heresies*, IV, 27, 1). He left Asia Minor and migrated to Gaul, where he became a presbyter in the congregation at Lyons. In 178 or thereabouts, he succeeded the elderly bishop, Photinus, who had been martyred while Irenaeus was apparently on a mission to Rome. The struggle against the gnostic heresy was the labor of his life. We hear of him somewhat later toward the end of the second century when he intervened to mollify Pope Victor (189-198) in his acrimonious dispute with certain eastern prelates over the date of the celebration of Easter. At that time Irenaeus wrote several of the bishops in Asia Minor and Pope Victor, urging them to make peace. This is the last we hear of Irenaeus, who must have died sometime after 200 A.D. It was he who gave to posterity invaluable information regarding the gnostics, especially Marcion and Valentinus, both of whom came to Rome ca. 140 A.D.

Gnosticism was truly the bane of the second century Church, threatening to undermine not only the doctrine of apostolic succession, but the doctrines of creation, the resurrection of the body, the developing doctrines of the Trinity and the Incarnation, and more. Irenaeus was a kerygmatic teacher rather than a speculative theologian. Although he learned much from Justin, he made no concerted attempt to blend Greek philosophy with the teachings of the apostles which he had learned from Polycarp. In his writings, the bishop of Lyons made use of Matthew, Mark, Luke, and John, the Acts, and the Pauline corpus to demonstrate his assertions and clarify his arguments. He apparently included *The Shepherd of Hermas* as Scripture, but excluded the letter to the Hebrews. Nor did he ever quote from III John, James, or II Peter. According to Henry Chadwick, Irenaeus was "the first writer whose New Testament virtually corresponds to the canon that became accepted as traditional."[17] His masterpiece, *Against Heresies*, is not especially easy to read because of its verbosity, repetitiveness, and lack of order. Though he did not seem to be able to organize his material effectively, he was most gifted in giving rather convincing explanations of the principal doctrines of the Church. Perhaps some of the difficulty we experience results from the fact that *Against Heresies*, which was written in Greek, is available to us only in a very literal Latin translation.

One of the most celebrated and widely discussed passages of the work deals with the position of the Roman church in the world Church. Scholars such as the eminent patrologist, John Quasten, hold that Irenaeus set forth his version of the Roman primacy in chapter 3 of book III of *Against Heresies*.[18] Irenaeus was stressing the importance of clarifying the chain of succession in the apostolic churches to show that the doctrine taught in these communities was precisely that which was handed down from the apostles themselves. He states:

> Since, however, it would be very tedious in such a volume as this, to reckon up the succession of all the churches, we do put to confusion all those who, in whatever manner, whether by an evil self-pleasing, by vainglory, or by blindness and perverse opinion, assemble in unauthorized meetings; (we

do this, I say) by indicating that tradition derived from the apostles, of the very great, the very ancient, and universally known church founded and organized at Rome by those two most glorious apostles, Peter and Paul; as also (by pointing out) the faith preached to men which comes down to our time by means of the successions of the bishops. For it is a matter of necessity that every church should agree with this church on account of its preeminent authority, that is, the faithful everywhere, inasmuch as the apostolic tradition has been preserved continuously by those (faithful men) who exist everywhere.[19]

It is indeed understandable how this passage has baffled scholars for centuries! Those who were wont to find in it a verification of the Roman primacy were able to interpret it in that fashion. However, there is so much ambiguity here that one has to be careful of over-reading the evidence. After this passage, Irenaeus went on to reconstruct the chain of Roman pontiffs from Peter to Eleutherus, who was reigning at the time *Against Heresies* was written.[20] There is no doubt about the fact that for Irenaeus, the Roman church was "very great," "very ancient," and "universally known to have been founded by the two most glorious apostles, Peter and Paul." But whether or not he judged it to be the only church that enjoyed "preeminent authority" (*potentior principalitas*) in the whole Church is the disputed issue. According to the noted historian Karl Baus, Irenaeus' point can be explicitated as follows:

The apostolic tradition is found most certainly in the communities which rest on a directly apostolic foundation; there are several of these and each of them has a stronger power, grounded in its apostolic origin for the ascertaining of truth, than any other Christian community whatever. But Rome stands out even from this series of apostolic foundations, because as is everywhere recognized, Peter and Paul were its founders. Then Irenaeus summarizes; with such a church of apostolic foundation every individual church must agree, because precisely such a church has always preserved the apostolic tradition. One of these churches is the Roman church; which is even in a particularly favorable position for establishing the apostolic tradition, but not exclusively so.[21]

Karl Baus' interpretation seems to be the one that is more faithful to the text and does not presume to read into it a meaning which might not be there. Hence, it neither overstates nor understates Irenaeus' position. For him, it is those churches of apostolic foundation that have the greater claim to authentic teaching and doctrine. Among those, Rome, with its two apostolic founders, certainly holds an important place. However, all of the apostolic churches enjoy what he terms "preeminent authority" in doctrinal matters.

We mentioned earlier that Irenaeus had an encounter with Pope Victor (189-198) over a dispute between Asia Minor and Rome regarding the date of the celebration of Easter. Apparently a priest named Blastus attempted to introduce at Rome the practice of commemorating Easter on the 14th of Nisan, rather than on the Sunday following, which was the established practice in Rome and elsewhere. Rome, which had initiated the paschal celebration rather late compared with the eastern churches, must have included Easter in its liturgical calendar in the third or fourth decade of the second century. Victor excommunicated Blastus and ordered that synods be held in every province of the Christian world to study the matter. It is significant that synods were indeed held almost everywhere and the results were that most provinces agreed with Victor on the Sunday celebration, save for certain churches in Asia Minor. Bishop Polycrates of Ephesus led the opposition against Victor, claiming that they had kept the 14th of Nisan from apostolic times. Victor's reaction was described by the historian Eusebius:

> Thereupon Victor, head of the Roman church, attempted at one stroke to cut off from the common unity all Asian dioceses, together with the neighboring churches, on the ground of heterodoxy, and pilloried them in letters in which he announced the total excommunication of all his fellow Christians there.[22]

Irenaeus and others interceded with Victor, insisting that all the Roman bishops down to Soter (ca. 166-174) had tolerated the 14th of Nisan practice and that the difference never precipitated a rupture of communion among the churches. We do not know what happened, but apparently the whole affair blew over. The issue of the date of the Easter celebration was not finally settled until the Council of Nicaea (325 A.D.), which related the following in the final paragraph of a letter appended to the canons of the council.

> We also send you the good news of the settlement concerning the holy pasch, namely that in answer to your prayers this question has also been resolved. All brethren in the East who have hitherto followed the Jewish practice will henceforth observe the custom of the Romans and of yourselves [i.e.. the churches in Egypt, Libya, and Pentopolis] and of all of us who from most ancient times have kept Easter with you.[23]

According to our count, this action of Victor was the first clear instance of the exercise of "world-wide" authority over the other churches on the part of the bishop of Rome. Although his action (ca. 190-195) was most likely ineffective in regard to changing the practice of the Asia Minor churches, it is apparent that he sensed that he had the power to intervene in the disciplinary affairs of distant provinces and impose his will on them.

Victor's intervention stood as the sole precedent, as far as we know, for the papal claim to universal disciplinary authority for more than fifty years, until the dispute between Cyprian and Pope Stephen (to be discussed later). Victor's successor, Zephrinus (198-217), was troubled by several trinitarian controversies during most of his reign. One of the principal thorns in his side was the Roman presbyter, Hippolytus, who rather ruthlessly opposed him at every turn and criticized him for being deficient intellectually. Zephrinus' principal objective was to steer a middle course between the modalism of Sabellius and the "binitarian" teaching of Hippolytus. Sabellius, who came to Rome at this time from north Africa, taught that the one God operated under three modalities, that of the Father, the Son, and the Holy Spirit. Apparently there was no distinction of persons, but only different modes of operation—creation, redemption, and sanctification—which were attributed to the one God. Hippolytus, on the other hand, having been won over to the Logos theory of Justin, spoke emphatically about the real distinction between the Father and the Word within the one divine nature. He seemed to be unwilling to call the Word "Son" until the Incarnation, and left little room for the distinct personhood of the Holy Spirit.[24] Toward the end of his pontificate, Zephrinus issued a statement on the subject which was probably drafted by his archdeacon, Callistus. It was the purpose of Zephrinus and Callistus to safeguard the monotheism of the primitive church against Hippolytus' binitarian tendencies and, at the same time, to maintain the divinity of Christ and his distinct personhood over against the Father versus the modalists.

In Rome at this time (unlike the Rome we know), there was a great deal of theological ferment and a great variety of opinions espoused. Gregory Dix, in the general introduction to his edition of *The Apostolic Tradition of Hippolytus*, comments:

> The Roman system [at that time] was very tolerant. Apparently any Christian arriving from any church, even one already under censures in another church, like Marcion, was allowed to open a lecture room and there to teach with the authorization of the church the version of Christian doctrine he had received or elaborated for himself to such hearers as he could attract. These "lecture rooms" were private ventures, hired and carried on by the lecturers themselves, who lived by the proceeds. Some of the teachers were clerics, others not. The hierarchy appears to have exercised very little in the way of censorship, and when one reflects on the number of early heresiarchs who were for years accepted teachers of the Roman church, and on the fact that apparently most catechumens received almost all their preparation for baptism in these establishments, the drawbacks of the system become apparent. Only when a teacher had demonstrated beyond a doubt that his creed really did differ in essentials

from that of the Roman church did the "presbyters" expel him from communion.[25]

Upon the death of Zephrinus, the popular archdeacon Callistus was elected bishop of Rome, much to the chagrin of Hippolytus who seems to have separated himself at this time from the main Roman church and formed a rival congregation, appointing himself its bishop. Callistus (217-222), quite probably born a slave, was the most powerful ecclesiastic in Rome during the pontificate of Zephrinus. He was not of a speculative bent in theological matters, but rather tried to affirm the traditional doctrinal positions. Because of his own difficult early life, he was sensitive to the pain and the needs of the poor. Callistus excommunicated Sabellius in an effort to eliminate some of the confusion regarding trinitarian issues, but the Roman congregation continued to have trouble with modalism for some time to come.

It was at this juncture, or perhaps some years earlier, that Hippolytus wrote his *Apostolic Tradition,* a document on church order of primary importance. There is some dispute over the place of origin of the work because it first surfaced in Coptic and Ethiopic versions. However, it seems very probable that the document does reveal important dimensions of the Roman congregation in the first half of the third century. It is extremely likely that the author was Hippolytus and that he has provided us with a picture of the liturgy and the canonical regulations, especially regarding the clergy, that prevailed in the early third century.

The work is composed of three parts, the first of which deals with the ordination of the bishop, the presbyters, and the deacons. It then outlines a variety of rules guiding the life of the laity, the catechumenate, and the rite of baptism and confirmation (Part 2). Finally, it sets out various Christian observances and practices such as regulations for fasting and prayer, etc., in some detail (Part 3). Part 1 begins with the norms concerning the election and confirmation of the bishop, who is initially chosen by the people. Then the people present the candidate who is to be confirmed or approved by the presbyters and any bishops who happen to be in attendance. The bishops then consecrate the candidate selected by laying their hands on him, with the presbyters witnessing in silence.[26] In the prayer of consecration, the episcopal functions referred to are feeding (shepherding) the flock, forgiving sins, and performing the eucharistic rite.

The ordination of the presbyter is effected by the imposition of hands by the bishops. The ordination prayer asks for the imparting of the spirit of grace and counsel that he may govern with a pure heart.[27] The deacon is to be appointed—we are not told by whom—and ordained by the bishop alone. He is not ordained for a priesthood, but for the service of the bishop, to take charge of property and those responsibilities entrusted to him under the bishop's authority.[28] There follow some brief directives for the recognition of confessors (i.e., those who have confessed their faith before civil magistrates but did not suffer martyrdom), and the appointment of widows, readers, virgins, and subdeacons.

The *Apostolic Tradition* also affords us a rare view of the liturgy of the third-century Roman church—the eucharistic celebration as well as the rites of baptism and confirmation.[29] Hippolytus died in exile in Sardinia around 238 A.D., quite possibly after having directed his followers to rejoin the main Roman congregation.

The most devastating and pervasive persecution leveled against the Church was instigated by Emperor Decius (249-51). Most of the first half of the third century was relatively peaceful for the Christians, save for periods during the reign of Septimius Severus (193-211), who made the fact of being a Christian an indictable offense, and that of Maximinus (235-38), who imprisoned or expelled a number of the leaders of the churches, such as Bishop Pontian of Rome (230-35), who was banished, along with Hippolytus, to Sardinia. Decius dreamed of revitalizing the Roman religion as a means of restoring and invigorating the Roman state. His ambitious plan was to summon all of the inhabitants of the empire to participate in a ritual sacrifice to the Roman deities to beseech blessings on the empire. Those who took part in the ritual were given a *libellus*, or certificate, which had to be shown to the governmental authorities within a certain period of time. Those refusing to take part were subject to imprisonment and possible torture. Decius was most likely anticipating a large scale return to the practice of the civil religion. Not surprisingly, there were massive defections throughout the empire on the part of Christians. Although there was evidence of martyrs everywhere, the number of defectors, or *lapsi*, was extremely high.

There were many Christians who were able to buy fraudulent certificates from government officials, thus exempting themselves from prison. On the other hand, most of those who had sacrificed—and they were numbered in the tens of thousands—did whatever they could to return to the good graces of the Church as soon as possible. The confessors, who had refused to sacrifice but for some reason were released after a short imprisonment, were approached by the guilty parties for letters of peace which, at least in some places, assisted them in the process of reconciliation with their local church. The persecution began in December 249 and, for the most part, lasted little more than a year. Bishops were the very first to be apprehended. Antioch, Jerusalem, and Caesarea saw their bishops martyred at the onset of the persecution. In January 250, the Roman Bishop Fabian (236-250) was put to death. Decius' plan to win back great numbers of people to the civil religion failed; first, because the Roman procedure of bringing forward everyone to pay homage to the Roman gods was understandably not all that efficient, and second, because the Church reversed its previous harsh stand, finding a way to restore great numbers of *lapsi* to the fold.

BISHOP CYPRIAN OF CARTHAGE (d. 258)

The defections in Africa were enormous according to Bishop Cyprian (*Epistle* 20, 2), who had removed himself to a hiding place not far from Carthage whence he could be free from the clutches of the civil officials and be able to manage, at least in some fashion, the affairs of his diocese by correspondence. Cyprian was apparently rather recently converted when he was elected bishop of the largest see in north Africa, and his election surprised a good many people. Well educated and most likely destined for a lofty government post, his mind-set had a decidedly legal turn which meant that he saw himself as a kind of curial bishop—one who would to some degree emulate the public presence and the concerns of the Roman consuls and pro-consuls. In his communications with his presbyters in Carthage, he made it clear that he did not want them to readmit the *lapsi* while he was absent. Rather, he desired that those who had lapsed do penance and remain outside the congregation until he would personally be able to preside over the manner of their reconciliation. One of his clerics, a certain Felicissimus, organized a band of presbyters in Carthage who were opposed to Cyprian's decision in this matter. Since the bishop's removal to a place of hiding was not fully understood or accepted by some whom he had left behind, it was apparently not difficult to organize this opposition against him. The opposition did not unduly disturb Cyprian, however, who continued to maintain a firm hold on his see. In the spring of 251—after thirteen months *in absentia*—he returned to Carthage and summoned a council of the bishops of the area to deliberate on the subject of the procedure to be followed regarding the readmission of the *lapsi*. Those Christians who had fraudulently obtained certificates without sacrificing could be readmitted on the basis of the penance that they had already done. However, those who had actually sacrificed to the Roman deities were to remain under penance, and the so-called letters of peace were no longer considered as a warrant for hastier readmission. Individuals who were in danger of death could always be reconciled, given the proper dispositions.

It is obvious from his letters that Cyprian had cordial relations with Pope Cornelius of Rome (251-53), who was banished from his see by the emperor Gallus (251-53) shortly after the emperor revived the persecution. The same could not be said of Cyprian's relationship with Pope Stephen (254-57), with whom he quarreled vigorously over the question of the rebaptism of converts from heresy. Following the tradition of the north African church going back to Tertullian (ca. 200 A.D.) and one of Cyprian's predecessors, Bishop Agrippinus (ca. 220 A.D.), converts were always rebaptized. Pope Stephen did not agree, because the practice at Rome was simply to admit those converts already baptized by means of the imposition of hands. It was most probably during those debates with Stephen that Cyprian further refined his understanding of the relationship between himself as the primate of the church in Africa, and the bishop of Rome.

Cyprian's views on the role of the bishop, church organization, and the relationship between the bishops and the Roman pontiff are set forth in some depth in his epistles and in his two monographs, *The Unity of the Catholic Church* and *The Lapsed*. His overriding vision of the Church was animated by the theme of the local church which gathered itself around the bishop: "the Church consists of the people who remain united with their bishop, it is the flock that stands by its shepherd. By that you ought to realize that the bishop is in the Church and the Church is in the bishop, and whoever is not with the bishop is not in the Church."[30]

In a letter to Pope Stephen, in the spring of 256, regarding the need to rebaptize heretics entering the Church, Cyprian says, "We are not forcing anyone in this matter; we are laying down no law. For every appointed leader has in his government of the church the freedom to exercise his own judgment and will, while having one day to render an account of his conduct to the Lord."[31]

There was in his view no jurisdictional power over the local bishop that could force him to legislate or rule in one way or another. He was responsible only to God. However, he was not to render decisions as an autocrat: "I make no reply on my own, for it has been a resolve of mine, right from the beginning of my episcopate, to do nothing on my own private judgment without your counsel [i.e., the presbyters] and the consent of the people."[32]

Cyprian's approach to consultation depended somewhat on the subject matter and on the circumstances, but generally for him it was the role of his clergy to offer counsel and that of his people to voice either agreement or disagreement. Then, in the end it was he who would decide.

The process to be followed in the selection and installation of the bishop was an issue involving the local presbyters, the people of the diocese, and the nearby bishops: "Divine authority is also the source for the practice whereby bishops are chosen in the presence of the laity and before the eyes of all, and they are judged as being suitable and worthy after public scrutiny and testimony."[33]

After quoting from the Book of Numbers regarding the selection of Eleazar by Moses and the choice of a replacement for Judas by the apostles in Acts, Cyprian declares:

> Hence we should show sedulous care in preserving a practice which is based on divine teaching and apostolic observance, a practice which is indeed faithfully followed among us and in practically every province. And that is this: when an episcopal appointment is to be duly solemnized, and the neighboring bishops in the same province convene for the purpose along with the people for whom the leader is to be appointed, the bishop

is then selected in the presence of those people, for they are the ones who are acquainted most intimately with the way each man has lived his life and they have had the opportunity to thoroughly observe his conduct and behavior.[34]

Once selected, consecrated, and duly installed, the bishop was in undisputed control. Although he was to deliberate with his presbyters regularly and consult with his people, he was really answerable—from a jurisdictional point of view—to no one but God. However, the bishop did see himself as operating within the context of the churches of his province. The provinces of the empire provided the basis for supra-diocesan organization, though there were some regional variations on that theme. Apparently by Cyprian's time, the practice of holding regional synods or councils was rather firmly established in north Africa. So far as we know, after the regional synod in the spring of 251 on the matter of the readmission of the *lapsi*, Cyprian, as primate of the north African church, convoked at least three councils (spring, 255; Easter, 256; September, 256) to ponder the question of the rebaptism of heretics. These gatherings involved the bishops of Proconsular Africa and occasionally the bishops of Numidia—representing in effect the majority of the north African church. Individual bishops though were not absolutely bound by the recommendations of the councils. They were free to legislate in their own dioceses according to their consciences, knowing that they were responsible to God for their enactments. The diversity in discipline which this caused did not of itself precipitate a fracturing of communion among the churches. Cyprian reminded a fellow bishop, Antonianus, of this:

> And you must remember that even amongst our predecessors here in our own province who judged that peace ought not to be granted to adulterers and they, therefore, shut off completely any room for penitence in the case of sins of adultery. And yet that did not cause them to withdraw from the college of their fellow bishops, nor to shatter the unity of the Catholic Church. . . . Accordingly, he who refused to grant peace to adulterers did not separate himself from the Church simply because others were granting such peace. Provided that the bonds of harmony remain unbroken and that the sacred unity of the Catholic Church continues unimpaired, each individual bishop can arrange and order his own affairs, in the knowledge that one day he must render an account to the Lord for his own conduct.[35]

In a letter written by Bishop Fermilian of Caesarea to Cyprian on the occasion of Cyprian's acrimonious dispute with Pope Stephen over the rebaptism of heretics, Fermilian points out that the Roman church is in no position to dictate what is or what is not traditional practice:

Anyone can see that those who are in Rome do not observe in all particulars those things that were handed down from the beginning; it is pointless therefore for them to parade the authority of the apostles . . . their practices are not all exactly the same as those in Jerusalem. This is as we find in very many other provinces: there is a great deal of diversity, just as the people and the places themselves vary. And yet there does not follow from this that there has been any departure at all from the peace and unity of the Catholic Church.[36]

Fermilian and Cyprian agreed that unity and communion do not necessitate uniformity in practice. The bishop of Caesarea furthermore chastised Stephen for his audacity in breaking communion with Cyprian over the issue of rebaptism. Cyprian affirms, in his *Unity of the Catholic Church*, that communion among the duly appointed bishops was critical to the life and growth of the Church:

Now this oneness we must hold to firmly and insist on—especially we who are bishops and exercise authority within the Church—so as to demonstrate that the episcopal power is one and undivided . . . The authority of the bishops forms a unity of which each holds his part in its totality. And the Church forms a unity, however far she spreads and multiplies by the progeny of her fecundity.[37]

In a letter written to Pope Stephen, most probably in 254-55, rather soon after Stephen's election and before the bitter dispute between them, Cyprian refers to the bond that exists among the bishops the world over, describing it in a forceful manner.

Now, dearly beloved brother, there is good reason why our body of bishops is at once so generously large and yet so tightly bound together by the glue of mutual concord and by the bond of unity: it is so that should anyone from our sacred college attempt to form a heretical sect and thus to savage and devastate the flock of Christ, there should be others to come to the rescue, and being practical and kind hearted shepherds, they should gather the Lord's sheep back into the fold.[38]

I believe that we are now in a position to inquire if there was in the ecclesiology of Cyprian any organizational layer—with jurisdiction—above the local bishop and the occasional gatherings of the bishops in provincial or regional synods. An incident occurred, probably in the middle of Pope Stephen's three-year pontificate (254-57), which is recorded in *Epistle* 67 of the letters of Cyprian. It seems that during the persecution of Decius, two Spanish bishops, Basilides and Martialis, had yielded to the pressure of imperial Rome and obtained certificates, which identified them as *lapsi*. They were deposed by their respective dioceses and new bishops were elected and consecrated, whereupon Basilides went to Rome and, possibly on the basis of a falsified story, won reinstatement from Stephen for both himself and Martialis. The two new Spanish bishops who were shocked by Stephen's decision sent letters to the north African churches in order to appeal to Cyprian and the other bishops of the region. Because there were apparently only two primatal sees in the West at that time, it was logical for the prelates to have recourse to Carthage after Rome had favored the fallen bishops. Cyprian and the African prelates with him praised the two Spanish churches for their action and encouraged them to remain faithful to the new bishops in spite of the claims of Basilides and Martialis.

A similar incident is recorded in Cyprian's *Epistle* 68 which is directed to Stephen himself. Bishop Marcionus of Arles was refusing to reconcile any of those who had lapsed in the Decian persecution. Upon hearing of this from Faustinus of Lyons, who had also apprised Stephen of this excessively harsh situation, Cyprian urged Stephen to contact Marcionus and urge him to change his ways so that those who had fallen might—after penance—be restored to the good graces of the Church. These two incidents—in Spain and Gaul—reveal rather fascinating data. First, we just alluded to the fact that the bishops of Rome and Carthage, ca. 250 A.D., were apparently the only two primates, i.e., bishops with wide territorial influence, in the West. Second, there does not seem to be any obvious subordination of Carthage to Rome. Cyprian counseled the people of the two Spanish dioceses to continue their allegiance to the newly elected and installed ordinaries, rather than the lapsed former bishops. He seemingly felt that his "solicitude" had just as much weight in Spain as did Stephen's. Regarding the case in Gaul, the bishop of Carthage urged Stephen—as a brother bishop—to make an effort to correct a cruel situation, probably because it was closer to the sphere of influence of Rome than to that of Carthage.

The question of the rebaptism of heretics wishing to enter the Church caused a mighty rift between Cyprian and Stephen. In the first synod on the question in north Africa (spring, 255), the African bishops, following their tradition going back at least two or three generations, remained firm in their policy to rebaptize. A second synod on the subject—involving an impressive number of prelates from Proconsular Africa and Numidia—was held around Easter of 256. The same stand was reaffirmed and a letter articulating the north African position was dispatched to Stephen (*Epistle* 72). The Roman bishop's response is lost but some shreds of his thinking are reflected in Cyprian's *Epistle* 74 to a fellow African bishop, Pompeius. Stephen's letter is described by Cyprian:

> There is much that is arrogant, irrelevant, self-contradictory, ill-considered and inept in what he has written; but he has even gone so far as to add this remark: "And so in the case of those who may come to you from any

heresy whatsoever, let there be no innovation beyond that which is handed down: hands are to be laid on them in penance."[39]

It is likely that peace between Cyprian and Stephen had been severed prior to the third African synod on the same issue in September of 256. *Letter 75*, written by Bishop Fermilian of Caesarea and included in Cyprian's collected epistles, was dispatched to the bishop of Carthage ca. the fall of 256. Fermilian alludes to Stephen's justification for insisting on the Roman tradition over the north African tradition. Apparently Cyprian had sent to Fermilian a copy of the letter he recently dispatched to Stephen, along with Stephen's response. The bishop of Caesarea says about Stephen's theological argument:

> At this point I become filled with righteous indignation at Stephen's crass and obvious stupidity. He is a man who finds the location of his bishopric such a source of pride, who keeps insisting that he occupies the succession to Peter, upon whom the foundations of the Church were laid.[40]

This could very well have been the first reference on the part of a Roman pontiff to any kind of superior, wide ranging power of governance over other churches based on the Petrine formula of Matthew 16:16-19. Is it possible that he could have taken the reference from Cyprian's *The Unity of the Catholic Church*, chapter 4? After the September synod of 256, Cyprian sent legates to Rome to sue for peace, but Stephen refused even to receive them or give them hospitality. Furthermore, during this dispute over rebaptism, Stephen must have "ruptured peace" with a number of eastern bishops as well.[41] However, the division between Rome and Carthage was short-lived. After Stephen died in 257 and Cyprian was martyred in 258, their successors seem to have forgotten about the rift.

The last observations of Cyprian to be dicussed are found in his work, *The Unity of the Catholic Church*, probably written in 251. The perennially discussed and debated chapter (or paragraph) four comes down to us in two versions. Quoting chapter 16:18-19 of Matthew's gospel (Christ's promise to Peter), Cyprian says:

> Although he assigns a like power to all the apostles [in Mt 18:18], yet He founded a single chair, thus establishing by His own authority the source and hallmark of the (Church's) oneness. No doubt the others were all that Peter was, but a primacy was given to Peter, and it is (thus) made clear that there is but one Church and one Chair.[42]

Some several years later, perhaps after his conflict with Stephen, he seems to have modified his text: "No doubt the other apostles were all that Peter was, endowed with equal dignity and power, but the start comes from him alone, in order to show that the Church of Christ is unique."[43]

In the context of his life and his convictions reflected in his actions and his writings, Cyprian's position can be paraphrased as follows: Peter received the power of the keys, the power to bind and loose, before the other apostles received the same powers. This priority—in time—symbolizes the unity of episcopal power which is held by all in the same way. The only difference is that Peter was granted the power a short time before the others. It must be said that the impact of Cyprian's symbolism is not entirely clear. He was not a speculative theologian but a preacher, trained more as a lawyer than as a rhetorician. His meaning, from the context of his conduct as a bishop, seems quite unambiguous. And those who see in *The Unity of the Catholic Church*, in the light of his entire episcopal life, an articulation of the Roman primacy—as we have come to know it, or even as it has evolved especially from the latter fourth century on—are reading a meaning into Cyprian which is not there.

SUMMARY

In the period from *I Clement* to Cyprian and Pope Stephen, there appears to have been only two Roman bishops who presumed to invoke jurisdictional authority over the dealings of distant churches: Victor (189-98), who attempted to sever communion with the churches in Asia Minor that were celebrating Easter on the 14th of Nisan rather than on the Sunday following; and Stephen (254-57), who broke peace with Carthage and a number of eastern churches regarding the rebaptism of heretics. In Victor's case, his action had little effect because those churches continued to celebrate Easter on their traditional day until the Council of Nicaea dealt with the issue in 325 A.D. Irenaeus' intervention seems to create the impression that Victor's action was precipitous and not consonant with Rome's own best traditions. In Stephen's case, his actions against the several churches were virtually forgotten within a few years after they were enacted, although Stephen's policy of not rebaptizing baptized converts was—after numerous refinements—settled on as the accepted policy of the Church. Although we do not have his own text, it was probably Stephen who was the first Roman pontiff to ground his assertion of jurisdictional authority over distant churches in Christ's promise to Peter (Mt 16:18-19), which was to become so terribly crucial in the definition of papal prerogatives in the latter fourth century and beyond.

CHAPTER 3

The Expansion of the Papal Office

257 to 590

After the death of Pope Stephen in 257 A.D., the Roman congregation was ruled for a period of less than a year by Sixtus II. From 258 to 260 the Church was still suffering under the persecution initiated by Valerian until his son, Gallienus, succeeded him as emperor in 260. Gallienus brought the decade of intermittent but severe persecution to a close and restored the Church's properties which had been confiscated under his father. After about two years of rule by the presbyters, the Roman church elected Dionysius (260-68) as pope, a Greek by birth and a leading clergyman on the Roman scene. It was Dionysius who supposedly assigned the responsibility for the Roman parishes and cemeteries to various members of the presbyteral college. Eusebius referred to him—quoting the words of Bishop Dionysius of Alexandria, a contemporary of Dionysius of Rome—as a man "of learning and high character."[1] The bitter conflict between Rome and the churches of Asia Minor over rebaptism had seemingly been brought to some kind of closure by this time. Pope Dionysius wrote to the Egyptian church to clarify what he thought were subordinationist tendencies in the teaching of his brother bishop, Dionysius of Alexandria, who was apparently making the Son of God a creature. The pope's exposition of Trinitarian doctrine has been preserved in a work of Athanasius on the decrees of the Council of Nicaea.[2] According to the fragment, Pope Dionysius proclaimed the distinction of persons—Father, Son, and Holy Spirit—in the unity of the Trinity.

> That admirable and divine unity therefore must neither be separated into three divinities, nor must the dignity and eminent greatness of the Lord be diminished by having applied to it the name of creation, but we must believe in God the Father Omnipotent, and in Jesus Christ His Son and in the Holy Spirit . . . Thus doubtless will be maintained in its integrity the doctrine of the divine Trinity and the sacred announcement of the monarchy.[3]

Pope Dionysius' presentation became one of the guideposts of orthodoxy in the Christological and Trinitarian debates of the fourth century and beyond. It has been noted by some scholars, e.g., John Quasten and J.N.D. Kelly, that Dionysius was perhaps the most outstanding of the Roman pontiffs in the third century.

The period between 260 and 303 A.D. was a time of exceptional peace and growth for the Church. The distinguished ecclesiastical historian, W.H.C. Frend, describes the situation in the capital thus:

> By the end of the [third] century there were believed to be no less than forty churches in the city. Beyond its boundaries, the Roman see was acquiring estates (*fundi*) perhaps by bequest before the outbreak of the Great Persecution in 303.
>
> The bishop's authority was extending throughout the whole hundred mile radius, administered by the prefect of the city. Cornelius held a council of sixty bishops with priests and deacons in 251, who must have been drawn from that area. Dionysius was credited with the establishment of further bishoprics.[4]

Leadership in Rome after Dionysius was rather unexceptional. We know precious little of the four prelates who spanned the period from 269 to 304. We are, however, quite certain that Pope Marcellinus (296-304) apostatized in the first wave of Diocletian's persecution in 303, apparently having offered homage to the Roman gods. By the sixth century, Marcellinus' defection was rather openly acknowledged.

Ramsay MacMullen estimates the population of the Roman Empire at the turn of the fourth century at about sixty million, and it is his conjecture that the Christian population at that time was approximately five million, with the great majority of Christians residing in the eastern provinces.[5] Although reminding us of the difficulty of estimating the population of the empire and its major cities because of the scarcity of data, A.H.M. Jones judges that "the inhabitants of Rome numbered between half and three-quarters of a million in the early fourth century."[6] Regarding the Christian population of the capital, the best early projection we have dates from the pontificate of Cornelius (251-53) who set forth in a letter—preserved by Eusebius—the number of clergy, widows, and needy in his diocese who were supported by the faithful. Scholars have projected that this would compute to a total of 30,000 to 50,000 Christians at the time of the persecution of Decius.[7] Granted the forty years of peace in the empire and in the capital beginning with Gallienus, it is not illogical to surmise that Rome's Christian population could well have almost doubled from 206 to 303 A.D.

Peace came to a frightening end in the nineteenth year of Diocletian's reign. In spite of all his military successes, he saw what Decius saw, i.e., that the core of the rejuvenation of the empire had to consist in the revitalization of the traditional Roman religion and its values. The general edict of February 303 heralded the onset of a new and perhaps the most devastating persecution. It ordered "the destruction of all Christian places of worship, the surrender and burning of all the sacred books, and it forbade all their assemblies for divine worship."[8]

Eusebius relates, "Such was the first edict against us. Soon afterwards other decrees arrived in rapid succession, ordering that the presidents of the churches [i.e., the bishops] in every place should all be the first to be committed to prison and then coerced by all possible means into offering sacrifice."[9]

Although the persecution raged with awesome furor in most of the eastern provinces of the empire from 303 until Galerius' Edict of Toleration in 311, the western sectors generally suffered less because the leaders in the West, e.g., Constantine and Maxentius, were not as ideologically committed to the persecution of the Christians. The Edict of Toleration issued by the senior Augustus, Galerius, and signed by the other imperial rulers, conceded that the harsh measures had not brought the Christians back to the practice of the Roman religion, and hence they were to be granted clemency, "so that Christians may again exist and rebuild the houses in which they used to meet, on condition that they do nothing contrary to public order."[10] The number of those martyred in this last great persecution has been estimated in the thousands and occasionally in the tens of thousands. After Constantine and Licinius had consolidated their power and had become sole rulers in the West and East respectively, they issued a lengthy ordinance granting religious freedom to all, Christians and non-Christians, and providing for the return of all confiscated property to the Christians.

Before initiating a discussion of the Church, and specifically the Roman see, in the Constantinian era and beyond, it is appropriate to reflect on the image and role of the Roman pontiff in the worldwide Church of some five million faithful at the beginning of the fourth century. In light of our discussion in Chapters 1 and 2, the more moderate position, i.e., that which claims less rather than more, is more consonant with the data presented thus far. The noted historian, Walter Ullmann, summarizes the situation in the introductory pages of his short history of the papacy in the Middle Ages:

> By the time of the settlement of 313 the Roman church had a somewhat superior but purely moral authority in comparison with the other churches, just as Rome itself carried greater weight than, say, a Milan or a Marseilles. There was as yet no suggestion that the Roman church possessed any legal or constitutional pre-eminence.[11]

Geoffrey Barraclough, another widely respected scholar, reached roughly the same conclusion in a work published at about the same time:

After Stephen [i.e., 254-57] there was little progress in the theoretical formulation of papal rights until popes Damasus (366-84) and Leo I (440-61). In practice Stephen's pronouncements had no visible effect. The church, in organization, was still a federation of episcopal churches, each with its own customs and usages, loosely ruled by synods, and only by straining the evidence can it be argued that any special authority was vested in the bishop of Rome.[12]

Concerning the Roman see, Barraclough adds, "its advantages as the church of the imperial capital and its ecclesiastical prestige, as the church of 'the two most glorious apostles, Peter and Paul,' reinforced each other. It is impossible to say with finality which came first, or which contributed more to its rise to pre-eminence."[13]

Although the observations of Ullmann and Barraclough do understate the pre-eminence of Rome c.a. 300 A.D. in the areas of widespread charitable assistance and, to some extent, doctrinal influence, they rather accurately portray the jurisdictional and constitutional situation of the Roman church and the papacy outside of some regional authority in central and southern Italy and, to a lesser extent, western Europe.

After Constantine had defeated Licinius in the fall of 324 and became sole emperor, he turned his attention to the religious crisis in the East which had been recently created by Arius, a presbyter of Alexandria, who had been condemned by a local council at Alexandria in 323 for his subordinationist views concerning Christ. According to Arius, the Logos, i.e., the Son, was inferior to the Father. Furthermore, Christ possessed no human soul, which had been replaced by the created, higher spirit, the Logos. It was the Logos who had assumed the human weakness of the flesh of Christ.[14] After his condemnation, Arius took refuge in Palestine and found support in Bithynia and elsewhere. Constantine summoned a general council to deal with this crisis which was splitting the East. The two most prominent prelates who gave Arius comfort were Eusebius of Caesarea, the noted historian, and Eusebius of Nicomedia.

EARLY CONCILIAR ACTIVITY

The first general council met at Nicaea in June of 325, in the presence of the emperor, with about 250 bishops in attendance. Almost all of those present were from the eastern provinces. Pope Sylvester (314-35) did not attend but was represented by Bishop Ossius of Cordova and two presbyters. This procedure set the precedent for the pope's representation at the first eight ecumenical councils. Nicaea proclaimed the Son to be of the same substance (*Omoousios*) with the Father, although no attempt was made to explain this unbiblical term. There were widespread divisions and doctrinal differences after Nicaea, with the aforementioned prelate, Eusebius of Caesarea, serving as the rallying point of the anti-Nicaeans. After almost two decades of debate, Pope Julius (337-52) urged Constans in the West and his brother Constantius in the East to convoke another general council to heal the conflict. (Constans had assumed power in Italy, while Constantius took over in the East after their father, Constantine, had died.) Bishops of both factions were invited to convene at Sardica in eastern Illyricum and the council was to open in the fall of 343.[15] The western prelates were the first to arrive, and when the eastern bishops came, they opted to have their own meetings rather than join their brothers from the West. The Council of Sardica turned out to be a western synod rather than a general council, and because the fathers decided not to issue any new creedal statement, they discussed and enacted canons on largely disciplinary matters. The canon that perhaps had the greatest impact in the West, canon 3c, reads as follows:

> If sentence should be given against a bishop in any matter and he supposes his case to be not unsound but good, in order that the question may be reopened, let us, if it seems good to your charity, honor the memory of Peter the Apostle, and let those who gave judgment write to Julius, the bishop of Rome, so that, if necessary, the case may be retried in the neighboring provinces and let him appoint arbiters; but if it cannot be shown that his case is of such a sort as to need a new trial, let the judgment once given not be annulled, but stand good as before.[16]

This canon was frequently cited in the West as a precedent for appeals to the pope, especially on the part of bishops who felt that they had been unjustly treated either by their metropolitan or by their provincial council. Although it had considerable significance in the western provinces, this norm was not acknowledged as having validity in the eastern churches. In fact, the canons of the Council of Sardica were generally ignored in the East.

Constantius, who ruled as sole emperor for both East and West from 353 to 360, made every effort to replace the Nicene Creed with a new profession of faith which left unclear the degree of resemblance between the Father and the Son. As a committed Arian, he wanted to settle for the assertion that the Son is like the Father, without explicating the nature or the degree of the similarity. According to Henri Marrou, perhaps the greatest historian of late Christian antiquity, this position was termed *homoeism*.[17] At the time of Emperor Valentinian who ruled the West (364-75) and his younger brother Valens (364-78) who ruled in the East, the pro-Nicaean sentiment—always strong in the western provinces—experienced a resurgence in the East through the efforts of the Cappadocians, Basil the Great, his younger brother, Gregory of Nyssa, and his friend, Gregory of Nazianzus. Shortly after Theodosius (379-95) succeeded Valens as emperor in the East, he convoked—along with Gratian, the emperor in the West—a general council to re-emphasize the creed of Nicaea in the hope that this would bring all the churches closer together dogmatically. Theodosius was a Spaniard by birth and a committed Nicaean. The council, which took place in 381 (i.e., Constantinople I), did reaffirm the creed of Nicaea and added a few statements regarding the full divinity of the Holy Spirit which had been questioned by a group of dissenters called the Pneumatomachians. Although the acts of the council's doctrinal decisions have not survived, seven disciplinary canons have been preserved in various collections of conciliar enactments.[18] The third canon, which was to serve as a point of endless disputes between Rome and Constantinople in the succeeding centuries, read: "Because it is new Rome, the bishop of Constantinople is to enjoy the privilege of honor after the bishop of Rome."[19]

When Constantine decided in 324 or thereabouts to move the seat of his government to Byzantium and rename it Constantinople, the seeds of the rivalry between old and new Rome had been sown. The rather harmless sounding wording of canon three of Constantinople I hardly gives evidence of this, but that brief statement was the beginning of a feud which would never really end.

The gifts and the privileges which Constantine showered on the Church, and especially the church in Rome, are legendary. He gave to the pope the magnificent Lateran palace as his residence and financed the construction of numerous churches and basilicas in Rome and elsewhere.

Best known are the extraordinary number, size and grandeur of the basilicas with which Constantine enriched the church in Rome, many of them assigned great endowments of land and other wealth, others in Aquileia to the north, Trier, Antioch, Nicomedia, Jerusalem, Constantinople, Cirta and Savaria. In some now-lost decree, he exempted church lands from taxation; he ordered provincial officials to make available materials and labor for construction; set up the system of gifts of food to churches, grain allowances to nuns, widows and others in church service, excused clerics from shouldering onerous, sometimes ruinous civic obligations, indeed, saw that they were given regular contributions from the fiscus.[20]

After the enactment of toleration for Christians, Constantine erected buildings, and granted exemptions and all varieties of subsidies. He also recognized the local bishop's court as a civilly acceptable means of settling disputes between Christians as well as those involving the clergy. And what is more, his sons continued these favorable dispositions. "Constantine's sons continued and extended their father's gifts to the Church—gifts of exemptions from taxes and inheritance rights, 'and ten thousand other matters, as he [i.e., Constantius] reviewed them, through which he supposed he might bring his subjects over to the faith.' "[21] It would be difficult indeed to overstate the transformation that this revolution created in terms of the growth in numbers of those converting to Christianity as well as those entering the ranks of the clergy.

The Church was becoming very affluent. Bequests and donations poured in from the living and from the estates of the deceased, while the exemptions from taxation and the various government subsidies allowed the ecclesiastical treasuries to swell. Fully half of the total revenues of the Church went to the support of the mounting legions of clergy. As a matter of fact, by the end of the fourth century, the Church was considered to be a heavy economic burden for the state, as the numbers of the clergy continued to expand.[22] Ambrose, Chrysostom, and Augustine frequently complained about insincere conversions as well as the inertia of many of the clergy.

The growth of the Christian population from 300 to 400 was truly astounding. A fair estimate of the number of Christians at the beginning of the fifth century could run as high as 20 to 25 million, with the great majority of them situated in the East. "So far as we can form an impression of numbers at the turn of the fourth to the fifth century, the entire Levant from the Euphrates south to Egypt was not much more than half converted."[23] Looking at the entire empire, however, MacMullen concludes, "the empire overall appears to have been predominantly non-Christian in 400 A.D."[24]

The cities were evidently the most heavily Christianized, while the rural areas—which by general agreement accounted for the great majority of the empire's total population—were not as yet widely evangelized. The region bordering the Aegean Sea was, according to Marrou, the most heavily populated, with Asia Minor apparently having the greatest concentration of Christians.[25] In the West, there were large Christian congregations only in Italy and northern Africa. Given those caveats, the growth of Christianity in the 300s can only be described as phenomenal. The increase within that period was probably in the range of 400 to 500 percent. It must be noted, however, that many of these converts were of the nominal variety. Large numbers became Christians for non-religious reasons, because in a high percentage of cases it was financially and/or socially more advantageous to do so.

> Around 350 very little separated a Christian from his pagan counterpart in Roman society. Dancing, rowdy celebrations, especially those connected with cemeteries, the theatre, games, resorting to baths, a variety of magical practices and the like, often aroused suspicion and provoked denunciation by bishops; but they were part of that vast "shared territory" which Christians inherited from the pagan past.[26]

By the time of Jerome (d. 420) and Augustine (d. 430), the question of what constituted authentic Christianity became quite pressing. Terms like "semi-Christians" and "paganized" Christians came into frequent use to illustrate what was happening to church affiliation.[27] Henri Marrou describes the overall effect of lived Christianity at this time on the larger society as marginal.[28] For example, exposure of newborn infants was apparently not yet clearly prohibited by the Church. Tyranny, cruelty, and torture continued within the Christianized empire. As a matter of fact, some feel that torture and cruelty were actually on the increase. Such was the state of things after almost 100 years of Christianization in the empire. It would be unfair, however, not to add that one-fourth of the wealth of the Church was given to the poor, who were becoming part of the retinue of the local bishop. With massive unemployment in the cities, especially in the East, the needy were attracted to the services that the Church provided for them. This mission to the poor and the destitute, centering around the bishop, constituted one of the most important contributions of the Church in the fourth century and beyond.

Turning our attention once again to the Roman congregation, whatever was said about the growing wealth of the Church applies *a fortiori* to the situation in Rome, where gifts and bequests to the Roman pontiff and his clergy were very much in evidence. The entry on Pope Sylvester (314-35) in *The Book of Pontiffs* (the *Liber Pontificalis*) lists pages of donations of church buildings and appointments, precious objects, lands, and income-bearing property of all sorts which were bestowed on the Roman congregation during his twenty-one-year reign.[29] A.H.M. Jones relates that one of the more notable pagan senators of Rome, Argorious Praetextatus, said—although in jest—to Pope Damasus (366-84), "Make me bishop of Rome and I will become a Christian tomorrow."[30]

Sylvester remains a rather uncertain quantity in the history of the papacy because we know so little about him. Other than presiding over the enormous increase of wealth which occurred during his years as pontiff, he did not do much to elevate the prestige of the Roman see. Pope Julius I (337-52), whom we encountered earlier in connection with the council of Sardica, was a forceful prelate who had the respect of the western bishops. Much of what he accomplished, though, was probably undone by his successor, Liberius (352-66), who subscribed to an eastern creed which had definite Arian undertones.[31]

After a hotly disputed election, Pope Damasus (366-84) began a line of strong-willed, talented, and influential pontiffs who would give permanent shape to the office over the next 100 years. He was not as influential in regard to his dealings with imperial Rome as was his contemporary, Bishop Ambrose of Milan, but he did concentrate on the task of forging stronger and more effective ties between Rome and the western churches. This endeavor was raised to another level under Pope Siricius (384-99), who utilized the instrument of decretal letters (i.e., authoritative written responses to questions submitted to him from various churches) to extend his power in the West. He frequently directed, or commanded, bishops in Gaul, southern and central Italy, and even in northern Africa to follow his proposed course of action. He referred to his responsibility for the Catholic world as a "solicitude" for all the churches, although his primatial position in the East was regarded as one of honor only.[32]

Pope Innocent I (401-17) addressed the churches of the West in the same tones as Siricius, although shortly after his death, the north African synod of 419 A.D. unambiguously restricted the rights of bishops and clergy to appeal to Rome.[33] It was Innocent who ordered that all major cases (i.e., *causae majores*), such as disputes between metropolitans and appeals from provincial councils, should be dispatched to Rome for settlement. The number of "major cases" was, however, not enumerated and hence was capable, over the years, of almost infinite extension.

POPE LEO I (440-61)

Although Damasus, Siricius, and Innocent made their contributions to the development of what could be called the beginnings of the medieval papacy, it was Leo I (440-61) who truly shaped the office and gave it a direction which determined its destiny for centuries. It is indeed ironic that we know so little about his life prior to 440 A.D. He was probably born in Rome of Tuscan parents, but his many letters and sermons reveal very little about his personal history. It can be said that he did not so much expand the prerogatives charted out by his predecessors since Damasus as to implement them in a consistent and thorough manner. As is the case with so many great figures, the circumstances of his time were extremely favorable to him. The north African church and its traditionally independent conciliar tradition had all but vanished with the collapse of the region, especially Carthage, to the Vandals. The Spanish church and its emerging provincial structure had suffered considerable damage at the hands of the Visigoths, leaving the Spanish bishops hardly any alternative but to have recourse to Rome in cases of dispute.

In spite of the pillages of Alaric, the Visigoth, early in the century, the often recounted threat of Attila the Hun in 452, and the devastation wrought by Gaiseric the Vandal in 455, Rome enjoyed the favor of the western emperor, Valentinian III (425-55) who, although generally weak as a leader, did enhance the prestige of the pope in the West by means of an edict which he issued in 445:

Inasmuch as the pre-eminence of the Apostolic See is assured by the merit of St. Peter, the first of the bishops, by the leading position of the city of Rome and also by the authority of the holy synod, let not presumption strive to attempt anything contrary to the authority of that See . . . we decree by perpetual edict that nothing shall be attempted by the Gallican bishops, or by those of any other province, contrary to the ancient custom, without the authority of the venerable pope of the Eternal City. But whatsoever the authority of the Apostolic See has enacted, or shall enact, let that be held as law by all.[34]

Although the effect of Valentinian's edict can be overstated, there is no doubt that it enhanced the authority of the Roman pontiff in the West. In the East, however, its effect was negligible.

Before beginning a review of Leo's writings on the papal jurisdictional role, it might be helpful to share an insight advanced by the French historian Pierre Batiffol earlier in the century and subsequently articulated by Yves Congar:

> Batiffol has proposed the very enlightening idea of three zones in which the papal *potestas* was exercised: (1) a zone around the city of Rome, immediately subject to Rome, (2) the zone of the West outside of Italy, and (3) a zone of universal extension, but concretely representing the East where Rome only intervened, but with authority, as arbiter of the whole communion and as judge in *causae majores*.[35]

These zones could be seen taking shape from the time of Popes Damasus and Siricius. Congar adds:

> And yet, when the popes of the fifth century addressed themselves to the bishops of the East, they did not do so in the same tone and manner they adopted when addressing themselves to the bishops of Italy, or even more generally, to the bishops of the West. To the West, the popes spoke in the tone of the decretals; the East was treated as an associate.[36]

The intent of at least some of the popes of the fifth century and beyond was seemingly to bring all the churches of East and West into one zone, where they would be able to rule "in the tone of the decretals." Congar argues:

> The development was oriented towards a certain abolition of the lines of demarcation between these different zones. The papacy tended to govern all the churches as if they were within her metropolitan competence and, from the liturgical point of view as well as from the canonical and, apparently, from the dogmatic as well, to bring them in line with herself. She succeeded in the West except, of course, in the countries affected by the Reformation . . . but never in the East.[37]

This policy which was undertaken by a number of Roman pontiffs, beginning in the fifth century and persistently though intermittently pursued in the succeeding centuries, was indeed an effort on the part of Rome "to govern all the churches as if they were within her metropolitan competence." This development—which certainly did not occur in one pontificate or in one or two generations—did indeed represent a major break with the organizational pattern of the first three or four centuries, and a discontinuity of significant proportions.

Pope Leo's view of papal authority is set forth in his Sermon III delivered on the anniversary of his episcopal consecration.

> The dispensation of truth therefore abides, and the blessed Peter, persevering in the strength of the Rock, which he has received, and has not abandoned the helm of the Church which he undertook. For he was ordained before the rest in such a way that from his being called the Rock, from his being pronounced the Foundation, from his being constituted the Doorkeeper of the kingdom of heaven, from his being set as the Umpire to bind and to loose, whose judgments shall retain their validity in heaven, from all these mystical ties we might know the nature of his association with Christ. And still today he more fully and effectually performs what is entrusted to him, and carries out every part of his duty and charge in Him and through Whom he has been glorified. And so if anything is rightly done and rightly decreed by us . . . it is of his work and merits whose power lives and authority prevails in his See.[38]

Leo saw himself as a veritable reincarnation of Peter who continued to speak and act through him.

As the sole metropolitan of all the dioceses in central and southern Italy, he directly applied the canon law to all sorts of cases involving the clergy (Epistle IV), the alienation of church property (Ep. XVII), the manner of reciting one's sins in preparation for penance (Ep. CLXVIII), and so forth. Leo ordered the bishops of Sicily to send representatives to the annual Roman synod each fall in order to foster correct teaching and proper ecclesiastical discipline (Ep. XVI). Regarding the churches in northern Italy, there are four letters addressed to the bishops of the province of Aquileia (which became independent of Milan shortly after 400 A.D.), one to Milan and one to Ravenna, which became the seat of the western emperor ca. 402. T.G. Jalland summarizes the activity of Leo in northern Italy: "even beyond the limits of its metropolitan jurisdiction, the Roman see in his [i.e., Leo's] time was regarded as the obvious center to which there should be recourse for the solution of points of uncertainty in matters of discipline, and for support in dealing with irregularities."[39]

Jalland notes that beyond his own sphere of metropolitan jurisdiction, Leo only intervened directly in the affairs of individual dioceses in those cases where he distrusted the respective metropolitan bishop's loyalty to proper canonical discipline.[40] His ordinary course of action was to respond to problems and inquiries through the appropriate metropolitan prelate.

The situation of the churches in northern Africa was desperate indeed after the fall of Carthage to the Vandals in 439. Unlike the Ostrogoths, the Visigoths, and the Burgundians, the Vandals were Arians who actively persecuted Catholics. In a letter to the bishops of Mauretania—written after the Vandals had invaded that country in 442—Leo deals with a whole range of canonical issues regarding ordinations and clerical discipline, and he concludes:

> But whenever other cases arise which concern the state of the Church and the harmony of priests, we wish them to be first sifted by yourselves in the fear of the Lord, and a full account of all matters settled or needing settlement sent to us, that those things which have been properly and reasonably decided, according to the usage of the Church, may receive our corroborative sanction also.[41]

While Carthage was operating as the primatial see, there was rather consistent and firm resistance to papal interference. As Jalland notes, "In the time of Celestine I [i.e., 422-32] the synod of Carthage did not hesitate to express its mind freely in regard to the intervention of that see [i.e., Rome] in its affairs. Now, however, its place had been taken by the papacy [i.e., after 439], and the primacy of Carthage had ceased to exist."[42]

The procedure of operating through the metropolitan of the province was normally followed by Leo in connection with his dealings with the churches in southern Gaul. However, there was one situation—involving Hilary, the metropolitan of Arles—which really irritated Leo because he was convinced that Hilary had exceeded his powers in deposing the bishop of Besançon, also a metropolitan. Leo examined the case in a Roman synod and judged that Hilary had acted on false information, and hence unfairly deposed Bishop Celidonius.[43] Pope Leo had responded to an appeal from Celidonius and undoubtedly judged this case to be a *causa major*. Finally in a letter to Theodore, the bishop of Forum Julii (i.e., Fréjus, near Nice), responding to his questions on penitential absolution, Leo begins: "Your first proceeding, when anxious, should have been to have consulted your metropolitan on the point which seemed to need inquiry, and if he too was unable to help you, you should both have asked to be instructed by us."[44] The pope concludes the letter with the following observation:

> These answers, brother, which I have given to your questions in order that nothing different be done under the excuse of ignorance, you shall bring to the notice of your metropolitan; that if there chance to be any of the brethren who before now have thought there was any doubt about these points, they may be instructed by him concerning what I have written to you.[45]

The methodology of operating through the metropolitans in Gaul is clearly articulated in the Fréjus case.

Although Leo apparently had minimal contact with the churches in Spain, northern Gaul, and Britain, eastern Illyricum and its primatial see of Thessolonica received a good deal of his attention because of their proximity to Constantinople. Since the days of Popes Damasus and Siricius, efforts had been made to retain that area as part of the Roman pontiff's sphere of influence. Leo was also very concerned about keeping eastern Illyricum under his control. There is no doubt about the fact that as one traveled eastward Rome's primacy of honor was recognized, but not much more. It was thus crucial for Leo to reaffirm the powers of Bishop Anastasius of Thessolonica as vicar of the pope in the region.

> Seeing that, as my predecessors acted towards you, so too I, following their example, have delegated my authority to you, beloved: so that you, imitating our gentleness, might assist us in the care which we owe primarily to all the churches by divine institution, and might to a certain extent make up for our personal presence in visiting those provinces that are far off from us . . . For as it was free for you to suspend the more important matters and the harder issues while you awaited our opinion, there was no reason nor necessity for you to go out of your way to decide what was beyond your powers.[46]

Leo's vision of his own role is strikingly reflected here. He inherits by divine institution the care or "solicitude" of all the churches, and this solicitude he fulfills—in regard to the province of eastern Illyricum—by means of his vicar, Bishop Athanasius of Thessolonica, whom Leo regards as taking his place in that distant jurisdiction. The letter further points up the jurisdictional hierarchy which Leo wants recognized in Illyricum and elsewhere. The local bishops should bring disputed issues to the semiannual provincial synod, which can then send out any appeals to the metropolitan, who is to have recourse to the vicar of the territory. The vicar is to remand whatever remains unsettled to Rome.[47] By way of a historical footnote, the two dioceses of Decia and Macedonia, the heart of eastern Illyricum, were formally transferred in 379 A.D. by the western emperor, Gratian, to his counterpart in the East, Theodosius. Previously they fell within the sphere of the prefecture of Italy, and hence were naturally within the pope's ambit. However, in spite of the best efforts of Leo, the Illyrian churches, including Thessolonica, moved inevitably into the realm of the patriarch of Constantinople.

A word needs to be added regarding Pope Leo's role in the Council of Chalcedon in 451. Some years before, he had sent a treatise in the form of a letter to Bishop Flavian, the patriarch of Constantinople (446-49), outlining his position on the Christological issues that had been recently raised by the old monk Eutyches of Constantinople. Leo affirmed the distinction of natures and the single personhood of Jesus in a rather flowery but not particularly

larly profound manner. The *Tome to Flavian*, however, did play a significant part in the formulation of the doctrinal decree of Chalcedon. The fact that Leo's work was in reasonably close agreement with the Christological position of Cyril of Alexandria (d. 444) no doubt helped to move the council forward to the articulation of their *Definition of Faith* in late October 451. In the very heart of the *Definition* we read:

> And because of those who are attempting to corrupt the mystery of the economy and are shamelessly and foolishly asserting that He who was born to the holy Virgin Mary was a mere man, it has accepted the synodical letters of the blessed Cyril, pastor of the church in Alexandria, to Nestorius and to the Orientals, as being well suited to refuting Nestorius' mad folly and to providing an interpretation for those who in their religious zeal might desire an understanding of the saving creed.
>
> To these it has suitably added against false believers and for the establishment of orthodox doctrine, the letter of the primate of the greatest and older Rome, the most blessed and most saintly Archbishop Leo, written to the sainted Archbishop Flavian, to put down Eutyches' evil-mindedness, because it is in agreement with great Peter's confession and represents a support we have in common.[48]

Historians consider that Leo's *Tome to Flavian* and its influence on the fathers at Chalcedon constituted the high point of the doctrinal prestige of the papacy in the East. The council also issued disciplinary canons in subsequent sessions, the most celebrated of which—for our purposes—is canon 28. The crucial sentence of the canon is:

> The fathers rightly accorded prerogatives to the see of older Rome, since that is an imperial city; and moved by the same purpose the 150 most devout bishops [at Constantinople in 381] apportioned equal prerogatives to the most holy see of new Rome, reasonably judging that the city which is honored by the imperial power and senate and enjoying privileges equalling older imperial Rome, should also be elevated to her level in ecclesiastical affairs and take second place after her.[49]

This canon was immediately rejected by the Roman legates at the council and was never approved by Pope Leo or any of his successors. Leo did belatedly ratify the council's doctrinal decrees in March 453, but he rejected canon 28 as running contrary to the venerable council of Nicaea and the most ancient traditions. It was the explicit contention of the popes at least from the time of Damasus that the unique prerogatives of the see of Rome were not the result of Rome's status as an imperial city but rather the result of St. Peter's singular ties to the Roman church.

Pope Leo was, by most estimates, the outstanding churchman of his time. His many letters and sermons reveal him as a person of remarkable pastoral and diplomatic talents, with a consistency and a balance in his dealings with emperors, patriarchs, bishops, and faithful, both of which are extremely rare. His relations with the churches of the West raised the status of the papacy to a level heretofore unknown. Although the East was unwilling to concede to him any more than a primacy of honor, Leo's reputation in the East towered over that of any of his predecessors. He truly deserved the title of Leo the Great.

DOCTRINAL DIVISIONS AFTER CHALCEDON (451)

The Roman Empire in the late fifth century was in a state of deep decline. Both East and West were ruled by the relatives of Theodosius I for more than half a century after his death in 395 A.D. The descendants were weak and indecisive at best at a time when both East and West were besieged by barbarian tribes—the Vandals, the Visigoths, the Ostrogoths, the Burgundians, the Huns, and other lesser clans. The losses suffered by the Roman armies in the West were staggering. This dramatically weakened the western empire financially. There were no revenues from Spain or north Africa, leaving the tax burden in Italy extremely heavy. The East was considerably better off. Asia Minor, Syria, and Egypt—the most affluent sectors of the empire—were relatively unscathed by the barbarian attacks. Although the fiscal policies of the East were more efficient and the tax revenues available allowed the eastern emperors to field more formidable armies and maintain stronger defenses, the religious divisions became more and more severe after the Council of Chalcedon. A.H.M. Jones describes the situation:

> The doctrinal decisions of the council led to more lasting troubles. It would no doubt have been difficult in any case to reconcile the two theological parties, but the Council of Chalcedon by adopting a formula which all theologians of the Alexandrian school could not but regard as Nestorian made the task impossible. In Egypt and Palestine the reaction was immediate and violent.[50]

When the eastern emperor, Theodosius II, died in 450, he was succeeded by a relatively unknown military tribune, Marcian (450-57), whose political position was enhanced by his marriage to Pulcheria, Theodosius' older sister. After Marcian, the East was governed by another unknown military officer, Leo (457-74), who was then succeeded by his son-in-law, Zeno (474-91). It was Emperor Zeno who made a special effort to address the religious divisions which were literally tearing the East apart. In Egypt, Palestine, Syria, and parts of Asia Minor, there was widespread and deepening opposition to Chalcedon.

With the help of Acacius, the patriarch of Constantinople, he drafted an imperial constitution, the *Henotikon*, or the decree of union, which was intended to downplay the definition of Chalcedon and thereby win back the Monophysites and others who were convinced that Chalcedon had unduly exaggerated the distinction between the divinity and the humanity of Christ, thus destroying the essential unity of the God-man. The *Henotikon* stressed the critical significance of the creed of Nicaea which was confirmed by the Councils of Constantinople (381) and Ephesus (431). It also subscribed to the chapters of Cyril of Alexandria, and it seemed to condemn any other symbol or definition of faith. "And we anathematize anyone who has held or holds any other opinion, either now or at any other time, whether at Chalcedon or at any synod whatsoever."[51]

Even the downplaying of Chalcedon did not satisfy the Monophysites, who wanted an explicit condemnation of that council. Pope Felix III (483-92) refused to subscribe to the *Henotikon* and, in a Roman synod of 484, excommunicated Patriarch Acacius, who in turn excommunicated Felix. This schism between the two sees—the first in Christian history—lasted until 519 A.D. Although there were no notable Christological controversies in the West, the political and economic situation had deteriorated profoundly since Pope Leo's time. The Roman army had lost control of Africa, Spain, Dalmatia, and all but the southwest corner of Gaul.[52] In 476 the puppet emperor, Romulus Augustulus, was deposed by a Scirian army officer named Odoacer who consolidated his position on the peninsula and called himself king of Italy. Emperor Zeno in Constantinople knew that something had to be done about this situation in the West because Odoacer was continuing to expand his power base into Sicily, Dalmatia, and beyond. He therefore commissioned King Theodoric of the Ostrogoths to recover Italy. Theodoric's powerful army forced Odoacer to retreat and retire to the enclave around Ravenna. The new eastern emperor, Anastasius (491-518), made Theodoric king of Italy and he ruled the West from 493 to 526.

Theodoric, who proceeded to settle his Ostrogoths in Italy, was careful to preserve the governmental structure of the Roman Empire as much as possible. Although he was an Arian, he was very tolerant of Chalcedonian theology. A.H.M. Jones says about him:

> Having once become king of Italy he became a very different man from the Theodoric who had brutally ravaged the Illyrian and Thracian provinces. Not only did he do his utmost to conciliate his Italian subjects, but he strove to maintain peace with all of his neighbors.[53]

The rupture of communion between Rome and Constantinople was a cause of great anxiety in both capitals. When Pope Gelasius (492-96) succeeded Felix III, he was keenly aware of all that had transpired since the *Henotikon*, because he was probably the archdeacon for both Popes Simplicius (468-83) and Felix III. A.K. Ziegler notes, "The new pontiff had not even sent a letter to Emperor Anastasius at the time he became pope. A word of complaint from the emperor himself sent by a returning embassy of Theodoric the Ostrogoth at length caused the pope to write."[54]

Gelasius' response has often been cited through the centuries as a veritable charter for the growth and expansion of the power of the medieval papacy. After attesting that he was pleased to write the emperor, Gelasius embarked on his memorable discourse on the two powers by which the world is governed:

> Two there are, august emperor, by which the world is chiefly ruled, the sacred authority (*auctoritas*) of the priesthood and the royal power (*potestas*). Of these the responsibility of the priests is more weighty in so far as they will answer for the kings of men themselves at the divine judgment. You know, most clement son, that, although you take the precedence over all mankind in dignity, nevertheless you piously bow the neck to those who have charge of divine affairs and seek from them the means of your salvation, and hence you realize that, in the order of religion, in matters concerning the reception and right administration of the sacraments, you ought to submit yourself rather than rule.[55]

The pope went on to reaffirm the condemnation of the old patriarch, Acacius, and insisted that the emperor also regard Acacius as a schismatic. Gelasius strongly affirmed that it is not the emperor's role to presume to tell the Roman pontiff what to do. A.K. Ziegler summarizes, "As for Gelasius' success in his own time, he failed utterly in his efforts to make the emperor heed and to put an end to the schism."[56]

Regarding the pope's position on "the two powers," A.S. McGrade notes, "There is not in Gelasius' writings a fully worked out doctrine either of the relation of spiritual to temporal authority or of the rightful power of the pope within the Church."[57] Gelasius' approach, however, was quite different from that of Pope Leo I.

> In dealing with the highest worldly authorities of his day, Leo implicitly acknowledges the autonomy of the secular, while at the same time treating his imperial correspondents as if he and they were acting, in religious matters, on the basis of mutual understanding and in pursuit of common values.[58]

After about thirty-five years of schism, Rome and Constantinople finally resolved their differences and were reunited. Pope Hormisdas (514-23) and Emperor Justin I (518-27) agreed to the condemnation of the late Emperors Zeno and Anastasius and the former Patriarch Acacius as heretics. Although Justin was a convinced follower of Chalcedon and his favorite nephew and successor, Justinian (527-65), was more inclined towards orthodoxy than to-ward Monophysitism, they were unable to overcome the profound doctrinal divisions in the East. This was a genuine frustration for Justinian and it plagued him throughout his life. He even tried to heal the rift on the basis of a Theopaschite formula which attempted to blur the lines drawn by the distinctions between the persons and natures in the Trinity and in Christ—the distinctions that had so rattled the Monophysites. Justinian had hoped that this formula, which spelled out nothing more than that "one of the Trinity has suffered for us," would satisfy the Monophysites, but even this was not acceptable to them.

In 533 A.D. Justinian launched an invasion of north Africa in an effort to win back the West from the barbarians. His most effective general, Belisarius, conquered Africa and then invaded Sicily in 535. When Belisarius occupied Rome unopposed, he encountered the very recently elected Pope Silverius (536-37), the son of Pope Hormisdas, who like his father, was an ally of the Ostrogoths who were controlling most of Italy. It is almost impossible to un-ravel the series of events that occurred at this juncture. Apparently Justinian's wife, the Empress Theodora, a convinced Monophysite, had prevailed on the papal representative in Constantinople, the deacon Vigilius, to accept her aid in promoting him to the papacy if he would then assist her in returning the patriarchate of Constantinople back into the hands of someone more amiable to the Monophysites. Some such deal was apparently cut and Vigilius made his way to Rome with orders from Theodora to Belisarius to insure his election as pope.[59]

> So Belisarius returned to Rome [from Naples] and summoned Silverius [the reigning pope] to his official residence, the Pincian palace, and tried to persuade him to renounce Chalcedon and embrace Monophysitism. When he failed, Belisarius charged the pope with writing treasonable letters to the Goths, promising to admit them to Rome.[60]

Belisarius then exiled Pope Silverius and insisted that the Roman clergy elect Vigilius (537-55) as the new pope. Silverius was brought back to Rome under guard, perhaps to be tried on the basis of his pro-Gothic sympathies, but there does not seem to have been a trial. According to *The Book of Pontiffs*, Vigilius "took Silverius into his own charge, so to speak, sent him into exile at Pontiae and fed him on the bread of affliction and the water of distress."[61] Silverius died in exile in late 537 A.D.

POPE VIGILIUS (537-55) AND THE "THREE CHAPTERS"

The almost twenty years of bitter warfare between the imperial army and the Goths, which left Rome and many parts of Italy in utter ruins, was finally over in 554. According to Justinian's Pragmatic Sanction concluding the hostilities, Italy became a province of Constantinople to be ruled by an imperial governor who was soon thereafter given the title of exarch. All during the lengthy Italian campaign, Justinian was attempting to reconcile the Monophysites with the adherents of Chalcedon in spite of the failure of his efforts in pushing the Theopaschite position. The emperor was finally persuaded that the only possible avenue to unity lay in the formal condemnation of several works of three theologians who were considered by the Monophysites to be their archenemies: Theodore of Mopsuestia (d. 428), Theodoret of Cyrus (d. 466), and Ibas of Edessa (d. 457). The treatises in question were referred to as the "Three Chapters." Justinian had become convinced that he had to engineer a formal condemnation of the "Three Chapters" to eliminate the Monophysites' objections to the doctrine of Chalcedon once and for all. In 544, the emperor promulgated an edict condemning the "Three Chapters" and prevailed on the four eastern patriarchs to subscribe to it. The bishops of the West, however, were opposed to the condemnation because they felt that it seriously compromised Chalcedon. At first Vigilius refused to subscribe to the edict, and on hearing this, Justinian had the pope rather surreptitiously transported to Sicily, where he remained until summoned to Constantinople in late 546, arriving at the capital in January 547. Pope Vigilius, who was not a man of particularly strong principles, responded in 548 with a written opinion which attempted to straddle the fence because he was aware that the emperor wanted from him a judgment of condemnation. Vigilius condemned the "Three Chapters" without prejudice to Chalcedon. This precipitated immediate and vigorous opposition from north Africa, Gaul, Milan, Illyricum, and Dalmatia. Vigilius felt that he had no other option but to advise the emperor to convoke a general council on the matter. Justinian grudgingly agreed and summoned a council which convened in May 553. Although the pope did not attend, there were some 160 bishops at the synod, the overwhelming majority of whom were from the East and in favor of the condemnation. In June 553, the Council of Constantinople II condemned the "Three Chapters." After six months of hesitation, Pope Vigilius approved the enactments of the council, anathematizing Theodore of Mopsuestia, condemning his writings and those of Theodoret and Ibas. Berthold Altaner comments on the condemnation of Theodore:

> M. Richard and R. Devreese have proved that the texts which were the cause of his condemnation as the father of Nestorianism in 553 are mostly spurious. His writings which have recently become known in a Syriac translation, show that he taught largely orthodox Christology, even though his terminology was still partly inadequate and liable to be misinterpreted.[62]

Vigilius, who had been under house arrest by order of Justinian for the better part of his sojourn in Constantinople, was now released and allowed to return to Italy, his homeland. On his way back to Rome, he died in Syracuse in June 555. This whole affair graphically and tragically illustrates Caesaropapism at its worst, with Justinian simply commandeering the pope, the patriarchs, and the bishops to do his bidding. Perhaps this whole sad affair would not have ended so miserably if Vigilius had been a man of greater integrity. Most of the churches of the West severed relations with Rome over the pope's condemnation of the "Three Chapters." Much of the work of Leo I and several of his predecessors to strengthen Rome's positions vis-à-vis the churches of the West had been at least temporarily undone by Vigilius' vacillation and weakness.

After the death of Vigilius, Justinian offered the deacon Pelagius the papacy if he would support the condemnation of the "Three Chapters." Pelagius, who had been with Pope Vigilius under house arrest in the East, must have accepted Justinian's terms and returned to Italy. The Romans were not at all happy with Pelagius (555-61). *The Book of Pontiffs* says cryptically that no bishops were found to ordain him: "monasteries and a large number of the devout, the prudent and the nobility withdrew from communion with him, saying that he implicated himself in the death of Pope Vigilius and so had brought great punishments upon himself."[63]

By the end of his pontificate, Pelagius had apparently persuaded central and southern Italy that the condemnation of the "Three Chapters" did not run directly counter to the definition of Chalcedon.[64] Opposition to the papal condemnation, however, ran high in the West for many years.

ITALY INVADED BY THE LOMBARDS (568)

After the death of Justinian in 565 A.D., serious military threats emerged in the East, forcing his successors to concentrate on the challenges in the eastern half of the empire and more or less ignore the West. This was especially true of Emperors Tiberius II (578-82) and Maurice (582-602). This change of emphasis played into the hands of the Lombards, who invaded Italy in 568. Most of the remaining imperial troops in Italy were drawn close to Ravenna to defend the exarch's residence and headquarters, leaving the central part of the peninsula and Rome especially vulnerable to attack. The popes remained loyal to the emperor in spite of the fact that they were left on their own to defend themselves against the formidable Lombards, who were a military threat and, as Arians, a religious threat as well. Under Pope Pelagius I and his successors, the extensive patrimonies and estates of the Holy See, which were per force neglected during the 535-55 hostilities, were to a considerable extent restored and revitalized. This resulted in increased revenues for the pontiffs, so that they were able to assume more and more of the governmental functions which were being abandoned by imperial officials. However, the demands of the time were almost more than the popes could manage. *The Book of Pontiffs* relates the following in its brief entry concerning Pope Benedict I (575-79): "At that time the Lombard nation invaded the whole of Italy, and the famine then was so extreme that a large number of walled towns even surrendered to the Lombards to relieve their want and hunger."[65]

Benedict was succeeded by Pelagius II (579-90), who was ordained without waiting for imperial confirmation, "because the Lombards were besieging Rome and causing much devastation in Italy."[66] A letter, cited by J. Richards, from Pelagius II in 584 to his ambassador (or *apocrisiarios*) in Constantinople, the deacon Gregory, rather graphically reveals the extent of the crisis in Rome:

> Unless God prevails on the heart of our most gracious prince [i.e., Emperor Maurice] to show to his servants the pity he feels and to grant us a commander or general, then we are lost. For the territory around Rome is completely undefended and the exarch writes that he can do nothing for us, being unable himself to defend the region around Ravenna.[67]

The conflict with the Lombards, which so frustrated Pelagius II, was to be a source of abiding frustration for his illustrious successor, Pope Gregory I, whom we shall deal with in the following chapter.

CONCLUSIONS

The period from the death of Pope Stephen I in 257 A.D. to the accession of Gregory the Great in 590 witnessed enormous changes in the role of the papacy. From Dionysius (260-68) to Damasus (366-84) and Siricius (384-99), the position of the Roman pontiff in the Church universal evolved dramatically. All of the gains from 366 to 440 A.D. were given a discernible shape during the influential reign of Leo I. In central and southern Italy, the pope was the sole metropolitan bishop, with his legislation and his synods exercising the controlling force in that area. Regarding the rest of the West—especially after the fall of Carthage in 439—he enjoyed what later came to be called a "primacy of jurisdiction," although he chose generally to exercise his governing prerogatives through the metropolitans of the various provinces. Only exceptionally did the pope interfere directly in the affairs of individual dioceses. There is practically no evidence to indicate that he attempted as a matter of policy to control episcopal appointments or the selection of the clergy for other significant positions in the dioceses. The pope did function as the final court of appeal in the West and consistently issued rulings on disputed issues of canon law and ecclesiastical procedure.

In the East, however, the situation was very different. There the pope was coping with the ancient traditions of the patriarchs of Antioch, Alexandria, Jerusalem, and the more recently acquired prestige of the patriarch of Constantinople. The Orient had always recognized—from the days of Ignatius of Antioch—a primacy of honor attached to the Roman see, but any sort of "primacy of jurisdiction" was another matter. The evidence we have reviewed up to 590 A.D. does not permit the attribution of any such jurisdictional powers to the Roman pontiff with regard to the eastern churches, and particularly with reference to the patriarchate of Constantinople. There were indeed occasional appeals from eastern bishops and synods which were dispatched to Rome for settlement, but other patriarchs also received such appeals. There was the acknowledgement at Chalcedon of the abiding significance of Leo's *Tome to Flavian*, but there is no undisputed indication of the awareness on the part of the eastern churches that Rome had the power to govern and/or control the affairs of those patriarchates. We shall see that this independence continued to deepen and expand in the succeeding centuries up to the moment of the tragic and permanent split between the eastern and the western traditions.

CHAPTER 4

The Pope Turns to the West

590 to 1000

It is indeed ironic that *The Book of Pontiffs* has so little to say about Pope Gregory I (590-604). The short commentary hardly does his writings justice, and makes no mention of his dealings with the East or with the western churches except to note that it was he who dispatched "Mellitus, Augustine, John and many other God-fearing monks . . . to preach to the English nation and convert them to the Lord Jesus Christ."[1] Gregory was born in Rome around 550 A.D. of well-to-do parents who lived on the rather fashionable Coelian hill. His father was a Roman official, and Gregory followed him into civil service. In 573, he was selected as the Prefect of the City, which was the highest civil office in Rome. A year later he renounced government service and established a monastery in the former family residence. He was ordained a deacon after some five or six years and soon thereafter was sent to Constantinople as Pope Pelagius II's special representative. As we discovered at the end of the previous chapter, Gregory's most urgent mission was to prevail on Emperor Maurice (582-602) to assist the Roman church in its bitter conflict with the Lombards who were about to overrun the former capital.

During a vicious (bubonic?) plague which struck Rome in 590, Pope Pelagius died and the deacon Gregory was elected to succeed him. Although he was not eager for the post, he was for more than thirteen years the most competent, inspiring, and effective pontiff since Leo I. His theological education was not outstanding, but his leadership was exceptional. Henri Marrou notes,

> For a long time people found it difficult to rank Gregory so high. They were too aware of what seems to be a reflection of his age, of that unhappy period when Italy, in her turn, was sinking into barbarism. The culture was impoverished and suffering from sclerosis. True, Gregory wrote essentially correct classical Latin, . . . but his mental equipment is strictly limited. . . . In matters of dogma, St. Gregory, like St. Leo, is very faithful to the Augustinian tradition. But these three men, Augustine, Leo and Gregory, are landmarks in a movement which must be called decadence:

from one to the next shades of thought are lost, difficulties no longer appreciated and a calm dogmatism emerges.[2]

As an administrator, however, in a very difficult time, Gregory was masterful. With the weakening of the imperial regime, more and more responsibilities of civil government were thrust on the bishops of Italy and especially on the bishop of Rome.

With the aristocracy broken and dispersed and the provincial government weak and preoccupied, it fell more and more to the bishop to undertake such responsibilities as the handling of refugees, the negotiating of treaties, the provisioning of cities and the making of defense dispositions. The people came to look upon the bishops, as they did the pope, to protect them from the wrath of the barbarians.[3]

The legislation of Justinian conferred on the bishops administrative powers in wide areas of civil government: "They [i.e., the bishops] were expected to oversee the treatment of prisoners, orphans, foundlings and lunatics, civic expenditures, public works, aqueduct maintenance and the supply of foodstuffs to the troops."[4]

POPE GREGORY I'S ADMINISTRATION

Gregory was adept at these administrative responsibilities, in addition to expanding and improving the management of the extensive patrimonies of the Roman church, which were in the process of being restored after the savage Gothic Wars by his predecessors, especially Pelagius I and Pelagius II. The patrimonies of the Holy See, which were spread throughout Italy, Sicily, northern Africa, Dalmatia, and southern Gaul, provided the popes with revenues which enabled them to perform all these costly tasks. Gregory often complained in his letters about the heavy administrative burdens he had to carry; but he really had no alternative because there was precious little help from the imperial officials in Ravenna, or from the emperor himself.

One can learn a great deal about the way in which Gregory exercised his role as pontiff from his 850 or more letters which have been preserved for posterity. He was regularly involved in the issues of the church in Sicily from the beginning of his reign. It could be said that he managed the affairs of the dioceses on the island very closely, using the agency of a papal legate. He was instrumental in the selection of bishops and ordered the bishops of Sicily to hold an annual synod to deal with ecclesiastical matters.[5]

The sees of Naples, Rimini, and Ravenna were also subject to Gregory's direct jurisdiction, at least in regard to major issues such as the selection of bishops. Milan, which had been decimated by the Lombards, also gradually came under his sway.

> The archbishopric of Milan, once Rome's most powerful ecclesiastical rival in Italy, had been virtually wiped out by the Lombard invasion. Although a handful of the clergy remained in Milan, the bulk of them, together with the archbishop, had taken up residence in the imperial stronghold of Genoa. This put Milan within reach of papal influence. The papacy had no authority over Milanese elections, but as a result of the changed circumstances of the see it began to assume such authority.
> This process of papal interference can be seen developing throughout Gregory's reign and must therefore be a Gregorian innovation.[6]

Jeffrey Richards has observed that Gregory was "reducing Milan to the status of one of the suburbicarian sees and assuming the right of oversight."[7] It is fair to say then that the pontiff saw himself as wielding metropolitan powers of jurisdiction over the greater part of the Italian peninsula, although the alienation of the northern provinces (i.e., Istria and what was left of Milan) over the "Three Chapters" incident and the papal compromises at and after Constantinople II (553) were still alive and active.

The vestiges of that same alienation were evident in northern Africa after the defeat of the Vandals and the restoration of church organization there by Justinian. However, the resurgence of Donatism in Africa was a greater problem for Gregory. Early in his pontificate he wrote to Gennadius, the chief imperial official in Africa, about this problem, urging him to enforce the laws already on the books against the troublesome Donatists (Bk. I, Ep. 74). In a second letter (Bk. I, Ep. 75), the pope urged Gennadius to admonish the bishops of Africa to settle on a primatial city for each province which would then be the fixed see of the primate, rather than having the senior bishop, regardless of the location of his see, serve as primate. (The province of Proconsular Africa had always had that arrangement, of course, with Carthage as its primatial see.) Gregory was not able to bring about such a change, at least in the province of Numidia, as is evident from his subsequent correspondence (Bk. II, Ep. 49). Gennadius, by the way, was lauded by Gregory in a letter sent in 590-91 for having restored and revitalized great portions of the papal patrimonial territories in Africa.

It is interesting to note the tone of Gregory's letter to Adeodatus, the primate of Numidia, in connection with a provincial synod which the Numidians were preparing around 592-93. Gregory was as always most gracious to the elderly bishop (Bk. III, Ep. 49) and recommended that he employ the good services of a certain Bishop Columbus of the same province should he need assistance. The only direction that the pope gave Adeodatus had to do with the qualifications for promotion to sacred orders in the area. Gregory was not demanding that certain ordinances be enacted. He rather exhorted the elderly prelate to do what he could to have these issues discussed and resolved at the forthcoming synod. The pope closed his letter, "When therefore the council which you are taking measures to assemble has, with the succor of God, been brought to a conclusion, gladden us by telling of its unity and concord, and give us information on all points."[8] Gregory also wrote Bishop Columbus imploring him to urge Adeodatus to have the qualifications for sacred orders reexamined at the synod since the matter was so critical for the life of the African church (Bk. III, Ep. 48).

The manner in which the pontiff dealt with the African bishops leads Jeffrey Richards to conclude:

> All the evidence suggests that both church and state authorities wished to keep the papacy at arm's length. Despite the fact that Gregory enjoyed a friendly correspondence with Archbishop Dominicus of Carthage, and that Exarch Gennadius earned papal thanks for settling farmers on the papal estates, papal authority in Africa was virtually non-existent. [Bishop] Columbus explained to Gregory that he was unpopular because of his role as the pope's agent.[9]

Gregory's attempts to exercise his solicitude in the Balkans and Dalmatia had about the same success as his dealings with the African provinces. His efforts to bring the church in Spain into the ambit of Rome were not successful either, even though he had struck up a friendship with Archbishop Leander of Seville while they were both in Constantinople some years before. Although Gregory sent Leander a pallium to remind him of his dependence on the papacy, this did not have much significance in Spain.[10] The Orthodox scholar John Meyendorff adds: "There was practically no Roman intervention in Spain and no appeals to the pope by Spanish bishops."[11] According to Meyendorff, the Spanish bishops kept their distance vis-à-vis Rome because "Gregory and his successors appeared very much as a close ally of the [Byzantine] empire, which occupied the South of Spain and was politically intolerant of the Visigothic kingdom."[12]

Gregory I's efforts in Gaul were somewhat more successful. In 594-95, at the request of the Merovingian king, Childebert II (575-96), he revived the custom of appointing a papal vicar for the churches under the dominion of Childebert (Bk. V, Ep. 53). The pontiff declared the following to Virgilius, the bishop of Arles: "And so we commit to your Fraternity, according to ancient custom, under God, our vicariate in the churches which are under the dominion of our most excellent son, Childebert, with the understanding that their proper dignity, according to primitive usage, be preserved to the several metropolitans."[13]

At the conclusion of his letter of appointment to Virgilius, the pope wrote,

"If any question of faith or perhaps other matters should arise among the bishops which cannot easily be settled, let it be discussed and decided in an assembly of twelve bishops. But if it cannot be decided after the matter has been investigated, let it be referred to our judgment."[14]

On the same day Gregory wrote to all the bishops of Gaul who were Childebert's subjects, informing them of the appointment of Virgilius (Bk. V, Ep. 54). He reminded all of the necessity to gather regularly in synods.[15] It seems that Gregory's efforts to initiate synodal activity for the purpose of instigating religious reforms in the Merovingian kingdom met with little success, and apparently there were no appeals from Gaul to the Roman see during Gregory's pontificate. On balance, outside of Italy, Pope Gregory's influence from a jurisdictional point of view was not seriously recognized in the West.

Let us now examine the pope's relationship with the eastern churches, especially the church in Constantinople. In what seems to be his introductory letter to the patriarchs of Constantinople, Alexandria, Antioch, and Jerusalem (Bk. I, Ep. 25), Gregory pleads his unworthiness and asks each for his prayers. "For while we are joined to you through the aid of prayer, we hold as it were each other by the hand while walking through slippery places, and it comes to pass, through a great provision of charity, that the foot of each is more firmly planted in that one leans upon the other."[16]

He then affirms his commitment to the four gospels and to the four great councils: Nicaea, Constantinople, Ephesus, and Chalcedon. And—as something of an afterthought—also expresses his veneration for the fifth council (i.e., Constantinople II). He concludes the introductory epistle with a doxology.

One of the principal preoccupations of Gregory's pontificate regarding Constantinople was his objection to the title "ecumenical" or "universal" patriarch, employed by John the Faster (582-95) and his successor, Patriarch Cyriacus' (595-606). The title, which was apparently used initially around the time of Pope Gelasius (492-96), was taken up again by John the Faster in 587 and promptly objected to by Gregory's predecessor, Pelagius II. Gregory wrote John a lengthy letter in January 595 (Bk. V, Ep. 18), begging him to stop using the title:

> If then he [i.e., Paul the Apostle in I Cor 1:13] shunned the subjecting of the members of Christ to certain particular apostles, . . . what will you say to Christ, the Head of the universal Church, in the scrutiny of the last judgment, having to put all His members under yourself by the appellation of universal?[17]

In the letter the pope reminded John that he had brought this to his attention many times before through his official representative, Sabinianus, but to no avail. After writing to the patriarch, Gregory dispatched a long missive to

Maurice (Bk. V, Ep. 20) in which he implored the emperor to order John not to use that title henceforth. We learn from a letter the pope wrote to Maurice's wife, Empress Constantina (Bk. V, Ep. 21), that the emperor had replied, requesting Gregory not to press the issue any longer because he, Maurice, did not intend to rebuke the patriarch or request that he drop the title.

Pope Gregory pushed the matter further by writing to Eulogius, the patriarch of Alexandria, and Anastasius, the patriarch of Antioch, urging them, "Wherefore let not your Holiness in your epistles ever call anyone universal, lest you detract from the honor due to yourself in offering to another what is not his due."[18]

In the previous paragraph the pope gives the reason for his admonition:

For as your venerable Holiness knows, the name of universality was offered by the holy synod of Chalcedon to the pontiff of the Apostolic See which by the providence of God I serve. But no one of my predecessors has ever consented to use this profane title, since if one patriarch is called universal, the name of patriarch in the case of the rest is derogated.[19]

Although the pope was apparently oversensitive to the use of a title which had been employed on occasion even by patriarchs of other sees, his words and his thoughts reflect a vision which was clearly not monarchical. He saw the five patriarchs as the regional heads of the Church, and for him it seems that the five were on something of an equal footing, with no one of them exercising a universal jurisdiction over the others. In a letter to patriarch Eulogius, however, he did draw together the three Petrine sees (i.e., Rome, Alexandria, and Antioch):

Wherefore, though there are many apostles, yet with regard to the principality itself, the See of the Prince of the apostles alone has grown strong in authority, which in three places is actually the See of one. For he himself exalted the See in which he deigned to rest and end the present life. He himself adorned the See to which he sent his disciple as evangelist [i.e. Mark]. He himself established the See in which, though he was to leave it, he sat for seven years. Since then it is the See of one, the one See over which by divine authority three bishops now preside, whatever good I hear of you, this I impute to myself.[20]

Although his meaning is not entirely clear, Pope Gregory envisioned the see of Peter as being the principal see which gives firmness and stability to all the other churches. But he held to a threefold location of the one chair of Peter, so that the one Petrine see seemed actually to be realized in three places—and that these three were somehow one. Save for just a couple of exceptions over his long pontificate, he never addressed any of the patriarchs in anything but a fraternal tone. He did not present himself as their superior, but as a brother, always sensitive to that special bond uniting the sees of Antioch, Alexandria, and Rome.

In spite of the fact that Gregory is one of the doctors of the Church, he could not be called a great theologian. As Altaner notes, "We do not find in him original ideas of lasting influence on the great questions of the faith; he consistently follows tradition, especially St. Augustine."[21] However, as a pastor and spiritual leader, there was no one to match him for centuries.

NEW DIFFICULTIES WITH BYZANTIUM (649 to 752)

The story of the popes following Gregory in the seventh century cannot be told without a bit of background as to what was occurring at that time in Byzantium. The worthy Emperor Maurice was assassinated by the lecherous Phocas who reigned from 602 to 610. "Maurice was one of the most outstanding of Byzantine rulers. His reign marks an important step forward in the transformation of the worn-out late Roman Empire into the new and vigorous organization of the medieval Byzantine Empire."[22] Phocas, a soldier and semibarbarian, represented a strong step backward. He headed up a military mutiny against Maurice and overthrew him. Heraclius, the son of the exarch of Carthage, sailed a fleet of ships into the port of Constantinople, deposed the tyrant Phocas, and was crowned emperor by the patriarch in October 610.

> The empire lay in ruins when the government was taken over by Heraclius (610-41), one of the greatest rulers in Byzantine history. The country [after the disastrous years under Phocas] was economically and financially exhausted and the worn-out administrative machinery had come to a standstill.[23]

Heraclius' most serious threat came from Persia, which shortly after his coronation occupied Syria, Armenia, and finally Egypt in 619. In 622, he counterattacked, liberating Asia Minor and Egypt. As he moved with his armies through the Middle East, he witnessed the religious divisions between the Chalcedonians and the Monophysites, and like Justinian, he aspired to find some way, some formula to bring them together again. His trusted ally was Patriarch Sergius (610-38) whom he called on to assist him in this endeavor. Sergius, who was probably a convert from Monophysitism, came upon a formula which he thought might bring together the opposing theological factions.

> Unfortunately, he [i.e., Sergius] does not seem to have been a truly great theological mind, and did not realize at once the implication of the

formula which he proposed as the basis for unity. The formula consisted in affirming that the hypostatic unity of the two natures in Christ, since it implied the unity of one active subject, presupposed one divino-human energy or activity in Christ.[24]

Sergius apparently convinced Emperor Heraclius that this formula, referred to as Monoenergism, would be acceptable to the Monophysites and possibly even to the Nestorians.

Some initial success was achieved in discussions with the Armenian Monophysites as well as with the anti-Chalcedonians in Syria. The efforts in Egypt resulted in a meeting of minds of sorts in 633, and excerpts from the compromise draft were sent to Pope Honorius, who replied by congratulating Sergius for his progress, in spite of some vigorous opposition. The pope agreed with the patriarch's suggestion that, although there were some problems with the assertion of only one energy or source of activity in Christ, the unity of the Savior could perhaps be explained most effectively by positing in him only one will. This approach would clearly exclude the possibility of two conceivably opposing wills existing in Jesus. Pope Honorius I (626-38) picked up on this suggestion and, in his response to Patriarch Sergius, declared, "Indeed the Deity could neither be crucified, nor experience human passions. But (according to the hypostatic union) one says that the Deity suffered and that humanity came from heaven with the Deity. Therefore we confess the one will of our Lord Jesus Christ."[25]

The formula was obviously not a successful one because the exclusion of the human faculty of will from Christ made it impossible to assert that he was fully human. A human nature without a human faculty of willing was very clearly opposed to the whole Christian tradition and to the definition of Chalcedon regarding the identity of Jesus. Emperor Heraclius' document of agreement of 638, the *Ecthesis*, quoted Pope Honorius' statement about the one will in Christ. The unity among Christians so desired by the emperor was never achieved because of a tidal wave that inundated Egypt, Syria, most of Asia Minor, Africa, and large sections of the Persian Empire within several decades after the death of Mohammed in 632. The sudden and devastating Islamic invasions rendered pointless the issue of the reunion of the Chalcedonians and the Monophysites for many generations. Pope Honorius died in 638 without having had the opportunity to clarify or retract his position. Pope Martin I (649-55) presided over a council at the Lateran in 649 which condemned the *Ecthesis* as heretical and anathematized Patriarch Sergius—who also died in 638—and two of his successors. No condemnations were levied against the late Emperor Heraclius, his successor, Constans II (642-68), or Pope Honorius. The noted church historian, Hans-Georg Beck, observes with regard to Patriarch Sergius: "To make him suffer for what people are unwilling to charge to Pope Honorius I is one of the indiscretions of church history."[26]

Emperor Constans II was bitterly opposed to the Lateran synod's declaration of the two wills in Christ because he had forbidden any further discussion of the issue of one or two energies and/or one or two wills in 648. Pope Martin was deported to Constantinople in 653 and tried in the patriarch's court. "The pope was defrocked, publicly divested of his episcopal ornaments, chained and humiliated. He died in exile in Kherson in the Crimea, on September 16, 655, and is venerated by the Church as a confessor."[27] Meyendorff adds: "The participation of the patriarch in these shameful events makes this period, morally, the lowest point in the history of the church of Constantinople."[28]

Both Popes Eugene I (654-57) and Vitalian (657-72) were able to sidestep confrontations with Emperor Constans II, who remained adamantly opposed to the Lateran decrees of 649. After the emperor's assassination in Sicily in 668, he was succeeded by his son, Constantine IV (668-85), who was not especially interested in the theological debates that so fascinated his father and grandfather. Given the empire's losses in the East at the hands of the Arabs, Constantine was most interested in strengthening his base in southern Italy and in the West, and thus he was eager to expand his ties with the pope. Accordingly he wrote Pope Donus (675-78), outlining his plan to call a council in Constantinople to settle the issue of Monoenergism and Monotheletism (one will in Christ) once and for all. Pope Agatho (678-81)—who had meanwhile succeeded Donus—was obviously pleased with the idea and dispatched a letter to the emperor outlining the Roman position on the issue. He omitted the deviant theories of his predecessor, Honorius I, declaring that the Roman church in the matter of Monotheletism "had never departed from the way of truth."[29]

The sixth ecumenical council, Constantinople III, convened in the imperial palace in November 680 under the presidency of the young emperor. Attendance was quite modest because of the fact that Egypt, Africa, Palestine, Syria, and most of Asia Minor were overrun by the Muslims. Giuseppe Alberigo summarizes the events of the synod:

> The doctrinal conclusions of the council were defined in the seventeenth session and promulgated in the eighteenth and last session on 16 September 681. The acts of the council, signed both by 174 fathers and finally by the emperor himself, were sent to Pope Leo II [682-83] who had succeeded Agatho, and he, when he had approved them, ordered them to be translated into Latin and to be signed by all of the bishops of the West. Constantine IV, however, promulgated the decrees of the council in all parts of the empire by imperial edict. The council did not debate church discipline and did not establish any disciplinary canons.[30]

The doctrine of the two wills in Christ was articulated as follows, "And we proclaim equally two natural volitions or wills in Him and two natural principles of action which undergo no division, no change, no partition, no confusion, in accordance with the teaching of the holy fathers."[31]

In the same decree, those who had held deviant opinions were explicitly condemned:

Theodore, who was bishop of Pharan, Sergius, Paul and Peter, who were bishops of this imperial city, and further Honorius, who was the pope of elder Rome, Cyrus, who held the see of Alexandria, and Marcarius, who was recently bishop of Antioch, and his disciple, Stephen.[32]

John Meyendorff adds:

The condemnation of Honorius did not raise any objection on the part of the Roman legates [at the council] or of Agatho's successor, St. Leo II (682-83). It was reaffirmed by the seventh council (787) and repeated by all popes at their consecration until the eleventh century.[33]

Emperor Constantine IV was followed by his young son, Justinian II (685-95; 705-11), who convoked a follow-up council in 691 in the Trullan hall of the imperial palace to deal with disciplinary issues which had not been dealt with in the last two ecumenical councils. The Council in Trullo, or the Quinisext Council, was an eastern synod which laid out the foundations for the subsequent development of an independent eastern canon law. George Ostrogorsky summarizes the results of the gathering:

From the historical point of view the most significant decrees of the Quinisextum Council were those revealing differences in matters of discipline in the eastern and western Churches, as for instance the permission of priests to marry, or the express rejection of the Roman fast on Saturdays. Scarcely ten years after agreement on doctrinal matters had been reached at the sixth General Council, fresh disputes now broke out between Rome and Byzantium. This time conflict did not arise over matters of faith, but over questions which revealed the divergent developments of the two world centers.[34]

Justinian II sent a copy of the 102 disciplinary canons that had been enacted to Pope Sergius (687-701), who refused to sign them because he considered them as lacking authority. Since the emperor's influence in the West did not allow him to do what his grandfather, Constans II, had done to Pope Martin I some forty years earlier, the emperor simply had to live with the pope's refusal. Justinian later renewed his efforts with Pope John VII (705-07) but met with no more success than he had with Sergius. *The Book of Pontiffs* tells a rather touching story of the visit of Pope Constantine (708-15) to Byzantium in 710.

> At that time the emperor [Justinian II] sent the pontiff Constantine a mandate in which he bade him to go up to the imperial city. In obedience to the emperor's commands, the holy man immediately had a fleet prepared to tackle the journey by sea. . . . When the lord emperor Justinian heard of his arrival, he was filled with great joy. . . . On the day they saw each other, the Christian Augustus, crown on head, prostrated himself and kissed the feet of the pontiff.[35]

After a seemingly pleasant visit of some days at Nicomedia, the emperor "renewed all the church's privileges and gave the pope leave to return home."[36] This was the last visit by a Roman pontiff to Byzantium until Pope Paul VI's pilgrimage to Istanbul in 1967.

The years after Justinian II were a touchy time for the empire. "From 711 to 717 the Byzantine empire passed through a period of short reigns, usurpations, instability and severe threats from the Arabs. The Greeks were neither willing nor able to pay much attention to Italy."[37]

It was while the Arabs were at the very walls of Constantinople (717-18) that the Lombards, under King Liutprand (712-44), went on the attack again in Italy, reviving the Lombard scheme of occupying all of the peninsula. After Emperor Leo III (717-41) had defeated the Arabs in the East, it was his intention to revitalize the imperial rule in Italy. One of his first moves was to impose a crippling tax on all the estates in the West, which would have severely damaged the papacy inasmuch as it was probably the largest landholder in Italy. Pope Gregory II (715-31), a gifted leader, simply refused to pay the additional levies which enraged Emperor Leo such that he tried to orchestrate a plot through his exarch in Ravenna to kill the pontiff, but the Romans and some of their allies thwarted the plan. In 726-27, the same Leo launched an attack against the cult of icons, which had become "one of the chief expressions of Byzantine piety."[38] According to Ostrogorsky, "it was contact with the Muslim world which first fanned the smouldering distrust of icons into open flame."[39] Although many eastern Christians considered the devotion to icons one of the foundation stones of their faith, others felt that the cult should be abolished because it distracted believers from the true objects of devotion, i.e., Jesus, Mary, and the saints.

Pope Gregory took a strong stand against Leo's orders against icons, as *The Book of Pontiffs* describes:

> In the mandates he later sent, the emperor had decreed that no church image of any saint, martyr or angel should be kept, as he declared them all accursed; if the pontiff would agree he would have the emperor's favor; if he prevented this being carried out as well he would be degraded from his office. So the pious man despised the prince's profane mandate, and now he armed himself against the emperor as against an enemy, denouncing

his heresy and writing that Christians everywhere must guard against the impiety that had arisen.[40]

In 730 Emperor Leo renewed his attack on the cult of icons, and Pope Gregory III (731-41)—another strong pontiff who succeeded Gregory II—held a synod in Rome with 93 bishops in attendance:

> The synod decreed that if anyone thenceforth, despising the faithful use of those who held the ancient custom of the apostolic church, should remove, destroy, profane and blaspheme against this veneration of the sacred images, viz. of our God and Lord Jesus Christ, of His mother, the ever-virgin immaculate and glorious Mary, of the blessed apostles and of all the saints, let him be driven forth from the body and blood of our Lord Jesus Christ and from the unity and membership of the entire church.[41]

Shortly thereafter, as Walter Ullmann notes:

> The emperor ordered the confiscation of all papal estates in Calabria and Sicily and separated the whole of Sicily and all the Balkan regions and transferred these districts to the patriarch of Constantinople, a measure that was never revoked. It was obvious that these two steps—the confiscation and the ecclesiastical reorganization—vitally affected the papacy both ecclesiastically and economically.[42]

THE POPES AND THE MEROVINGIAN KINGDOM

Meanwhile both Gregory II and Gregory III were having serious trouble with the Lombards, who had complete license in the northern and central parts of Italy. Regular pleas by the pontiffs to the exarch in Ravenna and to the emperor himself went unheeded. Thus, when the Lombards seized Ravenna in the late 730s, Gregory seemed to have no alternative but to request assistance from Charles Martel in Francia.

> The pope told the mayor of the palace [i.e., Martel] that as a true son of St. Peter he must rush to the defense of Peter's Church and the pope's "peculiarem populum." The Church of St. Peter was being oppressed by the Lombards and, after God, only Charles could help. The pope concluded by telling Charles that if he hoped to have eternal life he had to come to the defense of the Church.[43]

Charles Martel—at that time the virtual ruler of the Franks—did not respond to Gregory's call. Among other things, Charles had recently forged an alliance with the Lombard king and was unwilling to jeopardize it. Gregory's second request for help might have done some good because the Lombards were relatively quiet after that for several years. Thomas Noble speculates: "It may have been Boniface [i.e., St. Boniface] who suggested to Gregory the idea of an appeal to Charles. In 737 the great missionary visited Rome for a second time and stayed there nearly a year."[44]

It is difficult to overstate the effect that St. Boniface had in the forging of a lasting tie between the northern kingdoms and Rome. Boniface was sent to the Frankish realms in 722. By 741 the church in the Germanic nations was reorganized and Boniface turned his efforts to the western sectors. The transformation that Boniface effected eventually involved an assimilation of Roman theology, Roman canon law and liturgy, but most of all, what Boniface and other missionaries left behind was a lasting affection and reverence for the chair of Peter.[45] Gregory III could, in the late 730s, address Charles Martel as "a true son of St. Peter" and call on him to "defend Peter's church and the pope's own people."[46]

It is important to note that the papal territories had, in the course of the eighth century, changed from a network of patrimonies to a sort of nation-state, the Papal States. Thomas Noble contends that Popes Gregory II (715-31) and Gregory III (731-41) were responsible for easing the papal domain out of the Byzantine Empire.[47] The duchies of Rome, Perugia, and, to some extent, Ravenna had taken on the configuration of a distinct political entity which Gregory III—in the late 730s—was beginning to call a republic. Whether this occurred in the 730s or (more likely) sometime later, or whether this new territorial entity enjoyed a measure of political sovereignty or was a subject of the descendants of Charles Martel, is debatable. But the fact is that something new had come into being in the mid-eighth century which changed things for the papacy, because it had formally become a political player in the newly forming European arena. Geoffrey Barraclough evaluates this turn of events:

> At no time in the whole preceding history of the papacy had there been any suggestion that the bishop of Rome should exercise temporal power or rule like a king over a territorial state. If this claim was now made, it was no doubt in response to a particularly difficult situation. But the claim once made was never dropped. It runs like a red thread through papal history right down to the Lateran treaties of 1929, and for long periods in the middle ages . . . it played a part in papal policy and influenced the very character of the papacy itself.[48]

The precedent for this new temporal power is reflected in a document called the *Donation of Constantine*, which most experts consider to have been confected in Rome, probably in the Lateran writing office, in the mid-eighth century. The *Donation* masqueraded as the work of Constantine I, who suppos-

edly set forth in writing a series of permanent gifts and conveyances to Pope
Sylvester and his successors ca. 315-25 A.D. It begins with Constantine's nar-
ration of his miraculous cure from some type of leprosy through the intercession of the apostles Peter and Paul, and his subsequent conversion and baptism
by Pope Sylvester. As a result of his wondrous transformation, Constantine—
according to the document—decreed the following:

> We ordain and decree that he [i.e., Sylvester and his successors] shall have
> rule as well over the four principal sees, Antioch, Alexandria,
> Constantinople and Jerusalem, as over all the churches of God in all the
> world. . . . we grant and by this present we convey our imperial Lateran
> palace . . . we convey to the oft-mentioned and most blessed Sylvester,
> universal pope, both our palace as preferment, and likewise all provinces,
> palaces and districts of the city of Rome and Italy and of the regions of the
> West.[49]

This document—one of the most notable forgeries of the Middle Ages—although seldom "trotted out publicly to make or prove a point," does indeed
echo, "in a clear way the ideology of the Republic of St. Peter since the 730s."[50]

The *Donation* was formally unmasked as a forgery by an Italian Renaissance scholar, Lorenzo Valla, around 1440. It had meanwhile become very
widely known and had exercised considerable influence inasmuch as it was
incorporated into the Pseudo-Isidorian Decretals in the middle of the ninth
century (see pages 84-86 below). Furthermore, parts of the *Donation* have also
found their way into a number of the more influential medieval collections of
canon law. One should not be overly scandalized by this because in the Middle
Ages forgeries of this sort—asserting various claims to certain territories or
prero-gatives—were by no means uncommon. However, this forgery did provide, at least partially, the ideological groundwork for a discontinuity of sizeable proportions regarding the pope's understanding of his role in the world.
Beginning with the mid-eighth century or thereabouts, the popes came to see
themselves more and more as political and territorial potentates, as well as
spiritual primates. This rather different self-understanding, which deepened
and expanded over the years, gave the papacy a whole new look and took it in
directions hitherto hardly imagined. That this change or discontinuity was
inevitable, given the circumstances and exigencies of the time, does not alter
the fact that the discontinuity remains.

THE POPES AND CHARLEMAGNE

After the death of Charles Martel in 741, his sons Carlomann and Pepin
assumed the leadership of the kingdom of Francia, the Merovingian throne

having been vacant for some time. In 743, a Merovingian, Childeric III, was placed on the throne, and in 747 Carlomann saw fit to abdicate, leaving Pepin in sole charge as mayor of the palace. Shortly thereafter, Pepin requested that Pope Zachary (741-52) give a reply as to whether or not it was proper that the current king of the Franks, although he had no power, should continue to hold the royal office. Zachary responded that the person who held the power ought to be king. This set the stage for the election of Pepin by the Frankish nobles in 751. It is probable that Pepin needed the approval of the pope before the Frankish nobles would switch their allegiance to him.

It was during the reign of Pope Stephen II (752-57) that the Lombards, under their new king, Aistulf, took over Ravenna (precipitating the end of the exarchate) and were advancing against Rome. After the pope had appealed to the Byzantine emperor for help and it was clear that no help was forthcoming, he dispatched a plea for assistance to Pepin, who was still allied to the Lombard royal family which had friends among the Frankish nobility. Pepin invited Pope Stephen to visit him, and the pope made his way to Francia. *The Book of Pontiffs* relates in considerable detail Pope Stephen's visit.[51] Upon the pontiff's arrival, he met Pepin at Ponthion (south of Châlons-sur-Marne) in January 754. Pepin agreed to respond to the pope's entreaty:

> At that moment he satisfied the blessed pope with an oath that he would obey his orders and advice with all his strength, and that it would give him pleasure to restore by every means the exarchate of Ravenna and the rights and places of the State.[52]

Because it was mid-winter, Pepin persuaded Stephen and his retinue to spend some time at the monastery of St. Denis in Paris. In April at Quierzy (near Laon), the king and the "dignitaries of his royal power" confected a document laying out the pope's territorial claims in Italy.

> Historically, the great significance of the Quierzy document is that it displays unambiguously what could be called the pope's "maximum plan" for the territorial dimensions of the Republic. In the best possible circumstances, the Republic would have consisted of all formerly Byzantine central Italy, plus Lombard Tuscany and the two greatest Lombard duchies [i.e. Spoleto and Benevento].[53]

In July 754 at St. Denis, the pontiff anointed Pepin and his sons, and apparently solemnly enjoined the Franks always to choose their kings from the family of Pepin. This point may well have been what Pepin wanted from the pope.[54] Pepin then battled King Aistulf of the Lombards, defeating him in 756.

Pope Stephen was followed by his brother Paul (757-67), who had his own difficulties with the Lombards under their new king, Desiderius, who failed to hand over the duchies of Spoleto and Benevento as agreed. After Pope Paul's death, there was a good deal of internal turmoil in Rome precipitated by a battle for the control of the chair and the Republic of St. Peter, waged by the more powerful lay and clerical factions in the duchy. After no little trouble in the summer of 768, Pope Stephen III, a Sicilian who was not of a noble family, was elected and held the papacy until 772. In the spring of 769, Stephen held a synod at the Lateran basilica, which settled on the following procedure for the election of popes: "no layman should ever be presumed to be promoted to the sacred honor of the pontificate, nor even anyone in orders, unless he had risen through the separate grades and had been made cardinal priest or deacon."[55] Thomas Noble summarizes the rather lengthy enactment: "Henceforth the election was closed to Roman laymen: only the clergy could participate as electors, and only specified clerics were eligible for elections."[56]

Stephen's rather short reign ended in 772, and Hadrian I (772-95) was selected without the violence and turmoil that preceded the choice of Stephen. Hadrian was of noble ancestry and hence had no trouble with the Roman aristocracy. He did, however, have serious problems from the outset with King Desiderius. With the Lombard armies marching toward Rome, Hadrian pleaded with Charlemagne for help. (After Pepin's death in 768, Charlemagne and his brother Carlomann ruled the Franks, until Carlomann's death in 771 left Charlemagne the sole ruler.) With the support of the Frankish nobles, Charlemagne moved his army southward. In June 774, Desiderius was captured, the Lombard capital of Pavia was taken, and Charlemagne assumed the role as king of the Lombards, thus eliminating the threat from the Lombard royal family. "Hadrian and Charlemagne became and remained firm friends, and by the time of Hadrian's death in 795 the Republic [i.e., the Papal States] had assumed its basic territorial configuration."[57] According to the arrangements made between Charlemagne and Hadrian I, the duchies of Rome and Perugia, as well as the Roman Campania, were under the control of the pope, while Ravenna was under the joint control of the pope and Charlemagne. In 781, Pepin, Charles' son, became king of Italy, which consisted largely of northern Italy. The southern sections of the peninsula, Naples and Calabria, were still under the jurisdiction of Byzantium.

Although much has been made of the so-called Byzantine captivity or Byzantine period of the papacy from 687 to 752, because all but two of the thirteen popes elected during that period were Greek-speaking, Jeffrey Richards notes that this was not due to the influence of the emperor in Constantinople—because there is little evidence for that—but rather to the fact "that the composition of the (Roman) clergy had drastically changed during the course of the seventh century."[58] Many Greek-speaking Sicilians, immigrants and the sons of immigrants, made their way to Rome and became part of the Roman clergy. Also, the Arab invasions in the East, from 635-645 onward, propelled many Greek-speaking Christians from Syria, Asia Minor, and elsewhere to move westward. Thus, although it would be incorrect to infer an undue influence by the imperial court on the papacy during the years from 687 to 752, from 756 into the eleventh century the papacy was more often than not under the sway of one faction or another of the Roman nobility. As the papal domain assumed more and more the appearance of a political regime in the mid-eighth century, the noble families of the Roman duchy moved in to assume control. "[T]he Roman aristocracy, which must always have been represented to some degree in the clergy of the Roman church, gradually began to dominate that clergy and through it the Republic [i.e., the Papal States]."[59]

Thomas Noble further observes: "as an independent political entity was emerging, the Romans, and chief among them the nobility, took over its leadership. . . . The Republic of St. Peter saw the emergence of a 'noble Roman captivity' of the papacy."[60] It was this "noble Roman captivity" which did so much to politicize the papal office from 750 onward and inevitably modify its priorities. From 752 to 844, all the pontiffs but Stephen III (768-72) and Leo III (795-816) were members of various families of the Roman aristocracy.

THE ICONOCLAST CONTROVERSY

It was during Pope Hadrian's pontificate that the iconoclast controversy was finally settled through the Council of Nicaea II, the seventh ecumenical council and the last to be recognized by the Eastern church. The iconoclast struggle reached its peak during the reign of Emperor Constantine V (741-75), one of the most vicious and violent rulers ever to occupy the imperial throne. It was during his reign that the popes turned to the Franks after the demise of the exarchate of Ravenna in 751. After this, imperial power in central and northern Italy was virtually nonexistent. Leo IV (775-80) became emperor after Constantine V, serving as a kind of mollifying agent in the dispute over icons. Leo was a moderate man who continued to enforce the prohibitions against those favoring icon veneration, but not with the rigor of his predecessor. Leo died prematurely in 780, leaving his ten-year-old son to succeed him. Young Constantine VI became co-emperor with his mother, the Empress Irene, who gradually changed the policies against icon veneration which had been in force since the days of Leo III (717-41). Under the regency of Irene, preparations were made for an ecumenical council which would review the whole issue and eventually restore the use of icons in the East. As George Ostrogorsky, a Byzantine historian, notes, "The Byzantine government entered into negotiations with Rome and the eastern patriarchs, who all welcomed the change and dispatched representatives to the council."[61]

The council, attended by more than 250 prelates including the papal legates, handed down a definition regarding the desirability of venerating icons and sacred images of Jesus, Mary, and the saints.

The more frequently they are seen in representational art, the more are those who see them drawn to remember and long for those who serve as models, and to pay these images the tribute of salutation and respectful veneration. . . . Indeed, the honor paid to an image traverses it, reaching the model; and he who venerates the image, venerates the person represented in that image.[62]

After the definition, the council—which opened in August 786 and concluded in October 787—set down twenty-two canons on various disciplinary matters dealing largely with the selection and the conduct of bishops, priests, and monks.

Although Charlemagne was livid over the fact that he had not been asked to play a part in the council, he and Hadrian I had an otherwise constructive relationship for nearly twenty-five years. It was Hadrian I who sent Charlemagne a Roman collection of canon law (the *Dionysio-Hadriana*) in 774, and it was this collection that Charles ordered to be used officially in the Frankish church.[63] After the death of Pope Hadrian, the Roman nobleman *par excellence*, the clerical electors chose a career Lateran prelate who, however, was not an aristocrat, Leo III (795-816). From the outset Leo was opposed by the noble Roman families. He was accused of various serious crimes, attacked physically, and in 799 saw no alternative but to flee to Paderborn, seeking the protection of Charlemagne. There is little doubt that the Roman nobles were attempting to drive Leo out of office. Charles came to Rome himself late in the year 800, determined to hold hearings regarding the accusations of simony and immorality leveled against Leo, but not one of his accusers would come forward. "Finally Leo exculpated himself by oath of any wrongdoing, and on Christmas day in 800 he crowned Charlemagne emperor in St. Peter's."[64]

Ostrogorsky observes:

> The coronation of Charles the Great violated all traditional ideas and struck a hard blow at Byzantine interests, for hitherto Byzantium, the new Rome, had unquestionably been regarded as the sole Empire which had taken over the inheritance of the old Roman *imperium*. . . . In actual fact, from the year 800 onwards two Empires, an Eastern and a Western, stood face to face. . . . The *Oikoumene* [i.e., the universal Christian world] had split into two halves which in language, culture, politics and religion were poles apart.[65]

Another Byzantine scholar, John Meyendorff, views the growing separation as follows:

> In the sixth and seventh centuries, the Roman church was still playing the role of a link between East and West, as shown with particular clarity by St. Gregory the Great. It did so, however, at the price of certain inner

contradictions. Accepting the "pentarchy" by participating in the imperial Byzantine system, it was, at the same time, using the argument of Petrine apostolicity, whenever it could be used to assert jurisdiction. Perhaps this Janus-like equilibrium could have been maintained much longer, if the arrogance and the carelessness of the iconoclastic emperors of Byzantium had not condemned the papacy to become a western institution, tied to the Carolingian monarchy.[66]

THE PENTARCHY

Meyendorff's comments do indeed reflect what was happening in the Christian *oikoumene*. The pentarchy, or the coordinated rule of the five great patriarchs over all of Christendom, was an organizational structure which had grown up over the centuries. Although it was not formally proposed as an ecclesiological system until the eighth and ninth centuries by such scholars as Theodore the Studite (759-826), the pentarchical arrangement was implicit in the conduct of the ecumenical councils of Constantinople I (381), Chalcedon (451), Constantinople II (553), and Constantinople III (680-81). According to Meyendorff, the prelates at these councils were "seen as representing five patriarchates."[67]

> Authentic ecumenicity required the participation of these five patriarchs [i.e., Rome, Constantinople, Antioch, Alexandria, and Jerusalem], either in person or by proxy, or at least . . . in the form of a *post factum* approval. This system of "pentarchy," the governing of the universal Church by five rulers, equal in dignity, but related to each other by a strict order of precedence, was a Byzantine vision, enshrined in the legislation of Justinian.[68]

Yves Congar mentions that this theory of the pentarchy was assumed in Justinian's *Novellae* 123 and 131. (The *Novellae* were Justinian's laws enacted after the publication of his second code in 534.) His imperial statutes regarding the Church were customarily addressed to the five patriarchs.[69] The accord of the five reflected the unity of the whole Church. Congar notes that this was not essentially an anti-Roman ecclesiology, but rather an attempt on the part of the Byzantines to describe the organizational structure of the churches as they saw it.[70] As long as the papacy was sensitive to this reality—at least in its dealings with the East—the equilibrium between East and West was maintained. But when the assertions of the popes began to emphasize Petrine primacy to the exclusion of the coordinated rule of the five, then the papacy began to reduce itself to a western institution. This change did not occur during one pontificate or within a century of pontificates, but by the year 1000 or thereabouts, the papacy was essentially reduced to the status of a western institution. There were—as there are still—authentic universalist dimensions inherent in the papal office. These dimensions (e.g., the preeminent orthodoxy of the faith of Peter and Paul) were acknowledged by the East in the first millennium, as they are largely acknowledged today. But those very qualities were overshadowed by certain universalist jurisdictional claims which were not, and still are not, acceptable to the eastern churches.

Hardly anyone maintains that the pentarchy ever represented a well-defined organizational paradigm, but it was apparently very much "in the background" during the period of the great ecumenical councils. Although its disappearance cannot be attributed to one cause alone, with its departure came a growing, deepening lack of understanding between East and West. This loss, or discontinuity, if you will, is perhaps the most unfortunate of the discontinuities we have come upon thus far. And the papacy's growing inability to maintain equilibrium in its rapport with the East as its jurisdictional claims in the West increased, played no small part in this tragic, perduring division.

FRANCIA AFTER CHARLEMAGNE

Pope Leo (795-816) was able to stave off the attacks of the Roman nobles after his defense by Charlemagne in December 800. Before the newly crowned emperor left Rome, he ensured that Leo's principal detractors were sentenced to death. In the year 800 there were approximately 130 churches in Rome, of which twenty-eight were *tituli*, or parish churches, each with a lead titular priest and possibly two or three other titular priests. These titular priests made up the Roman *presbyterium* whose head was the archpriest, one of the most influential clerics in Rome. The priests who were the pastors of the twenty-eight parish churches, along with the seven Roman deacons and the seven suburbicarian bishops, were referred to, at least from the days of Pope Stephen II (752-57), as the cardinal priests, deacons, and bishops of the Roman church.[71]

After 810 or so, Charlemagne directed much of his effort to initiating dramatic ecclesiastical reforms in Francia. He provided for his succession by crowning Louis the Pious, his only surviving legitimate son, as emperor in 813. After Charlemagne's death in 814, a contingent of Roman aristocrats set out to undo Pope Leo once again, forcing the pontiff to appeal to Louis the Pious, who dispatched legates to Rome to settle the issue. However, Leo died shortly thereafter and was succeeded by a nobleman and career Lateran staffer, Stephen IV (816-17). During his short reign, Stephen traveled to Rheims to crown Louis and to renew and update the agreements entered into by his predecessors and the father and grandfather of Louis in 754 and 774.

The so-called *Pactum Ludovicianum* of 816 confirmed and expanded the pope's territorial rights in central Italy, including the duchies of Rome, Perugia, Ravenna, Lombard Tuscany, and even the duchies of Benevento and Spoleto. Louis guaranteed that he would protect these papal territories. The *Pactum* further stipulated:

> There will be no Frankish or Lombard interference in papal elections; a pope freely and unanimously elected by all the Romans (N.B. in practice, no doubt, the nobility, whose candidate Stephen had been) may be consecrated and his envoys will afterwards inform the king, so as to maintain the amity, charity and peace as under Charles (Martel), Pepin and Charlemagne.[72]

Papal elections were again open to all Romans, i.e., to the nobility, although the pool of available candidates remained the same. Only the cardinal priests and deacons of the Roman church were qualified to be elected. Thomas Noble comments, "After 816, however, contested elections, factional strife and often violence became the almost inevitable companions of papal elections. . . . The situation was finally rectified by the election decree of Nicholas II [1058-61] which basically returned the situation to what it had been between 769 and 816."[73]

After 816, the various families of the Roman aristocracy took control of the papal office, and this situation continued—except for several interventions by the Ottonines in the tenth and eleventh centuries—for more than 200 years. The principal attraction, of course, was the political and financial power that the papacy maintained over the Papal States. After a hotly contested election in 824 resulting in the selection of Pope Eugene II (824-27), Louis' elder son, Lothar, issued a decree, the *Constitutio Romana*, which reaffirmed the pact of 816, allowing the Romans, i.e., the nobles, to participate in papal elections. The Romans, however, were asked to swear a loyalty oath to the emperor that they would act fairly and according to proper canonical procedure as electors. If they acted otherwise, they were warned that they would be liable to punishment by the emperor. Louis and his descendants did indeed make every effort to avoid influencing the outcome of papal elections. This could not be said, however, of the Germanic emperors, the Ottonines, who followed them.

The Carolingian Empire did not fare very well after Charlemagne. Louis the Pious (814-40) decided in 817 to divide the kingdom among his three sons, Lothar, Pepin, and Louis the German, making Lothar co-regent. Another son, Charles, was born to Louis' second wife, Judith, in 823, and this created much anxiety among the elder sons, who eventually went to war against their father. Louis the Pious was defeated at Colmar in 833, but the fraternal strife continued. After the death of Pepin in 838, and especially after their father's death in 840, the hostilities continued among Lothar, Louis the German, and Charles who was called the Bald. The treaty of Verdun in 843 provided for the partitioning of the Frankish Empire among the three surviving sons. Lothar, who was emperor since the death of his father, received the middle (and richest) territory, Lotharingia (i.e., the Low Countries, Alsace-Lorraine, Burgundy, Provence, Switzerland, and Italy), while Louis the German took East Francia (roughly modern Germany), and Charles was awarded West Francia (roughly modern France). The popes were not at all pleased with this arrangement because they then had to deal with three Frankish rulers rather than one. The imperial crown was passed on to Lothar's son, Louis II, after Lothar's death in 855. Throughout the ninth century, the Roman pontiffs jealously guarded their prerogative of crowning the Frankish emperors. Paschal I crowned Lothar in 823, while three different popes bestowed the honor on Lothar's son, Louis II, who died without a male offspring in 875. Pope John VIII (872-82) then selected Charles the Bald to succeed Louis II as emperor. Historians commonly identify the total collapse of the Carolingian Empire with the death of Charles the Fat, the third son of Louis the German, in 887.[74]

THE ECCLESIOLOGY OF HINCMAR OF RHEIMS (CA. 850)

It is important to go back to the mid-ninth century to trace several critical developments that profoundly affected papal ideology from that point forward. We can appropriately begin with a description of the ecclesiology of Archbishop Hincmar, who presided over the see of Rheims from 845 until his death in 882. Hincmar, perhaps the greatest canonist of the century, was a vigorous proponent of the prerogatives of metropolitan bishops. He knew the canonical collection, the *Dionysio-Hadriana*, very well indeed and had assimilated its strong biases toward the rights of metropolitans over their suffragan bishops. Since the latter part of the eighth century in Francia, the role of the metropolitan had acquired a new prominence and importance. It was in the ninth century that the metropolitan dignity began to be affixed to the more notable sees rather than being granted as a personal title by the pope.[75]

Although hardly anyone can defend Hincmar's conduct with regard to some of his suffragans and even several bishops outside his metropolitan jurisdiction, his theological positions regarding the constitution of the Church are quite attractive. He did not conceive of the unity of the Church in terms of its being a papal monarchy. Rather he saw the universal Church as made up of an ensemble of local churches in communion with one another through a common faith and the celebration of the Eucharist. Hincmar often spoke of the Church in terms of *communio*.[76] For him, the churches were ruled by the Scriptures, the canons of the great councils, and the norms that were generally accepted by the whole Church, and not by the personal authority of the bishop of Rome, whose role was to intervene as arbiter of the *causae majores*.[77] Although affirming that Christ instituted a universal primacy in Peter, Hincmar stressed the fact that the Lord also directly empowered the other apostles who are succeeded by the bishops. Furthermore, the canons of the venerable councils, grounded in the Spirit, have instituted metropolitans at the head of the various provinces.

It was also Hincmar's view that a council could be "catholic" without being universal or ecumenical. Councils convoked by metropolitans or primates have occasionally attained great authority in the whole Church. He believed strongly in the concept of "reception," which Yves Congar elsewhere describes as "the process by means of which a church (body) truly takes over as its own a resolution that it did not originate in regard to itself, and acknowledges the measure it promulgates as a rule applicable to its own life."[78]

For Archbishop Hincmar, those decrees truly deserve the name "canons," which have received the approbation not only of the Apostolic See but of the great majority of the bishops of the entire world.[79] He was of the mind that the popes do not create laws. Rather, their function is to apply the conciliar canons in accord with changing historical circumstances. It is, he reasoned, one thing to legislate canons and quite another to apply that legislation to the appropriate subjects according to the needs of the time. The latter role he judged to be the responsibility of the popes, while the prior function belonged to the great councils. The noted medievalist, Eugen Ewig, summarizes Hincmar's views on the prerogatives of the metropolitans as follows:

> According to Hincmar, an archbishop [or metropolitan] had the right to convoke provincial synods, which he directed, to a place of his choice and to punish absent bishops, to appoint visitors during the vacancy of sees, to arrange the new election and consecration, to examine and confirm the bishop elect and to decide a disputed election. . . . According to Hincmar, the archbishop could also summon cases to his own tribunal and interfere at will in the administration of his suffragans. Appeal to Rome, however, was only possible after a provincial synod had passed sentence. . . . In Hincmar's view, ecclesiastical legislation was the business of general councils; he conceded to the [papal] decretals only a function of clarifying and implementing.[80]

THE *FALSE DECRETALS*

The views of Hincmar were clearly not those of his contemporaries, Popes Nicholas I (858-67), Hadrian II (867-72), and John VIII (872-82). For them the role of the metropolitan and that of the Roman pontiff were very different indeed. In Rome during the middle years of the ninth century, as the Carolingian dynasty became weaker and more partitioned decade by decade, papal ideology became more and more absolutist. Popes were not only crowning emperors, they were making emperors (e.g., Charles the Bald). They were intervening in political matters of every sort. They were becoming the key figures in the calculus of European affairs. One of the factors in this development was a canonical collection of conciliar enactments, papal letters, and decretals probably confected around 850 in northern Francia west of the Rhine, i.e., the *Decretals* of the so-called Isidore Mercator. Although the *Pseudo-Isidorian Decretals* were not the only forged collections produced at this time in the Gallo-Frankish north, they came to have the greatest influence over the centuries.

> The great forgery which is of particular interest in papal history was the so-called *Pseudo-Isidorian* collection of ecclesiastical law: in the preface the compiler called himself Isidore Mercator. The collection was concocted by an extremely able and gifted team of ecclesiastics. Although at least a third of the papal decrees and other legal material was pure invention, and although the remaining parts consisted of garbled or falsified as well as genuine material, it would be quite unhistorical to apply modern standards of moral evaluation to this product. The substance of that material was no invention. What was fabricated was the law. What was not fabricated was the doctrine or ideology that was embodied in the law. . . . this very large forgery fell on fertile soil because that soil had already been cultivated in precisely the direction in which the forged material pointed.[81]

Ascribing this collection of papal letters (going back to Clement I!), conciliar decrees, and papal decretals to St. Isidore of Seville (d. 636), they "surrounded their own concoction with an air of respectability."[82] Most scholars, I believe, agree with Walter Ullmann when he notes, "Pseudo-Isidore must be classed as one of the most influential fabrications in the history of medieval (and possibly also modern) Europe."[83]

Regarding the underlying ideology of *Pseudo-Isidore*, J. M. Wallace-Hadrill states:

> It plainly does reflect the anxieties of the provincial clergy and equally plainly reflects a vision of what the Church should be. In particular it champions the role of bishops as the masters of their own dioceses against the encroaching power of the metropolitans such as Hincmar. The natural protector of bishops was the pope. Therefore direct appeal to Rome was the last and proper recourse of every diocesan.[84]

The collection (henceforth referred to as the *False Decretals*) also attacked the intrusions of lay and royal jurisdiction into the sphere of the Church, and for the forgers, this problem too seemed to be most effectively addressed by an appeal to the power of the Roman pontiff. The true beneficiary of the *False Decretals* was no doubt the papacy, and especially Pope Gregory VII (1073-85) and his successors, whom we shall discuss in the next chapter.

POPE NICHOLAS I (858-67)

Nicholas I, who was born in Rome of an aristocratic family in the early years of the ninth century, enjoyed a very successful ecclesiastical career at the Lateran before being elected pope. It is quite clear that almost from the outset of his pontificate he had a copy of the *False Decretals* at his disposal, and cited from them in his letters. The leitmotif of this collection was that the formulation and development of Church life and organization evolved from the papacy. Everything proceeded from the chair of Peter—the authority of the councils, episcopal power and jurisdiction, and ultimately, all of ecclesiastical life. This ideology was perfectly consistent with that of Pope Nicholas, who translated his understanding of the traditional Roman "solicitude" for all the churches in an intensely jurisdictional manner. He, like Pope Leo I before him, saw himself as the veritable reincarnation of Peter. He would often begin his letters with the following greeting: "I Peter, the Apostle of God" say this and this.[85] Nicholas, however, went far beyond Leo in viewing the whole Church as a single people under the rule of the Roman bishop. For this pontiff, the authority of the Holy See was absolute and there was no appeal from his judgment. The papacy for him had the indisputable right to regulate the life of all the churches and to depose bishops without appeal. The pope was the source of the legitimacy of every law and of all sacerdotal power.[86] Congar attests that Nicholas had recourse to Pope Gelasius frequently in his correspondence and could truly be called a disciple of Gelasius, more so than of Leo I or Gregory I.[87] Pope Nicholas claimed that the power of metropolitans came from the papacy rather than from the conciliar canons and called to his tribunal all cases—in the first instance—involving bishops, resting his claims undoubtedly on the *False Decretals*. Furthermore, this pontiff asserted that he had the right to judge the patriarchs as he would judge any other bishop.[88] Councils also fell under his power, deriving their force of law entirely from papal approbation. In his debates with Archbishop Hincmar, he protested that the papal decretals obtained their authority from the pontiff alone, independent of any subsequent reception in the churches.[89]

One of Nicholas' most celebrated and tragic struggles was his contest with Emperor Michael III and Patriarch Photius of Constantinople. In 856 Michael was acknowledged by the imperial senate as having been emancipated from the regency of his mother, Theodora, and proclaimed the independent ruler of the empire. His uncle, Caesar Bardas, who became the true power behind the throne, negotiated with the old patriarch, Ignatius, forcing him to resign inasmuch as he was too committed to the policies of the previous regime and could not make the transition to the new order. In December 858, Photius—one of the greatest scholars of his time—succeeded Ignatius as patriarch. Pope Nicholas was unwilling to recognize the new patriarch because the transition was not canonically legitimate. The pontiff rebuked the emperor for granting Photius the right to succeed Ignatius without papal approbation. Nicholas identified himself in his letter to Emperor Michael as the supreme arbiter in all ecclesiastical matters:

It is immediately clear that the judgments of the Apostolic See, than which there is no greater authority, cannot be handled by any other tribunal, nor is it possible for any to sit in judgment upon its decision. Appeals are to be made to that See from any part of the world. Such is the meaning of the canons. But no appeal is allowed from that See.[90]

The pope then admonished the emperor not to render decisions in matters such as this that pertain to the Church:

Do not usurp the things that are her own; do not seek to take from her the things that are entrusted to her alone, knowing that everyone who has the administration of the affairs of this world ought to be kept away from sacred matters, to just the same extent as it is fitting that no member of the ranks of the clergy and the warriors of God should be immersed in any secular business. In fact we are utterly at a loss to understand how those who have been given the right to preside over only human, and not over divine affairs, may presume to sit in judgment on those through whom divine affairs are administered.[91]

It must be admitted that Pope Nicholas did have a point in opposing this effort on the part of Emperor Michael to make the patriarchate dependent on purely political contingencies. But for the pontiff to claim that he had the right to sit in judgment over the affairs of the patriarchate of Constantinople was not something that either the emperor or the patriarch could accept. I believe Ostrogorsky is correct when he says, "Nicholas I was intent on establishing the principle that as head of Christendom he was entitled to the last word in disputes over ecclesiastical matters as much in the East as in the West."[92]

Whereas in the course of this rather drawn out controversy, Photius appealed to the legitimate differences existing between one region and another in the Church regarding customs and disciplinary regulations of all sorts, Nicholas I insisted on drawing in the reins, strictly curtailing that disciplinary diversity and affirming that no particular custom or discipline could stand against a papal decision.[93] Although it would be almost 200 years before the definitive split between East and West, it was clear in the Photian conflict that neither Rome nor Constantinople was any longer capable of truly comprehending the other. The ideology of Nicholas I animated and informed his successor, Hadrian II (867-72), who was also the offspring of a noble Roman family. Like Nicholas, Hadrian saw the Christian world as a single *societas fidelium*, one congregation of faithful over which he presided. Kings, princes, and emperors must submit to the *sacerdotium*.[94]

CONSTANTINOPLE IV (869-70)

During Hadrian II's pontificate, a strange turn of events occurred in Constantinople. In September 867, Emperor Michael III was murdered by a Macedonian upstart who had won the emperor's favor and climbed into a position of power, superceding and eventually killing Michael's uncle and chief advisor, Caesar Bardas, in 865. This "clever and crafty peasant's son," Basil I (867-86), put himself on the imperial throne, deposed Photius, restored Ignatius as patriarch of Constantinople, and reopened relations with Rome.[95] He requested that the pope call a council to decide a number of issues arising out of the removal of Photius. A council was indeed held at Constantinople, from October 869 to February 870, in the presence of Pope Hadrian's delegates who presided at the sessions. The council (Constantinople IV) condemned Photius because he "engineered the expulsion of the most just, lawful and canonically appointed high priest, namely the most holy patriarch Ignatius."[96] The council fathers concluded their definition of faith by anathematizing Photius and then proceeded to issue twenty-seven canons on various disciplinary matters.[97] Giuseppi Alberigo, in his masterful work on the decrees and canons of the ecumenical councils, says regarding Constantinople IV:

> This council, designated as the eighth ecumenical council by western canonists, is not found in any canonical collection of the Byzantines; its acts and canons are completely ignored by them. Modern scholars have shown that it was included in the list of ecumenical councils only later, that is, after the eleventh century. We have decided to include the council for the sake of completeness.[98]

Four or five years after the council, Emperor Basil allowed Photius to return to the capital, and on the death of Patriarch Ignatius in 877, it was none other than Photius who succeeded as patriarch. Photius' second reign lasted until 886 when he was deposed again by the new emperor, Leo IV.

POPE JOHN VIII (872-82)

Pope Hadrian II was followed by John VIII, the last of the noteworthy pontiffs of the ninth century. John revived Hadrian's papal-hierocratic themes and raised them to another level. For him the Christian world—East and West—was the *res publica Christiana* and the Roman church held the *principatus*, the chief place, over all. The *res publica Christiana* has been given over to the care of the pope. It was Pope John, for example, who chose Charles the Bald to succeed Louis II as emperor of the West, and it was John who placed the imperial crown on his head on Christmas day, 875. He could have chosen someone else. As a matter of fact, it was the express wish of the late Louis II— who left no heir—that someone other than his uncle Charles be chosen to wear the imperial crown after him. But this was the kind of power and influence that Pope John VIII wielded, at least until the death of Charles the Bald in 877.

Yves Congar observes that according to John's letters, the Holy See claimed a unique authority over all the bishops of the world. John expanded the role of the papacy in the provision of episcopal sees—not by direct intervention in episcopal elections (which was to come later) but in a number of other ways. For example, he wanted to confirm every transfer of a bishop from one diocese to another. Also, after any residential bishop had been deposed, he wanted to examine and confirm the new bishop prior to his installation. John further insisted on carrying out and rendering the decision in cases of allegedly irregular episcopal elections. All these matters, which had been within the ordinary jurisdiction of metropolitans in the ninth century, Pope John arrogated to himself.[99] Walter Ullmann concludes his treatment of Pope John VIII with the following observations:

> John's pivotal idea was that contemporary society formed one body corporate and politic: it was an organic whole which was headed by him and which was to be ruled through the instrumentality of the *sacerdotium*. The emperor is created for the sake of the protection and defense of the Roman church, and he receives this empire through the medium of the pope as a *divinum beneficium* [i.e., a divine favor].[100]

Pope John VIII was assassinated in December 882 by a member or members of his own staff. According to Eugen Ewig, his pitiful demise was "an omen of an approaching dark epoch in papal history."[101]

After the death of Charles the Bald in 877, the collapse of the Carolingian Empire was virtually inevitable. This came with the death of Charles the Fat, the third son of Louis the German, in 882. The tenth century has been called the *saeculum obscurum*, the obscure century, by papal historians because of the deplorable depths to which the papacy descended in that period. Once the protection of the Carolingians had faded away, the papacy was left to its own devices. The venerable church historian, Ludwig Hertling, summarizes the epoch:

> Now there remained only the feuds of the Roman families, who sought to impose their own members as popes and to overthrow the popes set up by other families. The anarchy was so great that we know only the names of some of these popes, who were in office for only a few weeks or days, and we cannot always be sure whether they were legitimate popes.[102]

In such an environment it could not be expected that the ideological advances of the ninth century would be maintained, much less expanded. In the next chapter we shall see how the Ottonine kings from Saxony provided the impetus in the eleventh century for the restitution of the papacy and the creation of a climate in which the ideology of Gelasius I, Nicholas I, Hadrian II, and John VIII could not only revive but expand to new heights not even dreamed of in the ninth century.

SUMMARY

Pope Gregory I's many letters reflect his understanding of the authority he possessed in the East and in the West. Although his control over the churches in Italy was quite strong and he did have some influence over the churches in Gaul, the ecclesiastical organization in such places as Spain, north Africa, the Balkans, and Dalmatia was for the most part independent of papal control. His letters to the churches in the East reveal that he was aware that the five patriarchs (Rome, Alexandria, Constantinople, Antioch, and Jerusalem) were indeed the regional heads of Christendom, with no one of them exercising anything approaching jurisdictional authority over the others.

As the Byzantine emperors became less concerned about the West during the seventh and eighth centuries, due to pressing problems of their own, they offered the pope no security against his political rivals in Italy. It was in the eighth century that the popes began to move toward the Frankish kings in order to seek out military assistance against the Lombards. Under Popes Gregory II (715-31) and Gregory III (731-41), the duchies of Rome, Perugia, and in some respects, Ravenna, were beginning to converge as a distinct political entity which eventually came to be called the Papal States. This arrangement was acknowledged by Charlemagne, who offered protection to the popes and their lands.

In the ninth century, as the descendants of Charlemagne became more and more ineffective as rulers—allowing the original Carolingian Empire to disintegrate—popes such as Nicholas I and John VIII claimed ever expanding spiritual and temporal power over all the churches. These claims, however, were never really taken seriously in the East. As a matter of fact, by the end of the first millennium the papacy and the eastern churches were drifting unalterably apart.

CHAPTER 5

The Rise of the Medieval Papacy

1000 to 1300

⌒

King Conrad (911-18), the first non-Carolingian monarch of east Francia, designated Henry the Saxon (919-36) to be his successor in the presence of the Frankish and the Saxon people. In a true sense, it could be said that Henry ceased being a Saxon because he wholeheartedly embraced Frankish law and traditions. Having assumed the undisputed role as king of east Francia, he managed to establish his control over the duchies of Bavaria and Lorraine before his death. His son, Otto I (936-73), became a veritable emperor in the estimate of his contemporaries through his victories over the Hungarians and the Slavs. "It was . . . in Rome in 962 that Otto I received the title 'Imperator et Augustus,' thus renewing, as heir of the east Frankish Carolingians, the tradition of the Carolingian empire."[1]

Pope John XII (955-64) crowned Otto, making him *rex et sacerdos* with the obligation of watching over and caring for the church in his territory. The imperial title thus passed to the kings of Germany.

> The transformation of the church into a pillar of royal government in Germany was the work of Otto I (936-73), his son, Otto II (973-83), and his grandson, Otto III (983-1002). These three reigns, and that of Henry II (1002-24), saw royal control over churches and abbeys elevated into a principle of government.[2]

The church was the instrument by which the Saxon kings controlled the five principal duchies: Franconia, Saxony, Swabia, Bavaria, and Lorraine. At the same time, the church preferred to be under the direct dominion of the kings rather than being subjected to the conflicting claims and demands of the many dukes and counts of the territory. Under Otto I the popes began for the first time to take an oath of allegiance to the emperor. Pope John XII and Otto entered into a solemn agreement in 962 wherein Otto confirmed the Carolingian concessions and the papal territories, while Pope John in turn took an oath of loyalty to the new emperor. This arrangement—which prevailed for approximately 100 years—allowed Otto's successors to intervene in papal elections whenever the local situation in Rome got out of hand. This occurred frequently because the principal Roman families, the Crescentii and the Tusculani, were often unable to settle peaceably on a candidate for the papacy. Otto's grandson, Otto III, took advantage of this prerogative—nominating Gregory V (996-99) as the first German pope, and then Otto's former tutor, Gerbert, the archbishop of Ravenna, to succeed Gregory V as Pope Sylvester II (999-1003). Parenthetically, Yves Congar notes that Pope Sylvester's view of the papal office was quite different from that of Nicholas I (858-67) and John VIII (872-82) (whom we discussed in the last chapter). According to Sylvester, the Church was a communion of churches under the direction of the Holy See, but the Petrine ministry was not at all seen in the absolutist terms employed by Nicholas and John. Unlike them, Sylvester had a strong view of the episcopal function and of the indispensable authority of metropolitans.[3]

When Otto III died at the age of twenty-one, he was succeeded by his cousin, Henry II (1002-24), the last of the Saxons. Conrad II (1024-39), the first of the Salian kings, showed little interest in Italy. His emphasis was directed towards administrative changes and improvements within the German government. This shift left the fragile papacy once again under the control of the rival noble families in and around Rome, especially the counts of Tusculum. Conrad's son, Henry III (1039-56)—called by many the ideal Christian ruler—saw his responsibility as guardian and protector of the papacy far more clearly than his father. During the reign of Conrad II, the counts of Tusculum were literally in control of Rome. Popes Benedict VIII (1012-24), John XIX (1024-33), and Benedict IX (1033-44 or 46) were all members of the Tusculani family, and anything but exemplary pontiffs. While Benedict VIII was more a ruthless soldier than a spiritual leader, searching out and destroying the Crescentii, John XIX and Benedict IX obtained the papal office through overt acts of bribery and treachery.

In the fall of 1044, revolts broke out in Rome, probably spearheaded by the Crescentii, which drove the depraved Benedict out of the city. The Crescentii set up their own pope, Sylvester III, and shortly thereafter a third pope, Gregory VI, was chosen by the Tusculani after Benedict IX had apparently been persuaded (with the help of a substantial bribe) to abdicate. At this point, Henry III—who was in Italy at the time—called a synod at Sutri in 1046 at which Benedict IX and Sylvester III were deposed and Gregory VI (who apparently offered the bribe) was sent into exile in Germany. Henry designated the bishop of Bamberg as pope (Clement II, 1046-47), and on Christmas day, 1046, Clement crowned Henry emperor of the Romans.

Damasus II (1048), Leo IX (1049-54), and Victor II (1054-57) were all Germans who were animated by a similar reforming spirit.[4] Pope Leo IX, a relative of Henry, was the bishop of Toul at the time of his selection.

One of Leo's most important contributions was the recruiting of a group of outstanding reformers into the senior ranks of the Roman church. Some were from his own diocese of Toul, including Humbert . . . (who became cardinal-bishop of Silva Candida), Hugh Candidus . . . (appointed cardinal-priest of San Clemente) and Udo (papal chancellor). From elsewhere came Frederick, archdeacon of Liege and brother of Duke Godfrey of Lorraine (also papal chancellor) and the subdeacon Hildebrand, who now after the death of Gregory VI [1047] returned to the Lateran palace.[5]

THE REFORM PAPACY—LEO IX (1049-54)

Many historians today agree that the future character of the reforming papacy was determined by Pope Leo IX.[6] The so-called Gregorian line of reform popes—which stretches into the 1120s—began with him. Geoffrey Barraclough says,

It was the pontificate of Leo IX (1049-54) which saw the first rapid advance in the reconstruction of papal authority. Three times crossing the Alps to France and Germany, and holding synod after synod at which he legislated against abuse, Leo made the papal headship a reality.[7]

R. W. Southern states:

When we turn to consider the great change in papal pretensions after 1050, the personality of Leo IX, who was pope from 1049 to 1054, must first attract our attention. He was a quieter and much less controversial character than Gregory VII [1073-85], but nearly everything that we associate with the papacy in its most expansive period can be traced back to his initiative: the political alliance with the Normans; the exacerbation of relations with the Greeks; the reform of papal administrative machinery; the beginnings of a consistent plan of government through legates, councils and a vastly increased correspondence.[8]

The German papal historian, Friedrich Kempf, attests that it was Leo IX who initiated the development of the College of Cardinals as an organ of government of the universal Church while de-emphasizing their traditional liturgical roles in Rome.[9] Kempf adds:

Unlike his predecessors, Leo IX did not reside in Rome. Restless, like the secular rulers of the day, he traveled from country to country. . . . Reform synods interrupted his movements. Apart from Rome, where he held synods in 1049, 1050, 1051 and 1053, he deliberated with bishops at Pavia, Reims, . . . Mainz, . . . Salerno and Vercelli, . . . at Mantua and Bari.[10]

R.W. Southern's allusion concerning the worsening relations with the Byzantines brings us to a very painful incident which colored the history between Christian East and West for nearly 1,000 years. The encounter took place in July 1054 between one of Leo's chosen cohorts, Cardinal Humbert of Silva Candida, and the patriarch of Constantinople, Michael Cerularius. The Orthodox scholar, Timothy Ware, describes the situation between Rome and Byzantium in the eleventh century:

> As the eleventh century proceeded, new factors brought relations between the papacy and the eastern patriarchates to a further crisis. The previous century had been a period of grave instability and confusion for the see of Rome. . . . But under German influence Rome now reformed itself. . . . The reformed papacy naturally revived claims to universal jurisdiction which (Pope) Nicholas [858-67] had made. The Byzantines on their side had grown accustomed to dealing with a papacy that was for the most part weak and disorganized, and so they found it difficult to adapt themselves to the new situation.[11]

For a number of years prior to 1054, the Normans in southern Italy had been forcing the Greeks in their territories to follow the Latin rather than the Byzantine rite. In response, Patriarch Cerularius required that the Latin churches in Constantinople should adhere to Greek practices, and when they refused, he forced them in 1052 to close their doors. In 1053, possibly at the urging of the Byzantine emperor, Cerularius wrote to Pope Leo IX, requesting that an attempt be made to settle the dispute. Pope Leo dispatched a delegation, under the direction of Cardinal Humbert, which arrived in Constantinople in the summer of 1054. The encounter between Cerularius and Humbert could not have turned out more tragically. Cerularius, "the most strong-willed and ambitious prelate of Byzantine history," and Humbert, a man of "stiff and intransigent temper," were precisely the wrong players to effect a compromise, and no compromise was achieved.[12]

George Ostrogorsky describes the events that transpired in the summer of 1054:

> Encouraged by the attitude of the emperor, who appeared to be ready to sacrifice his patriarch for the sake of friendship with Rome, the papal legates laid down a bull of excommunication against Cerularius and his chief supporters on the altar of Hagia Sophia on 16 July, 1054. . . . With the consent of the emperor, he [Cerularius] summoned a synod which

returned blow for blow by excommunicating the Roman legates. The significance of this event was not realized until later. . . . Misunderstandings between the two ecclesiastical centers were all too common and no one was to guess that the quarrel of 1054 was of greater significance than the earlier disputes, or that it marked a schism which was never again to be healed.[13]

Timothy Ware adds a valuable comment regarding the reverberations of the event of 1054:

The dispute remained something of which ordinary Christians in East and West were largely unaware. It was the Crusades which made the schism definitive: they introduced a new spirit of hatred and bitterness, and they brought the whole issue down to the popular level.[14]

The closing years of Leo IX's pontificate were consumed in an effort to overcome the inroads of the Normans in southern Italy. Unable to elicit support from either Henry III, emperor of the Germans, or from Byzantium, the pontiff himself gathered together a papal army to fight the Normans. However, the expedition ended in disaster with the pope taken into captivity. He remained in Norman hands for almost a year, and died in Rome in April 1054 shortly after his release. The three key elements of ecclesiastical reform pushed relentlessly by Pope Leo throughout his reign were the battle against simony, the eradication of concubinage among the clergy, and the issue of lay investiture. The purchase of ecclesiastical offices and benefices and the practice of lay investiture (i.e., lay lords appointing individuals as pastors, abbots, bishops, etc., in their territories) struck at the very roots of the Church's spiritual mission. Brian Tierney describes the situation:

In every part of Europe ecclesiastical lands and offices fell under the control of lay lords. A petty lord regarded the village church and its lands as part of his estates, the priest as an estate servant like one of his stewards, to be appointed at will. A greater noble, greedy for the vast lands of some local abbey, would set himself up as its "protector" and assume the right to appoint its abbot. The complex of the estates belonging to the abbey then became just one more fief rendering service to the lord and subject to his rule. Some richly endowed bishoprics went the same way. . . . Few of the men who acquired ecclesiastical positions in this way cared anything for the spiritual duties of their offices.[15]

In this context it is not difficult to imagine scenarios in which ecclesiastical offices could be sold to the highest bidder. The widespread problem of concubinage was of course opposed to the western church's oft repeated injunction regarding celibacy for priests and major clerics.[16]

Leo IX was succeeded by another relative of Henry III, Victor II (1054-57), who was the last of the popes chosen by Henry from the German episcopate. It was during Pope Victor's reign that Emperor Henry died quite suddenly in 1056, leaving as heir a young son, Henry, who was put under the regency of his mother, the Empress Agnes, until 1065. After Victor's brief reign, Pope Stephen IX (1057-8) from Lorraine was elected by the clergy and people of Rome without any interference from the German court. After a short pontificate of less than a year, Stephen died while on a diplomatic mission to Florence. An interlude of eight or nine months preceded the election of Nicholas II, during which an antipope was chosen by the Tusculani family, but he soon renounced his claim to the papal office.

NICHOLAS II (1058-61) AND ALEXANDER II (1061-73)

Nicholas II, who was born in Lorraine, was the bishop of Florence when he was elected pope in December 1058. He was a reformer who came to associate himself closely with three of the architects of the reform movement in Rome: Peter Damian, Cardinal Humbert, and Hildebrand (who would later become Gregory VII). One of Nicholas' first acts was to summon a synod at the Lateran which reaffirmed the prohibitions against simony and clerical marriage. Also, a new decree on papal elections was enacted which set forth the following dispositions:

> When the pontiff of this universal Roman church dies the cardinal bishops shall first confer together most diligently concerning the election; next they shall summon the other cardinal clergy; and then the rest of the clergy and the people shall approach to give their assent to the new election, the greatest care being taken lest the evil of venality creep in by any way whatsoever. . . . The cardinal bishops shall make their choice from the members of this church if a suitable man is to be found there, but if not they shall take one from another church, saving the honor and reverence due to our beloved Henry who is now king and who, it is hoped, will in the future become emperor by God's grace.[17]

Another item of note was included in the election decree. Should the election not be held in Rome for whatever reason, the cardinal bishops, "together with the God-fearing clergy and the Catholic laity, even though they are few," were empowered to conduct the process.[18] Such an election would involve all the cardinals gathered in the location (outside Rome) along with at least the clergy and laity in the papal retinue.

The virtual elimination of the German king from the decision-making procedure represented a dramatic departure from the practice that had prevailed under Henry III. According to Colin Morris:

> It is unlikely that it [i.e., the new arrangement] was intended to exclude the emperor from any part in papal elections, but his role was reduced to a privilege granted by the Roman church, a change which marked a sharp difference from the days of Henry III, when the all important *tractatio* [i.e., the selection process] had been held at the imperial court.[19]

Pope Nicholas II's synodal legislation—confirmed by the 113 bishops in attendance—was promulgated through the western churches. When Nicholas died in July 1061, trouble was already brewing in Germany over the papal election decree and also the alliance which the pope had made in 1059 with Robert Guiscard and the Normans, acknowledging their right to much of southern Italy in exchange for an annual tribute and the assurance of Norman protection.

The cardinals then selected Bishop Anselm of Lucca, who became Pope Alexander II (1061-73). The new pontiff was enthusiastically supported by the Archdeacon Hildebrand who was the most powerful cleric in the curia after the death of Cardinal Humbert in 1061 and Peter Damian's retirement to a hermitage shortly thereafter. It is entirely possible that the archdeacon's ascendancy and the demise of Humbert made Rome a rather uncomfortable place for Damian. Colin Morris comments on the reign of Alexander: "The pontificate saw a steadily increasing intervention in the regions of Europe in the cause of reform, a policy implemented by the dispatch of legates and by the approval of military endeavors in support of the papacy."[20] The church in England, for example, was brought closer to Rome through the policies of William the Conqueror (1066-87), who was supported by Alexander. However, the pope's influence in Germany deteriorated dramatically after King Henry IV (1056-1106) reached his majority and assumed control ca. 1065. A violent dispute erupted between Henry and Pope Alexander over the choice of a new bishop for the important see of Milan. Henry had promoted one candidate and the pope backed another. The conflict had reached a boiling point at the time of Alexander's death in April 1073.[21]

POPE GREGORY VII (1073-85)

Gregory VII was without question one of the most important and yet controversial figures of the Middle Ages. While the eminent historian Erich Casper considers him "the greatest who has ever sat in Peter's chair," Geoffrey Barraclough is convinced that "Gregory died a failure, without having achieved any of his objects."[22] Hildebrand was apparently a Roman by birth, and perhaps a member of the Pierleoni family. He seems to have been educated in Rome and became a part of the retinue of the reformer, John Gratian, who was chosen pope (Gregory VI) in 1045 after Benedict IX had taken steps to resign. Hildebrand accompanied Gregory VI into exile in Germany, but returned to Rome with Leo IX in 1049. From 1049 to 1073 he was a key member of the reform team in the Roman curia.

In the early years of his papacy, Gregory seemed to withdraw into a very small circle of confidants, and this eventually alienated him from the College of Cardinals, who since 1050 or so had become much more intimately and regularly involved in papal decision making and the Church's central administration. The cardinals did not take this change of direction lightly. Their discontent erupted, and in 1084, thirteen of them, along with a number of leading curial officials, abandoned him. From the outset, Gregory depended heavily on his legates whom he dispatched to the various countries to carry out his reform. From the first year of his pontificate, the decrees of his annual Lenten synods were promulgated and then enforced by his standing legates in France, Germany, England, and elsewhere. His prohibitions against simony and clerical concubinage precipitated vigorous opposition among the resident clergy.

> Gregory was bitterly disappointed by the attitude of some bishops. In face of clerical opposition, Archbishop Siegfried of Mainz moderated the [papal] decrees (as did Lanfranc in England), and when Gregory sent his legates to publish them, [Bishop] Liemar of Bremen, who was no friend of simony, objected angrily to their activity. He described Gregory as a dangerous man, who ordered bishops about as if they were his bailiffs.[23]

Most students of the period agree that it was not Gregory's conscious aim to destroy the authority of metropolitans and make the bishops his "bailiffs," but his constant and notoriously undiplomatic interventions in diocese after diocese certainly created that impression among many local ordinaries. Leo IX's interventions did not have that effect as he pursued his reforming efforts, but Gregory's unbounded zeal and fiery rhetoric produced very negative results. He would often chastise bishops for their slowness in rooting out abuses, and then require that they come to Rome to render a personal accounting to him. "In England Gregory succeeded in alienating the devout and influential Archbishop Lanfranc of Canterbury, who grew impatient at the demands made on him to visit Rome."[24]

It was Gregory who not only considerably extended the use of permanent legates to effect his policies in England and throughout Christendom generally, but who also established the pattern of *ad limina* visits for local bishops (which became a general obligation under Gregory IX) and initiated the practice of the episcopal oath—thus tying each resident bishop more closely to the papacy. Although he probably did not directly intend by these measures to dilute the constitutional powers of metropolitans, these policies did clearly have that effect.[25] Friedrich Kempf, a preeminent Gregorian scholar, attests that Gregory VII believed (like a number of his predecessors) that Peter truly lived and acted again in him.[26]

There is an intriguing and much discussed document found in Gregory VII's register for March 1075. It is an undated list of twenty-seven propositions called the *Dictatus Papae*, the *Dictates of the Pope*. Although there is much debate among historians regarding the origin and purpose of the document, it seems fair to say that the statements reveal the mind of Gregory regarding the extent of papal prerogatives. Perhaps the document represented an outline of a canonical collection which was to be compiled in his lifetime but never was. Many, if not most, of these prerogatives are rooted in the *False Decretals* discussed in the previous chapter. Although some of the declarations seem rather innocuous, the cumulative effect of the twenty-seven is startling indeed. Gregory seemed to envision his role in almost exclusively juridical terms. A cursory reading of some of these "dictates" reveals his mind-set, as well as something of his temperament:

2. That the Roman pontiff alone is rightly to be called universal.
3. That he alone can depose or reinstate bishops.
4. That his legate, even if of lower grade, takes precedence, in a council, over all bishops and may render a sentence of deposition against them.
7. That for him alone is it lawful to enact new laws according to the needs of the time, to assemble together new congregations, to make an abbey of a canonry; and on the other hand, to divide a rich bishopric and unite the poor ones.
8. That he alone may use the imperial insignia.
12. That he alone may depose emperors.
18. That no sentence of his may be retracted by anyone; and he, alone of all, can retract it.
21. That to his see the more important cases of every church should be submitted.
22. That the Roman Church has never erred, nor ever, by the witness of Scripture, shall err to all eternity.
27. That the pope may absolve the subjects of unjust men from their fealty.[27]

Given the temper of the times, it is not difficult to see how a papal state of mind animated by such principles would encounter no end of opposition, both from ecclesiastics and from temporal rulers. Perhaps if Hildebrand had been endowed with a greater measure of diplomatic skill, he would not have encountered the animus which he eventually did face from bishops and princes alike. His problems with Henry IV (1056-1106) of Germany began with the unfinished business at Milan at the very outset of his pontificate. Henry, who controlled Lombardy and exercised his influence there principally through the bishops, wanted his man rather than the pope's man as archbishop of Milan, the primary see in Lombardy. Pope Gregory accused Henry of insubordination and disobedience because, by refusing to accept the papal candidate, he was obstructing the reform movement. The pontiff threatened the king with excommunication. Henry, in turn, branded the pope as an imposter inasmuch as he had been improperly elected, and called on him to step down. Gregory then excommunicated Henry at the Roman Lenten synod of 1076. The following October, the powerful German bishops—sympathetic at that time with the pope—warned the king that if he did not obtain reconciliation with Rome within four months, he would lose their allegiance and the crown. This occasioned the celebrated meeting in January 1077 between Henry and Gregory at Canossa where the pontiff released the king from his excommunication.

Although the German bishops remained loyal to Gregory VII in his early conflicts with Henry, the mood of Germany was very different several years later. In Gregory's 1076 condemnation of Henry, the pope also withdrew from him the governance of Germany, and it was not clear whether his deposition had been lifted when he was absolved from excommunication in the snow at Canossa. Since Henry's status as king was not at all clear in Germany, the pope and most princes (including the magnate-bishops) were looking forward to a council on German soil which would clarify the situation. However, the Lombards made it impossible for Gregory to travel to Germany:

> The Lombard bishops refused to withdraw their hostility against Gregory and insisted on negotiations being abandoned, thus making the journey effectively impossible. There, the opposition met at Forchheim on 13 March 1077, refusing to delay until the pope's arrival, and elected Rudolf of Swabia as king in Henry's place. The country was now in civil war.[28]

By the beginning of 1080 it was clear that Henry would eventually overcome the forces of Rudolf and that for the pope there was little hope of a peaceful settlement with Henry. In March of 1080, Pope Gregory anathematized Henry again.[29] This time there was not much support in Germany and northern Italy for Gregory's action. In June 1080 at Brixen, an assembly of bishops, after declaring that Gregory's election had been invalid, proceeded to elect as antipope the archbishop of Ravenna, who took the name Clement III. Gregory became more and more isolated, while Henry's prestige continued to grow:

Early in 1084 thirteen cardinals, much of the staff of the Lateran palace, and even the papal chancellor changed their allegiance to Clement III. On Easter Day 1084 Henry, along with his empress Bertha, received [in Rome] the imperial crown at the hands of Clement III.[30]

Pope Gregory received whatever protection and support he could from Robert Guiscard and the Normans to the south, but at the time of his death in 1085 in Salerno (under Norman protection), the pope was by all appearances a failure.[31]

Gregory has left us a precious collection of letters, "the first even approximately complete collection of the correspondence of a pope since that of his saintly predecessor, Gregory I, nearly five centuries earlier."[32] The letters dramatically reflect his reforming zeal and his persistent efforts to force the bishops to eradicate simony and clerical concubinage. Further, the acts of the Roman synod of 1078 contained in the register reveal his strong stand against the evils of lay investiture:

Whereas we have learned that investiture into benefices by laymen is practiced in many places and that in consequence great confusion has arisen in the church, whereby the Christian faith is being trampled under foot, we ordain that no cleric shall receive the investiture of a bishopric, an abbey or a church from the hand of an emperor or a king, or any lay person, man or woman. If he shall presume to do this, let him know that such investiture is invalid according to apostolic authority, and that he is subject to excommunication until he shall have made due satisfaction.[33]

Some insight into Gregory's harsh treatment of local ordinaries who failed to respond promptly to his mandates can be observed in a letter to Archbishop Liemar of Bremen:

You placed every possible hindrance in the way of our legates, Bishop Albert of Palestrina and Gerald of Ostia, whom we sent into your country to summon a convention of archbishops, bishops, abbots and pious clergy, and in our place, supported by our authority, to correct whatever needed correction. . . .You forbade the synod to be held and when you were summoned by them to Rome . . . you failed to appear.

Wherefore we summon and order you, by our apostolic authority, to present yourself at the synod [in Rome] . . . in the first week of the coming Lent for the correction of these and whatever matters need correcting. In consequence of the above mentioned offenses we suspend you from all episcopal functions until you appear before us.[34]

In the letter, Gregory referred to the archbishop as his "enemy" because he refused to accede to the reform synod called for by the pope. Whatever strategic reasons the archbishop may or may not have had for his action were not dealt with, at least in the letter. Liemar was suspended until he was to appear in Rome some months later. Gregory's zeal, in this and many other cases, is beyond dispute, of course, but the manner in which he carried out his reform policies was often seriously counterproductive. His negative mind-set regarding the bishops in the West, the civil rulers of his time, and even his contemporaries in Italy is painfully illustrated in a letter he sent in January 1075 to his old friend and confidant, Abbot Hugo of Cluny:

> When I review in my mind the regions of the West, whether north or south, I find scarce any bishops who live or who were ordained according to the law and who govern Christian people in the love of Christ and not for worldly ambition. And among secular princes I find none who prefer the honor of God to their own righteousness and gain. As to those with whom I live, Romans, Lombards and Normans, as I often say to them, I find them worse than Jews and pagans.[35]

In the longest doctrinal letter in the register (addressed to Bishop Hermann of Metz on March 15, 1081), Pope Gregory defended his action of excommunicating and deposing King Henry for a second time.[36] Gregory quotes Matthew 16:18-19 and infers from it the papal prerogative of deposing (unworthy) kings. He declares that the fathers and the general councils have acknowledged this papal power:

> They have not only accepted her [i.e. Rome's] expositions of doctrine and her instructions in [our] holy religion, but they have recognized her judicial decisions. They have agreed with one spirit and one voice that all major cases, all especially important affairs and the judgments of all churches, ought to be referred to her as to their head and mother; that from her there shall be no appeal, that her judgments may not and cannot be reviewed or reversed by anyone.[37]

After quoting Popes Gelasius, Julius, and Gregory I in an attempt to demonstrate the superior prerogatives of the Roman pontiff, he continues:

> Who does not know that kings and princes derive their origin from men ignorant of God who raised themselves above their fellows by pride, plunder, treachery, murder ... Does anyone doubt that the priests of Christ are to be considered fathers and masters of kings and princes and of all believers? Your Fraternity should remember also that greater power is granted to an exorcist when he is made a spiritual emperor for the casting out of devils, than can be conferred upon any layman for the purpose of earthly dominion.[38]

Various hierocratic ideals articulated in the *Dictatus* are embodied in this letter of Gregory to Bishop Hermann of Metz. It was St. Peter and his successors who possess the supreme jurisdiction over the *societas Christiana*. Emperors, kings, and princes are subject to the Roman pontiff, as are all the archbishops, bishops, clergy, and faithful. The 389 letters and documents in Gregory's register reflected these themes again and again. They echoed the ecclesiology of Nicholas I and John VIII and were taken up by the pontiffs in the next two centuries. As Friedrich Kempf notes, with Gregory VII the papacy had become a monarchy in political terms. "There remained merely the task of justifying it more precisely and guaranteeing and perfecting it."[39] Like Nicholas I before him, Gregory could not realize or implement his ideals to the fullest because he lacked the resources. His Lateran staff was small compared to what the papal entourage would amount to by 1150 or 1200. Best estimates are that his curia produced about two letters per week during his pontificate:

Neither Gregory's personal industry nor the political preeminence of his pontificate entails a high output of curial business by later standards. On the contrary, both suggest that his system of work was quite inadequate to his designs, and that he probably worked harder and with much less result than say, Alexander III [1159-81] a century later.[40]

Regardless of the verdict one renders concerning Pope Gregory VII, he did cast a very large shadow over the next half century after his death—so much that the period from 1073 to 1130 has often been called the Gregorian age. Although some authors, such as the eminent French historian Augustin Fliche, prefer to attribute the entire reform movement from 1049 onward to Gregory, the majority of historians today feel that this would be unfair to his predecessors, e.g., Leo IX, Nicholas II, and Alexander II, because they too had a major part to play in the reforms initiated in the eleventh century.

URBAN II (1088-99) AND PASCHAL II (1099-1118)

After Gregory's death in May 1085, the see of Rome was vacant for about two years before Gregory's remaining cardinals agreed on the choice of Abbot Desiderius of Monte Cassino, who took the name Victor III. However, after four rather tumultuous months in office, he died, at Monte Cassino because Rome was occupied by the antipope, Clement III. The reforming cardinals then chose Odo, the cardinal-bishop of Ostia, to succeed Victor. Odo, a French nobleman who had been a monk at Cluny, became Urban II. He had worked closely with Gregory and from the outset identified himself with the reform party.

Urban himself issued a resounding declaration of his loyalty to the principles of Gregory. He was, nevertheless, far from being an unimaginative imitator. He was more prepared than his predecessor to permit exceptions when they seemed advantageous. . . . they were facilitated by the growing clarity of the theory of dispensation . . . Urban also relied far more than Gregory on consultation. There is little in his letters about a personal relationship with St. Peter, and he spoke not as a man with a private illumination but as head of the Roman church after discussion with its clergy.[41]

Urban's diplomatic ability, along with his capacity for compromise, made him far more effective in the implementation of the reform movement than was Gregory.

The principal consultors of the pope had, by this time, come to be the cardinals, who were replacing the annual or biannual Roman synods as the pope's principal deliberative body.

An involved process of transformation shifted, during the eleventh century, the main functions of the Roman cardinal priests and bishops from liturgical duties and prerogatives to prominent roles in the government of the Church universal. This development was intimately connected with the great Reform whose phases and struggles would mold the history of a century, beginning with the accession of Leo IX (1049-54). . . . That the political rise of the cardinals in church government was but part of the fundamental changes brought about by the great Reform is now commonly accepted.[42]

Stephen Kuttner notes that by the last decades of the eleventh century, the cardinals (i.e., cardinal-bishops, priests, and deacons) had come to be the "Senators of the Church."[43] Geoffrey Barraclough considers Urban II as the creator of the papal curia; revamping the writing office, replacing the old financial administration with the camera, and utilizing the College of Cardinals as his supreme advisory body.[44] Barraclough further notes:

It would be difficult to exaggerate the importance of the changes Urban II inaugurated. The establishment of the curia as the pivot of the administration put the papacy on an equal footing with the rising states of feudal Europe; while at the same time the new conception of the pope's government as a court—for curia, as in the contemporary secular states, meant the central administration as a whole and a court of law—prepared the ground for the legal development which contributed so much to the rise of papal monarchy.[45]

At the synod of Piacenza in 1095, Urban reenacted Gregory's legislative agenda, and at Clermont in the same year, he proclaimed the First Crusade. Colin Morris says regarding Urban's pontificate:

> In the course of ten years Urban had immensely strengthened the position of the Gregorian line of popes. ... The programme enunciated by Gregory had been brought to much wider acceptance. This, however, was not the whole of his achievement. He began to build the papal administration on new foundations, and he turned papal policy away from its concentration on the empire. Certainly there were precedents for this, for the involvement in southern Italy and Spain dated back to the time before Gregory VII. Urban developed these relationships and added to them a much closer link to the French church, which reflected his own French origins.[46]

It was Urban's successor, Paschal II (1099-1118), who assumed the task of addressing the investiture controversy, especially in Germany, France, and England. The customary investiture of bishops and abbots with ring and staff by the king or prince was not acceptable to the Gregorian reformers since these acts expressed the conferral of spiritual authority which had to come from the proper ecclesiastical superior. The king or prince, on the other hand, was concerned about who would succeed as local ruler of the territory which was attached to the spiritual office (e.g., a diocese), because the prince or king was ultimately responsible for the government of the entire region. For example, the German king was not about to give up his right to control the appointment of his bishops because they were some of his most important feudal lords, wielding temporal jurisdiction over the territories they held from the king. "A compromise was indeed reached in England as early as 1107 by which the king gave up the practice of investing bishops with ring and staff while retaining the right to receive feudal homage for the land attached to their churches."[47]

Although Pope Paschal regarded this as only a partial solution, it did seem to work in England and France. The answer to the problem in Germany was not clarified until the synod of Worms in 1122, with Pope Callistus II (1119-24) and Emperor Henry V (1106-25) agreeing on a formula which was sealed by the Concordat of Worms. The pope's declaration reads:

> I, Bishop Callistus, servant of the servants of God, concede to you, beloved son Henry—by the grace of God August Emperor of the Romans—that the election of those bishops and abbots in the German kingdom . . . shall take place in your presence without simony or any violence; so that if any discord occurs between the parties concerned, you may—with the council and judgment of the metropolitan and the co-provincials—give your

assent and assistance to the party who appears to have the better case. The candidate elected may receive the "regalia" [i.e., the temporal rights and revenues connected with the benefice] from you through the sceptre and shall perform his lawful duties for them.[48]

The emperor, on the other hand, promised to surrender the right of investiture through ring and staff to the proper ecclesiastical officials, agreeing "that in all churches throughout my kingdom and empire there shall be canonical elections and free consecration."[49] Although the concordat did not solve the problem of royal interference in ecclesiastical elections, it did provide a practicable solution to a knotty ideological impasse. However, the emperor's influence on episcopal elections was not significantly reduced by this pact, because he could withhold his "assent" to a candidate and thus nullify the election, forcing the choice of another person—presumably someone more acceptable to him.

LATERAN I (1123)

The settlement at Worms in September 1122 was followed in the spring of 1123 by the first western general council, referred to as Lateran I. Although there were apparently no representatives from the eastern churches, about 300 western bishops, abbots, and religious took part. Giuseppe Alberigo makes the following observations on the "general" character of the gathering:

> The council is often called "general" in the letters and decrees of Pope Callistus II. It is reasonable, however, to doubt its ecumenicity. Indeed the manner in which the council was called and conducted by the pope and the fathers differed from that of the older councils. Moreover, several other councils, similar to Lateran I, were convened in the eleventh and twelfth centuries but were not termed ecumenical. The ecumenicity of this council seems, so far as we can tell, to have been confirmed later by the tradition of the Roman church.[50]

Lateran I—which began on March 18 and closed on April 6, 1123—addressed in twenty-two canons the reform of the Church in the areas of simony, clerical concubinage, the election of bishops, the subordination of religious to the local bishops in the pastoral care of the faithful, and the prohibition of marriage for priests, deacons, subdeacons, and monks. The Concordat of Worms was also given conciliar confirmation.[51]

Lateran I constitutes the beginning of a new epoch in the history of general councils. Although we are frequently inclined to group them together—stressing their similarities—those held after 1100 were very different from the ecumenical councils of the first millennium. R.W. Southern, for example, contrasts the three general councils held between 680 and 869 with the seven that took place from 1123 to 1312:

> Between the seventh century and the early twelfth the councils are few and, from a western point of view, insignificant. They were all held in Byzantine territory, and there were no representatives from the West except the papal legates, who played a minor role in the proceedings. The whole picture therefore is one of western inertia and papal impotence. Then for two centuries after 1123 the position is dramatically altered. There are no less than seven general councils culminating in the huge council of Vienne in 1311-12. All of them were summoned by the pope, who presided and was responsible for the decrees that were issued; all were held in the West; they were almost purely Latin; and the proceedings were of central importance in many fields of doctrine, [western] government and politics.[52]

These dramatic differences in the location, the shape, the composition, and the direction of general councils before and after 1000 A.D. point to the emergence of a discontinuity of global proportions. Western and eastern Christianity separated, drifted apart, like the separation of continents hundreds of millions of years ago. Initially the severance was not clearly perceived, even by the popes and the patriarchs. Some attempts were made—most of them politically motivated—to bring the two "continents" back together again over the next several hundred years, but to no avail. The causes of the division are manifold, no doubt. However, the papacy's growing involvement as a political player in the West, its narrowing vision of what constituted the *oikoumene*, and, perhaps most importantly, its loss of understanding of what it took to keep the bridges and the lines of communication open between East and West—these shifts contributed in a major way to the separation of the two Christian continents. Rather than being a largely unifying influence, the papacy must be considered as one of the principal agents of this most tragic division among Christians. What was originally destined as a source of harmony had truly become one of the major causes of dissonance.

INNOCENT II (1130-43) AND LATERAN II (1139)

With Lateran I the Gregorian period came to a close. It should be noted that from 1080 to 1121 there was a rather constant, though not unbroken, run of antipopes, who were for the most part the German emperor's men, causing the reforming line, i.e., the valid line, no end of difficulty and frustration. With the death of Honorius II in 1130, the Frangipani family, which elected Honorius, chose Innocent II to succeed him, while their rivals, the Pierleonis, chose a family member who took the name Anacletus II (1130-38). Although Anacletus had more power in Rome, Innocent II was much more widely acknowledged in northern Europe.

> The resolution of the schism was finally made possible by the death of Anacletus on 25 January 1138 . . . The victory of the Innocentians was a mark of the growing power of international opinion and of its limitations. It had sustained his cause effectively, but the resolution of the schism had to await its natural end through his rival's death.[53]

During the first eight years of his pontificate, Innocent II was not welcomed in Rome, which was controlled by Anacletus and the Pierleoni family. Innocent was forced therefore to spend most of those years in France, where he encountered Bernard of Clairvaux who proved to be an invaluable ally. Elizabeth Kennan, the noted medievalist, remarks, "Bernard's passionate endorsement of Innocent II was a major factor in the French decision to recognize him and reject the claims of his rival, Anacletus II."[54] Innocent's influence was growing in Germany also since the Concordat of Worms:

> The vast German church with its populous Rhineland dioceses and its important vantage for the missions to the East was at last brought into the sphere of papal influence. Free ecclesiastical elections elevated bishops sympathetic to the papacy in dioceses that were developing vigorously. Papal legates, now able to travel widely in German territories and intervene in diocesan affairs, brought occasional outside supervision to ecclesiastical courts. Grants of exception to German monasteries made the papacy a court of first instance in adjudicating many claims to monastic property.[55]

With the pope's prestige increasing in England as well under King Stephen (1135-54), the stage was set for a dramatic growth in papal influence throughout most of Europe. When Emperor Henry V, the last of the Salians, died in 1125, he was eventually succeeded by Conrad III (1137-52), the first of the Hohenstaufens (who were initially in accord with papal interests). The Concordat of Worms had enhanced the pope's position in Italy as well as in Germany. "The whole approach of the curia toward secular powers radiated a new confidence. Conrad was anointed by a papal legate."[56] One of Innocent's priorities, upon his return to Rome in March 1138, was the calling of the Second Lateran Council, which met in April 1139. Giuseppe Alberigo notes that the council was attended by more than 500 Latin bishops, abbots, and religious superiors, but he adds, "The council was called 'general' in the records and more frequently 'plenary' by Innocent himself. However, there is doubt about its ecumenicity for the same reasons that affect Lateran I."[57]

The thirty canons which the council enacted went over much the same ground as Lateran I and other recent synods, such as Clermont, Rheims, and Pisa. For example, there were canons against simony and against clerical marriage for subdeacons and those in higher orders. The practice of tithes from ecclesiastical benefices going to lay people was condemned, as was the practice of usury. Shortly after Lateran II, the monk Gratian from Bologna published the *Decretum*, or compendium of canonical texts, which was to serve as the foundation for the future development of canon law. This massive private collection of laws and prescriptions was drawn largely from Sacred Scripture, conciliar canons, papal decretals, Roman civil law, and the writings of the Church fathers. There were 324 passages taken from the *False Decretals*, of which 313 were forgeries. However, the work provided a critical base for the mass of legislation that would follow.

EUGENE III (1145-53) AND PAPAL CENTRALIZATION

The period after 1130 witnessed a dramatic rise in papal administrative and judicial activity. Innocent was the first to reserve whole classes of legal disputes to the papal curia for settlement. From that date, appeals from the various dioceses of Europe and from the monasteries and abbeys increased almost beyond counting, reaching the flood stage by the pontificate of Eugene III.

> It was in the decade from 1140 to 1150 that papal jurisdiction emerged as a perceptible fact in everyday European life. It is in these years we first begin to see it penetrating the lowest strata of the ecclesiastical structure as a matter of ordinary routine. . . . It is remarkable how little business the popes initiated in the great days of growth. They had no need to initiate. The business rushed upon them; they had only to invent the rules and reach the decisions.[58]

The positive result was that the whole range of church discipline—rights, duties, relationships between ecclesiastical entities, the prerogatives of the various office-holders, etc.—took shape in a reasonably uniform way. The overwhelming disadvantage was that the papal curia became predominantly a series of law courts. The other more central functions closer to the spiritual mission of the Church were relegated to a secondary position.

St. Bernard, who had been a mentor of Pope Eugene at the monastery of Clairvaux, spoke very candidly to his former pupil regarding his fears and anxieties concerning the papal court. Elizabeth Kennan notes that Bernard's little treatise titled *De Consideratione* (written to Pope Eugene) paints a graphic portrait of the abuses besetting the curia: "ambition and avarice among ecclesiastical officials, misuse of appeals to the curia, disruption of the hierarchy by intemperate granting of exemptions and failure by bishops and popes alike to enforce conciliar legislation."[59] Among the corrections Bernard felt should be made were the following:

> If you love justice, you do not encourage appeals but tolerate them. . . . Certainly appeals must be fostered and safeguarded; but only for those which necessity demands, not those which cunning devises. . . . Remove abuse and contempt will have no excuse. . . . You do well to refuse judgment on appeals, or rather to refuse protection to them, and return many of these problems to men who are acquainted with them, or who can more quickly become acquainted with them.[60]

He also warned that the excessive granting of dispensations and privileges was destroying the fabric of the Church.

> Are you still unaware of what I want to say? I will not keep you in suspense any longer: I speak of the murmuring complaint of the churches. They cry out that they are being mutilated and dismembered. There are none, or only a few, who do not suffer the pain of this affliction, or live in fear of it. Do you ask what this affliction is? Abbots are freed from the jurisdiction of bishops, bishops from that of archbishops, archbishops from that of patriarchs or primates. Does this seem good? I wonder whether this practice can ever be excused. In doing this you demonstrate that you have the fullness of power, but perhaps not of justice. . . .You have been appointed not to deny, but to preserve the degrees of honor, and of dignities and ranks proper to each.[61]

Through the fostering of appeals and the granting of privileges and dispensations from the established order, the institutional fabric of the Church, according to St. Bernard, was being broken down. Bishops, archbishops, and primates were losing their authority. Decisions and responsibilities were being gathered up into the papal curia, and this was breeding dissension, confusion, and resentment among the churches. In the curia itself there was apparently plenty to criticize. According to Bernard, the papal staff had more than its share of "blatant liars and wicked traitors" who were lining their pockets with silver to the disadvantage of those much less fortunate. The papal retinue was beginning to look more like the court of Constantine than the flock of disciples gathered around St. Peter. Bernard pleaded with Pope Eugene to curb and roll back some of these unfortunate developments, but as the events of the next several hundred years or so will reveal, things did not improve. Rather, they became worse. Apparently Pope Eugene himself spent much of his time in the hearing of cases.[62]

The problem proved too much for Eugene III, who was unable to stem the tide of this bureaucratic explosion. Because of unrest and civil disorder in Rome, the papal court was located in Viterbo. In 1143 a commune had been established in Rome which rejected the pope's temporal power, and the newly revived Roman senate considered itself to be a republic. Eugene had to cope with this situation throughout his pontificate. He died in Tivoli in July 1153 after making a pact with Emperor Conrad III's successor, young Frederick I (Barbarossa). Eugene was to crown Frederick emperor and Frederick in turn was to defend the pope and recover his territories. Eugene III was succeeded by Hadrian IV (1154-59), the only Englishman ever to be elected supreme pontiff. Hadrian crowned Frederick emperor in 1155, but the two had disagreements from the outset. Frederick was convinced that Hadrian conceived of the imperial coronation as an action that gave the pope a kind of temporal domination over the empire. The conflict was never resolved and led to a division among the College of Cardinals—the Sicilian party (who wanted to rely on Norman protection) and the imperialist sympathizers (who preferred imperial protection):

> During three days of intense negotiations after the funeral of Hadrian IV on 4 September 1159 rival groups of cardinals elected two candidates, Roland the papal chancellor as Alexander III and Octavian, cardinal-priest of St. Cecilia, as Victor IV. It was the third major schism in less than a century, following those of 1080-1100 and 1130-38.[63]

Frederick summoned a council in Pavia in 1160 to decide who was the validly elected pope. Alexander III refused to take part, and the council decided in favor of Victor IV (1159-64). Alexander then excommunicated Frederick and released his subjects from their obedience to him. Allegiance to Alexander came from Sicily, Lombardy, England, and France, while Victor was supported by the territories under the control of Frederick. When Victor died in 1164, some of the more prominent members of the German block went over to Alexander III, rather than pay homage to the imperial selection, Paschal III (1164-68). Callistus III (1168-78) followed Paschal III, but the imperial line was clearly losing favor with growing numbers throughout Europe. Colin Morris observes: "The western church was now closer to a state of permanent schism than at any time before the Great Schism of the fourteenth century."[64]

ALEXANDER III (1159-81) AND LATERAN III (1179)

Although it was clear that Alexander III's position was dominant, he was unable to return from France until the Peace of Venice (July 1177) when Frederick finally renounced Callistus III and made his allegiance to Alexander

III, after the pope lifted the emperor's excommunication. This third schism (1159-77) was not as long as the first schism (1080-1100), but was longer than the second schism (1130-38). In spite of this turmoil, the curia of Alexander was one of the busiest and most efficient in Europe. The judicial business continued to expand by leaps and bounds over the twenty-two years of his pontificate. He was the first of the great lawyer-popes which included Innocent III, Gregory IX, Innocent IV, and Boniface VIII.

They brought to their task clarity of mind, firmness of principle and a capacious practical wisdom. But they had the weakness of the lawyer at the head of affairs. They aspired less and less to provide the leadership which always seemed just beyond their grasp, and increasingly they devoted their energies to keeping the wheels of government turning.[65]

Upon his return to Rome in 1178, Alexander III began making preparations for a general council which would put an end to the schism and finally settle the dispute between him and Emperor Frederick. Three hundred fathers assembled at the Lateran—all Latins but one—in March 1179. Giuseppi Alberigo observes regarding the ecumenicity of Lateran III:

We do not have the same reasons for doubting the ecumenical nature of this council as we have for Lateran I and II. For the way in which the council was summoned and conducted by the pope, and the number of fathers who gathered from the whole Latin world and devoted their efforts to strengthening the unity of the Church and condemning heretics, resemble rather the ancient councils than Lateran I and II and exemplify the typical council of the Middle Ages presided over by the Roman pontiff.[66]

Concerning the enactments of the council, the final session on March 19, 1179, produced twenty-seven canons.[67] Canon 1 addressed the issue of papal elections, affirming that a two-thirds vote of the cardinals would be required to elect the new pope. The confusion that arose in 1159 when two popes were elected—Alexander III by the majority and Victor IV by a disgruntled minority—would thus be eliminated. Canon 3 established age requirements for episcopal and other ordinations, while canon 4 laid out rather precise arrangements for episcopal visitations within each diocese. According to canon 7, no charges were to be levied for the administration of the sacraments. The fathers (in canon 8) prohibited the assigning of clerical offices and benefices to candidates before the posts become vacant (i.e., expectancies). Clerics living in concubinage were required either to cease the practice or be deprived of their office (canon 11). One of the most potentially harmful abuses, that of pluralism, was confronted in canon 13:

Because some, setting no limit to their avarice, strive to obtain several ecclesiastical dignities and several parish churches contrary to the decrees of the holy canons, so that though they are scarcely able to fulfil one office sufficiently, they claim the revenues of very many, we strictly forbid this for the future. Therefore, when it is necessary to entrust a church or ecclesiastical ministry to anyone, the person sought for this office should be of such a kind that he is able to reside in the place and exercise his care for it himself. If the contrary is done, both he who receives it is to be deprived of it, because he has received it contrary to the sacred canons, and he who gave it is to lose his power of bestowing it.[68]

Had this canon been faithfully implemented by the popes and the bishops, the history of the next three or four centuries would have been very different indeed. Finally, Lateran III, in canon 18, prescribed that in every cathedral church a master was to be assigned to teach and instruct the clerics and the poor scholars of the area. The master was to be provided with a suitable benefice so that he could adequately provide for himself. This arrangement was only a start in the effort to broaden the educational base—especially among the clergy—but it was a significant step nonetheless.

The final canon addressed the rising tide of opposition groups on the margins of the Church, especially the Cathars in France. Christians were forbidden to trade with them or support them, and princes could subject them to slavery. The Cathars, the Waldensians, and others—although in many ways quite distinct from one another—were all searching for a return to the simplicity of life reflected in the gospels. They opposed the growing wealth and power of the organized Church and were dedicated to the restoration of the *vita apostolica*. These movements gathered momentum in the early 1100s and were a force to be reckoned with by the time of Lateran III.

In summary, Alexander III is remembered most for his decretal legislation. His enactments on a wide range of subjects constituted the largest single contribution made by any twelfth-century pope to the fabric of medieval canon law.[69] He was a tireless worker who sat daily in consistory with his cardinals, deliberating and deciding legal cases and affairs of state dispatched from all corners of Christendom. Lateran Council III, which was invoked by Alexander and directed by him in almost every detail, set the tone for the general councils of the Middle Ages. Since the promulgation of Lateran III's canon 1 in 1179, the cardinals have exercised the mandate to conduct papal elections from that time to the present. In spite of his many battles with Frederick I of Germany, which forced him to move his court out of Rome for the better part of eighteen years, Alexander's curia was one of the most progressive and efficient in all of Europe.

With all the curial expansion necessitated by the growth of papal administrative and judicial activity and the incessant struggles with Frederick I over the control of territory in Italy, the papal coffers were seriously depleted at the time of Alexander III's death in 1181. The battle between Frederick Barbarossa and the papacy over the control of the papal territories continued through a series of rather brief pontificates from Lucius III (1181-85) to Clement III (1187-91), the first of a rather long line of Roman popes, i.e., popes of Roman birth and education.[70] Barbarossa's death during the Third Crusade in June 1190 did not change matters significantly because his son, Henry VI (1190-97), followed his father's policies regarding the control of the church in Germany and the struggle over papal lands in Italy.

THE PAPAL SYSTEM OF JUSTICE

Before leaving the twelfth century behind, something more should be said about the way in which papal judicial activity had expanded since the 1120s and 30s. We recall what St. Bernard said around 1150 to his former pupil, Eugene III, concerning the excessive concentration on litigation at the papal curia. Although it is true that petitioners flooded into the pope's courts on their own initiative, Bernard's clear implication was that much of the increase was encouraged and fostered by the curial people themselves. Litigation was a source of considerable revenue for the curial officials. However, the greater the volume of litigation, the more judges, auditors, lawyers, notaries, and clerks were needed. This judicial activity could support itself somewhat, but the sheer volume put a terrible strain on the physical capacity of the courts. Although there was some use of judges-delegate before Alexander III, the practice of empowering judges in the various countries of Christendom to handle cases submitted to the pope, both on appeal and in the first instance, expanded notably with him. In England when the Constitutions of Clarendon (1164) were modified in 1172 at Avranches, King Henry—after having been absolved by the pope for his complicity in the murder of Archbishop Thomas Becket on December 29, 1170—promised that henceforth he would no longer impede appeals to Rome as long as the appellant intended no harm to the king or the kingdom.[71]

Bishop Bartholomew of Exeter (d. 1184) was one of the more active judges-delegate in England during the pontificate of Alexander III. During his outstanding career as a papal judge, he tried such cases as the crimes of clerics, actions involving the property rights of religious houses, the exemption of religious from the jurisdiction of the local ordinary, matrimonial cases, various disputes between bishops and their clergy, and many actions involving the contested possession of offices and benefices.[72] Although recourse to papal justice was a lengthy procedure and no doubt quite expensive, it enjoyed great popularity throughout Europe because it was a way of eliminating endless appeals and obtaining a definitive decision. The judges-delegate acted in the pope's stead "and therefore obtained a plenary jurisdiction over all things or people which affected the case."[73] Actions initiated before local ecclesiastical courts could normally be interrupted at any stage in the procedure, by either party, with an appeal to another tribunal, thus stalling indefinitely the original process. A papal judicial action could be started by either or both parties to the dispute appearing personally or through a procurator before the pope's curia. An auditor would hear the complaint and a qualified judge-delegate from the petitioner's locale would normally be appointed to hear the case. If the plaintiff alone appeared, he would be given a rescript initiating the action, and upon his return home, he would present the rescript to the judge selected to resolve the dispute.

Normally the rescript would contain three items: (1) a general outline of the case as presented by the plaintiff, (2) a statement of the law that would be applicable in such a trial, and (3) the formal appointment of the judge-delegate directing him to inquire into the facts and apply the law previously outlined according to the evidence. Upon receipt of the rescript, the judge-delegate would summon the parties to appear at some convenient location, e.g., London or Exeter. The parties would then secure the services of advocates and the process would begin. As a privileged agent of the pope, the judge enjoyed full power to bring the required witnesses forward, and usually the rescript contained a clause prohibiting any further appeal.[74] The use of judges-delegate reduced some of the clutter in the papal courts and brought about a relative uniformity of jurisprudence throughout the Christian West. However, it did significantly weaken the local courts and contribute to the process of papal centralization which was in many ways disabling and dismantling the subordinate structures of the Church, namely the local bishops and the metropolitans.

In the twelfth century, bishops were more and more frequently elected by the canons of the cathedral, and hence it is understandable that a large number of ordinaries were chosen from the cathedral chapters. Local clerics were usually selected, and often they were from the same family. The principal outside influence came from the king or the local prince who would with some regularity pressure the chapter to select a candidate favorable to royal or noble interests. There is not much evidence, however, for the existence of papal interference in episcopal elections in the twelfth century. Also, the royal or noble power would on occasion pressure the cathedral chapter to leave sees vacant for considerable periods of time, so that the episcopal revenues would, in large part, flow to the king or prince. However, the development of regular patterns of taxation of the churches, either by the royalty or the pope, did not occur until the next century.

There was good reason for the interest on the part of the royalty and the pope in the revenues from ecclesiastical property. "In 1200 something like one-fifth of the land in western Europe was in the hands of ecclesiastical institutions, which also had the right of receiving tithes, in effect a tax of ten percent on all monies."[75] Although this did not, in many cases, work out as well as it sounds, the control of financial resources by the dioceses and monastic institutions at this time was immense compared with contemporary standards.

The cathedral canons were usually from wealthy families, who tended to control the membership of the chapter. This meant that the bishops elected out of the chapters usually had aristocratic backgrounds and were not often naturally inclined to become involved in the regular instruction and supervision of their clergy.[76] In this connection, Colin Morris notes: "It is significant that as far as we know not a single bishop in Germany, France or England [in the twelfth century] was elected because he had been a successful parish priest."[77] Although there is little evidence of papal interference in the local diocesan episcopal election process, there was a growing tendency in the twelfth century for cathedral chapters to request papal confirmation of the elections after they had taken place. The growing centralization of canonical discipline and ecclesiastical procedure in the 1100s was accompanied by the increasing use of legates to carry out the pope's business in various parts of the Christian West. These legates were frequently curial cardinals who were delegated to carry out a certain mission, e.g., the promotion and supervision of regional reform synods, for a certain limited number of years. Another type of delegated papal jurisdiction was often conferred on a residential bishop or archbishop to perform, for a certain period, a limited number of responsibilities, such as the granting of various dispensations or privileges which had been reserved to the pope.

CELESTINE III (1191-98) AND INNOCENT III (1198-1216)

After the death of Clement III in 1191, the cardinals, to avoid another schism, chose an eighty-five-year-old cardinal, Giacinto Bobo, who took the name Celestine III. It was he who crowned the young German king, Henry VI (1190-97), as emperor in the first few weeks of his pontificate. Like his father before him and his son Frederick II, Henry strove year after year to gain control of the whole of Italy, including the papal lands. Because the expenses of papal government, especially during and after the reign of Alexander III, had been increasing far beyond its capacity to increase its revenues, the loss of additional funds from the pontifical patrimonies was a real threat to the popes. The business of the Roman curia, however, simply continued to expand: "As in previous pontificates, legal cases streamed from all of Christendom to Rome under Celestine III, especially since he solemnly declared that anyone who felt that he was threatened by others could and should seek justice at Rome."[78]

Worn out by more than fifty years of service in the papal court, Celestine

III died in January 1198. On the very day of his death the cardinals unanimously elected Lothario of Segni, a thirty-seven-year-old cardinal deacon, to be the next pontiff. Although Innocent III was a member of a noble Roman family and a nephew of Pope Clement III (1187-91), who made him a cardinal in 1190, he did not play a significant role in the pontificate of Celestine III. The stage was set, however, for a papal reign that knew no parallel since the days of Leo I and Gregory I. When Emperor Henry VI died prematurely in 1197, leaving a three-year-old son, Frederick, as his heir, a "period of darkness" set in for the German Empire.[79] Philip of Swabia, Henry's brother, stood loyal to young Frederick, and initially tried to establish himself as "guardian of the empire" until Frederick was ready to rule. Thinking that a long minority rule would be too debilitating, the leading German princes persuaded Philip to accept the German crown in 1198. Pope Innocent wanted someone more favorable to the papal cause, however, and claiming the right to dispose of the German crown, he sided with Otto of Brunswick who controlled the destinies of the empire from 1198 to 1212. In an effort to dislodge the Hohenstaufens, Innocent chose a Guelph (i.e., one favorable to the pope), but the choice of Otto did not work out as expected. He too had designs on the conquest of Sicily and was eventually excommunicated by Innocent in 1210.

During the period from 1199 to 1209, there was no effective German presence in Italy. The Papal States were under the reasonably secure control of Rome, with pontifical governors—normally cardinals—presiding over the papal territories. This meant that revenues increased as the civil administration of Rome and the Papal States underwent a thorough reorganization under Innocent. As vassals of the pope, Hungary, Poland, Aragon, Sicily, and England provided some revenues to the Roman curia in return for the pope's "protection." This dramatically indicates the rising prestige that the pope enjoyed in Europe. Innocent III was extremely involved in the politics of his day, not only in Germany, but in England and France as well. For example, he wanted to install Stephen Langton as the archbishop of Canterbury, and when King John of England refused, he excommunicated John and put the entire nation under interdict—which lasted for five years (1208-1213). Innocent also placed France under interdict for more than ten years because of Philip Augustus' long-standing marriage problems.

It was Innocent III who claimed for himself in a very special way the title "vicar of Christ." The term appeared in St. Bernard's *De Consideratione* around 1150 and was first used by Pope Eugene III. Another descriptive term which Bernard employed to emphasize papal prerogatives was the "fullness of power" (*plenitudo potestatis*).[80] This term was Innocent's favorite. He used it frequently. As a matter of fact, it was featured in his consecration sermon:

> In the sermon preached on the consecration of the pope, Innocent emphasized his splendid isolation, chosen as he was to be the steward of God's

household. "Only St. Peter," he says, "was invested with the plenitude of power. See then what manner of servant this is, appointed over the household; he is indeed the vicar of Jesus Christ, the successor of St. Peter, the Lord's anointed . . . set in the midst between God and man . . . less than God but greater than man, judging all men and judged by none."[81]

Helene Tillmann, in her classic biography of Innocent, clarifies the meaning of the *plenitudo*, as that phrase was employed by the pontiff.

The *plenitudo potestatis*, the fullness of power, which the Lord has assigned to the Roman bishop alone, is in no way a totality of all spiritual and temporal power, but, according to Innocent's oft repeated own statement, nothing else but the *plenitudo ecclesiasticae potestatis*, the fullness of ecclesiastical power, in the same way as the *plenitudo potestatis* which Innocent assigns to the emperor, denotes the fullness of temporal power. Innocent has not succumbed to the temptation of the medieval papacy to lay claim to both swords, the spiritual and the temporal one.[82]

Tillmann continues, "Although in Innocent's view, the spiritual power has a higher rank by far than the dignity of temporal power, he yet deems it God's will that the temporal power be autonomous in its domain, just as the Church is in its own sphere."[83] However, that is not the end of the story:

Though Innocent confesses in principle to the separation and independence of spiritual and temporal power, yet he laid claim to a conditional temporal power within the whole Christian world, a power which the pope exercises occasionally (*casualiter*) only and in respect of certain circumstances (*certis causis inspectis*), well knowing that such a measure is extraordinary.[84]

Innocent claimed that he was able to exercise this extraordinary temporal jurisdiction *ratione peccati* (i.e., by reason of sin): "Just as the actions of private persons, as regards their moral aspect, are subject to the judgment of the Church, so are the actions of rulers, not only concerning their private lives, but also as regards their public activities."[85] Although in theory this distinction has a measure of plausibility, in critical moments the lines of demarcation tended to blur somewhat. Even Helene Tillmann, who is most loyal to Innocent, admits that there were a number of egregious transgressions:

[Innocent] transgressed these limits in crucial moments, most conspicuously when he released those who had sworn their allegiance to Emperor Otto IV from their oaths [in favor of the young Frederick in 1212], when he prepared the same measure against King John of England [in 1208], and when he required that the papal recognition of Otto of Brunswick and the rejection of Philip of Swabia [in 1198] be binding on all subjects.[86]

The interdicts thrust on England and France, for example, were severe actions justifiable only by the heady ecclesiastical temper of the times. To keep whole nations deprived of the public celebration of the sacraments (save baptism and the last anointing) for years, simply for political reasons, is hardly comprehensible to the modern mind. But this reveals the awesome power of the papacy at its apogee. Gregory VII (1073-85) would have been exhilarated had he been in a position to exercise such power, but the time for bold strikes of this sort was not ripe in his day. Boniface VIII (1294-1303), on the other hand, fully expected to subject the royal power of Philip IV of France to his Petrine authority, but the political influence of the papacy in 1300 was in a state of serious decline. In Innocent's day, the papacy was the focal point of Europe. And he was clearly the right man at the right time—he was brilliant, energetic, ambitious, decisive, and utterly convinced that this was the pope's proper role in the affairs of Europe in the year 1200.

The more than 6,000 extant letters attributed to Innocent III constitute a precious record of his activities throughout his eighteen-year pontificate. The medieval historian Christopher Cheney paints an impressive picture of the pontiff as he is reflected in his ample correspondence:

The pope stands out as a man devoted to his pastoral task, uplifted rather than depressed by his responsibilities, teaching even when he is obliged to expostulate. The letters show him to be zealous for the faith, strong in legal science and subtle in diplomacy, and tirelessly active. The amplitude of expression and the narrative of events which the letters often contain, give them a unique importance as historical material.[87]

Pope Innocent's law courts were teeming with litigants, lawyers, and clerks, perhaps even more so than in Alexander III's day. Cheney has estimated that there were on average forty-five judicial actions per year coming to Rome from England alone, and some of them took years to settle.[88] Tillman notes,

Innocent three times a week held a consistory in open court in which he heard suits and petitions, examined himself the cases of major importance with the assistance of the cardinals, had the less important ones examined by the cardinals, and pronounced the judgments.[89]

Because the spiraling costs of litigation clearly exceeded the resources of the Roman curia, Innocent instituted a series of fees for the various services, and in addition, he allowed the litigants to give gifts to the officers of the court to supplement their income. The pontiff tried to care for the growing numbers of curial people by awarding them offices and benefices as they became vacant in the various dioceses throughout Christendom. Occasionally, he would confer on them the right to possess the next vacant post, e.g., a cathedral canonry, in some far-off diocese. Not infrequently a number of these benefices were conferred on the same person at the same time. In all such cases the recipient (of one or several benefices) would arrange with some cleric to perform the office(s) on his behalf for a portion—and often a rather small portion—of the revenue flowing from the benefice(s).

Understandably, this practice—which grew almost geometrically in the next two centuries—was not at all welcomed by the local clergy throughout Europe. Innocent let it be known, however, that he was able to intervene in this manner out of the *plenitudo*, the fullness of his ruling power. It was Innocent III who levied the first general tax on all the clergy in the West (1/40th of their income) in 1199 to finance the Fourth Crusade. He tried to respond to the complaints of the prelates gathered at the Fourth Lateran Council (1215) concerning the exorbitant and sometimes fraudulent charges assessed by the Roman curial officials for services rendered by proposing "to assign to the curia a revenue from every cathedral (one-tenth or one of the prebends, i.e., offices) with the objective of ending the extortion."[90] The proposal was not found acceptable by the bishops and hence was dropped. It is curious to note that throughout his reign, Innocent did not feel within himself the power, and/or the desire, to address some of the most damaging abuses of his day:

> The basic evils from which the medieval Church suffered were the claims of the nobility to the higher ecclesiastical offices and benefices, and the system of patronage and benefices together with the restrictions of the bishops' governmental power they entailed.[91]

Pope Innocent simply assumed these conditions as a part of the world in which he and his contemporaries lived. To change the traditional balance favoring the nobility to a more equitable arrangement was beyond his reach, and the granting of far-off benefices to absentee clergy working in the Roman curia seemed to be the only way to manage the situation which he inherited in 1198.

Innocent III's major geopolitical goal was to build around himself a substantial territorial state which could cope with Germany to the North and Sicily to the South.[92] Although he did significantly strengthen the Papal States and increase his revenues thereby, the enterprise was at best a limited success. Barraclough appraises the results:

> The establishment of an effective direct government (in the Papal States) was beyond Innocent's means; and the Papal States, far from assuring the papacy's independence, were during the two succeeding centuries more often to prove a millstone around its neck.[93]

Pope Innocent's dealings with the various rising nations of Europe were not particularly successful either because they left—in countries like Germany, France, and England—a great residue of negative feelings against Rome at a time when national spirit and national identity were beginning to assert themselves. Perhaps the most damaging results occurred in the East through the ravages of the Fourth Crusade, which overran Constantinople in 1204 and left a Latin emperor and a Latin patriarch in charge of the Byzantines.[94] Although one could hardly lay all of this at the pope's doorstep, he made little effort to correct this situation during his long reign. Furthermore, in canon 4 of Lateran IV, Innocent's council, the Greeks were told to "conform themselves like obedient sons to the holy Roman church, their mother."[95] This insensitivity to the Byzantine tradition must have left the Greeks in a state of utter dismay.

LATERAN IV (1215)

Perhaps the most important event of Innocent's pontificate was the Fourth Lateran Council which was held in 1215:

> The pope's summons had gone out to the Christian world in April 1213. Its objects were in the pope's words, "to uproot vices and implant virtues, to correct abuses and reform morals, to eliminate heresies and strengthen faith, to allay differences and establish peace, to check persecutions and cherish liberty, to persuade Christian princes and people to grant succor and support for the Holy Land from both clergy and layfolk." And, wrote the pope, "since these objects affect the whole body of the faithful," a general council was the appropriate instrument.[96]

The bishops and the major superiors of religious orders were invited to attend, and every cathedral chapter and collegiate church was directed to send a representative. Christopher Cheney notes that "a big advance was made on the idea of representation, although the function which prelates and delegates were to perform in the council remained obscure."[97]

Records indicate that there were over 400 cardinals, archbishops and bishops, along with approximately 800 other prelates, present. The sessions opened on November 11, 1215 and were concluded with the third and final session on November 30. The seventy decrees of the council were for the most part prepared beforehand and reflect the mind and the priorities of Innocent. In all probability they were read and adopted, not debated at the council.[98] However, most scholars who have studied the council in detail are of the mind that the enactments were to some extent at least a collaborative effort involving the prelates who were in attendance.[99]

Like the earliest ecumenical councils, Lateran IV began with a formal profession of faith which summarized the principal tenets of Christian belief. Decrees 2 and 3 concentrated on the rooting out of heresies in the West, while the fourth and fifth decrees dealt with the eastern churches. Innocent's insensitivity to the distinctiveness of eastern Christianity is revealed quite clearly in these enactments. For example, the eastern patriarchs are directed to receive the pallium from the pope. The pallium is an ancient liturgical vestment traditionally worn about the neck by archbishops and primates in the churches of the West as a sign of their papal confirmation and their allegiance to the papacy. For the patriarchs of the East to be asked to wear this western vestment was an insult, given their status and dignity within their own traditions. The remaining decrees dealt with western disciplinary matters, e.g., the reform of clerical morals, episcopal elections and the administration of benefices, the exacting of taxes, canonical trials, matrimony, tithes, and simony.[100]

It is generally believed that the most far-reaching pastoral enactment was decree 21, requiring annual confession and communion for all the faithful after reaching the age of discernment. Although not always honored, it probably did more to strengthen the adherence of Church members in the regular practice of their faith than any other canonical regulation of the Middle Ages. An effort was also made to raise the level of the preaching and instruction of the faithful (decree 10) and to provide more adequate educational resources for the seminarians and the priests of each diocese (decree 11). The legislative program of Lateran IV was on balance extremely thorough and well designed, compared with the first three Lateran councils of 1123, 1139, and 1179. Had the decrees been implemented more consistently, an effective program of reform could have been launched, and perhaps the history of the Church in the West would have taken a different turn.

The failure of Innocent III to secure from the bishops a more stable funding for his curial operations led him and his successors to the expansion of papal provisions and pluralism. During the twelfth and thirteenth centuries, more and more offices and benefices throughout the West were reserved in such a way that only the pope could fill them when a vacancy occurred. For example, if a thirteenth-century bishop of Exeter, England, died while in Rome, the pope was empowered to select the replacement, not the cathedral chapter in Exeter. The person chosen could well have been an official of the papal curia. He would become bishop of far-off Exeter but could conceivably remain in his post in the papal court. His pastoral responsibilities would then be delegated to a vicar, who would receive a part of the episcopal income, with the major share going to the curial official in Rome. Furthermore, although decree 29 of Lateran IV unambiguously reaffirmed the prohibition of Lateran III (canon 13) regarding the acquiring of more than one benefice with pastoral responsibilities attached, the practice of pluralism continued to expand, especially in the papal curia because it seemed an extremely effective way to provide more adequate financial support for the growing number of professionals employed there.

Although the legislation of Lateran IV clearly prohibited the granting of more than one benefice (with pastoral responsibilities) to a single individual, the pope—out of the fullness of his power—could rise above the common law and bestow several such benefices on a valuable official in Rome. These two practices—the awarding of pastoral offices *in absentia* and the holding of a number of them simultaneously, along with the dramatic increase in papal taxation—might well have provided needed revenues for the Roman curia, but at the cost of incalculable and irreparable harm to the vitality and morale of the local churches. The Fourth Lateran Council was truly focused on the need for reform in the Church, a theme that resounded through the enactments of the three previous Lateran councils. However, although Lateran IV was a legislative success, the reform of Church life and discipline was not forthcoming.

Pope Innocent III died in the summer of 1216, just six months or so after the close of his impressive council. He had reigned long and accomplished a great deal. His papacy, in the estimate of most, represented the highest level of papal influence in the West. His successors would try but never succeeded in attaining the heights he had achieved. Helene Tillmann concludes her masterful biography of Innocent III with the following observations:

> The person of a pope cannot solely be judged by the standards of excellent statesmanship, but must also, and above all, be measured according to the demands of the office and the dignity of Vicar of Christ. Innocent met these requirements in part. With holy ardour he strove for the reform of the clergy and of the Church; the purification of the sanctuary was his ardent desire and the object of constant efforts in his pontificate. . . . But it was not always the highest interpretation of his office which guided his actions, and the values of law and morality, which he had often high-mindedly advocated, he sometimes sacrificed to his political aspirations.[101]

HONORIUS III (1216-27) AND GREGORY IX (1227-41)

Cardinal Cencio Savelli, who was elected to follow Innocent III, was an extremely important functionary during the pontificate of Clement III (1187-91).[102] Savelli, who took the name Honorius III, has been described as a mild, peace-loving pontiff. One of his chief goals, however, was to protect the unity and the viability of the Papal States which had been secured under his predecessor. He also brought to term two other developments that had been initiated under Innocent, i.e., the official confirmation of the Order of Preachers in 1217, and the final confirmation of the Franciscans in 1223.

Innocent's allies in the movement of reform were the Cistercians who had formed sometime after 1100. Unlike the Augustinian canons who lived and worked in the cities but were not particularly influential, the Cistercians dwelt on the margins of society, occupying previously unsettled lands and giving themselves over to agriculture. Although they experienced a steady growth until about 1300, by 1200 they had become quite affluent—buying up more and more land—and found themselves being widely accused of covetousness.[103] And as they were not particularly effective preachers and pastors, their contribution to the reform movement was limited. The Dominicans and the Franciscans, i.e., the friars, were of a more pastoral bent. They situated themselves in the towns and were generally effective preachers and shepherds of souls. Their growth throughout Europe was simply phenomenal. R.W. Southern estimates that by 1300 there were 28,000 Franciscans and 12,000 Dominicans working throughout various parts of Europe and the Middle East.[104] It was the friars upon whom the popes in the thirteenth and fourteenth centuries largely depended to spearhead the tasks of preaching, instruction, and pastoral reform.

The conflict between the friars and the secular clergy erupted almost as soon as they encountered one another. The local bishops objected to the friars intruding into their jurisdictions, preaching and exercising pastoral care in their dioceses to the frustration of the secular clergy. Pope Honorius fortified both the Franciscans and the Dominicans with papal privileges, and from as early as 1220 ordered the bishops to allow the friars to preach and minister in their dioceses.[105] As we shall see in the discussions of the councils of Lyons I (1245) and Lyons II (1274), this issue was to constitute, along with papal reservations and pluralism, a serious and abiding source of contention between the papacy and the local hierarchy and clergy. In spite of the fact that Pope Honorius and his immediate successors were convinced that the friars represented their best hope for the realization of pastoral reform, they failed to cope adequately with the growing opposition between the friars and the local clergy. The conflicts between the hierarchy and the mendicants threatened the bishops' authority and increased the alienation between the local ordinaries and Rome.

This was a problem that Pope Honorius perhaps did not perceive because he was aged and rather sickly at the time of his election. Furthermore, he had spent practically his entire professional life in the curia, and hence never felt personally the local bishops' pain and frustration in this regard. When he died in 1227, he was followed by Ugolino of Segni, a nephew of Innocent III. Gregory IX (1227-41) was an energetic and extremely gifted canon lawyer who had studied at Paris and Bologna. The preoccupation of his pontificate was his battle against the Hohenstaufen, Frederick II (1212-50), who had been crowned emperor in St. Peter's in 1220 by Honorius. One of the primary objectives of Honorius' pontificate had been to launch the crusade called for by Lateran IV. For this he had looked to Frederick, but the emperor continued to postpone the project.[106]

Pope Gregory excommunicated Frederick in 1227 because of his countless delays in embarking on the crusade in which he had vowed to take part. The battle between the German emperor and the pope continued throughout Gregory's pontificate. Frederick's excommunication was renewed in 1239 by Pope Gregory for a number of reasons, including heresy, blasphemy, immorality, perjury, and other crimes, but the real grounds were political:

> A king of Sicily endowed with Frederick's unusual gifts and idiosyncrasies would have made an uncomfortable neighbor for the papacy at the best of times, but the popes could have put up with him if he had been content to stay in Sicily. What they could not permit was that any one man, whoever he might be, should rule over all Italy, north and south.[107]

The excommunication of Frederick on Palm Sunday, 1239, constituted something of a watershed. As Walter Ullmann describes it: "This was the signal for the outbreak of an ideological war which in fierceness, ferocity and depth of passion and disregard of all the accepted norms of warfare, has few, if any, parallels in medieval history."[108] Frederick wanted the pope to be put on trial before a general council. It was not so much the papal office he was attacking, but the person himself, whom he perceived as the personification of the Antichrist.[109] In his arrogance, Frederick wanted to occupy Rome and assume the role of the Roman emperor of antiquity. This solemn renewal of excommunication constituted Gregory's counterattack. The pope called Frederick a blasphemer and "the forerunner of the Antichrist."[110] As Frederick's armies encircled Rome, ready to occupy the city, Gregory died, an old but by no means broken man, in August 1241.

Gregory IX's unceasing battles with Frederick II should not obscure the contributions of his pontificate. In 1234 he promulgated the *Liber Extra* which "became the first, official, authentic, uniform, universal and exclusive law book of the Church."[111] The work contained 2,139 papal decretals issued since the publication of Gratian's *Decree* ca. 1140, including 195 of Gregory's own enactments. The *Liber* was divided into five books and purported to contain all the legislation in force since Gratian. Any legislation after 1140 not found in the *Liber* was abrogated. Gregory's contribution was invaluable because the *Liber* not only organized and synthesized the legislation after Gratian, but clarified countless issues that were dubious or in dispute. It was Gregory IX who definitively reserved the canonization of saints to Rome and constituted the *ad limina* visits of bishops to the Holy See as a general obligation. Further, his important decretal of 1235 gave official sanction to the missionary movement—promoted mainly by the Franciscans and the Dominicans—to proclaim the gospel outside of Europe.[112]

For a long time there seemed to be just two worlds, Christianity and Islam, but by 1250 or so—with the invasion of Genghis Khan into eastern Europe—whole new worlds appeared. Europeans became aware of the Mongols and other great populations to the East which had not yet been evangelized. Pope

Gregory IX gave shape and impetus to this critical development.

Another institution to which Gregory IX made a large contribution was the Inquisition. The Cathars, the Waldensians, and others continued to be active in southern France, northern Italy, Germany, and Spain. Although their tenets differed, all of them were protesting the growing wealth of the Church and advocated a return to the simple life portrayed in the gospels. Popes Alexander III (1159-81) and Lucius III (1181-85) promulgated legislation officially initiating the inquisitorial approach vis-à-vis heretics.[113] These procedures were expanded, perfected, and given additional force in the third decree of Lateran IV in 1215. In 1229, with the cooperation of the young King Louis IX of France, the national council of Toulouse established the first permanent college of judges with the task of seeking out and punishing heretics. After this the Cathars went underground.[114] Gregory IX put the final touches on the inquisitorial process in 1231 with the constitution, *Excommunicamus*:

> Public and private discussions of faith among the laity were forbidden, and ecclesiastical burial was denied to those put to death [N.B. a finding of guilt was penalized by death at the stake]. Immurement or life imprisonment for penitent heretics, prohibition of any appeal to other tribunals, denial of any legal assistance for the accused, and finally social ostracism of the descendants of the condemned—to the second generation they lost the ability to hold any ecclesiastical offices—were among the fundamental components of this legislation.[115]

In the following year, 1232, Pope Gregory turned over the Inquisition to the new orders, especially the Dominicans, who became forever identified with this terrifying procedure. In spite of its organization and its almost universal application, the Inquisition "was unable completely to eradicate heresy."[116] At this time the menace of heresy was viewed as a highly infectious disease which had to be eradicated by the most stringent of remedies. The problem, however, was that when such Star Chamber techniques were employed, the flagrant injustice and the unbridled cruelty quickly reached epidemic proportions.[117] For example, it was Pope Innocent IV who sanctioned the use of torture to elicit the confessions of alleged heretics.

INNOCENT IV (1243-54) AND LYONS I (1245)

When Pope Gregory died in Rome in August 1241, he was followed by Celestine IV, who lived for only three weeks. A long vacancy ensued after Celestine's death until Cardinal Sinibaldo Fieschi was elected in June 1243. Innocent IV, a masterful canonist, took up the battle with Frederick II from the outset of his pontificate. In the summer of 1244, he and his court fled from

Rome to Lyons where he was safely out of the grasp of Frederick. Innocent wasted no time in summoning a council which opened at Lyons in June 1245.[118] The principal participants were the Italians, the English, the French, and the Spanish, because Frederick had kept most of the German prelates away. Innocent engineered the council to depose Emperor Frederick in the third and final session on July 17, 1245—much to the chagrin of the fathers who felt that such action was without precedent.[119]

The sentence of deposition outlined in considerable detail the crimes of Frederick, i.e., perjury, violation of the peace, sacrilege, and heresy, and concluded thus:

> We therefore, . . . denounce the said prince, who has made himself unworthy of the empire and kingdoms and every honor and dignity and who also, because of his crimes, has been cast out by God from Kingdom and empire; we mark him out as bound by his sins, an outcast and deprived by our Lord of every honor and dignity; and we deprive him of them by our sentence. We absolve from their oath forever all those who are bound to him by an oath of loyalty, firmly forbidding by our apostolic authority anyone in the future to obey him or heed him as emperor or king, and decreeing that anyone who henceforth offers advice, help or favor to him as to an emperor or king, automatically incurs excommunication.[120]

Frederick fired back a response, addressed to all the kings of Christendom, insisting that this whole process of deposition was illegal and invalid. He asserted that he was neither summoned to the council nor proved guilty of "any deceit or wickedness." He warned the other Christian kings that any of them might be the object of a similar abuse of power. He railed against the lavishness of the papal court, "supported and enriched by your tithes and alms" and told his fellow princes that "to deprive such men of the baneful wealth that burdens them to their own damnation (would be) a work of charity."[121]

Following the lead of Gregory IX, Innocent defended his action against Frederick, grounding his claim to make and depose kings and emperors in the eighth-century forgery, the *Donation of Constantine*.

> He [i.e., Christ] established not only a pontifical but also a royal monarchy in the Apostolic See, handing the reins at once of heavenly and of earthly Empire to St. Peter and his successors. . . . Constantine received from the Vicar of Christ, the successor of St. Peter, the divinely regulated power of the Empire, that he might henceforth use it legitimately to punish the wicked and praise the good.[122]

Innocent IV won the battle with Frederick by surviving him. After Frederick's death in 1250, the pope returned to Rome. The papal battle against the

Hohenstaufens, however, was by no means over because Innocent and his successors continued to put obstacles in the way of Conrad IV, Frederick's son.[123]

In Geoffrey Barraclough's judgment, the pontificate of Innocent IV represents the start of the long decline leading to the abuses of Avignon and to the Western Schism.[124] It was Innocent IV who brought the practice of the papal provision of canonries (i.e., positions in the chapters of canons) to full term. The cathedrals in many parts of Europe were becoming more and more affluent.

> This growth in wealth and power made the cathedrals the target for papal provisions. . . . Under Alexander III papal nomination or provision was a frequent method of appointment, and the numbers continued to grow until the flood gates opened under Innocent IV (1243-54).[125]

The practice of laying a claim to the first vacant canonry in a certain church (i.e., an expectancy), prohibited by canon 8 of Lateran III (1179), was frequently employed by the popes in the mid-thirteenth century. They would simply use their fullness of power to dispense from the universal law which continued to bind bishops and metropolitans, giving the pontiffs a veritable monopoly regarding expectancies. This papal dispensing power could be helpful in other ways:

> A papal dispensation could free the candidate from many of the objections which could be urged against him, such as non-residence, plurality of benefices, or being under age, and thus leave the local church with no legal grounds to resist a provision which was clearly a pastoral abuse.[126]

BISHOP ROBERT GROSSETESTE OF LINCOLN

Robert Grosseteste, the bishop of Lincoln, England, since 1235, began to be concerned about the growing numbers of nominees for benefices and prebends (i.e., endowments) who had no intention of settling in England to carry out their ecclesiastical responsibilities. He felt that it was an abuse to accept a post and then farm out the duties to someone else who was occasionally unqualified and/or unworthy. Most of the revenues of the benefice or prebend would then flow to the absentee beneficiary, leaving but a fraction to support the function and the functionary at home. Grosseteste, then in his latter seventies, visited the papal court in 1250 to complain to Innocent and the curia about these and other abuses which were "drying up" the Church:

> The instrument of this desiccation was the papal curia which choked the system with privileges, exemptions, the creation of legal tangles, the

tolerance of evils and active support of evil-doers, in order to forward the family interests and political ambitions of the pope and cardinals.[127]

He pointed to such devices as papal exemptions, the flood of appeals to Rome, and the conferral of pastoral responsibilities on unworthy or unqualified sub-jects as the causes of the breakdown of pastoral care everywhere. The problem, he said, was the papal curia.

> He tells the curia that they are worse than those who crucified Christ. They had not known what they were doing, and would not have done it if they had known. But the curia knows what it is doing, and it had set itself up as a model for the whole world. It is, he says, the textbook for the world, provoking in others the destruction of souls, a contempt for eternity and the glorification of transitory things . . . What greater event could there be than this general corruption of Christendom? What cause could be found for so great an evil as this? Only the greatest thing in Christendom— the papacy.[128]

There is no evidence of any formal papal response to Bishop Grosseteste's impassioned plea for reform. However, two years later the following event occurred:

> Then came the final crushing affront to all that he had believed in and worked for as a bishop. Innocent IV sent letters, not to Grosseteste himself, whom he clearly now regarded as unmanageable, but to the papal agent in England and to the archdeacon of Canterbury, instructing them to put the pope's [unworthy] nephew in possession of a canonry and benefice in Lincoln, and declaring null and void in advance any attempt to grant his benefice to anyone else.[129]

THE PAPAL DECLINE AFTER INNOCENT IV

After the death of Innocent IV in 1254, the papacy continued to decline. From 1254 to 1294 there were eleven popes and as many as five long vacan-cies—one of them lasting nearly three years. Correspondingly, the College of Cardinals was increasing in power and influence, and was largely under the domination of the Colonnas and the Orsinis. There was throughout Christendom more and more open criticism of the papacy due to its abuse of papal reservations of benefices, the ever increasing numbers of appeals to Rome, and its taxation policies. The first general taxes on the churches were assessed in 1199 and 1215 for the support of the Fourth and Fifth Crusades. By 1250 the papal power to tax the churches and the clergy had been well established and its relentless expansion was becoming widely resented.[130] More and more frequently the bishoprics and the major benefices throughout the West were being filled by papal candidates and this too precipitated rising opposition. The bitter battle with Frederick II had not only grossly politicized the papacy but had driven it more and more under France's sphere of influence. From the mid-thirteenth century the face of Europe was changing profoundly. Nationalism and the use of vernacular languages were burgeoning. Local histories, chronicles, laws, and royal edicts were beginning to appear in the vernacular. With the Angevins in England, the Capetians in France, and the Hohenstaufens and Hapsburgs in Germany, we witness the rise of the nation-states.

The opposition to papal centralism, therefore, took on a more national character. The smoldering resentment against the ceaseless expansion of papal provisions and the ever increasing tax burdens imposed by Rome broke into flames in the second half of the thirteenth century. The relative weakness of the papacy during those years provided little leadership when leadership was sorely needed. Pope Alexander IV (1254-61), a nephew of Gregory IX, tried to reverse some of Innocent's damaging policies regarding papal provisions but with little success. Urban IV (1261-64) was the Latin patriarch of Jerusalem when he was elected pope. With the College of Cardinals down to eight members, he, a Frenchman, named more than a dozen cardinals—about half of them Frenchmen of considerable ability. Clement IV (1265-68), another Frenchman, issued a decretal in the first year of his pontificate, *Licet ecclesiarum*, which laid a firmer foundation for future popes to centralize even more the conferral of ecclesiastical offices and benefices, a movement that was to reach its medieval high point in the fourteenth century.

> Though this decretal did not reserve many benefices, it set the precedent for later popes to revolutionize the medieval Church. The practice of reservations, as much as any single factor, stimulated the hostility to the papacy that would culminate in the Protestant Reformation.[131]

GREGORY X AND LYONS II (1274)

After Clement's death at Viterbo in November 1268, the papal office was vacant until September 1271 when Tedaldo Visconti was elected, taking the name Gregory X (1271-76).[132] Gregory's heart was set on the reform council which opened at Lyons on May 7, 1274, and was concluded—after six sessions—on July 17.

> Probably there were present about 300 bishops, 60 abbots and a large number of other clergy, many of whom apparently were theologians (Thomas Aquinas died while on his journey to Lyons), as well as King

James of Aragon and delegates sent by the rulers of France, Germany, England and Sicily. The Greeks arrived late, on 24 June, . . . Meanwhile a delegation of Tartars had also arrived. Although the number of participants does not seem to have been especially large, the whole church world was present either in person or through representatives, and it was evident that the council, as Gregory X had wished, was universal and ecumenical.[133]

The attempt made by the council to secure a reunion with the Byzantines was largely motivated by political considerations because the Byzantine emperor, Michael VIII Paleologus, wanted and needed the pope's assistance against the threats of Charles of Anjou, the king of Sicily, who longed to dominate the entire Mediterranean. Michael was therefore ready to agree to almost anything, including the Roman primacy, to secure that help. However, his clergy and people back home were of another mind entirely. They simply refused to go along with the concessions which the emperor had made. Without an effective union with the Byzantines, the question of a crusade to aid the Holy Land receded into the background, especially after the death of Gregory X in January 1276.

The most important conciliar item, the reform of the Church, seems to have been the one that received the least attention. Pope Gregory announced at the final session that he was disappointed that discussion had not been sufficient to formulate and enact any really significant reform legislation.[134] The council did, however, promulgate a new set of regulations governing papal elections which still serves as a foundation for the selection of pontiffs today.

The cardinals were not to wait for more than ten days from the pope's death for the arrival of the absent [cardinals]. The election was to occur in the place where the pope died. The cardinals were to stay together, cut off from all contact with the outside world, until they completed the election. The longer the election took, the more scanty should their provisions become.[135]

Constitution 18 unfortunately reversed the prohibition of canon 13 of Lateran III and Decree 29 of Lateran IV regarding the holding of a plurality of offices with the care of souls attached.[136] Robert Grosseteste of Lincoln likely turned over in his grave as this constitution was formally enacted by an ecumenical council within a generation after his death! The papal dispensing power took precedence over all—even the basic demands of pastoral care.

Pope Gregory had sincerely wished that the council address the most damaging issues that were affecting the Church of his day. To this end, before the council he had dispatched a circular to all bishops and major religious superiors asking for reports on conditions that should be especially dealt with in the conciliar deliberations. Some of the responses are still extant. According to Geoffrey Barraclough, the responses reveal the following:

> These reports cast a revealing light on the state of western Christendom at the beginning of the last quarter of the thirteenth century; in particular, they reveal the disorder introduced into the Church by papal support for the mendicants against the secular clergy, and the bitter feelings aroused thereby, as well as the weakening of the position of the parish priests toward the laity resulting from the preferences given to the friars. Nor is there any hesitation in attacking the abuses of the Roman curia. But in the last analysis there is a curious hesitancy about all these writings. It is seen that the papacy is responsible for many of these evils in the Church, but at the same time there seems to be no hope of betterment except through the pope. In effect, the papacy is asked to reform itself.[137]

THE GROWING INFLUENCE OF THE CARDINALS AND THE ABDICATION OF CELESTINE V (1294)

After Gregory's death in January 1276, the next three popes reigned for a total of sixteen months, from January 1276 to May 1277. Because not one of them had enough time to accomplish much, the position of the College of Cardinals grew even stronger during this period. Nicholas III (1277-80), an Orsini, attempted to return to the policies of Gregory X by collaborating more closely with Rudolf of Hapsburg (1273-91), thus neutralizing in part the expansionist influence of the house of Anjou in Sicily.[138] After a vacancy of more than six months, another French ecclesiastic, Martin IV, was elected as a result of the heavy influence of Charles of Anjou on the consistory. "The French Martin IV (1281-85) . . . placed himself unreservedly at the services of [the house of] Anjou, . . . this final phase of the Church's development in the thirteenth century was under the sign of dependence on Anjou and France."[139]

In 1281 Charles of Anjou was at the peak of his power and was extremely close to reinstituting the Latin empire in Constantinople. All his dreams came crashing down, however, in March 1282, when the Sicilians revolted, driving Charles and his forces to Naples and the mainland once and for all. The Sicilians offered King Peter of Aragon the crown of the Kingdom of Sicily, while Charles was relegated to Naples. This revolution, called the Sicilian Vespers, left Charles a defeated man. Both he and his creation, Pope Martin IV, died in 1285.

The pontificate of Honorius IV (1285-87) was uneventful. While he tried to reopen dialogue with Rudolf of Hapsburg, the effort did not amount to much, either for the papacy or for the Hapsburgs. After an eleven-month vacancy, the small College of Cardinals elected a Franciscan friar who called himself Nicholas IV (1288-92), the first Franciscan to be chosen pope. He most probably was persuaded by the Orsinis in 1289 to enact formally the informal thirteenth-century practice of allotting half of the papal revenues to the College of Cardinals. It was largely because of their desire not to further dilute their revenues that the cardinals rather consistently urged that their numbers be kept small. After the Franciscan pope, there was a vacancy of more than two years.

> The election of 5 July 1294, two years and three months after the death on 4 April 1292 of Nicholas IV, fell on a man who did not belong to the college, where the rivalry of Colonna and Orsini would not allow anyone to obtain the required two-thirds majority. But it was not a happy choice.
> . . . The pope elect [i.e., Celestine V] had been a Benedictine, but later, as a hermit, he had founded an eremitical community, which had been incorporated into the Benedictine order by Urban IV [1261-64].
> . . . A year earlier [i.e., in 1293], the founder, more than eighty years old, had relinquished to others the direction of his community.[140]

Pope Celestine was hailed by some—who were convinced that the final age of the world had already dawned—as the "angel pope," i.e., a man of gospel ideals who had a deep commitment to the return of the simple apostolic life. The venerable monk, however, was absolutely incapable of managing the position. After consulting with Cardinal Benedict Caetani, the foremost canonist in the college, as to whether or not a pope could step down, he settled his mind and abdicated in December 1294.

SUMMARY

The prestige of the papal office had plummeted from the heady days of Innocent III (1198-1216) to the pathetic interlude of Celestine V. The College of Cardinals augmented their power and vastly improved their financial condition in the thirteenth century. The papal curia had clearly moved into France's sphere of influence, preparing the way for the transition to Avignon. The centralizing tendencies continued in spite of the weakness of the papacy in the latter half of the century, with papal provision, papal taxation, and the papal courts expanding their activities.[141] The consequences of this centralization will become more painfully obvious in the next chapter.

CHAPTER 6

The Worldly Papacy

1300 to 1523

Ten days after the resignation of Celestine V on December 13, 1294, the cardinals gathered in Naples to elect a new pope. The curia had moved to Naples only two months before at the behest of Charles II, king of Naples, who controlled the hapless but well-intentioned Pope Celestine. On the second day of the conclave, Benedict Caetani was elected and took the name Boniface VIII (1294-1303). The next nine years would prove to be one of the most tumultuous epochs in the history of the papacy. Historians have been trying for centuries to ferret out the causes of Boniface's tragic regime, but there is still no satisfactory explanation. The times would have required a man of exceptional vision and flexibility, but Benedict Caetani did not possess these gifts. He was, by contrast, a proud and arrogant man who looked at life "through a rear-view mirror." He viewed the world much as Innocent III and Innocent IV did in the thirteenth century. But the world had changed very much indeed. France, England, and Germany—as well as Aragon and Castile—were coming to see themselves, not so much as units of one European Christendom, but as unique, sovereign, and separate states with their own language, culture, and political agendas. Although this rise of the nation-states continued to evolve and come to term in Europe during the fourteenth and fifteenth centuries, the foundations were discernible at the time of Boniface's pontificate. A new world order was taking shape and Boniface was unable to read the "signs of the times."

THE PAPACY OF BONIFACE VIII

After Benedict Caetani had completed his legal studies at the University of Bologna, he spent the next thirty years or so advancing up the curial ladder—from one responsible post to another—until he was appointed cardinal-deacon by Martin IV in April 1281.[1] Ten years later he was ordained a priest after his career had elevated him into the inner circle of the Sacred College. In spite of the canonical prohibitions, Benedict had taken care to amass a considerable personal fortune along the way, acquiring a great number of lucrative benefices which he shared with the members of his family. "Already Benedict was securing that considerable personal fortune which did so much to increase his power, and which was to lead to so much criticism."[2]

Troubles began for Boniface not long after his coronation in January 1295. He evoked the wrath of the Colonna family and especially the two Colonna cardinals, James and Peter, with his rough and overbearing behavior, as well as his long-standing penchant for enriching the Caetani clan with wealth garnered from ecclesiastical benefices and endowments. The Colonna cardinals issued several written protests directed to the faculty of the University of Paris— and intended for the ears of the French king, Philip IV (1285-1314)—outlining their problems with Boniface. In their third manifesto of June 1297, they called him a tyrant who illegally usurped the papacy by persuading Celestine to resign.[3]

The Colonnas accused Boniface of diminishing the honor of the cardinals by refusing to take the customary counsel with them on matters of significant curial business, and by continuing to reserve the granting of more and more benefices exclusively to himself. Although the last two accusations were largely true, the earlier one concerning the forced resignation of Celestine was quite likely a fabrication. Boniface did not force Celestine to retire, nor is it clear that he mistreated him during that period prior to the resigned pope's death in May 1296. Moreover, the majority of the theologians at the University of Paris did not agree with the Colonnas that a pope could not resign. It was their judgment that a Roman pontiff could freely step down for a good reason. Prior to the controversy with the Colonnas, however, Boniface had to respond to the efforts of the kings of France and England to tax their clergy without obtaining the previous permission of the pope. Canon 46 of Lateran IV (1215) reaffirmed the provisions of canon 19 of Lateran III (1179) which required that the pope should be consulted before any taxes were assessed against clerics and ecclesiastical benefices, even when the common good required such assessments. At that time England and France were in conflict over Gascony, both claiming that they were involved in a just war. Boniface could have allowed the issue to pass, as a number of previous popes had done, but he chose to intervene, issuing a confrontational bull, *Clericis laicos*, in February 1296.

That laymen have been very hostile to the clergy antiquity relates; and it is clearly proved by the experiences of the present time. . . . Nor do they prudently realize that power over clerics or ecclesiastical persons or goods is forbidden them: they impose heavy burdens on the prelates of the churches and ecclesiastical persons regular and secular, and tax them . . . and in many ways they try to bring them into slavery, and subject them to their authority. And, we regret to say, some prelates of the churches . . .

acquiesce in such abuses, . . . without obtaining license from the Apostolic See.[4]

Boniface then proceeded to threaten the secular rulers and the cooperating prelates with a sentence of automatic excommunication which was to be reserved to the pope alone. Edward I (1272-1307) responded with stern anti-Church measures in England, but the more vehement reaction came from Philip IV of France who forbade the export of all monies and gold from France to the Papal States—thus cutting off a large portion of the pope's regular revenue almost overnight. This was the beginning of a savage conflict between Boniface and Philip the Fair which was to continue until Philip's death in 1314—even though Boniface died in 1303. Boniface watered down the restrictions of *Clericis laicos* in July 1297, permitting Philip to tax the clergy in cases of necessity, even when the Roman pontiff had not been consulted.[5] The damage, however, had been done. Philip was at war with Boniface. The second phase of the hostility was occasioned by Philip's action against the bishop of Pamiers in southern France, Bernard Saisset. Saisset had aggravated the archbishop of Toulouse, Pierre Taillefer, on a number of occasions and angered several people close to the king because of his loose talk. In addition, Saisset was known to be a friend of Boniface. In a rapid series of moves, Philip threw the bishop of Pamiers into prison in Paris and was ready to try to convict him of sundry crimes. Saisset promptly appealed to the pope, who replied in December 1301, informing the king of his position: "Let no one persuade you that you have no superior or that you are not subject to the head of the ecclesiastical hierarchy, for he is a fool who so thinks, and whoever affirms it pertinaciously is convicted as an unbeliever and is outside the fold of the Good Shepherd."[6]

The papal communication was twisted out of context by some of Philip's aides, and it was reported to the clergy and the people of France that the pope was asserting superiority over the French king in both spiritual and temporal matters. This was more than the king could bear, and the clergy of France were largely behind him. Boniface called a council for the French bishops to be held in Rome in the fall of 1302, which about half of the French prelates attended. No reform measures were agreed on at the November sessions which were followed soon thereafter by the issuing of Boniface's famous (or infamous) bull, *Unam sanctam*, perhaps the most memorable medieval document on the relationship of spiritual and temporal power. According to French historian Jean Rivière, there are two parts to the document: "One can distinguish two related parts, one following the other: one poses the principles from which the other draws the consequences: the first sets forth the constitution of the Church, the second describes the powers that flow from it."[7] Rivière proceeds to outline the tenets of Boniface's bull:

According to the formula of the old symbols, the Church is one, holy, catholic and apostolic; this is a dogma imposed on the Christian. . . . this first article of faith is soon joined by a second which completes it: outside the Church there is neither grace nor salvation . . . From these premises he immediately draws the alluring conclusion: the Church, being of only one body, must also, on pain of being a monster, have but one head. This unique "head" is obviously Christ. But Christ is continued in the person of his vicar: Boniface therefore returns to Peter, and to his successors, to strengthen him in his role as chief.[8]

Boniface draws his conclusions from these premises in the second part of the document: "At the outset the pope claims a double domain, spiritual and temporal. He expresses himself in the metaphor of the two swords."[9]
Unam sanctam articulates the doctrine of the two swords as follows:

Both then are in the power of the Church, the material sword and the spiritual. But the one is exercised for the Church, the other by the Church, the one by the hand of the priest, the other by the hand of kings and soldiers, though at the will and suffrance of the priest. One sword ought to be under the other and the temporal authority subject to the spiritual power.[10]

After declaring that the earthly power can be judged by the spiritual, and the supreme spiritual power can be judged only by God, he concludes with the following oft quoted (and debated) formula: "Therefore we declare, state, define and pronounce that it is altogether necessary to salvation for every human creature to be subject to the Roman pontiff."[11]

Although there is nothing much new in Pope Boniface's memorable declaration that had not been said before by the likes of Innocent III and Innocent IV, the clarity and succinctness of its claims did precipitate a vicious response from King Philip and his chief minister, William Nogaret. They renewed their call for a general council to summon Boniface to the bar for his alleged crimes. They wanted to convict him of heresy, murder, and other sundry offenses so that they might have him condemned and deposed before the whole Christian world. The extent of Philip's wickedness was almost without bounds, as we shall observe again in his dealings with the Templars during the pontificate of Clement V (1305-14). At Anagni during the summer of 1303, Boniface drew up a bull of solemn excommunication against Philip which he apparently intended to promulgate sometime in the fall. Before that could occur, William Nogaret, Philip's trusty hatchet man, and Sciarra Colonna, a brother of Cardinal Peter Colonna, put together an expedition of mercenaries who broke into the town of Anagni on September 7, 1303, and proceeded to invade the papal palace in order to take Pope Boniface captive. They taunted and struck him, demanding his resignation, but the pontiff refused. It was their intent to take him by force so that he could be called up before an ecumenical council to account for his alleged offenses. The townsfolk of Anagni, many of whom seemed at first to welcome Nogaret and his troops, turned against them after two or three days and routed them from the palace and from the city. After this traumatic experience Boniface was left a dispirited and broken man. He was taken to Rome and died a few weeks later on October 11, 1303.

Boniface has been compared to Innocent III, Gregory IX, and Innocent IV as one of the outstanding pontiffs of the High Middle Ages. He is remembered as an expert canonist who in 1298 skillfully compiled the *Liber Sextus* which brought the canon law of the *Liber Extra* (1234) of Gregory IX up to date. In his writings he consistently gave papal power and papal prerogatives a very wide interpretation, as did many of his predecessors in the thirteenth century.[12] Boniface continued to reserve the conferral of more and more benefices and endowments throughout Christendom to the Holy See, expanding thereby the taxing power of Rome. Perhaps more than any of his predecessors, he engaged in the transferring of bishops from one see to another, thus providing himself with the opportunity to appoint bishops to the newly vacated sees and to tax all of the new appointees.[13] These fees (the *servitia communia*) usually amounted to one-third of the first year's income from the newly conferred benefice or endowment.

> By the end of the thirteenth century it had become exceptional for the appointment to a see, . . . whatever the origin of the choice, not be made in the form of a [papal] provision. Devolution, translation, resignation, illicit cumulation, technical flaws in collation or—a rather disingenuous phrase—"various causes," were some of the headings under which Rome claimed the right to decide the matter. Wherever there were such grounds, there the pope had a "major cause" upon which he alone was efficient to adjudicate. Boniface exploited these opportunities to the full.[14]

At the time of Nicholas III (1277-80) the papal court consisted of a little over 200 officials. Under Boniface the staff expanded to more than 300, which must have increased his costs appreciably.[15] Boniface had little difficulty with the issue of simony inasmuch as it was his view that since all goods, spiritual and temporal, were under his control, he was unable to commit simony.[16] One of the posthumous accusations leveled against him was that in his governance of the Church, everything was for sale. This assuredly contributed to the growing discontent with the papacy and the Roman curia throughout the Christian world. The pontiff was simply unaware of the unrest and the frustration which surrounded him on all sides. This was due in great part to his personality which

consistently exuded arrogance and haughtiness, causing him to expose to frequent public ridicule the foibles of the cardinals, prelates, and visiting dignitaries. Boniface had many enemies and no friends. T.S.R. Boase, his outstanding English biographer, says about the man whom he sincerely venerated:

> He had the gift of sonorous phrases, and there were brave gestures in all
> his actions. His learning was praised by all his contemporaries. . . . He had
> too the arrogance and the cruelty of self-confident force. Personal
> elements meant little to him: he had no self-criticism to realize how dislike
> grew around him, and how his rough disregard broke loyalties and
> undermined his greater plans. To his own enemies relentless, he could not
> curb his temper to make or retain friends. Disease [perhaps gall stones]
> had made him impatient, pride forbade him to be careful. . . . There were
> great things by him forgot: the Church was to him an institution almost
> without function beyond government. . . . his skill in judgment was not
> tempered by personal sanctity . . .[17]

Although Boniface's humiliation at Anagni in September 1303 was de-
plored throughout Europe, and although common consensus viewed it as an
outrage wrought by King Philip IV of France on the Vicar of Christ, something was lost there which would never be entirely regained. The aura of the
thirteenth-century papacy had been tarnished, never to be restored to its previous luster.

Ten days after the death of Boniface, the cardinals gathered in conclave and
elected Cardinal Nicholas Boccasini on the first ballot. Boccasini, the former
minister general of the Dominicans, had been one of the two cardinals with
Boniface that fatal September at Anagni. The new pontiff, Benedict XI (1303-
04), was not a strong man either physically or temperamentally. He freed the
Colonna cardinals from the ecclesiastical penalties imposed on them by
Boniface, although he did not completely restore to them all of their possessions. Conflicts which he was unable to settle remained in the Sacred College.[18] After a five-month stay in Rome, where he was frustrated by the battles
among the noble families, he transferred his residence to Perugia, where he
died in July 1304. Benedict was buried in the Dominican church there.

CLEMENT V AND THE COUNCIL OF VIENNE (1311-12)

The next conclave, which began shortly after Benedict's death, stretched
out for eleven months. The fifteen cardinals were hopelessly divided into two
camps, neither side wanting another Boniface VIII. By December 1304 it was
obvious that no one of the cardinals could garner two-thirds of the vote, so

they began to search out a candidate who was not a member of the college. On June 5, 1305, the archbishop of Bordeaux, Bertrand de Got, was elected by the required two-thirds majority. De Got, who took the name Clement V (1305-14), was also a rather weak figure, and Philip IV was aware that he had a compliant pope. It seems that Clement never had any real intention of taking up residence in Rome immediately. He wanted to remain in France in order to assist in forging the peace between France and England. Although he had arranged to hold his coronation at Vienne, he changed his plans at the behest of Philip IV and was crowned in French territory at Lyons. During the coronation procession, a wall collapsed, injuring the pope. After this incident, his health—which was never robust—was in a state of constant decline.

> From the beginning of his reign, Clement V revealed characteristics which were to be evident throughout: a weak, impressionable personality, a vacillating diplomatist and a man of compromise, he was a completely unworthy opponent of Philip the Fair, who possessed an inflexible will and was accustomed to bring into play all the resources of a coldly calculating temperament. The pope was to use every stratagem and prevarication, only to have concessions wrested from him in the end. . . . It is only fair to state, in Clement's defense, that he was a sick man during the whole of his pontificate. He suffered cruelly from a disease that is thought to have been cancer of the bowel or stomach.[19]

It seems that Philip IV was urging Clement to convoke an ecumenical council from the day of the pontifical coronation in November 1305. The French king wanted to see Boniface VIII tried posthumously for his alleged crimes, and it was also his wish that the status of the Knights Templar be investigated because of the "scandalous character" of their lives. The reason for the king's vendetta against the Templars is still not entirely clear, in spite of numerous attempts on the part of scholars over the years to pinpoint his motives. Philip's desire to appropriate their great wealth in terms of lands and money was probably his prime motive because he was forever in dire financial straits. In April 1307 the king met Clement at Poitiers in order to lay out what he expected of the pope. He wanted Boniface tried for his transgressions, all of Boniface's measures against France annulled, and full compensation awarded to the Colonnas for their losses suffered at the hands of the Caetani pope. Although Clement rather artfully delayed the action against Boniface, it was becoming very clear that he was terrified of Philip and that Philip would eventually have his way on almost every issue. An interesting story has been related by the German historian Karl August Fink concerning the reaction of the ten new cardinals whom Pope Clement had created in December 1305. The event must have occurred some time after King Philip's sudden and unforeseen arrest of all the Templars in France in October 1307. Clement then promptly ordered their arrest in all the countries of Europe.

A story from this period relates that the ten cardinals thus far created by Clement came to him to give back their red hats. In accepting them, they said, they had incorrectly thought that like all previous popes, he was the lord of the world, superior to the Emperor and to kings; but actually he was the servant of the king of France, who in his arrogance had committed a grave crime against the renowned order.[20]

Philip the Fair was attempting to extort confessions from the Templars under the pressure of the most cruel and inhumane torture. Hearing of the nature of the king's investigations, Clement ordered all the interrogations of Templars stopped everywhere. This made Philip so violently angry that he launched a blackmail campaign against the pontiff. Further, he demanded another meeting with Clement in the summer of 1308, at which time he insisted on the condemnation of the Templars, the announcement of a date for a general council, the condemnation of Boniface, and the canonization of the hapless Celestine V. By this time the pope's will was broken. He could no longer resist Philip's demands.[21] Accordingly, Clement agreed to convene a general council, open the process against Boniface VIII, and allow the bishops and the inquisitors to proceed against the Templars. The council was set for Vienne in October 1310. Local commissions in the dioceses of Europe were to commence investigations into the conduct of the individual Templars, while the papal commission, controlled by Philip, was to evaluate the status and conduct of the order itself.

Perhaps a word is in order concerning the origin and nature of the Knights Templar. In 1120 or thereabouts, a group of knights from Champagne and Burgundy settled in Jerusalem and established a religious order for the defense of the Holy Land and the protection of the pilgrims who were journeying to the territory. After Acre (a seaport in the north of Palestine) had fallen in 1291, the Holy Land was essentially lost to the West, and the Templars were driven back to Europe where they owned much land and controlled an abundance of monetary resources. By 1300 there was no longer a religious reason for their continued existence. They had, however, become skilled money managers in Europe. Their houses were built and maintained as fortresses so they were ideally suited to act as trustee bankers and brokers for the holding and transfer of funds from one part of Europe to another. As a matter of fact, they had acted as bankers to the kings of France for 100 years. After their role in the Holy Land had come to an end, they began to lose favor. Had they made a secret deal with the Muslims for the surrender of the Holy Places? The eminent French historian G. Mollat describes their situation:

A religious order cannot become a financial power and a creditor of kings without arousing jealousy. Temporal prosperity almost inevitably produces a slackening of discipline, excites pride and favours the deterioration of moral standards. By the end of the thirteenth century public opinion had turned against the Templars. They were said to be backward in almsgiving. They were reproached with having forsaken the course of the Crusades, and secretly accused of having made a pact with the Infidel. . . . There was talk of the Knights' greed and unscrupulousness, of their passion for self-aggrandizement and their rapacity. Their insolent bearing was a byword. They were said to be given to drunkenness.[22]

The alleged guilt of the Templars was established only in France and only on the basis of confessions extracted by the most cruel torture and the threat of death to those refusing to confess their "crimes." The Knights were asked if they were required to spit on the cross during their initiation ceremonies, if they were encouraged to sodomy, to the adoration of an idol, and expected to deny Christ three times. Torture, plus the certain prospect of burning at the stake should they be unwilling to confess, did precipitate confessions on the part of the members of the order in France, but in the rest of Europe they were found to be innocent of all accusations even after the application of torture. Because the gathering of confessions even in France was a slow process, the opening of the Council of Vienne was postponed until October 1, 1311.

It was in 1309 that Pope Clement moved his court to Avignon, which was at the western edge of the Comtat Venaissin, the only papal territory on the French side of the Alps. Avignon had been held, however, by Charles II, king of Sicily, since 1290. Although the move to Avignon was a most significant change of course for the papacy, it must be said that the residence of Clement's predecessors in Rome was for a long period intermittent at best. Mollat quotes L. Gayet, a nineteenth-century French scholar: "In the 204 years from 1100 until 1304, the popes spent 122 years away from Rome and eighty-two in Rome: that is, forty more years away from Rome than in it."[23]

Mollat further notes that between 1099 and 1198, the pontiffs spent fifty-five years away from Rome and more than eight of those years in France.[24] The move to Avignon then, albeit momentous, was not completely without precedent.

The Council of Vienne finally opened on October 16, 1311. Although there were other stated objectives for the gathering, e.g., the preparation for a crusade and church reform, the chief task was the settlement of the issue of the Templars. Clement's selection of delegates for the council was rather different from the procedure followed in the previous Lateran councils. Only 231 ecclesiastics were invited. The council opened with twenty cardinals, four patriarchs, about 100 archbishops and bishops, and a number of abbots and priors.[25] The preliminary work was to be done in consistories, while the decrees were to be promulgated in the plenary sessions. In January 1312, the decision of how to deal with the Templars was still being debated. At that point, Philip took matters into his own hands.

> Meanwhile in March 1312 Philip held a general assembly of his kingdom in Lyons, his object being to disturb and steamroller the minds of the council fathers and of the pope himself. Secret bargains had been made between Clement V and the envoys of Philip IV from 17 to 29 February 1312; the council fathers were not consulted. By this bargaining Philip obtained the condemnation of the Templars.[26]

On March 22, 1312, Pope Clement delivered to the commission of cardinals the bull, *Vox in excelso*, ordering the suppression of the Knights Templar. The decision was approved in the second plenary session on April 3, 1312.[27] After the property of the Templars had been consigned to the Hospitallers of St. John (another military order) on May 3, 1312, the council was formally closed on May 6. King Philip and his successors must have been extremely disappointed because within ten years, the Hospitallers did indeed take over almost all of the resources—land, buildings, and monetary assets—of the Templars.[28]

Although certain enactments were published after Clement's death, in April 1314, by his successor, John XXII, it is not easy to determine which of these were conciliar decisions and which were later pronouncements of Clement. It is Giuseppe Alberigo's judgment that there were thirty-eight decrees which were approved by the council fathers in the third and final plenary session of May 6, 1312.[29] These were not edited, corrected, and published until after Clement's death. They dealt with such matters as the conferral and management of benefices and endowments, the renewal of Boniface VIII's legislation regulating the respective rights of religious and seculars in the areas of pastoral care, a warning against excessive harshness by inquisitors, and another effort to unite the two warring factions of the Franciscans, the Spirituals and the Conventuals.

The Council of Vienne stands as a tragic example of a general council that was convened, conducted, and closed under extreme political pressure. The influence of Philip IV of France was in evidence from beginning to end. The council's major enactment—the elimination of the Templars—was a sad mistake.

> The absence of proof, the improbability of the charges, the contradictory nature of the statements, the brutal methods used at the inquiry, the number of recantations, the courage of those who defended the order—all go to prove the Templar's innocence. Their trial was a trumped up

affair, and bears the unmistakable mark of William of Nogaret. The relentless pursuit of the Templars shows the same tactics as those employed against Boniface VIII.[30]

There was no time to address fully and honestly the crying needs of church reform. Clement V orchestrated the gathering away from a full airing of the problems that were tearing the Church apart—the excessive centralization of decision making into the papal curia which was emasculating local church government, the overpowering burden of papal taxation, the scandal of pluralism and the ever expanding papal control over the conferral of benefices (often to absentee prelates), the favoritism shown to religious at the expense of diocesan organization, and so forth. The list of abuses was long and painful, but there was only time to abolish the Templars who, in the judgment of the majority of historians today, were largely innocent of the charges brought against them. Regarding the strong-arm tactics of Clement V at the council, Mollat notes, "An English chronicler declared—with some little exaggeration—that the Council of Vienne 'did not deserve the name of council, for the Lord Pope did everything on his own authority.' "[31]

Pope Clement's health deteriorated rather dramatically after 1309, causing him to live in almost total seclusion for months at a time. The threat of a lawsuit against Boniface VIII caused him the greatest anxiety up to and through the Council of Vienne. It was to his eternal credit, however, that he was able to defer and finally dodge that awesome threat. Also, it must be said that he was not as ineffective in dealing with the empire and the German kings, Albert I and Henry VII, as he was with France and Philip IV. He was called on occasionally to act as arbitrator in Europe and he performed effectively. Clement was an able canonist who added a seventh book, the *Clementinae*, to the medieval collection of church law. He was a man with an affable manner and an easygoing, pleasant disposition (when he was not oppressed by illness), but he was a notoriously poor manager. His lack of supervision over the curia and the papal offices and his unfamiliarity with curial procedures resulted in disastrous consequences. Inefficiency and unbridled greed were everywhere in evidence. Furthermore, Clement's nepotism was almost unrivaled. Five members of his family were created cardinals, while others were awarded some of the richest benefices in Christendom.[32] At the end of his life he handed over about three-quarters of the monies in the papal treasury to his relatives—leaving only a fraction of the total on deposit for his successor. K.A. Fink concludes his treatment of Clement:

When en route to his beloved Gascony, Clement died at Roquemaure near Carpentras on 20 April 1314, the unlucky pope bequeathed an evil legacy to his successor: Rome abandoned, the government of the church shamefully dependent on France, a College of Cardinals consisting mostly of Frenchmen, and a curia bloated and plundered by narrow nepotism.[33]

JOHN XXII AT AVIGNON (1316-34)

The conclave that gathered after the death of Clement V lasted, with interruptions, from the beginning of May 1314 to August 1316. The cardinals were divided into three nearly irreconcilable factions—Gascons, French, and Italians—and could not settle on a mutually acceptable candidate for two years. Jacques Duèse was seventy-two when he was elected on August 7, 1316, but he was one of those pontiffs who managed to defy the odds and lived a long and active life. As a matter of fact, he was ninety years old when he died in December 1334. John XXII inherited a papal court that was in almost complete chaos after Clement V's disorganized pontificate and the papal vacancy of nearly twenty-eight months. The papal treasury was all but depleted because of Clement's nepotism, so John proceeded to build an incomparable fiscal system based on the reservation of benefices and on the continuing expansion of papal taxation. In 1316, he extended the reservation of benefices even beyond the limits of Clement V, almost doing away entirely with the election of local bishops by cathedral chapters. In 1317, John canceled the dispensations granted by Clement enabling curial cardinals and other officials of his court to hold several benefices, and limited them to two each. The vacated benefices, of course, were then reserved to the pope for conferral on other candidates.[34] At the same time, taxes and fees assessed against the beneficiaries were dramatically increased during John's papacy so that he was able to amass enormous sums of money which were expended on his efforts to gain control once again of the Papal States and on meeting the expenses of the expanding curia. Although John himself was a man of simple tastes and life style, he was overly generous and showed undue favoritism to his relatives, thus preserving the damaging practice of nepotism. The Inquisition flourished under John XXII, with record numbers of Catharists, Waldensians, and Fraticelli burned at the stake.

One of the great battles of the Johannine papacy was waged against the Franciscans who were dividing off into two groups, the Spirituals and the Conventuals. The Spirituals were committed to a more drastic form of poverty patterned on the life of their founder, St. Francis, whereas the Conventuals were reconciled to the communal ownership of simple churches and monasteries to support their apostolate. The Fraticelli, or Spirituals, who were forming independent associations in Italy and southern France, were bitterly opposed by Pope John who had those unwilling to rejoin their Conventual brothers seized by the Inquisition and imprisoned or burned.[35] The Spirituals were a genuine thorn in the pope's side because they were extremely vocal in their condemnation of the lavish life style at the papal court. They claimed that the Church—and especially the curia at Avignon—was beginning to look like the "whore of Babylon." After a general Franciscan chapter in May 1322 at Perugia had declared that the poverty of Christ and the apostles was absolute (i.e., they did not own anything either individually or collectively), John XXII condemned the Perugia declaration as heretical in 1323, thus raising the conflict to a higher level.[36]

The Franciscan general, Michael Cesena, was summoned to the papal curia to explain his own views, but after being unduly detained, he began to fear for his safety and fled from Avignon, seeking protection at the court of King Lewis of Bavaria which was sitting at that time in Pisa. Although the relations between Pope John and the majority of the Franciscans had healed in a year or two, Cesena and those who had joined him in the entourage of King Lewis remained strongly opposed to the pope. After Cesena had declared the pope a heretic, John excommunicated him and his companions in April 1329. This conflict played into the hands of Lewis of Bavaria, who used it to further his own ends. After King Henry VII of Germany died in 1313, a bitter rivalry arose between Frederick of Austria and Lewis as to who was to be the undisputed "King of the Romans." Even after Lewis had defeated Frederick at Mühldorf in 1322 and had himself crowned emperor in Rome by a civil magistrate, Pope John refused to recognize him as emperor. The pope excommunicated Lewis in March 1324 for exercising imperial authority without papal approval and forbade his subjects to obey him as their king. In his Declaration of Sachsenhausen two months later, Lewis labeled John a heretic and called for a general council to put the pope on trial for his unorthodox views concerning Franciscan poverty and for using ecclesiastical sanctions for purely political ends. The pope responded by deposing the king and placing his lands under interdict. Lewis in turn presumed to depose John and appointed a Franciscan, Nicholas V, as pontiff in Rome. After Lewis left Rome in 1328, however, Nicholas soon made his peace with Pope John. The struggle between the papacy and the German kings reached a point of no return with the issuing of the Golden Bull by Lewis' successor, Charles IV (1347-78). This formal document, which set out the procedure henceforth to be followed in electing the German emperor, made no reference whatsoever to the need for papal confirmation of the election. Yves Renouard, a foremost student of the Avignon papacy, observes: "The notion that Church and Empire were separate came to be generally accepted by the princes and by the public at large. In a nutshell, from 1350 on papal supremacy over the Empire was an idea with no practical consequences."[37]

John XXII represents a study in contrasts. Although he personally lived rather simply, his nepotism went beyond all reasonable limits.

John XXII carried family affection and esteem for his compatriots to excessive lengths. He lavished worldly goods on his brothers, sisters, nephews, nieces, his kindred and all those who were connected closely or distantly with the Duèse family.[38]

It must be said that he had a facile mind and exceptional energy for a man of his years, but he was unfortunately first and foremost a politician.[39]

BENEDICT XII (1334-42) AND CLEMENT VI (1342-52)

After John XXII died on December 4, 1334, the twenty-four cardinals chose Jacques Fournier on the seventh day of the conclave. Benedict XII was a Cistercian who had developed quite a reputation as a theologian at the University of Paris. Although John XXII had frequently spoken of the possibility of returning to Rome, this was probably never a real option for Benedict. In the first months of his pontificate, he began the construction of a new papal palace in Avignon, and in 1339, he directed that the papal archives (which were lodged at the time in Assisi) be transported to Avignon. He completely reversed the practice of nepotism followed by his predecessors and vigorously dedicated himself to the reform of the religious orders which had become quite lax in matters of discipline and life style. Unfortunately, however, the results were minimal. Benedict made some attempts at curial reform, but his time in office was not sufficient to ensure any significant level of success. Although he did revoke all grants of endowments *in commendam* (i.e., where the beneficiary took the revenues of a post but was not bound by its responsibilities),[40] he excluded the cardinals—the greatest offenders in this regard—from the prohibition. He also curbed expectancies (i.e., the papal power to confer an endowment that was expected to become vacant soon).[41]

> Although he curbed the excessive use of expectative graces, he extended the Holy See's reservation to include a greater number of benefices than his predecessors, and thus was in danger of seeing the reappearance of the very expectative graces he was rebuking.[42]

Benedict was a good man who genuinely desired to initiate badly needed reforms, especially in the curia. As a matter of fact, one of his first acts was to require bishops and other ecclesiastics with pastoral benefices to leave Avignon and observe the requirement of residence. This, of course, did not touch the cardinals, and we are not even sure how strictly the mandate was pursued. He was, however, seen in his day as a reformer who had the will to instigate change, but his limited vision as to what could be done hampered his effectiveness.[43] In the political arena, Benedict was unable to prevent the onset of the Hundred Years War between the French and the English in 1337. Actually, by his extreme partiality to the French from the very beginning of his pontificate, he alienated the English.[44]

Pierre Roger, the cardinal archbishop of Rouen, was selected to succeed Benedict on May 7, 1342. Clement VI (1342-52), a Benedictine, had been chancellor of France under Philip VI (1328-50) until he was appointed cardinal in 1338. He brought the courtly life style to Rouen and transferred it to Avignon after his election. Canon Mollat describes the choice of the new pontiff:

> They [the cardinals] were weary of the rigid, austere, autocratic government of Benedict XII, and had considered the opposite qualitites that characterised Pierre Roger—his urbanity and gentleness, his pliant temperament and aristocratic airs. They hoped that under him they would enjoy a tolerant, easy-going and bountiful regime.[45]

It can be said that the cardinals were in no way disappointed with their choice. Clement's court was easily the most lavish in all of Europe. The papal feasts and tournaments and fancy balls were the talk of the continent. The court was amply populated with painters, sculptors, poets, and literary people, perhaps like no other anywhere. The wealth and resources carefully gathered by Benedict XII were quickly squandered. The expense of the luxurious court, the completion of the splendid new papal palace begun by Benedict, and the purchase of the town of Avignon from Queen Joanna of Naples put the Apostolic Camera in a deficit position for years to come. Clement is said to have genuinely enjoyed the pomp and bustle of his court.

> Under Clement the curia was scarcely to be distinguished from a secular court. He delighted to display his sovereign power through a gorgeous retinue, quite in accord with the saying applied to him—that his predecessors had not known how to be popes.[46]

But there is no doubt that the last three Avignon popes—Innocent VI, Urban V, and Gregory XI—all struggled under the heavy burden of debt which they inherited from Clement, who also had to spend large sums of money to combat, with little success, the continuous insurrections in the Papal States. Due to his marked partiality to France, nations like England and Germany continued to drift away from Avignon's sphere of influence. Clement was undeniably a French pope through and through.

During the first attack of the Black Death (1347-49), Pope Clement was particularly generous and responsive to the needs of the people in southern France and the county of Venaissin where he lived. Avignon is said to have been especially devastated during the period—losing nearly fifty percent of its population. It must also be noted that the papal reservation of benefices and endowments reached a high point under Clement VI.[47] Needless to say, this situation increased the unrest and frustration in the Church and further emasculated the authority of the local bishops. Meanwhile the papal curia increased from over 300 people under Boniface VIII in 1300 to well over 500 by 1335-40. Yves Renouard has made the following inventory of officials and others attached to the papal court in the days of Benedict XII and Clement VI:

> On the average there must have been about 500 papal officials. Despite the building of two successive palaces side by side to accommodate the various departments they could not all fit inside. . . . Most of the officials took lodgings in the town; as well as the pope's officials there were the staffs of the cardinals: at least thirty persons each for twenty-three cardinals means nearly a thousand people. (With 500 papal officials that gives us 1,500.) But two-thirds of all these were laymen—a thousand or so laymen. . . . These thousand or so laymen, though, had often enough families of their own, wives, children and dependents, all living in the town. So the whole total of papal and cardinals' staffs was probably about 3,000 souls.[48]

Clement VI died in Avignon on September 6, 1352. Karl August Fink evaluates this pontiff's tenure "as the most splendid representative of the Avignon regime, if by this expression are understood grand-scale expenditures, a court of princely luxury and unbridled favoritism of relatives and countrymen."[49]

INNOCENT VI (1352-62) AND URBAN V (1362-70)

Clement was succeeded by the cardinal-bishop of Ostia, Etienne Aubert, who called himself Innocent VI. Aubert and twenty-four other cardinals in the conclave of December 1352 bound themselves to a pre-election agreement (called an election capitulation) which was to become very commonplace during the rest of the fourteenth, fifteenth, and sixteenth centuries up to the Council of Trent (1545-63). The capitulation of 1352, to which all the cardinals agreed under oath, stipulated that the new cardinals were to be chosen only with the consent of the existing group, that there were never to be more than twenty, that a two-thirds consent was required for the alienation of property of the Papal State, and that the papal treasury would hand over half its revenues to the College of Cardinals according to Nicholas IV's regulation of 1289. Like many of his successors, Innocent—after his election—made it clear that, as far as he was concerned, the capitulation was null and void. These pre-election agreements were attempts "to restrict papal power which was becoming more extensive every day."[50] From the latter half of the thirteenth century especially, the cardinals were acquiring an ever greater share in the papal decision-making power. One discovers more and more frequently that the popes' documents made reference to their having elicited at least the counsel of the

Sacred College before rendering this or that decision. Although some pontiffs such as Boniface VIII largely ignored the cardinals, this was by no means typical behavior for the popes of this era.

Innocent VI, who was known to have the blessing of the king of France, was easily the first choice of the conclave. He was a canonist of note, having taught for some years at the University of Toulouse. Although he was about seventy years old when elected and not in good health, he managed to surprise the cardinals who elected him by reviving the reform policies of Benedict XII. The cardinals probably chose him because they thought he would maintain the easygoing arrangement that prevailed under Clement VI, and hence could be molded to their wishes without much difficulty.[51] Innocent was especially severe with the Franciscan Spirituals, forcing the Inquisition to hunt them down as heretics and persecute them all over Europe. Because of Clement VI's profligate spending, Innocent was constantly in dire financial straits, having to borrow from any available source, even the cardinals.

A truce between England and France, causing an intermission of several years in the Hundred Years War, precipitated another crisis for the Avignon curia. In the spring of 1357, hundreds—perhaps thousands—of mercenary soldiers employed by England were discharged and left to wander about France in search of food, lodging, and booty. They roamed about central and southern France pillaging and burning churches, religious houses, and monasteries, picking up whatever treasures they could carry off. Avignon was extremely at risk since it constituted an ideal target for the marauders. Innocent VI set about building a wall and fortifications around the city, and in the meanwhile bought off as many mercenaries as he could, thus further aggravating his financial plight.[52] These struggles, which lasted for several years, took a heavy toll on Avignon and on the elderly pope's health. He died in September 1362. But it was in Innocent's reign that the situation in Italy was notably improved through the pacification efforts of Cardinal Gil de Albornoz, who was named papal legate for all of Italy in 1353. The former archbishop of Toledo and primate of Spain had come to Avignon in 1350 to work with Clement VI.[53]

Although Pope Innocent never left Avignon, he had prepared the way for a return to Rome. His successor, Urban V (1362-70), did negotiate the journey but returned to Avignon before he died. Urban was not a cardinal when he was unanimously elected in September 1362. He was actually the abbot of a prestigious Benedictine monastery in Marseilles, and had previously distinguished himself as a civil and canon lawyer, as well as a highly successful religious superior. As pope, he continued to live as a monk, but felt a certain insecurity vis-à-vis the cardinals at Avignon. He made some effort to re-establish the reform programs of his predecessors.[54] Urban was popular largely because of his basic goodness, but his generosity, e.g., to students and schools, led him deeper into debt. "He thought it necessary to indulge in excessive liberality which involved the papal treasury in heavy debts and was to lead him to borrow from the cardinals and to decree financial measures that were oppressive for the clergy."[55] Unlike several of his predecessors at Avignon, Urban genuinely desired to return to Rome, and actually set out in April 1367. Although he entered Rome in October 1367, the pontiff spent most of his three years in Italy in places like Viterbo and Montefiascone, not far from Rome. While residing in the Holy City, Urban made his home at the Vatican. "The Lateran palace was uninhabitable and Urban therefore took up residence at the Vatican where the popes have resided ever since."[56]

It is not entirely clear why Pope Urban left Rome in September 1370. Perhaps he felt that because the war between France and England had broken out again, he could more effectively mediate for peace with Charles V (France) and Edward III (England) from the vantage point of Avignon.[57] In spite of his reputation for simplicity and virtue, Urban did not take any steps to reverse the governmental centralization which had accelerated so dramatically at Avignon.

As holy a pope as Urban V considered papal provision as fully justified in law and he extended reservation without distinction to patriarchates, archbishoprics, monasteries and nunneries—that is, to all major benefices, in 1363. Gregory XI continued this practice. By the second half of the century, then, all appointments to all major benefices belonged entirely to the pope and so did appointments to many minor benefices as well.[58]

GREGORY XI (1370-78)
AND THE AVIGNON ADMINISTRATION

Gregory XI was forty-two years old when he was elected pope on December 30, 1370, eleven days after the death of Blessed Urban V.[59] A nephew of Clement VI, Gregory had been a curial official at Avignon for twenty years. In fact, Clement had made him a cardinal at nineteen. The new pope was an expert canon lawyer extremely dedicated to church reform. In this connection, he activated the Inquisition against various unorthodox movements in southern France, Sicily, and Germany, because heresy was spreading again like wildfire through Europe. It was at this time that the English scholar John Wyclif began to propagate his ideas regarding the church of the predestined versus the hierarchical church, which met with considerable enthusiasm in various sectors of Europe, e.g., Bohemia. Gregory convinced himself that the only effective way to control the Papal States was to govern the territories from Rome. A number of his predecessors at Avignon failed to see this, but should have come to the same conclusion years earlier. Gregory XI left Avignon in the fall of 1376 and entered a joyous and grateful Rome on January 17, 1377. However, due to poor health and the Roman climate, he died on March 27, 1378.[60]

Before considering the fateful papal election of 1378 which erupted into the Great Western Schism, several concluding observations are in order regarding the nearly seventy-year Avignon papacy. The two root causes of the problems besetting the pope and the curia after 1300 seem to have been the striking expansion of expenditures on the part of the popes and the cardinals, and the creeping centralization of decision making into the pope's hands. That is, more and more responsibility for critical decisions was being taken from the local churches and shifted to the papal court. These factors precipitated the explosion of the size of the curia and occasioned the shocking rise in the revenue demands laid on the whole of western Christendom. Although there was a causal relationship between the centralization of the decision-making processes and the surge in expenditures, there were other reasons for the rising costs. As the papal court settled into Avignon after Clement V, a luxurious life style evolved rather quickly and substantially increased the demands for funds. Also, the popes throughout their stay in Avignon consumed exorbitant amounts of money on military ventures in Italy to quell the multiple wars and insurrections in the Papal States, whence they once derived a major share of their income. For example, it is said that John XXII during his eighteen-year pontificate spent about two-thirds of his total revenues on military expeditions in Italy.[61] Scholars such as Canon Mollat and Yves Renouard have described in some detail the sumptuous character of the papal court: the expensive clothing, the tapestries, the paintings and sculptures, the gold and silver utensils, the luxurious feasts, and so forth.[62] The cottage industries surrounding the papal court had exploded the population of Avignon from 5,000 to 6,000 inhabitants in 1300 to something close to 30,000 by 1376.[63] (Paris at that time had a population of about 100,000.) A poignant observation by Professor Renouard is worth noting:

> The pope's residence at Avignon, far from the tombs of the apostles, the luxurious palace with its treasury lodged in its strongest tower, the complicated administration, the numerous courts, all seemed symptomatic of irredeemable worldliness. What was the Vicar of Christ doing raising taxes, equipping armies, reconquering lands? Was he any different from any other king? His spiritual office seemed obscured by his temporal concerns and his example justified every sort of abuse.[64]

The factors contributing to the centralization of decision making were largely two-fold: the ongoing expansion of the activity of the papal courts, and the phenomenon of the reservation of benefices and endowments. The judicial business, which was decried by St. Bernard already in or around 1150 as a tragic distraction deflecting the pope from his primary spiritual offices, continued to grow over the intervening 200 years into a dizzying maze of courts and offices, officers and clerks. Avignon had become a lawyer's paradise, teeming with job hunters of all sorts who were seeking to better themselves with whatever benefices and endowments they might acquire. The evolution of papal reservations seems to have begun with Pope Innocent II (1130-43). The first general reservations (i.e., over certain classes of benefices and/or endowments) began with Clement IV (1265-68). Boniface VIII and Clement V added further categories of reserved benefices to the list, and John XXII codified the previous enactments. And as we have seen, Urban V and Gregory XI extended papal reservations to include practically every major benefice and a considerable number of the minor benefices of note in western Christendom.

The elective process, respected and cherished by the early Church, was simply disappearing. The rights and the responsibilities of the bishops and the local church communities were ebbing away. Whole layers of ecclesial government, sacred from sub-apostolic times, had been for all practical purposes emasculated. From the second half of the eleventh century, the Gregorian reform had significantly weakened the position of the metropolitans as intermediate decision makers because the pope and his traveling legates were assuming that role. Then, the rights of the clergy and later the cathedral chapters to select the local bishops, and the local bishops' rights to choose their major benefice holders and officers, were disappearing as key decision-making prerogatives were removed from local authorities and carried off to the papal curia. Oh yes, there were abuses and delays and injustices perpetrated by the decision makers at the local levels, but these paled compared to what was happening and would happen under the centralized papal system. William of Durant, the bishop of Mende in southern France, bitterly denounced the growth of papal reservations at the Council of Vienne: "Guillaume of Durant called for the suppression of papal provisions; otherwise, he said, 'order in the Church will be set to naught.' "[65]

All of this unceasingly expanding activity at Avignon was expensive, and the popes were not able to draw from the Papal States the levels of revenue available to them in previous centuries. Hence the need for increasing other sources of revenue. The logical first targets were the benefices and endowments conferred by the Holy See. The common services (*servitia communia*) which were to be paid on the occasion of the nomination, confirmation, or translation of bishops and abbots were originally voluntary, but with Boniface VIII they became actual assessments. These fees could amount to a sizeable fraction of the appraised value of the benefice or endowment conferred. In addition, there were substantial fees for any services rendered by the papal curia as well as fees to be paid at the time of a prelate's *ad limina* visits. Then there were the papal taxes levied in the beneficiary's own country. The annates were revenues collected from the new beneficiaries appointed by the pope out of their first year's income. By Gregory XI's time, almost all bishops and abbots had to pay the annates which then amounted to a substantial share of the first year's revenue.[66] Further, there were, since Innocent III, tithes or taxes for the support of the crusades or other extraordinary expenses, and these usually amounted to ten percent of the assessed value of the beneficiary's property.[67]

Perhaps the grizzliest aspect of the papal financial system was the collection process. There were thirty-one collectories in Christendom, fifteen of them in France. Each financial district had a certain number of treasury agents whose task it was to collect the revenues due and to dispatch the funds to Avignon. The chief collectors had to return to Avignon to make a detailed account of their activities every two years. These principal collectors had awesome authority, including the power to excommunicate delinquents for nonpayment.[68] It is not particularly difficult to imagine how these heavy tax burdens and the odious collection procedures caused a mountain of aggravation and resentment everywhere.

> Parliaments in England protested bitterly against papal exactions. In France the incumbents expressed their opposition by hindering the collectors in the carrying out of their duties. From the reign of Philip VI [1328-50], the pope's agents more and more frequently ran up against the king's officers who defended the interests of the taxpayers. . . . In Germany, collectors were so frequently being seized and cast into unsavory prisons that, in 1347, one of them had great difficulty in recruiting any assistants. . . . the clergy's opposition to the payment of papal taxes was greater in Germany than in any other country.[69]

K. A. Fink concludes his treatment of the Avignon curia by noting:

> The unclerical management of the Avignon government, which was continued and multiplied during the Great Schism in two and then three obediences, led to a serious decline in confidence in the curia and in ecclesiastical authority.[70]

THE GREAT WESTERN SCHISM

At the time of Gregory XI's death in March 1378, there were sixteen cardinals in Rome (four Italians, eleven French, and one Spaniard), while six remained in Avignon. The local Roman citizenry, afraid that they would lose the pope again, made it clear to the sixteen cardinals in Rome that they wanted an Italian pontiff. As the prelates were gathering to open the conclave on April 7, 1378, the heads of the urban regions made their case in rather unambiguous terms. Apparently, early on there was an interruption, or perhaps more correctly, an invasion of the conclave by some of the citizens, causing several of the cardinals to retire to their residences for a time. After the consistory reconvened, not one of the sixteen cardinals could obtain the required two-thirds majority. Hence they chose an outsider, Bartholomew Prignano, the archbishop of Bari, on April 8, 1378. Bartholomew, who became Urban VI, had been regent of the chancery in Rome under Gregory XI and thus was something of a known quantity to the cardinals in the Holy City.

> The real problem begins after this very dubious election, since the cardinals took part in the enthronement, treated Urban VI (1378-89) as pope, at least outwardly, presented their petitions to him, and sent notifications of the election to the princes. Thereby, so one often reads, tacit consent was given and the cardinals lost their right of protest against "pressure" in the election.[71]

On Easter Sunday, April 18, 1378, Urban was crowned in the presence of all the cardinals in Rome and, on the following day, the cardinals sent a letter to their six colleagues in Avignon informing them of the election.[72]

From the outset, however, there was trouble between the pope and the Sacred College. Urban decided to initiate his reforms by attacking the rich life style of the curia. He upbraided the cardinals publicly, attacked them personally, and frequently employed abusive language and insults against them and other curial officers. The cardinals—who must have looked on Urban as an outsider because he had not been a member of the lordly college—deeply resented the pontiff's harsh and high-handed conduct: "The cardinals could never be reconciled to the somewhat austere and severe life in Rome, nor could they have submitted to the tactless, dictatorial manner of the pontiff who owed them everything."[73]

All but four of them left Rome in June and took up residence at Anagni. As a matter of fact, the curia was transferred there, and Urban intended to follow. He went to Tivoli instead, perhaps because of what he was hearing regarding the unrest at Anagni. On July 20, 1378, the Anagni contingent dispatched a letter to the Italian cardinals with Urban, ordering them to make their way to Anagni inasmuch as the Holy See was declared vacant. "On 9 August they issued their famous *Declaratio* from Anagni, in which they announced to the whole of Christendom that the election of Urban VI was null and void and that the Holy See was declared vacant. Urban himself was cited to come to Anagni, since he was a criminal who wrongfully usurped the throne of St. Peter."[74]

In mid-September the Anagni group was joined by the Italian cardinals at the palace of the duke of Fondi, south of Rome, and they elected Robert of Geneva as pope. Within the week, Urban created twenty-eight new cardinals to constitute for himself a new college because all of his original cardinals had deserted him. Robert of Geneva, who called himself Clement VII (1378-94), was excommunicated by Urban on November 29, 1378. Although the principal curial officials went over to Clement, he was unable to take possession of Rome, and left Italy for Avignon in May 1381.

The question of the validity of Urban's election has been vigorously debated over the intervening centuries. Many historians, such as Walter Ullmann, hold for the validity of Urban's claim, while others, such as the Tübingen scholar K. A. Fink are of the mind that the election was conducted under coercion and hence was not valid.[75] Debates, hearings, and investigations were conducted in several places in the years after 1378 with no definitive result. According to Fink, this issue constitutes "one of the most difficult problems of late Medieval Church History."[76] Urban was recognized as the true pope throughout Italy, England, most of the German Empire, Hungary, and the Nordic countries, while Clement could eventually claim the allegiance of France, Naples, Savoy, Scotland, and later, Aragon and Castile. Religious orders and many dioceses were split down the middle, with some adhering to Urban and others to Clement.[77] The amount of damage—even permanent damage—which this schism left in its wake can hardly be overstated. "In retrospect one cannot but come to the conclusion that this division of allegiance to the 'heads' of Christianity greatly accelerated the break-up of Western Christendom in the sixteenth century."[78]

Pope Urban died in Rome and was succeeded by a Neapolitan cardinal, Peter Tomacelli, who took the name Boniface IX (1389-1404). In Avignon, Clement died in September 1394 and was succeeded by Peter de Luna (Benedict XIII, 1394-1423), who lived for almost thirty years, utterly convinced that he was the true pope. Charles VI of France was of the mind that both should abdicate, but Benedict XIII staunchly advocated a settlement through arbitration because he was so sure of the validity of his claim. Boniface IX in Rome, however, was consistently unwilling to mediate the issue. Even as late as 1404, Benedict XIII made efforts to meet with Boniface IX, with no success. In October 1404, Boniface died in Rome, and the cardinals in the Holy City chose Innocent VII to succeed him. Within two years, Innocent died and was replaced by a Venetian cardinal, who identified himself as Gregory XII (1406-15). These were the two protagonists—Gregory in Rome and Benedict in Avignon—when the cardinals of both persuasions met in March 1409 at Pisa to address and bring to a conclusion this tragic and destructive impasse which had lasted more than thirty years.[79]

There were twenty-four cardinals, four patriarchs, eighty archbishops, and eighty abbots, the proxies of an additional 100 bishops and 200 abbots, the generals of the major religious orders, and a great number of theologians and canonists at Pisa.[80] This was no minor event by any means. After more than two months of deliberations and hearings, the council was prepared to take the momentous step. On June 5, 1409, both popes were declared notorious schismatics and obdurate heretics. Obedience was withdrawn from both claimants, and the Roman see was declared vacant.[81] The cardinals of both persuasions proceeded to elect a new pope, the archbishop of Milan, who became Alexander V (1409-10). The council closed on August 7, 1409. Alexander died in May 1410 and was succeeded by John XXIII (1410-15). Although today most church historians hold that Pisa was not a true ecumenical council and hence the depositions and the new papal election were meaningless,[82] this position was not shared by the majority of ecclesiastics at the time.[83]

CONCILIARISM

In spite of the fact that the *pars sanior* between 1409 and 1415 were convinced that the Pisan line represented the true papal succession, there remained much confusion and disagreement over the issue. Benedict XIII (Avignon) and Gregory XII (Rome) still had their adherents, so the crisis in many ways became more pressing than ever. Now the Christian people had to deal with three papal claimants. Since 1378 there had been a vigorous and broad-based debate over the underlying constitutional issues. Who was competent to decide which of the three claimants was the true pope? As a matter of fact, the question went even deeper than this. Brian Tierney, the eminent medievalist, states:

> The original dispute of the rival popes broadened into a constitutional crisis in which the most important problem to be resolved was no longer which of the rival claimants should be Pope but whether the papacy itself should continue to govern the Church in the old way.[84]

For a long time—perhaps 200 years or more—there had been the feeling, or more correctly the conviction, that universal Church reform could be most effectively addressed in an ecumenical council. As we have seen, the issue had been raised at Lateran II (1139) and at every one of the five general councils up to and including Vienne (1311-12). There was something about the force and effectiveness of a council which could summon the full strength of the Church and render itself present in order to identify what needed to be done and to chart out a corrective course, in a way that no other experience or agent could. In spite of the longstanding and clear teaching concerning the papal "fullness of power" which had enjoyed widespread acceptance from the twelfth century, the matter of Church reform called for a wider expression of "solicitude" on the part of a representative body of the whole Church. The early canonists (i.e., the Decretists, or commentators on the *Decretum* of Gratian, 1140) assumed that although the Church itself could never err in declaring the faith, the pope alone did not enjoy that prerogative since *de facto* previous pontiffs had fallen into error.

In Decretist thought there were at least two institutions through which the inherent authority of the whole Church could be expressed, the papacy and the General Council; and in questions of faith and other matters which affected the well-being of the whole Church, the authority of the Council was preferred to that of the Pope.[85]

It is this teaching on the superior authority of the council (including the pope) over the pope alone in matters of faith and in questions impacting the well-being of the whole Church that came to be called the conciliar theory. The conciliar position evolved from there, however, in the fourteenth century. The troubles of Boniface VIII and especially the events of the Great Schism had much to do with this. How was a crisis of such historic proportions to be addressed and solved?[86] The evolution of the conciliar position was what prepared the way for the Council of Pisa (1409), and eventually for the Council of Constance (1414-18). Scholars from the University of Paris and elsewhere were publishing studies on this issue from 1380 on. Conrad of Gelnhausen, a professor at Paris, issued a work called the *Letter of Concord* in May 1380 in which he articulated perhaps the first full rendering of the conciliar theory.

The Church is constituted by the pope and the faithful . . . The pope is only a secondary head of the Church, her primary and principal head being Christ himself. . . . even if there were no pope at all, the body and members of the Church would continue to exist . . . In short, the congregation of all Christians is superior to the pope. . . . Consequently, the whole of Christianity is the only rightful judge who can terminate the present dispute.[87]

Conrad believed that a general council, which would depose the two popes (there were only two in 1380—one in Rome and one in Avignon) and provide an occasion for the election of another pontiff by the cardinals, was the only viable solution. He then added:

If, for instance, the pope persisted in heresy, proved incorrigible and would not consent to the convocation of a general council, Christianity would be entitled to summon a council against the will of the pope, who could and should be indicted in this council.[88]

There was, in Conrad's judgment, no legal obstacle to the convocation of a general council without papal authorization.[89] Other scholars published similar theories over the next twenty or thirty years in which limitations were placed on the papal plenitude of power—at least in emergency situations. The authority and prestige of the College of Cardinals, in evidence particularly since the second half of the thirteenth century, did not seem to benefit from the restrictions placed on papal authority in most of these writings. Rather, it was the general council that received the greatest attention as the final court of appeal and the supreme convocation of the universal Church.

Another strand of canonical thought which evolved in the thirteenth century also served, according to Brian Tierney, as a ground for the development of the conciliar theory. Although these canonists (i.e., the Decretalists, or commentators on the collections of papal decretals from 1234 on) did not apply their thinking on the structure of ecclesiastical corporations to the papacy because they concentrated on the relationship of the local bishops to their chapters of canons, their views did have a pervasive effect in the fourteenth century on the developing understanding of the universal Church as a corporate body.[90]

> As the idea of the Church as a corporate entity in the more legalistic sense became accepted, there was always the possibility that it might be restated in a form that would lay all the emphasis upon the due participation of the members rather than on the unique authority of the head. . . . There was the doctrine that the Pope could not legitimately act against the general well-being of the Church, and that, at least in the case of heresy, he could be deposed by the Church.[91]

There is little doubt that the conciliar doctrines of the fourteenth century were considerably affected by the thirteenth-century theories of the canonists.[92]

Since Boniface VIII's epic struggles with Philip IV of France, theologians also had been focusing their attention on the theology of the Church and on the nature of papal power. Giles of Rome, for example, in his treatise, *On Ecclesiastical Power*, written in 1301, provided Boniface with the theories on the extension of papal prerogatives that he employed in his bull, *Unam sanctam*, in November 1302. John of Paris, on the other hand, who published his *Regal and Papal Power* in 1303, limited somewhat the scope of the pope's authority, affirming that both the pontiff and the civil ruler received their authority directly from God. Regal or princely power was not channeled through the pope, as Giles had taught. William of Ockham (d. 1347?), an English Franciscan, maintained as well that secular and ecclesiastical authority were separate and complementary. Regarding the structure of the Church, he taught that although the Church was established by Christ as a monarchy, the *Ecclesia Universalis* was above the pope, and it alone (not the pope) would never fall into error.[93]

Another imposing figure in the debate on the nature of papal power was Marsilius of Padua. In his influential work, *The Defender of the Peace*, completed in 1325, he taught that although sacramental authority is from God, institutional authority (whereby the clergy are assigned to specific pastorates, ranks, etc.) is from man.

Thus the whole body of believers, and not the priesthood alone, must control excommunication, the designation of priests to particular posts, the filling of ranks in the priestly hierarchy, including the office of "head bishop" or pope, the distribution of benefices and other economic matters affecting the clergy, the election of general councils, and the enforcement of the council's definitions of articles of faith.[94]

The pope as "head bishop" has the role, according to Marsilius, of notifying the faithful if there is an emergency of faith requiring the summoning of a general council, which has to be done by a secular legislator (e.g., the emperor) who alone has the required coercive power. The pope's role is to direct the deliberations of the council and publish the results.[95] Marsilius' position was too heterodox to have much influence on the formulation of the more moderate conciliar theories which commanded the field at Pisa (1409) and Constance (1414-18), but his emphasis on the notion of sovereignty residing ultimately in the Church people did have some indirect effect on the development of conciliar thought.

THE COUNCIL OF CONSTANCE (1414-18)

These were the principal currents of canonical and theological opinion that prevailed during the first two decades of the fifteenth century. We have attempted to illustrate the confusion and the frustration which existed at the time throughout the Christian world due to the continuing uncertainty as to who was the true pope. John XXIII of the Pisan line seems to have had the largest allegiance inasmuch as France, England, and several Italian and German states were behind him. Apparently Gregory XII (Rome) was in a much weaker position since the Council of Pisa, but Benedict XIII (Avignon) with his followers on the Iberian peninsula and in southern France was still a force to be reckoned with. The only way in which this division could be healed was through the convocation of a general council. It was King Sigismund of Germany (1410-38) who took the initiative and persuaded John XXIII to call a council. "To him [i.e., Sigismund] belongs the chief merit for having brought the council into being and for its accomplishments."[96] The council was opened on November 5, 1414 at Constance. Its purpose was "to attend to the peace, exaltation and reform of the Church and to the quiet of the Christian people."[97] These goals would only be achieved through the reunion of all three allegiances under one pontiff. During 1415, the numbers in attendance grew so dramatically that Constance could justifiably be called the greatest ecclesiastical congress in the Middle Ages.[98] Voting was conducted by "nations," based on the five most widely used languages (i.e., German, French, Italian, Span-

ish, and English), and the cardinals voted as a separate "nation." In spite of the
fact that the Council of Pisa was rather generally acknowledged at that time as
valid and that the Pisan line of popes represented for perhaps the majority of
Christians the true succession, the resignation of all three popes and the election of another pontiff by the cardinals seemed to be the only way to bring
about a definitive end to the conflict. In March 1415, John XXIII was the first
to volunteer to resign, but before doing so, he fled the council, hoping perhaps
to derail it. At the third session on March 26, the council fathers confirmed
the validity of the convocation and asserted that the council had in no way
been dissolved by John XXIII's departure, nor would it dissolve itself "until the
present schism has been entirely removed and until the Church has been reformed in faith and morals, in head and members."[99] Session five on April 6,
1415, made the most controversial and the most vigorously debated declaration regarding the relationship between papal and conciliar power.

> It declares that, legitimately assembled in the Holy Spirit, constituting a
> general council and representing the Catholic Church militant, it has
> power immediately from Christ, and that everyone of whatever state or
> dignity, even papal, is bound to obey it in these matters which pertain to
> the faith, the eradication of the said schism and the general reform of the
> said Church of God in head and members.[100]

This statement of the superiority of the legitimately convoked council over
any other power, even papal power, when gathered together to declare the
faith and to effect the general reform of the Church was perfectly consonant
with the current moderate conciliar theory which taught that the council was
an occasional legislative body and, in an emergency such as this, the superior
of the pope. The declaration should not be construed as an expression of radical conciliar thought which viewed the council as the normal, regular juridical
sovereign of the Church.[101] This extreme position, which was to become the
characteristic stance at the Council of Basel (1431-38), was not expressed in
the decree, *Haec sancta synodus*, of April 6, 1415. The fathers at Constance,
"legitimately assembled in the Holy Spirit," simply articulated here what had
to happen. One of the three popes was the true pontiff, but it was impossible
for them to determine which of the three he was. Therefore, to solve the dilemma, these three had either to resign or be deposed so that a new pope could
be elected. The council simply had to assume the sovereign power over the
three claimants in order to break the deadlock. In this, and presumably in any
similar situation, the council was the body that represented the universal Church
which needed and demanded a solution to the impasse.

John XXIII was brought back to Constance and put on trial. His immoral
life and alleged crimes were exposed, and the council deposed him on May 29,

1415. Although he was regarded as an unworthy pope, he was not judged to have been an unlawful or invalidly elected pope.[102] Gregory XII (Rome), who desired to convoke the council himself, was permitted to do so on July 4, 1415, and then he resigned. Benedict XIII (Avignon) refused to resign and was deposed two years later. During the intervening period from 1415 to 1417, discussions took place on various reform measures, but few conciliar reform decrees were enacted. There was, however, a great deal promulgated regarding the condemnation of the late John Wyclif and his writings. Also, Wyclif's disciple, John Hus, who had been invited to present himself before the council, was condemned and sentenced to burn at the stake in July 1415. It was the process against Benedict XIII that consumed many months, beginning in November 1416, and concluding on July 26, 1417, with his deposition. It is curious to note that while the council spoke of John XXIII before his deposition as "our most holy lord pope John XXIII,"[103] both Gregory and Benedict were referred to—prior to their resignation or deposition—as "those whom their allegiances claimed to be pope."[104]

After the deposing of Benedict XIII in July 1417, the way was clear for the election of a new pontiff. That summer there was a heated dispute over the council's priorities from that point on. Should the new pope be elected first or should the council promulgate reform decrees before proceeding to the papal election? The former view carried the day, and the election of the new pope was to take precedence. However, there were a few decrees enacted before the election process began, the most significant of which was the one on the frequent holding of general councils. This enactment of October 9, 1417, set forth a schedule for the regular celebration of general councils:

> We establish, enact, decree and ordain, by a perpetual edict, that general councils shall be held hereafter in the following way. The first shall follow in five years immediately after the end of this council, the second in seven years immediately after the end of the next council, and thereafter they are to be held every ten years forever.[105]

The rationale for the regular holding of councils was stated as follows:

> Thus by a certain continuity, there will always be either a council in existence or one is expected within a given time. If perchance emergencies arise, the time may be shortened by the supreme pontiff, acting on the advice of his brothers, the cardinals of the Roman church, but it may never be prolonged.[106]

The foundation for this enactment is laid out in the opening paragraph of the decree, *Frequens*:

The frequent holding of general councils is a preeminent means of cultivating the Lord's patrimony. It roots out the briars, thorns and thistles of heresies, errors and schisms, corrects deviations, reforms what is deformed and produces a richly fertile crop for the Lord's vineyard. Neglect of councils, on the other hand, spreads and fosters the aforesaid evils. This conclusion is brought before our eyes by the memory of past times and reflection on the present situation.[107]

Frequens is a clear statement of the role of councils in the Church. It is a forceful expression of the modified conciliar position, articulating a constitutional principle for the future. There should always be a council either in session or anticipated within a relatively short time. In case of an emergency, i.e., a danger to the well-being of the Church, the pope, after consulting with the cardinals, can shorten the time until the next council, but it should never be prolonged. *Frequens* rates among the more seriously neglected and ignored authentic conciliar decrees in the Church's history. Its validity as a conciliar enactment is clear because even Martin V (the pope elected at Constance) obeyed it, although reluctantly. *Frequens* would have acted as a significant deterrent over the years against the resurgence of papal absolutism. Further, one can only imagine what an effect regular general councils would have had in anticipating or at least coping with the Reformation of the sixteenth century in a timely manner.

It is most unfortunate that at the Council of Basel (1431-38), the radical conciliar theory (which saw the council as the normal, ongoing juridical sovereign in the Church) took center stage and pushed the moderate conciliar position (which understood the council as an occasional legislative body and, only in the gravest emergencies, the superior of the pope) into relative oblivion. It could be said that as a result of the events at Basel, the constitutional development of the Church experienced the throwing out of the baby (i.e., moderate conciliarism) with the bath water (i.e., the radical conciliar position).

The final session of Constance, before the beginning of the papal election process, outlined on October 30, 1417, eighteen areas where broad reform was required and suitable remedies should be legislated before the close of the council. These articles addressed the need for reform regarding the selection of cardinals, the papal reservation of benefices and endowments, papal taxes and assessments, the reservation of cases to papal judges and the control of appeals, papal dispensations, the disposition of papal revenues, indulgences, and tithes.[108] The conclave opened on November 8, 1417, and three days later, Cardinal Oddo Colonna was elected. In March 1418, seven reform decrees were promulgated in the name of the new pontiff, Martin V (1417-31). These, however, dealt with only a fraction of the issues pinpointed for immediate attention in the fortieth session of October 30, 1417. The other pressing grievances were addressed through diplomatic treaties, or concordats, with the individual nations.[109] At the second-to-last session on April 19, 1418, the place of the next general council—due to meet in five years—was scheduled for Pavia. The final session of Constance adjourned the proceedings on April 22, 1418. Giuseppe Alberigo notes the following with regard to the early sessions of this council:

> With regard to the ecumenical nature of the sessions, there is dispute about those before the election of Martin V and also about the significance and force he gave to the matters transacted by the council. The decrees, notably those of sessions 3-5 and the decree *Frequens* (session 39), appear to proceed from the council's teaching. Objections have been made to them on the grounds of the primacy of the Roman pontiff. There is no doubt, however, that in enacting these decrees there was solicitude and care to choose the true and sure way ahead in order to heal the schism, and this could only be done by the authority of the council.[110]

Largely because of the two decrees on the relationship between the pope and the general council (i.e., *Haec sancta synodus* of April 6, 1415 and *Frequens* of October 9, 1417), Constance was not generally accepted for a considerable period as an ecumenical synod.[111] When the notion of the absolute power of the papacy in the Church became widely accepted after Trent and the glory days of the Tridentine reform (1563-1605), Constance and Basel did not fare well. The papalist theologians later reconciled themselves with Constance and also with Basel by asserting that *Haec sancta synodus* (articulating the relationship between pope and council) was not a valid conciliar decree inasmuch as it was enacted prior to July 1415 when the "true pope," Gregory XII (Roman line), was allowed to summon the council before resigning. After this, they claim, the council was validly convened. And because neither Martin V nor his successor, Eugene IV (1431-47), ever specifically approved *Haec sancta synodus*, it never became a true conciliar decree. *Frequens*—prescribing the frequency of general councils—could be rather easily disposed of as a mere disciplinary decree which did not touch the constitutional fabric of the Church, although it was passed after July 1415.

There are several problems with this position. First, it would be historically inaccurate to assert the clear validity of the Roman line of popes between 1387 and 1415. According to Brian Tierney, "it was impossible in 1415 to know with certainty who was the true pope."[112] As a matter of fact, the fathers at Constance in 1415 were more inclined to assert that John XXIII (Pisan line) was the true pontiff. Secondly, the claim that neither Martin V nor Eugene IV specifically approved *Haec sancta synodus*, and therefore it was not a genuine conciliar decree, lacks historical precision. Again, according to Tierney: "The idea that *Haec sancta* should be presented to the pope for his *ex post facto* approval never presented itself to Martin V or to the fathers of the council or to anyone else."[113]

Finally, it is not necessary to hold, as some do, that *Haec sancta synodus* was an irreformable dogmatic definition which stands in opposition to the pope's absolute primacy defined at Vatican I (i.e., *Pastor aeternus*, 1870).

> Even if *Haec sancta* had always been held in honor and *Frequens* fulfilled to the letter, the pope, controlling all the central machinery of Church government, could hardly have become a mere executive agent of a council that met every ten years. Probably no one at Constance had any such intention. But it was entirely possible, without any such intention, to claim for the general council a regular role, in association with the pope, in the great task of reforming the Church that lay ahead. This was one of the purposes of *Haec sancta*.[114]

In another related study, Dr. Tierney adds:

> None of the moderate conciliarists at Constance denied that, in some sense, sovereignty (*plenitudo potestatis*) resided in the pope. . . . But the conciliarists also insisted that sovereignty also inhered in some other sense in the universal Church and in a universal council representing it. Thus, the whole conciliar theory, as it was developed by its principal exponents, was based on the idea of "divided sovereignty." It seemed clear that when there was no true pope, the whole power of the Church could be exercised by the fathers of a council. It was not so clear where the balance of power would be once the new pope was elected.[115]

It was unfortunate indeed that Martin V and Eugene IV were so "obdurately opposed" to the approach to constitutional development suggested by *Haec sancta synodus*, which, in the judgment of Tierney and others, had to be valid.[116]

In April 1415, the council had simply no alternative but to promulgate a decree clarifying its own authority so that it could move forward to the healing of the schism. The words of *Haec sancta synodus* were ambiguous and, according to Tierney, they were understood to be ambiguous when the decree was enacted.[117] This decree and the deliberations of Constance provided—in that moment of extreme crisis—an occasion, an opportunity for momentous constitutional development within the Church. If Pope Martin and his successors had been genuinely willing to work within the context of *Frequens*, the conciliarism at Basel might well have proved to have been much more moderate than it was, and the Church would in all probability have had a very different constitutional history from the fifteenth century to the present, and it would undoubtedly have a different face today. Geoffrey Barraclough appraises this critical moment:

> It is a serious criticism of the popes that none made any attempt to see whether the conciliar program would work. In this way they missed the

last chance for reform, while there was still time—for voluntary reform. ... That, really, was the tragedy of the medieval papacy. The conciliar movement gave it its last opportunity. The trouble with the popes was that they were too clever to take it, but not clever enough to see the consequences of not taking it. Their efforts were so concentrated in outmanoeuvering the council, when they should have been profiting from the fervour for the welfare of the Church—which, behind all the intrigues and political jockeying for position, was a real force throughout the conciliar epoch—to restore their position.[118]

MARTIN V (1417-31), EUGENE IV (1431-47), AND THE COUNCIL OF BASEL (1431-38)

Oddo Colonna was the first and only member of his famous family to be elected pope. The Colonnas, like the Orsinis, had been powerful Roman clans for centuries. In 1408, Oddo had left the service of Gregory XII (Roman line) in order to join the preparations for the Council of Pisa and remained loyal to John XXIII (Pisan line) until the spring of 1415 when John fled from Constance. It is fair to say that Martin V, who had spent his life at the curia, was not interested in a meaningful relationship with the moderate conciliarists at and after Constance. His view of the papacy did not allow for the notion of divided sovereignty. He settled the delicate areas of the papal reservation of benefices, papal revenues, and dispensations with the major powers individually by means of concordats with the French, Spanish, German, and English nations, which, except in the case of England, were to terminate after five years. After that time, the *status quo ante* was generally restored. He took cardinals from all three obediences to put together his curia, with the majority of major officials coming from Avignon because they had the more established traditions. Within a few weeks after the closing of the council on April 22, 1418, the pope made his way to Florence, but was unable to enter Rome until September 1420 due to the civil conflict in and around the city. When the papal forces had finally subdued the local war lord, Braccio of Montone, in 1424, Pope Martin was in a position to recover and reorganize the Papal States, thus restoring to a great degree a principal traditional source of papal revenue. Renovations began almost immediately in Rome and its environs. The major churches, the streets, bridges, and the city's fortifications were notably improved during the pontiff's reign.[119] As the concordats expired, he returned to the old system of papal reservations, provisions, and taxation which had prevailed at Avignon, thus recouping in large measure the former revenues of the Holy See.

It was with considerable reluctance that Martin convoked the Council of Pavia in 1423. There was little security in that location—some twenty miles south of Milan—because it was quite close to the stronghold of the Viscontis.

Hence the gathering was soon transferred to Siena which was near to the Papal States. Because the attendance was not at all impressive, the pope closed the council with the promise that the next synod would be held seven years hence according to the decree, *Frequens*. Before his death in February 1431, Pope Martin reluctantly convoked the Council of Basel and appointed Cardinal Julian Cesarini as its president.[120]

On March 3, 1431, the cardinals chose Gabriel Condulmer, a nephew of Gregory XII, as the next supreme pontiff. They were tired of Martin's authoritarian ways and wanted someone who would be more responsive to their advice and counsel. Eugene IV (1431-47) was not a particularly gifted individual. From the outset, the pope mistrusted the projected council at Basel and attempted to dissolve it before it got under way. He was not successful, however, because most of the cardinals were in favor of the convocation, and Cardinal Cesarini, the president, simply moved forward with the deliberations. Eugene finally reconciled himself with the conciliar proceedings in December 1433, although it was by then obvious to one and all that he was not in the least in favor of it. Whether or not the pope's unwillingness to make peace with the conciliar idea precipitated the radicalization of the events at Basel is hard to determine. Undoubtedly the uncooperative attitude and the manifest reluctance of Martin V had also done much since 1418 to sour and embitter the conciliarists. In any event, the moderate conciliar position which prevailed at Constance almost immediately gave way to the more radical variety at Basel. It was the delegation from the University of Paris that apparently spearheaded this emphasis. Antony Black, an eminent conciliar scholar, states:

> The most revolutionary step of all was the council's replication of the entire structure of papal administrative and judicial machinery. . . . The ferocity of the struggle [between the pope and the council] owed much to the fact that, after the reconciliation with Eugene in 1434, none of this machinery was dismantled.[121]

Basel identified itself, almost from the beginning, as the normal, regular, juridical sovereign in the Church. Although a respectable number of major prelates had joined the proceedings by the summer of 1432, as the years progressed the participation at the council shifted from the higher to the lower clergy (i.e., deans, priors, archdeacons, and university clergy). According to Black, after 1437, university and junior clergy comprised more than fifty percent of the delegates at the council.[122]

The participants at Basel were divided into several committees where most of the discussion and the formulation of enactments took place. General assemblies were held about once a week, at which the proposals of the deputations or committees were voted upon. A two-thirds majority of the delegates was required for passage.[123]

The overwhelming difference between Basel and other councils was, of course, that the vote was not confined to bishops and abbots. Provosts, deans, priors, doctors and masters, rectors, vicars, canons, parish priests, . . . attended the council and were incorporated as full voting members.[124]

The objectives of the council were announced at the opening session on December 14, 1431. The delegates proposed to address three issues: the elimination of heresies (especially the Hussite heresy), the establishment of peace and accord among the nations and the reform of the Church.[125] In June 1432, they invited the Bohemians to Basel for discussions, and in light of the unfortunate treatment of John Hus at Constance, the council fathers promised the Hussites safe passage to and from Basel along with fair and impartial treatment while they were in attendance. Some 300 Bohemian representatives presented themselves in January 1433 to deliberate with the council delegates.

> The Bohemians left Basel on 14 April [1433], but the negotiations were continued at Prague and led to an agreement on the four articles of Prague . . . concerning the chalice for the laity, free preaching, the punishment of those guilty of serious sins and a far-reaching renunciation of ecclesiastical property. This agreement, the so-called *Prague Compactata*, was promulgated on 5 July 1436 in the presence of the Emperor (Sigismund) at the Diet of Iglau and was ratified by the Council of Basel on 15 January 1437. The *Compactata* were not ratified by the (papal) curia and were annulled in 1462. But this settlement of the Bohemian affair was a great success for the council.[126]

After the pacification of the Hussites in 1437, support for the council waned in Germany and France, as did the financial assistance from King Charles VII of France and the German Emperor Sigismund because the threats to their territories posed by the Hussites had been neutralized. Between 1433 and 1436, however, it must be said that a good number of positive reform measures were enacted at Basel. The decree, *Frequens*, was reaffirmed in considerable detail, and the obligation to hold a general council every ten years was emphasized as the most effective way to promote church reform (April 1433). In November 1433, a lengthy presentation on the regular holding of diocesan and provincial synods was enacted as another means of "cultivating the Lord's field."[127] Some of the other reform decrees passed during this three-year period were:

(a) a proposal to search out and discipline clerics living in concubinage (January 1435)
(b) a provision against frivolous judicial appeals (January 1435)
(c) a strong prohibition against excessive papal fees levied on recipients of benefices and endowments (June 1435)

(d) regulations concerning the procedure to be followed in papal elections and specifications on the number and qualifications of cardinals (June 1435)

(e) the abolition of general and specific papal reservations (March 1436)

Although some of these decrees, especially the one regarding the elimination of papal reservations, could have been structured in such a way that their financial effects could have been gradually assimilated over time by the pope and his curia, the reform measures did address the major sectors of concern laid out at Constance in October 1417, prior to the election of Martin V.

After 1437 the council became more and more radical and hence lost even more of its support from bishops and princes throughout Europe.

> The prospect of a sovereign council with full legislative, administrative and judicial powers held no attraction for states capable of exercising their influence on the existing curial regime; and the council was beginning to appear less accommodating than the papacy.[128]

The possibility of a reunion with the Greeks, much discussed at this time in both the papal curia and at Basel, provided Pope Eugene with an enormous tactical advantage. The Byzantines and their emperor, John VIII, were in dire need of military assistance from the West because the Ottoman Turks were threatening to take over what was left of Byzantium. The emperor was willing to discuss dogmatic concessions if they would open the way to western military assistance against the Turks. The pope, on the other hand, wanted more than anything else a recognition of his primacy from the Greeks which he could use as a potent weapon to minimize the influence of Basel. Both the council and the papal curia were vying for the attention of the Greeks. Each wanted to be the chief western participant in the coming dialogue. However, the pope had this advantage: the Greeks preferred to deal with him and were insisting on meeting in Italy rather than at Basel or some other northern location.[129]

The voting at Basel in May 1437 as to the location of the meeting with the Greeks ended in a stalemate. Although two-thirds of the delegates opted for a location selected by the council, there was a substantial minority which favored an Italian location. In September 1437, Pope Eugene ratified the minority decision and directed that the council be transferred to Ferrara. This marked the end of the first (and authorized) phase of the Council of Basel, and, as a matter of fact, the end of conciliar deliberations on church reform. The transfer took place in January 1438. The delegates who chose to remain behind continued to act as a synod, but support for the Basel proceedings continued to dwindle. In June 1439, the 300 delegates, among whom were probably only seven bishops, formally declared Pope Eugene a schismatic and "deposed" him. Word of this came to Eugene IV in July, and he responded on September 4, 1439, calling the convocation at Basel "a pretended council" and excommunicated all who opposed and continued to oppose the transfer of deliberations to Ferrara (and thence to Florence where the council was moved in January 1439).[130] In 1440, the delegates at Basel elected their own pope, Felix V, the last of the antipopes, who abdicated in April 1449 and died in Geneva in January 1451. The remnant of the synod finally transferred itself from Basel to Lausanne in 1447. The failure of Basel and the relationship between Basel and the events of the Reformation in the sixteenth century provide an intriguing occasion for speculation. Antony Black observes:

> The historical consequences were momentous. Not only was the Church left unreformed. The aspirations of all those who pinned their hopes on the general council were disappointed; the gap between what many believed to be constitutional justice and existing forms of Church government widened. This was particularly significant for the middle clergy of Germany; areas such as Saxony, Switzerland, southern France, above all the German and Swiss cities which had sent numerous supporters to Basel, would be fertile ground for the sixteenth century Reformers.[131]

CONCILIAR PROCEEDINGS AT FERRARA AND FLORENCE

Returning to the events which occurred after the council was transferred to Ferrara in January 1438, the delegates dedicated themselves almost entirely to the reunion of eastern Christendom with Rome. Theological deliberations began with the Greeks in June over such issues as the *Filioque* clause (relating to the procession of the Holy Spirit from the Father and the Son), which was added to the western creed in the early Middle Ages and hence not acceptable to the East; the doctrine of purgatory, which was foreign to the Greeks; the matter and form of the Eucharist; and finally, the primacy of the pope. This last topic was extremely important politically for Pope Eugene because he urgently felt the need to reaffirm his supremacy due to the events at Basel.

> The Emperor opposed the discussion [re: the primacy of the pope] but in the interests of union he had to exert considerable pressure on the Greek participants. The Greeks regarded as the highest tribunal in the constitution of the Church the pentarchy, the traditional five patriarchates of Rome, Constantinople, Alexandria, Antioch and Jerusalem. They were fully prepared to concede to the Patriarch of Old Rome the privileges he had enjoyed before the outbreak of the Schism [i.e., 1054]. There could

be no question of the primacy of jurisdiction. But in barely three weeks the Greeks were compelled to yield on a broad front. However, this was not a genuine solution, as the various possibilities of interpretation showed and still show.[132]

Before the completion of the so-called decree of union on July 6, 1439, as mentioned, the Council of Ferrara had been moved to Florence where the final agreement with the Byzantines was worked out. Although the deliberations involved Pope Eugene IV and Emperor John VIII, along with his patriarch, Joseph, and several eastern metropolitans, there were very few western bishops, other than a number of Italians, to represent the western church. George Ostrogorsky, an Orthodox historian, relates the following regarding the results of Ferrara-Florence from the Greek perspective:

> On the surface the pro-union party seemed to have gained a still greater victory than in the days of the Council of Lyons [i.e., Lyons II, 1274], for on this occasion the Emperor had appeared before the council in person and together with the highest representatives of the Byzantine Church had openly professed the Roman faith. But in reality the decisions taken at the Council of Florence were of no effect. . . . The Byzantine people protested against the decrees of Ferrara and Florence with passionate fanaticism, and while all the exhortations of the pro-unionists were ignored, the fiery sermons of Mark Eugenius (the metropolitan of Ephesus—a strong anti-unionist) found everywhere a most enthusiastic response.[133]

Ostrogorsky judges that the decree of union at Florence was even less effective than the agreement of Lyons II in 1274. In fact, the Russian branch of the Orthodox church viewed the conversion of the emperor and the patriarch of Constantinople as "an incredible act of treachery." The Russian metropolitan, who had been appointed by the patriarch of Constantinople and was a member of the pro-union party who participated in the agreement at Florence, was deposed on his return by the Grand Duke Basil II and imprisoned. "From now on Russia chose its Metropolitan itself and turned its back on apostate Byzantium, which had forfeited all claims to leadership in the Orthodox world by its betrayal of the true faith."[134]

Of particular interest to our study is the statement of papal primacy that concluded the decree of union with the Greek church, issued in July 1439:

> We also define that the holy apostolic see and the Roman pontiff holds the primacy over the whole world and the Roman pontiff is the successor of blessed Peter prince of the apostles, and that he is the true vicar of Christ,

the head of the whole Church and the father and teacher of all Christians, and to him was committed in blessed Peter the full power of tending, ruling and governing the whole Church, as is contained also in the acts of the ecumenical councils and in the sacred canons.[135]

This declaration can be compared with the definition of papal primacy at Vatican I (1870), to be discussed in Chapter 8.

The conciliar fathers issued the decree of union with the Armenians on November 22, 1439, setting forth, among other things, a good summary of late medieval sacramental theology. The envoys of the Armenian patriarch subscribed to the decree and promised to "faithfully obey the ordinances and commands of the Apostolic See."[136] The decrees of union with the Copts (February 2, 1442), the Syrians (November 30, 1444), the Maronites and the Chaldeans (August 7, 1445) seem to have concluded the business of the council. "We do not know when the council ended, but it is probable that the work of the council ceased in the same year, 1445."[137] In the estimate of most historians of the eastern churches, these decrees of union—although entered into by Pope Eugene with optimism—did not have much tangible effect.

The entire papacy of Eugene IV was clouded and more or less defined by the events at Basel. However, the deliberations and the decrees of union forged at Ferrara and Florence (1438-45) must have been viewed with great pride by Eugene in the closing years of his life. He did not live long enough to see how ineffective they really were. There were many problems he had to leave to others to address. For example, France had placed itself in a position of ambiguity vis-à-vis the papacy by, on the one hand, adopting the *Pragmatic Sanction* of Bourges in 1438 and, on the other, refusing to go along with Basel's condemnations of Pope Eugene in June 1439. The *Pragmatic Sanction*, which became the law for the church in France, adopted many of the reform decrees of Basel.[138] This enactment transformed into French national law by order of King Charles VII certain valuable reform ordinances of Basel relating to such matters as the prohibition of the papal reservation of benefices which deprived the rightful collators of their prerogatives, the rigid curtailment of the pastorally devastating practices of pluralism and absenteeism among benefice holders (including many foreigners), the drastic reduction of appeals to Rome, and the elimination of many of the excesses of papal taxation.[139] Germany also straddled the fence between pope and council to protect itself from incurring the wrath of either faction. Although certain decrees of Basel were adopted by the German Electors as the law of the land in the *Instrumentum acceptationis* of 1439, the so-called *Vienna Concordat* of 1448 proved quite favorable to the papacy, softening appreciably the demands of the *Instrumentum*.[140]

The death of Pope Eugene IV on February 23, 1447, after a long and rather painful reign of sixteen years, closed an epoch in papal and ecclesiastical history. Although the traditional view of Eugene's papacy has given him much credit for preserving Rome from the evils of conciliarism, another evaluation is emerging even from historians generally favorable to the papacy.

> While with Pastor and Gill, one may be happy to regard him as the papacy's savior from the dangers of "conciliarism," the failure of reform is also his responsibility, for it had become all too clear that without a council there could be no reform. From the viewpoint of Church history the decisive turning point from the Middle Ages to modern times occurs around the middle of the fifteenth century. Rome had prevented reform and in return soon received the Reformation.[141]

THE RENAISSANCE POPES—FROM NICHOLAS V (1447-55) TO INNOCENT VIII (1484-92)

On March 6, 1447 the cardinals, after they had submitted themselves to an election capitulation which was probably similar to the one used in 1431, selected Thomas Parentucelli, the cardinal archbishop of Bologna, as the new pontiff. Thomas, who called himself Nicholas V, was not a scholar of note, but truly loved scholarship and surrounded himself with a considerable number of academics. He encouraged and sponsored the humanists who were beginning to prefer Rome even to Florence.

> The humanist patronage of Pope Nicholas V (1447-55) began the transformation which was to turn Rome into a cosmopolitan center of art and learning, capable by the end of the century of rivalling and surpassing Florence. The Vatican library was founded; there were grandiose plans for rebuilding St. Peter's and parts of the city.[142]

Nicholas V could indeed be called the first of the humanist popes, although the title did not carry any negative connotations when applied to him that were justified later. He was the founder of the Vatican library, providing it with more than 1,000 Greek and Latin manuscripts. He also initiated ambitious programs of reconstruction in the city of Rome which had fallen into disrepair due to the many civil disturbances during the long reign of Eugene IV.

On May 29, 1453, Constantinople, the city dedicated by Constantine I as the New Rome in May 330, fell to the Ottoman Turks. This was the day that the Venetians called "the darkest day in the history of the world."[143] The fall of Constantinople alarmed the pope and filled a good many Europeans with fear and horror. Nicholas felt obliged to declare a holy war and mount a crusade against the Turks.

When Pope Nicholas V called for a holy war in September of 1453, his appeal was answered by forthright declarations of support. . . . But it was merely a gesture: no nation offered tangible support, and the proposed crusade collapsed.[144]

Countries like France, England, Spain, and Germany were becoming less and less conscious of their obligations as part of "Christendom" and more concerned about their own national growth and well-being. What affected Christendom was not nearly as important to them as what affected their own national interest. The pope too was beginning to narrow his own vision. The peace of Lodi, in April 1454, aimed at securing the peace of Italy within the territorial limits which prevailed among the five Italian powers at that time. Rather than confronting the urgent issues of church reform, the papacy, beginning with Nicholas V, was more concerned with the reestablishment of its monarchical form of government and with the local provincial politics of the Italian peninsula.[145]

Pope Nicholas died on March 24, 1455, and was followed by a seventy-seven-year-old Catalan cardinal, Alfonso Borgia, who, as Callistus III (1455-8), brought good intentions to the office, but little else. Callistus reinstated the practice of nepotism on a grand scale, making two of his nephews cardinals, including the infamous Rodrigo Borgia (later to become Alexander VI). It was this family, the Borgias, as much as any other that gave the Renaissance papacy its reputation as the most unworthy succession of pontiffs since the *saeculum obscurum*, the tenth century.

Callistus' successor, Pius II (1458-64), was a gifted theologian and humanist who had taken part in the Council of Basel. He was one of those who remained behind at Basel after the "pars sanior" had joined forces with Pope Eugene IV in 1438 at Ferrara. Aeneas Silvius Piccolomini was finally reconciled with Pope Eugene in 1445 and was made a cardinal by Callistus in 1456. In the election capitulation preceding his election as pope, he had agreed, like the others, that if he were chosen, he would wage a crusade against the Turks, reform the curia, and assure for the cardinals a significant share in the decision-making processes of the pontifical court. Pius was unsuccessful in mounting a crusade against the advancing Turks in 1459 and again in 1463. As in the case of his predecessor, Nicholas V, there was no meaningful response from the rulers of Europe. He did succeed, however, in persuading King Louis XI of France (1461-83) to annul the *Pragmatic Sanction* of Bourges in 1461.[146] One of the grand ironies of his pontificate was his publication of the bull, *Execrabilis*, in January 1460. After spending a good share of his life as a devoted conciliarist, and indeed of the more radical variety, he issued the following prohibition:

We enjoin that nobody dares under whatever pretext to make such an appeal [i.e., to a general council] from any of our ordinances, sentences or

commands and from those of our successors ... If anyone ... shall
contravene this ..., he shall "ipso facto" incur the sentence of anathema,
from which he cannot be absolved except by the Roman Pontiff and at the
point of death.[147]

This injunction apparently had little effect because the practice of appealing
from a papal decision to a general council was employed with some regularity
throughout the rest of the fifteenth century. Pius planned to reform the practices of the curia, but never got to put his program into effect. His papacy
ended at Ancona, where he died in August 1464.

Pius was followed by Paul II (1464-71), Peter Barbo, the cardinal of Venice,
who renounced his sworn commitment to the pre-election capitulation almost
immediately after he was selected pope. Barbo was a man of modest talents
who applied force and intimidation to get his way, thus incurring the enmity of
those, both princes and prelates, with whom he dealt.[148] Paul II died unexpectedly in July 1471 at the age of fifty-three and was followed by an illustrious
gentleman, Francis della Rovere, a Franciscan, who also proceeded to ignore
the pre-election capitulation promises he had made to his fellow cardinals.
Della Rovere, Sixtus IV (1471-84), was a Renaissance man *par excellence*. He
built new streets and avenues in Rome, a new bridge across the Tiber (the
Ponte Sisto), new churches, and his crown jewel, the Sistine Chapel. Sixtus'
contributions to the development of the Vatican library almost equaled those
of Nicholas V, making it "the greatest and best organized center of all available
manuscript material."[149]

Unfortunately, however, Pope Sixtus IV was an egregious nepotist who made
six of his nephews cardinals and bestowed great riches on untold numbers of
his relatives. Karl A. Fink relates that the majority of the thirty-four cardinals
whom he created were "hardly worthy men" who aggravated further the "secular-
ization of the papacy and of the Sacred College."[150] Fink also notes that Sixtus
"bears a heavy responsibility for the history of Christianity and of the Church."[151]
He needed funds to pay for his lavish court, the scores of artists and humanists,
all his relatives, the many building projects, and the mercenaries employed for
his military expeditions. To meet these ever increasing demands, he created an
incalculable number of new curial posts which were sold to those who coveted
the honors and could pay an exorbitant price for them. He also resorted to the
frequent granting of indulgences to enrich the papal treasury. Pope Sixtus IV
does indeed bear a heavy responsibility for the precipitous decline of the papacy after 1450. There seemed to be no stopping the devaluation of the figure
of the pope into that of just another Italian prince who not only considered
himself as such, but who was treated as such by his contemporaries.[152]

Innocent VIII (1484-92) was elected to follow Sixtus as a result of a deadlock in the conclave between the forces of Rodrigo Borgia, the nephew of

Calixtus III, and those of Cardinal Julian della Rovere, a nephew of Sixtus IV. John Baptist Cibo, a rather indecisive Genoese, was the compromise candidate sponsored by Julian della Rovere. This election "can scarcely be regarded as other than transparent bribery and simony."[153] Julian della Rovere was clearly the power behind the throne throughout Innocent's pontificate which had no focus, other than the spending of vast sums of money on the luxurious papal court and on wars with Naples and Florence. Not even the multiplication of marketable papal offices and similar practices were able to supply sufficient funding for Innocent's ventures.[154]

ALEXANDER VI (1492-1503)

The nadir of papal corruption and abuse, however, was reached with Alexander VI, who was also elected in a divided conclave—the Borgia faction versus the della Rovere faction. The depths to which the College of Cardinals had sunk in the latter fifteenth century is graphically revealed in the selection of Rodrigo Borgia as pope. The fact that he had fathered at least six illegitimate children prior to 1492 did not seem to have been an obstacle to his election. Further, it is evident that simony was involved in this conclave as well because prior agreements regarding curial posts, benefices, and endowments in return for votes were concluded before the election. Rodrigo Borgia was the wealthiest Italian cardinal of his day, for he had maximized all the opportunities that came his way after he had been appointed cardinal and vice-chancellor, at the age of twenty-six, by his uncle in 1456. Two of his children, Caesar (b. 1475) and Lucretia (b. 1480), are the stuff out of which the wildest romance novels are concocted. Alexander VI provided well for his offspring, showering them with riches, positions, and protection. The debauchery and the scandals of his papal court provided ample material for the gifted Florentine Dominican preacher, Jerome Savonarola. It was Savonarola's political power in Florence that especially provoked the wrath of the pope inasmuch as the noted monk sided with France against the Italian League. (France at that time was urging a general council to replace Alexander.) The pope eventually had Savonarola condemned as a heretic by an ecclesiastical tribunal and executed in May 1498. The German church historian, Joseph Lortz, says, "He [Savonarola] can be viewed as the expression of the incarnation of the best attempts at reform in the fifteenth century."[155] In August 1503, Alexander died unexpectedly, probably of the Roman fever, but possibly the result of a successful assassination venture that may well have been intended for someone else. It is indeed difficult for us at this distance to conceive of Rodrigo Borgia as occupying the chair of Peter. How could the Renaissance papacy have descended to such depths?[156]

JULIUS II (1503-13) AND LEO X (1513-21)

After the death of Pope Alexander, the cardinals—whose numbers almost doubled during his reign—demanded a council within two years as part of their election capitulation. Although the previous capitulations since 1484 had called for a general reform council at some undetermined future date, the arrangement in 1503 set out a more precise time line. "A contrary tendency made its appearance after the pontificate of Alexander VI. Their experiences during the Borgia pope's reign convinced the cardinals of the necessity of the early convocation of a council."[157]

In spite of the fact that they were threatened by the prospect of deep curial reform imposed on them from the outside, even cardinals, many of whom were "less than worthy men," felt the need for a general ecclesiastical reform which, by rather broad consensus in the fifteenth century, could only come from an ecumenical council. Pope Pius III (1503) was elected out of that conclave and indicated a genuine desire to promote reform. Pius III, a nephew of Pius II, died after only twenty-six days in office. The election of Julian della Rovere, which took place on November 1, 1503, was undoubtedly another simonaical exercise, like those preceding the selection of Innocent VIII and Alexander VI. Julius II was much more a warrior than a pope. His principal aim was to promote the independence of Italy—still ruled by the five principates—which was threatened by foreign domination, especially by France. In the process, he alienated Louis XII of France (1498-1515) in 1511, and Louis responded by having his cardinals summon a council at Pisa in the summer of 1511 which would have as its principal objective the deposing of Julius. The German emperor agreed with the idea but sent no delegation to Pisa. Although up to this point the pope had shown no interest whatsoever in the notion, he quickly summoned his own council to meet at the Lateran in the spring of 1512. This synod, called Lateran V, held five sessions under Julius II and seven under his successor, Leo X (1513-21). As far as Julius was concerned, the council had served its purpose when the synod of Pisa dissolved shortly after the opening of Lateran V in May 1512.[158]

THE NEED FOR COUNCILS

Before reviewing the rather minimal results of the Fifth Lateran Council, it would be valuable to trace briefly the theological developments since the Council of Basel-Ferrara-Florence regarding the relationship between the power of the pope and that of the council. One should not be led to believe that after 1450 or so the conciliar theory had disappeared entirely. Although that might be true of the radical variety which prevailed at Basel (except perhaps for France), this was in no way the case concerning the moderate conciliar position. Even the cardinals, who had much to lose from a reform council, expressed the desire for a general synod every time they entered a conclave to elect a new pontiff after 1450. At the heart of this lay the almost universal conviction that the renewal of the Church, in head and members, could not happen except through an ecumenical council. This mentality was quite close to the theological position of the moderate conciliarists, who still held to the decree, *Frequens*. Most theologians and canonists of that period felt that the vitality and good order of the Church called for universal synods in times of great need. Although they might not hold for their convocation every ten years, councils were seen as a necessary, indispensable counterpoint to papal sovereignty. Such fifteenth-century scholars as Panormitanus (d. 1445), the cardinal archbishop of Palermo, took the following stand regarding the right of appeal from the pope to a council:

> In his opinion, appeal from the pope to the council is lawful not only when the pontiff falls into heresy, but also when he gives scandal, or by mandate or juridical sentence alters the status of the universal Church and thereby endangers her good order.[159]

The eminent historian Hubert Jedin continues to outline Panormitanus' position:

> The latter case was the most elastic of all, for it meant that a state of emergency, which only could be remedied by a council, might be brought about not only by a *crimen* of the pope, or by schism in the Church, but by grave danger to the good order of the Church in consequence of some measure taken by her supreme head.[160]

Even Cardinal Torquemada (d. 1468), whose *Summa de Ecclesia* (1448-49) was an early precursor of nineteenth-century manual theology which exalted the sovereign power and—in many cases—the "undivided sovereignty" of the pope, said regarding emergency situations: "If the Christian faith or the welfare of the whole Church is in danger, and the pope obstinately refuses to convene a council, he renders himself suspect of heresy."[161] This condition would automatically create the need to convoke a council, and it is the cardinals whose right it is to proceed with the convocation.[162]

The popes after 1450, however, more often than not opposed the idea of a council. Pius II, Sixtus IV, Alexander VI, and Julius II prohibited appeals to general synods because they feared a curtailment of their authority and a diminution of their prerogatives. They saw themselves as absolute monarchs who should not have to submit to an ecumenical convocation because they were convinced that they were the only ones who should and could manage and correct the Church's course when such changes were needed. The history of the 100 years from Florence to Trent is a tragic reflection of how wrong those Renaissance popes were, and how blind they were to the corruption and abuses that were festering around them which helped trigger the Reformation and the division of Christendom in the West. The perennial risk of undivided sovereignty—wherever and whenever it appears in human institutions—was succinctly portrayed by Lord Acton in his letter to Bishop Mandell Creighton in 1887: "Power tends to corrupt; absolute power corrupts absolutely."[163] It is no matter whether one speaks of absolute power in the civil sphere or in the Church. History has abundantly demonstrated the applicability of Acton's words within the ecclesiastical domain. In the judgment of Brian Tierney, the moderate conciliarists of the fifteenth century

> did not deny that, in some sense, sovereignty (*plenitudo potestatis*) resided in the pope. . . . But they also insisted that sovereignty inhered in some other sense in the universal Church and in a general council representing it. Thus, the whole conciliar theory as it was developed by its principal exponents was based on an acceptance of the idea of "divided sovereignty."[164]

LATERAN V (1512-17)

The Fifth Lateran Council, according to Giuseppi Alberigo, was never very well attended by the bishops and prelates outside of Italy. Actually, this absence of full representation has occasioned disputes "about whether the council was ecumenical."[165] The first five sessions (May 1512 to February 1513), which were presided over by Pope Julius, concentrated on the actions of the Pisan council and the revoking of the *Pragmatic Sanction* which limited papal authority in France. Pope Leo X (1513-21) directed the proceedings in the remaining seven sessions. Session VIII (December 1513) featured a dogmatic declaration of the immortality of the human soul. Session IX (May 1514) dealt with the reform of the curia and the College of Cardinals: "The decisions on the reform of the curia produced almost no effect because of the timidity and the inadequacy of the recommendations, especially since the papacy showed slight inclination to carry the matter through."[166]

As an instance of this timidity, here is the advice given to the cardinals in the bull on the reform of the curia relating to the issue of nepotism:

> It is entirely unfitting to pass over persons related to them by blood or by marriage, especially if they are deserving and need help. To come to their assistance is just and praiseworthy. But, we do not consider that it is appropriate to heap on them a great number of benefices or Church

revenues, with the result that an uncontrolled generosity may bring wrong to others and may cause scandal.[167]

Sessions X, XI, and XII dealt with other matters of reform which, in the light of the crises of the day, seem now to be rather irrelevant and secondary. Lateran V was very closely and tightly managed by Popes Julius II and Leo X, as well by the Roman curia. Whether it was a truly representative ecumenical council remains a disputed question. However, one issue beyond dispute is that Lateran V did not honestly and courageously confront the crying needs of the Church for reform in head and members. The rapidly rising floods of the Protestant Reformation were about to crash through the dangerously weakened dikes, and the Church would never be the same again.

SUMMARY

The humiliation of Boniface VIII at Anagni by the forces of Philip IV of France in 1303 was clearly one of the darkest moments in the history of the popes in the Middle Ages. Boniface's claims regarding his spiritual and temporal power over kings and princes were no more sweeping than those made by several of his predecessors in the thirteenth century, but Philip IV was not about to submit to *Unam sanctam*. With Pope Clement V, the papal sojourn at Avignon began in 1309 and lasted for nearly seventy years. The Avignon papacy, with its luxurious life style and exploding bureaucracy, multiplied almost beyond counting the financial demands placed on the various dioceses, chapters, parishes, monasteries, and religious houses all over western Christendom. Papal reservations of benefices were expanded to the point where almost every major office and a great many minor offices throughout the entire western Church were now conferred by the pope, giving him hitherto unheard of opportunities for levying taxes and fees on the officeholders. This escalated the general unrest and notably increased the level of frustration everywhere.

Gregory XI ended the Avignon papacy, returning to Rome in 1377. However, within six months after his death in 1378, there were two popes—one in Rome and the other in Avignon. This arrangement resulted in deep divisions in every nation, with some dioceses and religious institutions pledging their allegiance to Rome, while others were sworn to Avignon. To solve this pathetic situation, cardinals from both camps met at Pisa in 1409, creating a third papal line which only further exacerbated the state of things. It was the Council of Constance (1414-18)—a masterpiece of moderate conciliarism—that finally brought the scandalous and extremely corrosive Great Western Schism to an end. Popes Martin V (1417-31) and Eugene IV (1431-47) managed to thwart the moderate conciliarists and returned the papacy to its monarchical moorings. The last half of the fifteenth century witnessed the rise of the Renaissance popes, who proceeded to shrink the office down to the size and shape of a regional Italian duchy, whose lord and ruler manifested less and less interest in the wider concerns of the Christian world. The stage was now set for the cataclysmic Protestant Revolt.

CHAPTER 7

The Evolution of Papal Absolutism

1523 to 1869

Francesco Guicciardini's portrait of Leo X, written in the 1530s, is a classical reflection of the Renaissance papacy:

> Not only was he profligate with money, but with all those graces which are in the power of a pope: which he conceded with so little restraint that he caused the spiritual authority to become defiled, upset the style of the court, and by spending too much, put himself in a position where he was always looking for money by extraordinary means. . . . The same Leo was most devoted to music, to jests and to buffoons; in suchlike amusements he immersed his soul and spent most of his time that otherwise would have been devoted to great enterprises and ends, for which he had a most capable intellect.[1]

Leo was fearful of the thoroughgoing reform in head and members called for by many in Europe. He himself ruled the Papal States and Florence, while he made every effort to secure Parma, Piacenza, Modena, and Reggio for his brother. Leo's nepotism was scandalous beyond all measure. His lavish life style and luxurious court were the talk of the continent. The number of vendible offices in the curia multiplied during his reign, and even the office of cardinal could be purchased for the right price. Simony was rampant in Rome throughout his pontificate.

Elsewhere, there was great dissatisfaction and unrest in the Church, especially in Germany. King Ferdinand of Spain (d. 1516) was advocating that a general council be held every ten to fifteen years. Pope Leo must have thought that the turmoil beyond the Alps and the cries for reform would eventually abate as they had many times before. In the first year of his pontificate, two young Camaldolese monks presented him with an elaborate study which took the Renaissance popes to task for their heavy involvement in politics and for the needless expansion of the Roman bureaucracy. They advocated the holding of diocesan and provincial councils on a regular basis and the calling of an ecumenical council every five years. Along with countless others at that time, they viewed the general council as the indispensable agent for curing the grave ills of the Church. Pope Leo was simply unwilling to take the necessary steps to initiate reform. He felt that a strong representation of the French, the Spanish, and the Germans at Lateran V would force changes in the practices of the Roman curia which would overturn the status quo to which he and the cardinals were wedded. As a result, Lateran V turned out to be a nonevent which scholars such as Karl August Fink and Giuseppe Alberigo fail to recognize fully as an ecumenical council due to its inadequate representation.[2]

Leo's need for money led him to the most bizarre extremes. He created hundreds of needless curial posts which he then sold off to the highest bidders. In 1515, the pope cut a deal with young Albert of Brandenburg—who already held two bishoprics and had recently been elected archbishop of Mainz—to allow him to hold all three German sees for the fee of 25,000 gold florins. The young Hohenzollern borrowed the money from the Fugger bankers to consummate the arrangement. To repay the loan, Rome allowed him exclusive rights in the territories of Mainz and Brandenburg to publish Leo's new indulgence which was to provide funds for the rebuilding of St. Peter's in Rome. The pope and the curia would get about one-half of the proceeds of the sale of the indulgences, while the other half would go to Albert to allow him to repay the debt to the Fuggers. It was the infamous Dominican, John Tetzel, who led the charge in the publication of the indulgence for Albert, and it was Tetzel's scandalous preaching that urged Martin Luther to speak publicly against this notorious abuse in the spring of 1517.[3] That this tragic transaction between Albert of Brandenburg and Pope Leo's curia was an act of high simony there can be little doubt. Leo's extravagances left the curia nearly bankrupt when he rather suddenly died of malaria in December 1521, while the church in Germany was on the brink of schism.

The thirty-nine cardinals who met in conclave to choose a successor to the Medici pope were deeply divided, but to the surprise of many, they elected Cardinal Hadrian of Utrecht, the bishop of Tortosa, Spain, although he was not a participant at the conclave. He was, however, very well connected to the house of Hapsburg inasmuch as he had been young Charles V's tutor and was regent for the youthful emperor from 1516 to 1517. Hadrian was a good man who must have constituted a considerable threat to the Roman curial establishment which considered him something of a barbarian. The Dutchman was a scholar of some repute, having taught theology at Louvain for a number of years. He had no time for the lavish indulgences of the papal court, reduced the excessive expenditures, and cut back on the number of curial officials, thereby incurring the wrath of those who preferred the opulent style of Julian and Leo. Although Pope Hadrian VI (1522-23) seriously underestimated the gravity of the situation brewing in Germany under Luther's leadership, he correctly diagnosed the deplorable situation that had been choking the effectiveness and the credibility of the Holy See for generations. In an instruction which he gave to his emissary to be delivered at the Diet of Nuremberg (1522-23), Hadrian opened his heart:

> You will say (publicly before the entire Christian world of the time) that we freely confess: God permits this persecution of His Church on account of the sins of men, and especially of prelates and the clergy. . . . Holy Scripture declares aloud that the sins of the people are the consequences of the sins of the priesthood. . . . We know all too well that for many years things deserving of abhorrence have taken place around this Holy See. Sacred things have been misused, the commandments transgressed; in everything there has been a turn for the worse. Thus it is not surprising that a malady has spread from the head to the members, from the popes to the hierarchy. We all, prelates and clergy, have gone astray from the right path, and for long there has been none that has done good. . . . To God, therefore, we must give all glory and humble ourselves before Him.[4]

It was agreed at Nuremberg that the reform of the Roman curia should be undertaken and a general council should soon take place on German soil in order to address these grievous divisions. This was not the pope's only crisis, however, for the Turks were threatening again in eastern Europe and thus he felt compelled to raise funds through the imposition of new taxes and levies, although these measures were compromising his deeply held principles of reform. Hadrian VI died after thirteen months in office, hardly able even to begin the work which he saw had to be accomplished to save the Church from further disaster. There is a touching epitaph on Hadrian's tomb in the church of Santa Maria dell' Anima, just off the Piazza Navona in Rome, which reads: "Unfortunately, even for the best man, much depends on the age in which he lives."[5]

CLEMENT VII (1523-34)

The conclave following the death of Pope Hadrian finally reached a decision after two long months, electing Cardinal Giulio de Medici, an illegitimate son of one of the de Medicis, who was raised by his uncle, Lorenzo the Magnificent. At the time of his election, Clement VII held the post of Roman vice-chancellor, a position which had been bestowed on him by his cousin, Leo X. Although Clement's life style was somewhat more appropriate than Leo's, he was weak and indecisive as a leader and could not be trusted by either France or the Empire because he was forever changing allegiances. Charles V urged him a number of times to call a general council to discuss the rapidly deteriorating situation in Germany precipitated by Luther and his followers, but Clement always found a way to delay a decision. According to the Reformation scholar, A.G. Dickens,

> Clement never bluntly refused a general council, yet he beheld the prospect with something approaching terror: he even feared that he would be deposed from his office on the grounds that he had been born out of wedlock, and that his election had been attended by simony.[6]

Clement's principal motive in seeking aid from France was his fear of being overcome by the Hapsburgs who frequently had control of both Naples and Milan. In 1526 the pope joined the League of Cognac with France, Venice, and Florence against Charles V, but discovered that he was left to stand alone against the emperor. Angered at the pope's vacillating allegiance, some 20,000 of Charles' troops brutally sacked Rome in May 1527. This event—the famous *Sacco di Roma*—was viewed by many as a divine punishment for the sins and scandals of the Renaissance papacy. Clement finally made his peace with Charles V in June 1529 when he was certain that the emperor would not insist on the convocation of a general council. The pope then crowned him emperor at Bologna in February 1530, the last crowning of a Holy Roman Emperor by a pope. Another example of Clement VII's indecisiveness was the wavering stand he took regarding the annulment petition submitted to him by the English king, Henry VIII. Initially it seemed that he was siding with the king, but then Clement brought the action to Rome, and finally in 1533, he declared Henry's divorce from Catherine and his subsequent marriage to Anne Boleyn invalid. Erwin Iserloh summarizes the unfortunate pontificate of Clement VII:

> He died on 25 September 1534, called by von Ranke "probably the most calamity-ridden of all the popes who ever occupied the Roman See." It was especially mischievous that he took no decisive step toward the renewal of the Church, but rather refused the overdue council and felt that the unity of the Church could be assured by political means, by a subtle diplomacy.[7]

PAUL III (1534-49)

Alessandro Farnese, dean of the College of Cardinals, was elected after a short conclave on October 13, 1534. Pope Paul III represented a curious blend of the old and the new. Although he had been a cardinal since 1493 and had a mistress who bore him several illegitimate children, his life took something of a turn at the time of his ordination to the priesthood in 1519. After that he counted himself among the reform cardinals. As pontiff he awarded the red hat to such reformers as Reginald Pole, John Fisher, Gasparo Contarini, Gian

Pietro Carafa, and Giovanni Morone. It was men like Pole, Contarini, and Morone who, along with Paul III, spearheaded the developments resulting in the Council of Trent. In the summer of 1536, the pope established a commission to study church reform and placed it under the direction of Cardinal Contarini. The group submitted their study, the *Consilium de emendanda Ecclesia*, to the pope in March 1537. The document pulled no punches, blaming Rome for most of the troubles affecting the Church. The principal abuses noted were:

1. the poor training of the clergy
2. the bestowal of benefices largely for the convenience of the clergy, with little thought for care of souls
3. the accumulation of benefices with the care of souls and the neglect of the obligation of residence
4. the accumulation of benefices with the care of souls, even by curial cardinals
5. absenteeism on the part of officeholders
6. the excessive granting of dispensations which vitiate the common law
7. the destruction of the care of souls in dioceses by the relatively unrestricted activity of regulars
8. the sanctioning of countless cases of simony in the conferral of ecclesiastical offices[8]

The *Consilium* was truly a notable piece of work which anticipated many, indeed the principal, reform decrees of the Council of Trent. Paul made some effort to implement a few of the reforms in regard to absenteeism, e.g., by ordering the absentee bishops living in Rome back to their dioceses, but not much came of his efforts. The Roman establishment was not yet ready to surrender to reform, and the will of Pope Paul to impose the needed changes was ambivalent, as was his attitude toward cleaning up his own house. During his long reign he was a consistent nepotist, showing great generosity to his relatives, especially his illegitimate son, Pier Luigi, to whom he gave the dukedom of Parma. After Paul III, the Farneses were ranked among the more affluent of the Italian families. There was, however, a reforming side to Paul III. The quality of many of his appointees to the Sacred College did eventually turn the tide in Rome in favor of change.

THE RELIGIOUS REVOLT IN GERMANY

To embark on the story of the efforts to address the expanding crisis in northern Europe, we shall have to trace briefly the events that transpired in Germany after Martin Luther offered his ninety-five theses for debate on October 31, 1517. In the following summer, the Diet of Augsburg was convened by Emperor Maximilian I (1493-1519) to deal with, among other things, the religious disputes in Germany. Pope Leo X's delegates were Cardinals Lang and Cajetan. According to the distinguished Reformation scholar, Heiko Oberman, it was Cajetan's responsibility to work out some solution to the Luther dilemma without alienating the Saxon elector, Frederick the Wise, who was Luther's sovereign.[9] Since the aging Maximilian was nearing the end of his reign, a new emperor would have to be elected soon, and the pope did not want to alienate Frederick. Cajetan interrogated Luther at the end of the diet and came to the conclusion that the hitherto relatively unknown Augustinian monk was indeed a heretic and should be bound over and taken to Rome for trial in light of his views on justification, the priority of Sacred Scripture, indulgences, and other issues. Frederick, however, continued to uphold the monk's right to pronounce on these questions because, as a professor of Sacred Scripture, he was authorized to express his views regarding the interpretation of the biblical text.[10]

In June 1520 Pope Leo issued the bull *Exsurge Domine*, which outlined some forty statements in Luther's works that were identified as heretical. The monk was given sixty days to recant, but he remained silent. Hence, on January 3, 1521, Luther was formally excommunicated. Prince Frederick continued to protect Luther up to the time of the Edict of Worms, May 26, 1521, which placed the monk under an imperial ban. The new emperor, Charles V, who had been elected in June 1519, summoned Luther to appear before the Diet of Worms in March 1521. The monk was asked to identify his writings and then to repudiate what he had written.[11] Luther's oft quoted response was eventually heard around the world:

> Unless I am convinced by the testimony of the Holy Scriptures or by evident reason—for I can believe neither pope nor councils alone, as it is clear that they have erred repeatedly and have contradicted themselves— I consider myself convicted by the testimony of Holy Scripture, which is my basis; my conscience is captive to the Word of God. Thus I cannot and will not recant, because acting against one's conscience is neither safe nor sound. God help me. Amen.[12]

Charles V's imperial ban was issued May 26, 1521:

> We enjoin you all "not to take the aforementioned Martin Luther into your houses, not to receive him at court, to give him neither food nor drink, not to hide him, to afford him no help, following, support or encouragement, either clandestinely or publicly, through words or works. Where you can get him, seize him and overpower him, you should capture him and send him to us under tightest security."[13]

Some weeks before, Luther had been returned under protective security to Wittenberg and hidden in the Wartburg castle where he remained until March 1522.[14] The leadership of the reform movement at Wittenberg was assumed by Andreas Karlstadt during Luther's absence, but it soon became clear that the Reformation was from the outset a protest with many divergent voices.[15] In the next couple of years, Luther wrote two important works in response to an attack by Erasmus of Rotterdam, who questioned Luther's dim view of free will. His responses (*On the Freedom of the Will*, 1524, and *The Bondage of the Will*, 1525) laid out his position on predestination and his consequent denial of free choice in human beings once and for all. According to the Reformation historian Bernhard Lohse, "Luther . . . never substantially changed the position he took in the controversy with Erasmus."[16]

Since the conclusion of the Diet of Worms, Charles V had been involved in a war with Francis I of France (1515-47), but as soon as that was resolved he returned to Germany to take up once again the religious dispute which he sorely wanted to resolve at the Diet of Augsburg in 1530. It was Philip Melanchthon (1497-1560) who was largely responsible for the drafting of the Augsburg Confession which was presented to Charles at the diet. (Luther was, of course, under the imperial ban and thus could not attend.) Charles found the confession unacceptable, and the Edict of Worms was reaffirmed at Augsburg. This, however, constituted a significant threat to the Protestant states in Germany and they reacted by establishing the Smalcald league.[17] The formation of the league resulted in the veritable division of Germany into two opposing camps. Indeed, wars and skirmishes did result between the two factions. The French were pleased to see Germany divided and helped out the Smalcald league whenever they could against the emperor.[18] (The final resolution of this long conflict was not achieved until the Peace of Augsburg in 1555.)

Pope Paul III attempted to convoke a general council at Mantua in May 1537, and then at Vicenza in May 1538, but both efforts failed because the secular princes were not ready. Although Charles had urged Paul to call a council earlier, he began to feel that his policy of conversations with the Protestants in Germany had a greater chance of success in bringing the sides together. There were colloquies between Catholics and Lutherans at Hagenau, Worms, and Ratisbon in 1540-41 over such issues as original sin, justification, the role of Sacred Scripture, Mass, and the Eucharist. By the end of May 1541, it was obvious that the conversations had collapsed.[19] Even the argument on justification drafted at Worms was rejected by Luther and by the Roman curia as well. Cardinal Contarini, who had worked so hard to bring about a reconciliation between the parties, returned to Rome and found himself accused by Carafa and others of compromising with the enemy. Gasparo Contarini, the pope's legate at a number of these conversations, died under a cloud of controversy within the year. It was after these German colloquies that

Pope Paul III established the Roman Inquisition, which he put under the control of six cardinals. Gian Pietro Carafa eventually assumed the leadership and could be called the spiritual father of this new Roman dicastery.[20]

THE COUNCIL OF TRENT BEGINS (1545-47)

Although the emperor Charles V still preferred to negotiate directly with the Protestant leaders, and Francis I was wary of cooperating in any way with Charles (or even with the pope for that matter), Paul did manage to convoke a general council at Trent, a German city, for March 1545. Delays, however, postponed the first session until December 13. Thirty-four delegates gathered in the cathedral of St. Vigilius, under the papally appointed presidents, Cardinals Reginald Pole, Giovanni del Monte, and Marcello Cervini.[21] Some forty or fifty theologians were also in attendance. They were not voting participants as they had been at Basel, but only consultants. At the second session on January 7, 1546, a number of the bishops expressed concern as to whether or not such a small and unrepresentative gathering of delegates was capable of deliberating and settling these issues which involved the well-being of the whole Church. Hence some wanted to delay the discussions until greater numbers of fathers had arrived. It was at this second session that the decision was made to treat dogmatic questions and disciplinary matters more or less simultaneously, with first consideration being given to dogma at the behest of the pope.[22] Attendance began to increase at the third session with forty-one delegates present, and at the fourth session (April 8, 1546) decrees were issued; i.e., the statement that divine revelation has come down to us "in written books and in unwritten traditions which were received by the apostles from the mouth of Christ Himself, or else have come down to us, handed on as it were from the apostles themselves at the inspiration of the Holy Spirit."[23] The second promulgation established that the Latin Vulgate edition of the Bible "is to be regarded as authentic,"[24] that is, it was the official text to be used in public readings and sermons, but the council added that this text should be thoroughly revised. The council also placed restrictions on and established penalties against printers and publishers of biblical texts who proceeded without approval of the local ordinary.

Session five (June 17, 1546) directed its attention to the nature of original sin, correcting Luther's view on concupiscence.

> This concupiscence the Apostle [i.e., Paul] sometimes calls sin, but the holy council declares that the Catholic Church has never understood it to be called sin in the sense of being truly and properly such in those who have been regenerated, but in the sense that it is the result of sin and inclines to sin.[25]

The second decree of session five laid out seventeen disciplinary enactments which made provision for preaching and instruction to be carried out regularly in every diocese, parish, monastery, convent, and school. Provision was also made for the formation and licensing of the preachers and teachers, which functions were to be performed under the care of the local bishop. The fathers realized at the outset that the neglect of these duties had led to many of the maladies afflicting the sixteenth-century Church.

Due to a brief resumption of the Smalcald War in the summer of 1546, conciliar deliberations were interrupted, and hence the decrees of the sixth session were not ready for voting and promulgation until January 1547. One of the doctrinal masterpieces of Trent was the *Decree on Justification* which was issued on January 13, 1547. Among the seventeen chapters of the document, chapter seven took up the question of the internal effects of justification. Martin Luther taught that through Adam's fall, "our person, nature and entire being are corrupted. . . . Man's acts reveal that his entire nature is impure, that is, there is nothing in us except sin."[26] For Luther, justification was really "God's act of crediting, imputing or recognizing [the sinner] as righteous, that is . . . the act through which God grants a man value in relationship to Him. . . . The righteousness of Christ is imputed to the sinner."[27] Chapter seven affirmed the Catholic position that the actual justification of the sinner "consists not only in the forgiveness of sins but also in the sanctification and renewal of the inward being by a willing acceptance of the grace and gifts whereby someone from being unjust becomes just."[28]

The second decree of session six was disciplinary legislation dealing with the obligation of residence for bishops and other clergy. The Spanish delegates urged a clarification on the matter of episcopal residence. Was the requirement to reside in one's see an obligation flowing from divine law or human law?[29] If it was a divine law requirement, the pope would have no right to dispense from it, and hence all the rampant pluralism concerning the holding of dioceses by cardinals and bishops in the Roman curia would be indefensible because not even the pope can dispense from divine law. This issue would persist for years and would eventually be left for the pope to address. The fathers did attest to the fact that ecclesiastical discipline in the area of residence had to a considerable extent collapsed. This was not going to be easy to remedy because not only Rome but the secular princes were deeply involved in the practice of supporting their officials at court with the revenues from benefices which had been bestowed on perennial absentees, with the pastoral care falling to substitutes who were paid only a fraction of the proceeds of the benefices. Financial penalties were levied by the council against those bishops who were absent from their dioceses for more than six consecutive months in a year, and the ordinaries were obliged to enforce the obligation of residence on their clergy.[30]

In the seventh session (March 3, 1547) work was completed on the sacraments in general, as well as on a more detailed treatment of baptism and confirmation. This sacramental doctrine was articulated with almost juridical brevity and was largely directed against Luther and his followers. The seven sacraments were declared as having been directly instituted by Christ, although the biblical bases of this assertion were not identified. The second decree, which addressed disciplinary issues, attacked the abuses of pluralism on the part of bishops, requiring that they choose one see and abandon the other (or others) within a fixed period of time. If they failed to do so, all but the most recently conferred see would be declared automatically vacant.[31] Local ordinaries were charged with the responsibility of requiring those holding several incompatible benefices in their dioceses to present their dispensations for inspection, and it was the ordinary's responsibility to provide competent vicars for the care of souls and adequate compensation for them.[32] The bishops were directed to visit every parish—even those of exempt religious—each year to inquire into the way in which pastoral care was administered and into the state of repair of the church and its buildings.[33] The reform decree also laid on local ordinaries the obligation to examine and test all clerics before ordination as to their knowledge and suitability, and to ordain them personally.[34]

On March 11, 1547 (session eight), the council fathers voted to move the deliberations to Bologna, allegedly because of the threat of typhus at Trent.[35] The imperial delegates remained at Trent, however, but as a matter of fact the questions on the other five sacraments and the additional disciplinary topics could not be adequately resolved because of the small number of delegates at Bologna. Session nine (April 21, 1547) simply postponed deliberations until June because of the scarcity of delegates, while session ten (June 2, 1547) resulted in another postponement for the same reason. Although some of the delegates and theologians continued their discussions on the Eucharist, penance, and the Mass at Bologna, Charles V was insisting that the council reassemble at Trent. In January 1548 he registered a formal complaint with Paul III regarding the transfer to Bologna. According to Hubert Jedin: "Imperial circles were already weighing the continuation of the council by means of the minority that remained at Trent."[36] To ward off any such possibility the pope suspended the discussions at Bologna as of February 1548, thus ending the first period of the Council of Trent.

Pope Paul III died at the age of eighty-one in November 1549. He was truly a Renaissance prelate and a pope who brought the Farnese family into lasting prominence. Although his nepotism followed him to the end of his long life, there was something about him which clearly distinguished him from the likes of Leo X and Clement VII. In spite of his ambiguities, Paul was at heart something of a revolutionary who created the cardinals who would initiate the painful task of church reform. Perhaps the most significant thing that one could say about Alessandro Farnese is that he convoked and, through his presidential delegates, guided the Council of Trent to a successful beginning.

THE SECOND PERIOD OF TRENT (1551-52)

The conclave after the death of Paul III was a slow and circuitous affair involving a bitter division between the French and the imperial parties. After ten weeks, a compromise was struck, and Giovanni del Monte, one of the presidents of the first period of Trent, was elected. Charles had not wanted him because he considered del Monte responsible for the transfer of the council to Bologna. Julius III (1550-55), sensitive to the objections of the emperor to his election, decided that the council should be resumed, and that it should be reassembled at Trent. After the arrival of the German prelates in September 1551, the council resumed its work on October 11. The complement of delegates from Germany and Switzerland had increased by thirteen bishops, thus reducing the dominance of the Italian contingent which had generally controlled the first ten sessions of the council. The French, however, were still not willing to participate. In the decree on the Eucharist issued at session thirteen, chapter one defined that,

> after the consecration of the bread and the wine, our Lord Jesus Christ, true God and true man, is truly, really and substantially contained in the propitious sacrament of the Holy Eucharist under the appearance of those things which are perceptible to the senses.[37]

Later in chapter four, the fathers became more specific on the nature of the change:

> By the consecration of the bread and wine, there takes place the change of the whole substance of the bread into the substance of the body of Christ our Lord, and of the whole substance of the wine into the substance of His blood. And the Catholic Church has suitably and properly called this change transubstantiation.[38]

This teaching was to enunciate the Catholic position regarding the Eucharist against the Reformers such as Luther and Zwingli who held to either a spiritual as opposed to a real presence (Zwingli) or to a co-presence of Christ in the untransformed bread and wine (Luther). The reform decree of session thirteen also outlined the expanded powers of local ordinaries in the handling of various kinds of criminal cases.

In session fourteen on November 25, 1551, the doctrine of the sacraments of penance and extreme unction were outlined in order to correct the Reformers, particularly Luther, who held that there were strictly speaking only two sacraments: baptism and the Lord's Supper.[39] The council defined that there are three actions that constitute the matter of the sacrament of penance: contrition, confession, and satisfaction, and that the action of the priestly minister is a truly judicial act, "declaring to the penitent that his sins are forgiven."[40] The corresponding reform decree laid out in some detail the powers of the local bishop over the clergy of his diocese. Many of the immunities and privileges which formerly protected the clergy, and especially the religious clergy, were curtailed so that the local ordinary could more effectively govern his people. Also, the rights of patrons of certain churches were to be subjected to the jurisdiction of the local bishop so that in matters such as the selection of officeholders, the bishop's authority and judgment would prevail.

After a rather unproductive several months, the council was suspended on April 28, 1552, due to the hostilities between Maurice of Saxony, who was aided by the French, and Charles V. The prelates at Trent became frightened as the battle moved into southern Austria, forcing the emperor to flee from Innsbruck, and hence they decided to suspend conciliar deliberations for a period of two years. As a matter of fact, the intermission lasted almost ten years, until January 1562.

Pope Julius III, although a reformer of sorts, was in many ways similar to his predecessor in that he freely bestowed the wealth of the Church on his relatives and thoroughly enjoyed the pleasures of the Roman court throughout his life. Up to this point none of the enactments of Trent had been officially promulgated by the pope. Although many bishops in Spain and Portugal had begun to implement the reforms enacted so far, Julius never made any overtures in that direction. As far as reforms in Rome were concerned, other than the feverish activity of the Roman Inquisition (under Cardinal Carafa) to eradicate heresy, very little had changed. The Datary was still grinding out dispensations and privileges, while the pluralism of the curial officials went on almost uncontested. It is true that Julius did appoint a reform committee to initiate a revision of the Datary, but the progress was very slow. The flood of dispensations from the Datary was simply destroying ecclesiastical discipline. According to Leon Cristiani, one could say that the laws were simply occasions for the extremely lucrative relaxation of discipline through the awarding of dispensations.[41] After the death of Julius III in March 1555, the reform cardinals carried the day in the next conclave, electing Marcellus Cervini, one of the co-presidents at Trent in 1545. Cervini had every prospect of bringing his reform mentality with him into the papacy. Unfortunately, Marcellus II's pontificate lasted only twenty-two days. He whom Hubert Jedin called, "the first pope of the Catholic reform," never had an opportunity to make his contribution.[42]

PAUL IV (1555-59)

The reform block in the College of Cardinals selected another reform candidate, Gian Pietro Carafa, the Neapolitan who headed the Roman Inquisition. Paul IV, who was nearly eighty when elected, had been an aggressive reformer since 1524 when he founded the Theatine order with Gaetano di Thiene. Although a morally strict man, he was unspeakably harsh and even cruel to those who disagreed with him. Paul IV engaged in nepotism, leaning very heavily on an absolutely worthless nephew, Carlo Carafa, and several other relatives. His unwillingness to correct these tragic appointments in a timely fashion, as well as his persistent severity and cruelty, made him an object of derision and hatred at the time of his death. Had he not been elected pope, perhaps history would have viewed him in a rather different light. For Paul IV the resumption of the Council of Trent was always out of the question.[43] His triumphalistic view of papal supremacy was some two or three centuries out of date. It was Paul who created the Index of Forbidden Books in 1559, condemning the complete works of Erasmus and all translations of the Bible into the vernacular languages. In the first year of Paul IV's pontificate, the Peace of Augsburg brought to a close the bitter wars between the Protestant princes and the forces of the empire in Germany. After 1556 Charles placed the empire in the hands of his brother, Ferdinand I (1556-64). According to the provisions of the Augsburg agreement, Catholic territories were to remain Catholic and Lutheran territories were to remain Lutheran. The religion of the prince would determine the religion of the territory (*cujus regio, ejus et religio*). Subjects who could not live with this arrangement would simply have to move to another territory. The peace was to remain in force until a permanent and definitive settlement could be agreed to.[44] Eventually the Reformed or Calvinist churches were able to participate in the detente established in 1555, but this did not become official until the Peace of Westphalia in 1648. The Peace of Augsburg had a profound effect on the Hapsburg Empire, which thereafter became nothing more than "a mere federation of territorial states."[45] Charles lost his spirit after Augsburg, leaving the imperial crown to Ferdinand and the Spanish crown to his son, Philip II (1556-98).

THE THIRD PERIOD OF TRENT (1562-63)

Apparently the cardinals had had enough of the reforming popes after the death of Paul IV, for they selected, as the successor to Carafa, Gianangelo Medici from Milan in a conclave which lasted more than three months. Pius IV (1559-65) had never been a member of the reform wing of the College of Cardinals. He was a jurist of some distinction who had fathered three natural children in his younger days and, as pope, had no misgivings about providing financially for his relatives. One of the family, however, a nephew from Milan named Charles Borromeo, proved to be of great assistance to him especially during the third period of the Council of Trent. Pius intended to reopen the deliberations at Trent, but the manner in which this was to be achieved proved to be somewhat delicate. Philip II of Spain—now the most formidable power in Europe—wanted a continuation of the old council, while Emperor Ferdinand I and Charles IX of France opted for the summoning of a new council. The pope's bull of convocation of November 29, 1560, tried to please both factions but really did not satisfy either.[46] The theological winds in Europe had shifted since the Peace of Augsburg. Inasmuch as the curial people in Rome had all but given up hope of saving Germany at that point, attention was directed to what was occurring in France. In the summer and fall of 1561, there was a real fear that France was drifting into Calvinism. After the death of Francis II in 1560, the nation was ruled by young Charles IX (1560-74) under the regency of his mother, Catherine de Medici, a niece of the late Pope Clement VII (1523-34).

The third period of the Council of Trent opened on January 18, 1562, with 109 voting delegates in attendance—a more auspicious beginning than the inaugural gathering in December 1545.[47] The first two sessions in 1562 did not discuss issues of great import, but the meetings in May reopened the question of episcopal residence. Was the obligation of residence binding under divine law (and hence not under papal authority) or was it an ecclesiastical regulation over which the pontiff could exercise his jurisdiction? Because the council was hopelessly split over the issue, Pius IV did not choose to intervene directly but made it clear through his presidential legates that he was not pleased with the direction of the debate.[48] The issue was eventually remanded to the pope for his decision, but no decision was ever handed down. On July 16, 1562, the question of communion under both kinds was addressed, and the council defined that communion under one species was sufficient because Christ is received whole and entire under either species.[49] Both Emperor Ferdinand and the duke of Bavaria had asked that communion under both kinds be allowed. Leon Cristiani adds: "In fact, the concession was granted but it gave rise to so much inconvenience that those who availed themselves of it soon gave it up."[50]

The reform decree of July 16, 1562, confronted a number of critical issues. It was ordered that no money was to be collected by bishops for ordinations, and no one was to be ordained without a benefice. Ordinaries were permitted to establish new parishes as long as there were adequate revenues to support them, and bishops were able to combine and/or close parishes for good pastoral reasons.[51] The obligation of ordinaries to visit and inspect all places of worship once a year—even those run by religious orders—was reaffirmed.[52]

The sacrifice of the Mass was taken up for definition in September 1562. At the session on September 17, there were 183 delegates present to approve the decree on the Mass which was identified as an unbloody sacrifice where only the manner of offering is different from the sacrifice of Calvary.[53] Private Masses (where only the priest communicates) were not disapproved, nor was it deemed advantageous to celebrate Mass everywhere in the vernacular.[54] (Private Masses and liturgies in Latin were viewed as abuses by many of the Reformers.) The disciplinary decrees gave greater control to the local bishops regarding the finances of the cathedral and collegiate churches of their dioceses, along with greater jurisdiction over the chapter of canons. Furthermore, anyone diverting church revenues to private purposes would incur the penalty of excommunication which was not to be lifted until full restitution was made.[55]

The next session, set for November 12, 1562, was thrown off course due to the arrival of the French delegation of thirteen bishops, headed by the cardinal of Lorraine, Charles de Guise. The issue of the rights of bishops versus the prerogatives of the pope flared up again at the instigation of the French and the Spanish bishops, and almost broke up the council. A compromise was struck by the newly appointed president of the council, Cardinal Giovanni Morone, whereby the issue of papal primacy was not to be addressed by the council.[56] The November session was postponed until July 15, 1563, at which time the council's doctrine on the ministerial priesthood was articulated.[57] The priesthood of all the faithful alluded to in I Peter 2:9 was not denied, but it certainly was not affirmed, much less embellished by Trent.

The reform decrees of July 15, 1563, outlining in considerable detail the discipline of the clergy, were set forth in eighteen rather lengthy canons. The duty of residence for all clerics—cardinals, bishops, and pastors alike—having the responsibility for the care of souls was reaffirmed. The regulations regarding ordinations were clarified as to who was to ordain, the qualities of the ordinands, and the examinations that were to precede the ordinations. These obligations were placed on the shoulders of the local ordinary. Priests were not to be allowed to hear confessions until the bishop had examined them for competence, and no one was to be ordained without a definite church assignment.[58] Finally, there was new legislation regarding seminary training:

> Hence the holy council decrees that every cathedral, metropolitan and greater church is obliged to provide for, to educate in religion and to train in ecclesiastical studies a set number of boys, according to its resources and the size of the diocese: the boys are to be drawn from the city and diocese, or its province if the former do not provide sufficient, and educated in a college chosen for the purpose by the bishop near to those churches or in another convenient place.[59]

This college was referred to as "a perpetual seminary of the ministers of God."[60] Directives were given for curriculum and for the financial support of the institution, and should each diocese be unable to support a seminary due to a lack of resources, the provincial synod was to make adequate provision for all the dioceses in the province. Although it took decades, even centuries, for these ordinances to become effective throughout the Church, and in spite of the educational weaknesses that frustrated (and continue to frustrate) the system almost everywhere, this legislation was probably the most important disciplinary measure coming out of the Council of Trent. The two other reforms—the requirement of residence for all those with pastoral responsibility and the reaffirmation of the prohibition against pluralism—were also critical, but nothing was more vital to the restoration of the Church than the statutes providing for the seminary education of the clergy.

In the second last session of Trent on November 11, 1563, the sacramental nature of marriage and its indissolubility were defined. Two reform decrees followed. The first enacted a legal form for the celebration of marriage which was then to be promulgated from parish to parish throughout the Catholic world. This manner of promulgation led to countless difficulties which really were not resolved until the 1917 *Code of Canon Law.* The second reform decree largely covered ground which had been covered before in previous sessions, but the selection of candidates for the episcopate was outlined in some detail. The provincial synods were to select the more worthy candidates whose names were then to be submitted to the pope, "so that with full knowledge of the matter and information about the persons, he may himself make the best provision for the churches."[61] Provincial councils were mandated every three years, while diocesan synods were to take place every year. The remaining disciplinary canons of the second reform decree were aimed at strengthening the powers of the local bishop vis-à-vis his clergy, the religious, the lay patrons, and even the pontifical delegates should they interfere needlessly in his judicial procedures. Local ordinaries emerged from Trent as a much stronger cadre of pastoral leaders, although the role of the metropolitan was diminished. This reinforcement of the local bishop contributed significantly to the Catholic restoration which was initiated after Trent. The role of the papacy in church governance was left rather undefined by the decrees of Trent, but the local ordinaries had expanded jurisdiction and a new lease on life.

The final session of the council, session twenty-five, on December 3 and 4, 1563, issued brief dogmatic statements on the existence of purgatory and on the merits of appealing to the intercession of saints. There followed a disciplinary decree on religious and religious orders which gave to the local ordinary wider responsibilities regarding the implementation of these norms. A concluding set of general disciplinary statutes repeated many of the issues that had been articulated in previous sessions. Chapter one, however, addressed to the local bishop, but curiously not to the cardinals, the following admonition:

> The council wholly forbids them [i.e., the bishops] to try to improve the living [conditions] of their relatives and household from Church revenues, since the apostolic canons forbid them to give to relatives the property of the Church which is God's; but if these are poor they may give to them as to other poor people but not divert or scatter Church property for their sake.[62]

Many a noble family in Italy and other parts of Christendom had been enriched handsomely over the centuries in violation of the aforementioned "apostolic canon"! Regarding the matter of dispensations (i.e., relaxations of the law in special cases), chapter eighteen noted:

> Dispensations may be given in some cases, when pressing and good reasons and an occasional greater good so demand; they are to be given after the case has been examined with great wisdom and free of charge by those who have the power of dispensation; any dispensation granted otherwise is to be regarded as fraudulent.[63]

Had the Roman curia (especially the Datary) been more sensitive to this matter, the history of the later Middle Ages would have taken some very different turns.

On December 4, 1563, the final day, a decree on indulgences was enacted which approved their conferral, but warned that "all base gain for securing indulgences, which has been the source of abundant abuses among the Christian people, should be totally abolished."[64] The council then left the matters of the censuring of books, the issue of a Tridentine catechism, and the revision of the Missal and the Breviary to the pope, "and so by his wisdom and authority be completed and published."[65] The final paragraphs of the acts of Trent deal with several matters of note. The fathers declared that "since no hope is left that the heretics, invited so often even under the safe conduct they asked for and so long awaited, are ever going to come here, it has at last become necessary to close this holy council."[66]

After the princes and other civil rulers were requested to assist in the implementation of the conciliar decrees in their respective territories, the final matter of the reception and interpretation of the council's enactments was treated:

> If any difficulty arises over the reception of these decrees, or any matters are raised needing clarification (which the council does not believe to be the case) or definition, the council is confident that, in addition to other remedies it has put in hand, the pope will ensure that the needs of the provinces are met for the glory of God and the peace of the Church, either by summoning persons who are suitable for the matter, particularly from the provinces where the difficulty has arisen, or even by holding a general council if he thinks this necessary, or by whatever means he thinks best.[67]

Then the fathers, after listening to a reading of all the acts from session one through session twenty-five, voted to send the decrees to the pope for his confirmation. On January 26, 1564, Pius confirmed the acts of the council and on June 30, 1564, he formally promulgated them in the bull, *Benedictus Deus*. In

August 1564, the pontiff established the Congregation of the Council and gave it responsibility for interpreting the decrees of Trent.

Before moving forward, something should be said about the work of the Council of Trent. Due to the circumstances that prevailed in the heat of the Protestant Revolt, no real dialogue was established with the Reformers during the council. To assign precise blame for this failure would be difficult, but there was ample culpability on both sides. It must be noted also that the attendance on the part of the episcopal delegates at Trent was not truly representative of western Christendom.

> Judged by any regional and mathematical criteria, it could not be pronounced representative of western Christendom. At every session the Italian prelates vastly outnumbered the rest, for in Italy almost every minor city had its bishop. The Teutonic peoples of Europe were represented throughout by a tiny handful of members, while French bishops and statesmen both inside and outside the council spoke with contempt of its unrepresentative character. Of the 270 bishops attending at one time or another, 187 were Italians, thirty-one Spaniards, twenty-six French and two German. Of the 255 ecclesiastics to sign the final acts no fewer than 189 were Italians.[68]

Although it is indeed true that not all the Italians were the pope's men because the bishops from Milan, Naples, and Sicily, for example, were occasionally more responsive to the wishes of their temporal rulers, the great majority of the Italians could be counted on to side with the papacy on issue after issue. In spite of the fact that the popes were not present at Trent or Bologna, their authority was clearly felt throughout. The council was the pope's council, and the papacy emerged much stronger and more decisive that it was before 1545. The monarchical dimension of the supreme pontiff was reasserted during the eighteen years of the conciliar period so that, in a sense, the modern papacy could be said to have taken shape from the Council of Trent.[69] Although Trent constituted a victory for certain Catholic theological positions, e.g., Thomism, and something of a defeat for others, e.g., the Augustinian views on grace and justification and the biblical humanist overtures of such as Erasmus, one can readily agree with Professor Dickens when he says:

> Even those who judge Trent to have defined too sweepingly, and to have reacted too automatically against anything remotely savouring of Protestantism, may still think that the sheer weight of its intellectual achievement entitles it to a place of honor in Christian history. The canons and decrees remain one of the greatest monuments of committee-thinking in the whole history of religion.[70]

The Catholic historian, Joseph Lortz, has raised an intriguing question regarding the inevitability of the Protestant Reformation toward the end of his book entitled, *How the Reformation Came* (1964). Was the Tübingen scholar, Johann Adam Möhler, right in saying that everything would have worked out and corrected itself in time? Apparently Möhler was of the mind that one could not be a Catholic without admitting this possibility. Joseph Lortz has admitted that some sort of reformation had become a historical necessity, but he sidestepped the issue of the possibility of its being generated from within.[71] The facts, however, seem to point to the impossibility of a genuine reform from the inside. Without the agency of a Martin Luther or someone like him, it is fairly clear that the mind-set of the papacy and the Roman curia was not likely to change. Their financial world was built on pluralism and the fact that they were absent from their lucrative pastoral benefices because of the requirements of the curial posts in Rome. Many of the popes understood the roots of the problem and the underlying corruption of the Roman system for centuries before the revolt of Luther, but even the strongest and the most resolute of them, like Innocent III, were not up to enforcing the necessary changes. The four Lateran councils from 1123 to 1215 provide irrefutable evidence that the evils besetting the Roman curia and the Roman system of ecclesiastical government were well known. The criticisms continued at Lyons I (1245) and Lyons II (1274) although they were not directed at the pope personally.[72] However, in the proposals for reform received from the bishops of the Christian world by Clement V in preparation for the Council of Vienne (1311-12), the attacks were directed at the whole Roman system, not excluding the pope.[73] The problems of pluralism, nonresidence, and excessive taxation to support the Roman bureaucracy had been evident to all for several centuries before the revolt of Luther. Consequently, one finds it rather impossible to affirm with Professor Möhler that things would have corrected themselves in time from within. Even those who "think in centuries" would, it seems, have difficulty finding plausible historical precedents for such a claim. Further, to hold that one cannot be a Catholic without affirming this possibility is gratuitous indeed, and grounded in an ecclesiology that has become (or is becoming) obsolete. But more of this later.

THE SHAPE OF EUROPE AFTER TRENT

At the conclusion of Trent in December 1563, the religious landscape of Europe had changed considerably since the 1520s. In England, after King Henry's attempt to nullify his marriage with Catherine of Aragon had failed, he made Anne Boleyn his queen in January 1533. Rome declared that his first marriage was valid, and that declaration precipitated Henry's 1534 Act of Supremacy wherein he proclaimed himself head of the church in England, thus accelerating the Anglican schism. There followed a grand scale confiscation of church property, with the monasteries as the principal targets. A very large share of the revenue from the monastic lands accrued to the crown.[74] In this context Owen Chadwick observes:

> Everyone agreed that in all countries of Europe, the Church, as a collection of corporations, possessed too much wealth for the health of the state, that some diversion was necessary and that material transfers of property are always painful.[75]

After Henry's death in 1547, his son, Edward VI (1547-53), succeeded to the throne. During Edward's short reign, England moved toward Calvinism under the direction of Thomas Cranmer. Mary Tudor (1552-58) followed her brother Edward, and relations with Rome were reestablished. Elizabeth I (1558-1603) took care to preserve the episcopal system, but the Catholic prelates were replaced. She reinstituted the Act of Supremacy in 1559 which made her head of the Anglican church.

The state of affairs in Germany was even more perplexing. Lutheranism spread across the land through the efforts of Luther's disciples from the 1520s on. Luther's death in 1546 at Eisleben did not slow the conversion process in any way. Bishops and archbishops would convert to Lutheranism and take with them the property they administered as Catholic ordinaries. By the middle of the sixteenth century, northern Germany was largely lost, while in the South, Austria and Hungary remained largely Catholic. The Peace of Augsburg (1555) made the implementation of Trent very difficult.

> To avoid the appearance of violating the Religious Peace, the Catholic estates maintained a cool reserve in regard to the council. . . . Hence, apart from a few starts, the Tridentine reform made general progress [in Germany] only from the turn of the century.[76]

According to Hubert Jedin, pluralism in the holding of offices in Germany continued for a very long time.[77] In the Scandinavian countries, Lutheranism prevailed, as did Calvinism in the Swiss cantons of Berne, Zurich, Basel, and Geneva; while Lucerne, Fribourg, and Zug remained Catholic. The Netherlands were divided into the Catholic south (Belgium) and the Calvinist north (Holland). In France, Holland, and Scotland, the Protestant movement took on a Calvinistic appearance between 1559 and 1567.

John Calvin (1509-64), who was born in France, studied theology, then law and then literature at Paris, Strasbourg, and Basel. In 1536, he published his *Institutes of Christian Religion* which he revised and enlarged many times throughout his life. He made his name in Geneva where he lived from 1536 to

1538, and then from 1541 until his death. Geneva literally became a theocracy under him for he succeeded in making the state a total servant of the church. Calvin's theological positions were in many ways more severe than Luther's. For example, he admitted to nothing more than a symbolic presence of Christ in the Eucharist, professed absolute predestinationism, and discarded Luther's principle of the private interpretation of Sacred Scripture. His rule in Geneva was imperious, harsh, and intolerant, but his influence was considerable in Switzerland, France, parts of Germany, Holland, England, and Scotland. Calvin's followers, who were referred to as Reform Protestants, were generally less interested in his theocratic views and returned, for the most part, to the original Protestant principle of private interpretation in their treatment of Scripture.

The religious situation in France was characterized by the severe repression of Protestants during the reign of Henry II (1547-59). By 1560 the Calvinists, or Huguenots, were a significant element in the country's political landscape. In the 1560s and 1570s, they numbered nearly three million out of a total population of nineteen million or more. Although a majority of the city folk remained Catholic, the noblemen of the countryside and the merchants in the towns were attracted to Calvinism.[78] The religious conflict began under King Charles IX (1560-74), who succeeded his brother Francis II in December 1560. Charles was ten years old when he became king and was under the regency of his mother, Catherine de Medici. When the royal edict of 1562 prohibited the Huguenots from worshiping publicly in the towns, the religious wars began. Henry III (1574-89), who followed after his brother Charles, was stabbed to death allegedly by a Dominican friar in August 1589, leaving the Bourbon, Henry of Navarre, a Huguenot, as the legitimate heir to the French crown. King Henry IV (1589-1610) came to the conclusion that he could only bring peace to the country by becoming a Catholic, and thus he was received as a Catholic in July 1593. In 1598, he promulgated the Edict of Nantes whereby the Protestants were given liberty of conscience, but their ability to worship publicly was limited. Catholicism from that time was confirmed as the established religion of France.[79]

Because the Catholic Church in Spain and Italy did not experience the ravages of the Protestant Reformation like their neighbors in the North, the reforms of Trent were implemented much more quickly. Pius IV reduced his curial staff by twenty to twenty-five percent, and the Jesuits were put in charge of the visitation of the parishes in the diocese of Rome. From 1564 to the end of the century, there must have been more than 100 diocesan and provincial councils, while local and regional seminaries multiplied dramatically in Italy.[80] Philip II (1556-98) of Spain accepted the Tridentine decrees for his territories in July 1564, but he did so "without prejudice to his royal prerogatives."[81] That is, he waited until he was given assurance that his control over the conferral of the majority of the benefices of his realm would remain intact. Dozens of diocesan and provincial councils were held in the forty years after Trent, and a considerable number of seminaries were founded in the Spanish jurisdictions.[82]

As mentioned, the situation in Germany was quite different, for the bishops were hesitant about infringing on the prerogatives of the secular princes. In the Catholic cantons of Switzerland there were also many delays in the implementation process. Regarding Austria and Hungary, the Hapsburg emperor Maximilian II (1564-76) was not at all cooperative, and hence it was up to the bishops of the empire to introduce the reform decrees and establish seminaries.[83] In France, there was little difficulty in the assimilation of the dogmatic decrees, but there was considerable objection to the promulgation of the disciplinary statutes. The chief opposition came from the numerous Gallican jurists in Parlement whom the French kings were simply unable to override. Hence, the publication of the disciplinary decrees did not occur until 1615 when the bishops took matters into their own hands, ordering the holding of provincial councils within six months, and diocesan synods shortly thereafter, so that the enactments of Trent could be officially promulgated in France.[84] The establishment of seminaries in France came later through the influence of such men as Jean Olier, Jean Eudes, and St. Vincent de Paul in the seventeenth century.

PIUS V (1566-72) AND GREGORY XIII (1572-85)

Before Pius IV died in December 1565, he published the ten rules worked out by the fathers at Trent to govern the Index of Forbidden Books. Some years before that, he had published decrees reforming the Rota, the Papal Chancery, and the Apostolic Camera. On January 7, 1566, after a conclave of almost three weeks, the cardinals elected a Dominican, Michael Ghislieri, who became Pius V. Ghislieri was a very austere man, a protégé of Carafa, who had been appointed head of the Roman Inquisition in 1558 by Paul IV. As pope, he relied heavily on the Inquisition to eradicate heresy wherever he thought he encountered it, and the number of Inquisition cases during his pontificate increased dramatically—often culminating in public executions. Pius V's court "was as austere and frugal as was the pope himself."[85] The Roman Catechism appeared in September 1566 and within a short time was translated into all the European languages with the exception of English. (Apparently the first English translation was printed in Dublin in 1829.[86]) The purpose of the catechism was to raise the level of education of pastors and clergy whose task it was to instruct the faithful. The revision of the Breviary (1568) and the Roman Missal (1570) completed two other tasks left for the pope by the final session of Trent. It was to his credit that Pius did significantly curtail the use of indulgences and dispensations during his pontificate. However, his bull of excommunication and deposition of Elizabeth I of England only exacerbated the plight of Catholics in Britain.[87] More than his predecessor, Pius IV, or his successors, Gregory XIII or Sixtus V, Pius left a rather stern, indelible imprint—for better or for worse—on the Church, which it bears to this day.

> Endowed with full powers to interpret and implement the Tridentine decrees, the papacy recovered that commanding position within the Church which it has never since relinquished. ... Its confident and authoritarian spirit, incarnated by the grim St. Pius V, also captured gentler personalities like his successor, Gregory XIII.[88]

Ugo Buoncompagni of Bologna was elected to succeed Pius V, to a considerable extent through the influence of Philip II of Spain, who was then the most powerful monarch in Europe. As a new cardinal in 1565, he had been dispatched as a legate to Spain where he greatly impressed the Hapsburg king. Gregory XIII (1572-85) did not share the rigid and uncompromising mentality of his predecessor. For example, he permitted Ernst of Bavaria to accumulate no less than five bishoprics in clear opposition to the repeated prohibitions of Trent regarding pluralism and nonresidence.[89] Gregory, however, did actively promote theological education in Rome, making it "a center of theological scholarship and of the training of clerics for the universal Church."[90] Perhaps his greatest contribution to the progress of Tridentine reform and to the growth of papal centralization was his transformation of the various ecclesiastical nunciatures and legations throughout Europe and elsewhere into effective instruments of papal influence. The evolution of the nunciatures after Trent, according to Marcel Pacaut, can be divided into three phases: the period from Trent to Gregory XIII (1563-72), the pontificate of Gregory XIII, and the period from 1585 to 1648.[91] Although Paul IV (1555-59) engaged to some extent in the establishment of nunciatures, his unfortunate relationship with Philip II forced the closure of several locations under the jurisdiction of the Spanish king, leaving at his death only the offices in France, Portugal, and Naples. Pius IV (1559-65) reopened a number of those in Spanish territories and initiated offices in Turin, Florence, and Switzerland. Under Pius V (1566-72) there was something of a retrenchment in the utilization of legations due to his lack of appreciation for diplomatic efforts of any kind. But with Gregory XIII a dramatic development of the institution took place. He established a critical legation at Cologne which became pivotal for the partial resuscitation of the Catholic Church in northern and western Germany where the damage inflicted by the Reformation had been devastating. Also, he laid the foundation for a permanent office in Belgium and did what he could to establish some sort of presence even in Protestant areas like England.

The nuncios and legates brought together the resident clergy, established (where they could) liaisons with the secular rulers, and spearheaded the implementation of the decrees and directives of the Council of Trent. They also served as conduits of information from Rome to their territories and from the territories to Rome. M. Pacaut has affirmed that almost all of the delegations existing at the beginning of the French Revolution were either established or in the planning stage during Gregory's pontificate.[92] Actually, his successors from Sixtus V (1585-90) to Urban VIII (1623-44) did little more than refine the organizational plan that Gregory had formulated. It must be said that the nunciatures and legations had a profound effect on the promulgation and the implementation of the Tridentine reforms over the next couple of centuries, and were an indispensable agent in the growing centralization of the Church around the papacy which took place after Trent. The English historian H. Outram Evennett writes:

> The nuncios quickly became the vital links between the Counter Reformation papacy in Rome and the progress of the Counter Reformation outside Rome, and their extreme importance in the history of Catholicism at this period is now winning increasing recognition. . . . Primarily diplomatic agents, they had to urge the secular powers to support the new reforms, to take up the fight against Protestantism as vigorously as possible, and on the whole to follow the line of policy desired by Rome. They were also empowered to act as direct ecclesiastical agents: to concern themselves with the direct promotion through the local hierarchies of reforms in the clergy and the laity, of the establishment of seminaries and so forth, and with the importation of the new Roman spirit.[93]

According to Hubert Jedin, the transformation of the nunciatures into vehicles of church reform was Gregory XIII's major contribution.[94]

SIXTUS V AND THE REORGANIZATION OF THE CURIA

Sixtus V (1585-90) was a farm worker's son from the region around Ancona who joined the Franciscans at an early age. Although he became an important ecclesiastic and a cardinal under Pius V, his influence waned precipitously during Gregory's pontificate. After Gregory's death, however, his influential friends saw to his election as pope. Sixtus' most important contribution was the reorganization of the Roman curia. In 1588, he created fifteen permanent congregations of cardinals, each with distinct responsibilities. Six of them focused on the administration of the Papal States, and nine dealt specifically with the spiritual government of the Church. (At the time of the promulgation of the 1983 *Code of Canon Law*, there were nine congregations, although their responsibilities had changed over the years.) Taxes and other revenues had to be increased from the papal territories because the other sources of income from the various Christian countries, derived from dispensations, annates, tithes, conferrals of benefices, etc., had been markedly reduced since Trent. Sixtus was an excellent administrator who not only dedicated himself to the reorganization of the Roman political and ecclesiastical administration, but he put the papacy once again on a sound financial basis—although this meant increased financial burdens for his territories. During his years as pope, he rebuilt the Lateran, completed the cupola of St. Peter and the church of the Gesu, and began the construction of the Quirinal palace which was to be the papal summer home. In addition, he reduced the expenses of the papal court by about fifty percent, decreasing the curial staff from 1,000 to about 500 persons. A.G. Dickens refers to Sixtus as the greatest practical organizer ever to occupy the papal throne.[95]

As a result of the distribution of responsibilities to the fifteen congregations and the assigning of several cardinals to each, the government of the Church began to operate through the congregations.

> The consistory [i.e., the meeting of all the cardinals with the pope] declined in importance, as did the Chancery, which functioned henceforth only as a dispatching office. The claim to co-rule, pressed by a numerically small oligarchy of cardinals in the late Middle Ages and even under the Renaissance popes, was definitively destroyed.[96]

After the death of Pope Sixtus V in August 1590, Jedin notes that the "Tridentine generation" died out with the brief reigns of the three popes who succeeded one another in 1590-91.[97] The thirty years after the close of Trent had transformed once and for all the papal office and papal administration. Making the most of the mandates given by the council to implement and interpret the conciliar decrees, Pius V, Gregory XIII, and Sixtus V had initiated a centralization of church rule which has survived to this day. Their enforcement of the reforms of Trent—in some cases through an episcopate with widely augmented powers and in other cases through the papal nuncios—served as the foundation for this development. Liturgy, discipline, and theology were rendered more uniform which to some extent was good, but uniformity often blurs the richness of diversity. This was the state of the Church at the close of the sixteenth century.

CLEMENT VIII (1592-1605) AND THE GRACE CONTROVERSY

The papal election following the death of Innocent IX in December 1591 was, like the three preceding conclaves, heavily influenced by the Spanish crown. Ippolito Aldobrandini, a rather ponderous but pious man, emerged as the new pontiff, taking the name Clement VIII. With him the movement of Tridentine renewal began to dissipate, although he did see to the publication of the new Vulgate and new editions of the Breviary and the Roman Missal. Clement reactivated the unfortunate and demoralizing practice of nepotism, enriching several of his nephews and the Aldobrandini family in general on a grand scale. It was during his reign that the doctrinal disputes on grace, predestination, and free will between the Jesuits and the Dominicans reached a critical stage in Rome. A generation earlier, Pius V (in 1567) had condemned seventy-nine propositions from the writings of Michael Baius, a Louvain professor, who propounded a theology of grace and justification that reflected an Augustinianism of the strictest form. In spite of the fact that Trent had left certain questions on grace open for discussion, its basic theses, i.e., justification amounting to a radical transformation in man—an ontological change—and man being truly capable of cooperating in his own justification, had eliminated some previously viable theological options regarding the theology of grace.[98] Baius would not have been able to subscribe wholeheartedly to these Tridentine positions. For him justification was not a renovation of the whole being. The "divinization" of the Christian was ignored and medicinal grace had won out over elevating grace.[99] Henri Rondet, an eminent French theologian, observes regarding Baius: "Though he might sometimes have read Augustine with the eyes of Augustine, he read him more often with the eyes of Luther or Calvin."[100]

Baius did submit to Pius V, but his strict Augustinian views appeared again in the publications of Cornelius Jansen (d. 1638) and Paschal Quesnel (d. 1719) to cause difficulties and controversies reaching far beyond the issues of grace and free will.

The Jesuit–Dominican conflict boiled over on the occasion of the publication of Jesuit Luis de Molina's book, *Concordia*, in 1588. Molina's attempt to reconcile the efficacy of grace with human free will was largely directed against the positions taken by Dominic Bañez, O.P., in his commentary on St. Thomas published in 1584. While Molina was stressing the free will of man, Bañez placed his emphasis on the sovereignty of the divine will. Bañez charged that Molina was Pelagian, while Molina asserted that Bañez's teaching on "physical premotion" was similar to the positions held by Luther and Calvin.[101] Pope Clement initiated a series of hearings in the latter 1590s to resolve the dispute. The protagonists both died before the acrimonious debates concluded (Molina [d. 1600] and Bañez [d.1604]).

> The famous discussions lasted for nine years, but they ended with an admission of impotence. Paul V [1605-21] had to content himself with imposing silence on the two parties, without settling anything at all. As Bossuet would later say, the Church held on to the two ends of the chain; man is free and the grace of God is all powerful. Efforts to investigate the

mystery were not forbidden, but the two parties had to stop tearing themselves to pieces.[102]

Paul V did not choose to render a decision in this matter, except to say that the teaching of the Dominicans was not Calvinism and the teaching of the Jesuits was not Pelagian.[103]

PAUL V (1605-21) AND THE WANING OF REFORM

After Leo XI's very brief pontificate of less than a month in April 1605, Camillo Borghese of Siena was selected by the conclave as a compromise candidate after Spain had exercised its veto against Cardinal Robert Bellarmine. Paul V, who was only fifty-two years old when he became pope, was like Clement VIII a committed nepotist throughout his reign. As a matter of fact, the prodigious wealth of the Borghese family originated with his pontificate.[104] Paul's rather outdated views on the use of papal power prompted him to place the city of Venice under interdict as a result of a bitter conflict with the republic over several jurisdictional disputes from April 1606 to April 1607. The penalty was largely ignored, however, both by the republic and by the majority of the Venetian clergy. It was Paul who first censured Galileo for teaching the Copernican theory of the solar system, but he was rather farsighted in promoting the Church's missionary efforts, and even in approving the use of the vernacular in the liturgy of China. Paul's successor, Gregory XV (1621-23), was also dedicated to the growth of world missionary activity, establishing the Congregation for the Propagation of the Faith to which he delegated the care and oversight of all the missions, including the mission fields in America, Asia, and Africa, as well as the oriental churches united with Rome (e.g., the Maronites, Ruthenians, Armenians, and others). Further, this new office supervised the Catholic minorities in the countries of Europe, such as England, Scotland, Holland, and the Scandinavian countries, where official Catholic hierarchies no longer existed or were permitted to exist.[105] The Propaganda became in effect the headquarters of the Counter Reformation.

The church historian Ludwig Hertling provides a trenchant observation regarding almost all of the popes from 1605 to 1799 which is worth noting here:

The popes of the sixteenth century from Paul III on had for the most part been distinguished men, with sharply cut and expressive faces, very different from one another, yet almost all of them men of action who did much that was important in mostly brief reigns. In the sixteenth century the voice of the pope was again heard in the Church and in the world. In the seventeenth and eighteenth centuries everything was different. The age of giants was followed by an age, not of dwarfs, it is true, but of *epigoni* [i.e., lesser, uncreative people]. . . . They were not blind to the evils and the perils of the age. But the Catholic governments had gradually spun so tight a net around them that they could no longer stir.[106]

Gregory XV's successor was Cardinal Maffeo Barberini, a Florentine, who was, like many of his predecessors, a committed nepotist, appointing a brother and two nephews as cardinals, and taking care to enrich the Barberini family. One of the central events that occurred for the most part during the pontificate of Urban VIII (1623-44) was the Thirty Years War in Germany. Unlike the previous Emperors Ferdinand I (1556-64) and Maximilian II (1564-76), who were not of a mind to employ force against the Protestants, Rudolf II (1576-1612) adopted a rather belligerent stance against them. Emperor Ferdinand II (1619-37)—firmly convinced of the divine mission of the Hapsburgs—initiated the Thirty Years War against the Bohemians, with the aid of Bavaria, and without any help from Pope Urban. Ferdinand had in mind to take back all the German lands lost to the Catholic Church since 1552, and was quite successful during the first phase of the war (1618-29). Indeed, by 1629 practically all the Calvinist territories had been recovered. In southern Germany there were only a few pockets of Protestantism left, while in the North—which had become almost completely evangelical—large sections had been recovered by the Catholics. The second phase of the conflict (1630-32) reversed the Catholic successes almost completely, due to the intervention of King Gustavus Adolphus of Sweden and his forces. Gustavus was probably fearful that the Catholic victories would threaten Lutheran Sweden. The Catholic armies were thrown back, and the third phase of the bitter conflict (1632-48) turned into a political battle between France and Sweden on the one hand, and the Austrian Empire and Spain on the other. The French were pleased to help Sweden in order to weaken the Hapsburgs. One of the most devastating of religious wars ended with the Peace of Westphalia in 1648. The landed possessions of the Catholic Church were dramatically reduced, especially in the North. The Netherlands and Switzerland were recognized as independent states, and the Reformed church, i.e., the Calvinists, were afforded the protection of the Peace of Augsburg, along with the Catholics and the Lutherans.[107]

Pope Urban VIII condemned Galileo for a second time in 1633, forcing him to renounce publicly his views on the Copernican system. The baroque period reached its zenith in Rome during Urban's pontificate, especially through the outstanding work of Gian Lorenzo Bernini (1598-1680) and Francesco Borromini (1599-1667). In a way Pope Urban brought about a return of the Renaissance papacy. The Romans, though, felt oppressed by his extravagance and were overjoyed at his passing in July 1644. Urban's successor, Innocent X (1644-55), pursued the Barberinis in order to recapture some of the wealth that had been showered on them by Urban. He sequestered many of their possessions until he could determine whether or not they had been unduly enriched by the goods of the Church. Unfortunately, Innocent X also succumbed to nepotism, bestowing many ecclesiastical favors and goods on his family, the Pamfilis. The new pope was most displeased with the Peace of Westphalia because it definitively sanctioned religious pluralism in Germany and secularized a great portion of church land and possessions. Probably the most far reaching action he took was his condemnation in May 1653 of five propositions allegedly extracted from the work, *Augustinus*, published in 1640, after the death in 1638 of the author, Cornelius Jansen. Jansen had taught at Louvain (and also in France) until he became bishop of Ypres in 1634. Henri Rondet has described the Louvain scholar's views:

> For Jansenius, the whole of humanity, solidary with the sin of Adam, should rightly be damned. God rightly leaves a whole part of the *massa damnata*—the most considerable part—[to] go straight to the depths of hell.... The huge majority of infidels, sinful by nature and deprived of the grace which could help them escape sin, is on the way to hell. For since grace is gratuitous, it cannot be given to all men. Infidels do not have it, nor has it been given to the Jews, nor is it given to all sinners.... In the last analysis, only the predestined are saved—that is, those whom God has predestined before all time. Christ did not die for all men; the contrary position would be Semipelagian.[108]

Antoine Arnauld (1612-94), the leader of the Jansenists, responded to Innocent X's condemnation of the five propositions by saying that although only the first was taken from *Augustinus*, the others were as a matter of fact orthodox and accurately reflected the thinking of St. Augustine on grace.[109] The battle was joined which would persist throughout the seventeenth century and the eighteenth as well. Hubert Jedin has referred to the 1653 condemnation of Jansen as the most significant doctrinal decision of the seventeenth century.[110] Innocent's papacy was negatively affected not only by his suspicious, indecisive, and unsociable temperament, but especially by the excessive influence which he allowed his sister-in-law to exercise over his decision making.[111]

THE SEVENTEENTH-CENTURY POPES AND FRANCE

Fabio Chigi, who represented Innocent X at the deliberations leading up to the Peace of Westphalia, was elected to the papal office after Innocent. Alexander VII (1655-67) was initially opposed to the bestowing of favors on his relatives but was persuaded by the curia that the pope's family should live in comparative affluence, and thus he began favoring his people with benefices and lands. His relations with France went from bad to worse. Almost from the outset he deferred to Cardinal Mazarin's wishes regarding the selection of bishops in France. After the death of Mazarin in 1661, the twenty-two-year-old Louis XIV—who had been nourished on Gallican ideas—made it even more difficult for the pope, who simply had to comply with the king's episcopal appointments. Pope Alexander's cardinalatial selections strongly favored Italians, as had been more or less the case since the days of Sixtus IV (1471-84). In 1665, Alexander's Holy Office condemned forty-five propositions smacking of probabilism which had been submitted by the professors at Louvain as an attack of sorts against the Jesuits, although the system of probabilism was not condemned.[112] In spite of his diplomatic experience, Pope Alexander was unable to manage the Papal States effectively. After his death, his Secretary of State, Cardinal Giulio Rospigliosi, was elected to replace him after a short conclave. Clement IX (1667-69) was a man of frail health and did not last long. To his credit he was not a nepotist, but his relationship with Louis XIV was not any more successful than that of his predecessor.

The next conclave was a good deal more complex, lasting four months. The French cardinal who carried the king's veto excluded two candidates and the lead Spanish cardinal ruled out two more. It has been rightly said that the Catholic powers intervened more in this conclave than in any since the Council of Trent. Clement X (1670-76), who was eighty years old when elected, was largely under the control of his niece's father-in-law, whom he had appointed a cardinal. It was during Clement's reign that the Turks, who were threatening to overrun Poland, were decisively defeated in November 1673 by an army led by John Sobieski, who had received significant financial aid from the Roman curia. Sobieski was elected king of Poland about six months after his famous victory at the Dniester River. The pope's diplomatic overtures toward France were not nearly as successful, for Louis XIV managed to convince him that France's current war with Holland was aimed at restoring Catholicism to that country. As a matter of fact, Louis' objective was expansionism, pure and simple. As that conflict progressed, Louis needed more and more money, and so he began to confiscate church property, claiming the right to appropriate the income from the vacant sees of France. Although this was a serious violation of the rights of the Church, Clement X said or did nothing to curb the practice. He was unable to act in the political arena and indeed had no desire to be bothered with such matters. Ludwig Hertling has observed in this connection that the Catholic governments at that time preferred frail old men on the throne of Peter.[113]

Clement was succeeded by Innocent XI (1676-89), who is regarded by many as the most notable pontiff of the seventeenth century. The Odeschalchi pope was beatified by Pius XII in 1956. He was personally free of nepotism, but was unable to eradicate the practice from the College of Cardinals. Theologically the pope was somewhat sympathetic to Jansenism and rather critical of the

Jesuits. In 1679, he condemned sixty-five propositions against probabilism, largely put together by the Louvain faculty.[114] Like his predecessor, the pope came to the assistance of John Sobieski in battling the Turks. In September 1683 at Vienna, Sobieski forced them to retreat, and there is little doubt that Vienna owed its liberation principally to the efforts of Innocent XI.[115] The second diplomatic challenge had to do with his relationship with Louis XIV of France. Unlike Clement X, Innocent fought Louis every step of the way regarding the king's appropriation of ecclesiastical property and the channeling of the revenue from vacant sees to the royal treasury. After warning him twice to leave church revenues alone, Innocent's third warning contained the threat of excommunication. At that point Louis arranged for an assembly of the French clergy which formulated and enacted in March 1682 the famous Four Gallican Articles which were dispatched to all the bishops of France for their approval. The first and the fourth articles read as follows:

I. . . . We declare that kings and sovereigns are not, by God's command, subject to any ecclesiastical power in temporal matters; that they cannot be deposed, directly or indirectly, by the authority of the heads of the Church; that their subjects cannot be dispensed from obedience, nor absolved from the oath of allegiance.

IV. Although the pope has the chief voice in questions of faith, and his decrees apply to all churches and to each particular church, yet his decision is not unalterable unless the consent of the Church is given.[116]

These two propositions embody the basic tenets of the Gallican position. First, the sovereign is supreme in temporal matters, and the popes cannot directly or indirectly interfere with the relationship between the ruler and his subjects. Second, although the pope has universal jurisdiction over all the churches, his decrees (i.e., those relating to faith or morals) must be confirmed by the consent of the Church in order to be irreformable.

Innocent XI rejected the articles in April 1682 and refused henceforth to confirm the appointments of episcopal candidates who subscribed to them. By January 1688, thirty-five sees were vacant in France.[117] Possibly the most tragic decision that Louis XIV made in his seventy-two-year reign was his October 1685 abrogation of the Edict of Nantes promulgated by his grandfather, Henry IV, in 1598. All Protestant churches were to be destroyed; all ministers were to leave France within two weeks; and all newborns were to be baptized Catholic.[118] The result of the action was that over three million Protestants left France out of a total population of nearly twenty million. Those who left were mostly artisans, craftsmen, and merchants, representing a terrible loss for France. Louis had come to the conclusion that the existence of more than one recognized religion was destructive of national unity, and that the only way to realize the desired political cohesion was to eradicate the dissenters by force. Although he did not receive much negative criticism as a result of his decision at the time, there is no doubt that resistance and opposition developed against him throughout Protestant Europe because of this action.

Innocent XI was venerated by the people of Rome almost from the day of his death in August 1689. This speaks well of him because during his reign, he was not especially popular due to his repeated restrictions on public entertainments in the Holy City. Burkhart Schneider comments:

> His charity, extreme conscientiousness and austere piety were acknowledged. . . . Always intent upon safeguarding and defending the rights of the Church, he was not very open to the advice of others and at times persisted all too rigidly in his own views. Moreover, he never spent any time abroad, so that his knowledge of the political situation was insufficient. While he was an excellent administrator with a special skill in financial matters, he was lacking in knowledge of human nature and even in theological education.[119]

The next two popes, Alexander VIII and Innocent XII, were old men when elected. Pietro Ottobuoni (1689-91) was nearly eighty, and Antonio Pignatelli (1691-1700) was seventy-five. Alexander, a famous Rotal judge whose decisions were quoted for centuries, was agreeable to both France and Austria. Although he was relatively successful in his dealings with Louis XIV, he succeeded in alienating the Austrian emperor, Leopold I (1658-1705). Alexander revived the practice of nepotism, bestowing many benefits and goods on the Ottobuoni family. In the closing months of his reign, he declared the Gallican Articles null and void, which made very little difference in France. To counteract the propositions against probabilism condemned by his predecessor, Alexander condemned thirty-one Jansenist positions which were excerpted from the writings of theologians in Belgium.[120] The conclave following Pope Alexander's death in February 1691 lasted five months. Because the representative of the Austrian Empire used his veto to rule out the frontrunner, the cardinals settled on a compromise candidate, Cardinal Pignatelli, who had been a much traveled nuncio, and was archbishop of Naples since 1687. Innocent XII attacked nepotism with perhaps the most important reform decree of his papacy.[121] Unfortunately, the positive effects of his action did not survive beyond his reign. Innocent's rapport with the aging Louis XIV of France was reasonably successful. The king's military and political situation in Europe was weakening year by year and that certainly made him more docile. The pontiff ratified all the episcopal appointments made by Louis after 1682, and the king in turn promised to revoke the obligation he placed on newly appointed bishops to subscribe to the Four Gallican Articles, but he never delivered on that promise.[122] Gallicanism was the prevailing Church–state position in France until the French Revolution.

CONFLICT OVER THE SPANISH SUCCESSION

The death of Charles II of Spain in 1700 precipitated a crisis of major proportions among the European powers because Charles left no heir. Would Philip of Anjou or an Austrian Hapsburg succeed to the Spanish throne? The pope favored Philip of Anjou and this upset the Hapsburgs. Philip became Philip V of Spain (1700-21; 1725-46), but this seriously upset the balance of power in Europe for many years. The conclave after the death of Innocent XII was quite short due to the situation in Spain because the succession question had not been solved until after the election of the new pope, Clement XI (1700-21). Giovanni Albani was apparently the most powerful cardinal during the pontificates of Alexander VIII and Innocent XII, so it was not surprising that he was elected, even though he was only fifty-one years old. Clement XI also favored Philip of Anjou of the French dynasty over one of Emperor Leopold's sons of the Hapsburg line. Most of the European powers sided with Philip, but Austria obtained the support of England, Holland, and Prussia. War in Europe was a definite possibility over the Spanish succession issue, and after the death of Leopold I (1705) the situation worsened under Leopold's son, Joseph I (1705-11). Austrian troops invaded the Papal States in May 1707, and by January 1709 Pope Clement was forced to surrender to the Austrian army. Furthermore, he had to recognize Joseph's brother, Charles, as king of Spain. As a result, Philip V of Spain broke with the pope, putting Bourbon Spain into six years of schism. Joseph I's premature death due to smallpox opened up the Austrian throne for his brother, Charles, who ruled the empire from 1711 to 1740. The Peace of Utrecht (1712) and the Peace of Rastatt (1714), ending the War of the Spanish Succession, were disastrous for the papacy. While Austria acquired Sicily, the territories of Parma and Piacenza were lost to the pope. Italy became the battleground for Austria, France, and Spain, the so-called "Catholic" powers. These peace treaties were dramatic indications of the declining political prestige of the papacy because the decisions were made without consulting the pope. Owen Chadwick says regarding Clement's papacy: "More calamities happened during this pontificate than under any pope since the Reformation. In large part, they were calamities of circumstance which under some popes might have been more and worse."[123]

CLEMENT XI (1700-21) AND *UNIGENITUS* (1713)

The most critical doctrinal issue of Clement's reign was the renewed conflict over the variations of Augustinianism which surfaced again in the works of the Oratorian, Paschal Quesnel (d. 1719), who taught at Paris and Orleans, and then fled to Brussels and finally to Holland. According to Quesnel, there is no grace outside the Church, and the true Church is the Church of the saints, outside of which sinners and infidels are rejected.[124] According to Quesnel and the Jansenists, pagans, Jews, and separated Christians received no grace and hence were simply lost. Alexander VIII had condemned this position in 1690, and the Church responded again in 1713 with the publication of the bull, *Unigenitus*, which, according to Henri Rondet, revealed Rome's determination to be finished with a sect that attacked the universal value of the redemptive activity of Christ.[125] Quesnel's book, *Moral Reflections on the New Testament*, had been condemned by Clement XI in July 1708, five years before *Unigenitus*. The 1713 bull set forth 101 propositions extracted from Quesnel's book which were then condemned in a kind of global fashion, with no attempt to critique the heterodoxy or demerits of each statement. *Unigenitus* was indeed a most unfortunate pronouncement.[126] According to Owen Chadwick, "the bull did not distinguish propositions which were false from those which were only harmful, or offensive to pious ears."[127] Louis Cognet describes *Unigenitus* as follows:

> The 101 articles selected for condemnation from a list of 155 were arranged in such a way as to furnish a sort of summary of Jansenist doctrine. But a number of these articles could be authenticated by means of patristic texts; some of them in fact seemed to be quotes from the most esteemed of the Fathers. . . . in the eyes of many readers the bull seemed to go beyond Quesnel and actively condemn Augustinianism, to which many of the theologians and the faithful continued to adhere passionately, considering it one of the cornerstones of Christian thought.[128]

Even though Louis XIV wanted the French bishops to accept the bull, there was considerable opposition to it, led by the archbishop of Paris, Cardinal Noailles. Actually, some French dioceses refused to accept *Unigenitus*. It can indeed be said that the bull took a longstanding theological controversy and transformed it into a fierce debate on the nature and the limits of the teaching authority of the pope. *Unigenitus* was widely viewed as an instance of a teaching error by the pope.[129] Serious discussions were carried on for decades over the notion of the pope's infallibility. This conflict over *Unigenitus* no doubt weakened the reputation of the teaching authority of the papacy not only in France, but elsewhere, especially in Germany. The issue of papal infallibility remained as a subject of theological debate until Vatican I in 1869-70.

Pope Clement's enthusiasm for the Church's missionary activity in India, China, and the Philippines took what many consider an unfortunate turn when he ruled three times (1706, 1710, and 1715) against the use of local rites in the liturgies of the Chinese missions which Pope Alexander VII had sanctioned in 1656. In 1717 the Chinese government ordered the missionaries who refused to use the local rites to be expelled and their churches destroyed.[130] For the rest of the eighteenth century, Christianity was officially curbed in China. Pope Clement's latter years were clouded by illness which began to debilitate him as early as 1710. Although some criticize him for indecision and lassitude in carrying out his policies, many of his failures can be attributed to the circumstances of the age in which he lived. Clement died in March 1721 after a pontificate that perhaps lasted too long.

The next three pontiffs constituted a rather sorry trio because each was afflicted either by illness, advanced age, or, in one case, by disinterest. Innocent XIII (1721-24) had been forced to resign the see of Viterbo due to poor health two years before he was elected pope. In the conclave, the emperor's representative vetoed the favorite, Cardinal Paolucci, Clement XI's Secretary of State, because he was thought to have been the author of the former pontiff's policies which were unfavorable to Austria. The new pope was an ideal compromise candidate because he was not expected to live long. However, Innocent XIII's chronic illness rendered him incapable of any effective leadership, especially during the two years prior to his death in March 1724.

After a conclave of almost two months, another compromise candidate was chosen in the person of Cardinal Vicenzo Orsini, O.P., the archbishop of Benevento. Orsini was seventy-five years old when elected and had very little diplomatic or political experience. The affairs of state were left to a certain Niccolo Coscia whom Orsini had taken with him from Benevento. Benedict XIII (1724-30) was badly betrayed by Coscia, who revived the simonaical practice of selling ecclesiastical offices on a grand scale, and was also guilty of avarice and mismanagement of every sort. The pope would not listen to the numerous and pressing complaints against Coscia, but allowed him to proceed unfettered as Secretary of State while Benedict himself preferred to concentrate on the pastoral concerns of the diocese of Rome: visiting the sick, administering the sacraments, and occupying himself with catechetical instructions. In spite of his priestly efforts, he was disliked by the Romans, principally because of the notorious Coscia.

Pope Benedict XIII's successor was yet another compromise candidate who was chosen after the conclave had been at loggerheads for about four months. Cardinal Lorenzo Corsini (Clement XII, 1730-40) was seventy-eight years old when he became pontiff. He was able to put the papal finances in order to some extent, and managed to have Coscia jailed. In 1732 he became blind, and during the last several years of his reign, he was bedridden. The last half of Clement XII's pontificate was a disaster in that control over the Papal States was lost, and the conduct of papal business suffered greatly from a lack of direction. He died in February 1740.

Before treating Benedict XIV, the most notable of the eighteenth-century popes, it might perhaps be helpful to sketch a collective portrait of the careers of the seventeenth- and eighteenth-century pontiffs before their elevation to the papal office. Most of them were educated in civil and canon law and began their ecclesiastical careers as advocates or court officers at the Roman Rota or the Signatura. Most often they were not in major orders at the time that they embarked on their legal careers. Then—especially in the seventeenth century— they were appointed to one of the nunciatures for a tour of duty of two or three years. Often they served as nuncios in several places, the most prestigious locations at that time being Vienna, Madrid, and Paris. Their role as nuncios was to see to the implementation of the Tridentine decrees, to strengthen the authority of the local ordinaries, to examine the qualifications of local candidates for the episcopacy, and to serve as conduits for information and instructions between the location where they were stationed and the Roman curia. There were some unfortunate exceptions but, as a rule, they did not intervene in the affairs of the local churches unless there was evidence of negligence or abuse of power on the part of an ordinary. After a number of years of successful service in one or more legations, they were frequently awarded with the cardinal's red hat either during or shortly after their diplomatic careers. They were then, in most cases, given the responsibility of a diocese for some years before returning to Rome to serve in a congregation or some other significant curial position.

In the eighteenth century, although they were generally trained as lawyers, the majority of the pontiffs had no previous experience in the diplomatic corps, because the function at that time had receded in importance. After some time in one or another of the Roman offices, they typically served as bishops of dioceses before they were brought back to Rome as cardinals to take a significant post in the government of the Church. Looking at the ages of the popes from 1605 to 1800 at the time of their election, fifteen of the nineteen pontiffs were over sixty-five, and seven were over seventy years of age. It is clear that the great powers—France, Spain, and Austria—had insisted on elderly and frequently infirm men for the papal office, and to accomplish this, they employed their veto, or at least the threat of it, to rule out more vigorous and younger candidates. Even the distinguished Rotal judge, Charles Lefebvre, had to acknowledge that the frequency of these aged and often infirm men occupying the chair of Peter in the seventeenth and eighteenth centuries led invariably to a certain "paralysis" of the system.[131]

BENEDICT XIV (1740-58)

One of the outstanding exceptions to the rule was the sixty-five-year-old archbishop of Bologna, Prospero Lambertini, who was elected in August 1740 after a trying conclave which lasted six months. Benedict XIV was, according to Charles Lefebvre, without a doubt the most capable and successful pontiff in the eighteenth century.[132] He was open to the scientific advances occurring at that time, enjoyed a correspondence with Voltaire, did not play favorites, and avoided any tendency to nepotism. Lefebvre added that Benedict XIV was absolutely convinced of the necessity of expanding the authority and prestige of the Holy See, and set himself to the task of ordering more precisely the functions of the various Roman offices and dicasteries. He revitalized the *ad limina* process which had fallen into disuse, and he repeatedly urged the importance of residence for local ordinaries. As secretary of the Congregation of the Council in 1725, Lambertini revamped the questionnaire for the periodic bishops' reports so that more pertinent information on the local churches could be collected in Rome. During Benedict's pontificate, the first printings of translations of the Vulgate into the vernacular languages were sanctioned, as long as they were approved by Rome and included appropriate commentaries.[133] German, French, and Polish translations had long been available in spite of the 1559 prohibition. (One must add, however, that it was not until 1893 that Bible reading with more attention and freedom was especially recommended to the faithful by Leo XIII.) Although Benedict's accomplishments were numerous, the concordats that were signed during his pontificate were not always favorable to the interests of the papacy. For example, the agreement with Spain confirmed the king's right to appoint almost all of the 12,000 benefices within the jurisdiction of the Spanish monarch.[134] Also, it must be said that Benedict was not a good judge of character. For example, he shared confidences with the French Cardinal de Tencin which became public knowledge at the French court to the disadvantage of several of Lambertini's more sensitive diplomatic efforts. The eminent papal historian, Ludwig Pastor, identifies his activity as a legislator as Benedict's greatest contribution to the Church:

> From the very beginning he seems to have set himself the task of finishing what was incomplete in ecclesiastical statutes, of clearing up uncertainties, of filling in gaps, and of recalling what had been more or less forgotten. In this way it might be said of him that he rounded off the modern, post-Tridentine development of Church discipline.[135]

Benedict XIV's enactments dealt with such matters as marriage, the liturgy, and the reduction of the number of feast days of obligation. He also addressed the procedure involved in the censorship of books. The Congregation of the Index and the Congregation of the Inquisition "had been blamed for having, in many cases, condemned books without giving a hearing to their authors."[136] The pope intended that authors of good repute be given an opportunity to respond to objections raised against certain passages in their works. It was also his intention to sit in personally on the final session before definitive judgment was rendered on the works under discussion. (Would that Benedict's recommendations had been followed throughout the years!)

Another development that profoundly affected the Church in the eighteenth century and that gathered momentum during Benedict's pontificate was the swelling tide of opposition against the Jesuits. The pope's own feelings regarding the Society were apparently rather ambiguous. Ludwig Pastor's narrative confirms this. On the one hand, Pastor says that Benedict was "not unfavorable" to the Jesuits, and that no pope "had so many Jesuits around him as Pope Benedict." On the other hand, the historian attests that "it was generally thought that Benedict had little love for the Jesuits."[137] In any event, Rome became a major center of opposition against the Jesuits during Benedict's pontificate. Even as early as the pontificate of Clement XI (1700-21), Rome had reversed its earlier stand of accommodation to local customs and practices in the mission fields, thereby initiating an assault on the Jesuits' efforts at evangelization in the Far East. It seems that the leading Jansenist and anti-Jesuit agent in Rome for many years was Cardinal Domenico Passionei, who was about sixty years of age when Benedict was elected pope. Lambertini was not especially fond of Passionei whom he considered a collector of books rather than a scholar, and something of a dilettante.[138] Passionei seems to have adopted Jansenist leanings while he was in Paris and in Belgium as a minor diplomat early in the century. It is a distinct possibility that Passionei was the author of the plot to destroy the Jesuits. As a matter of fact, Pastor notes regarding Cardinal Lambertini before he became pope:

> It is related of Benedict XIV himself, that before he became pope he frequently expressed the opinion that Jansenius was a chimera invented by the Jesuits and that it was they who induced Clement XI to promulgate the bull, *Unigenitus* [1713]. In view of the pope's lively and unrestricted way of speaking, it is not impossible that he may have let slip some similarly sounding remarks which were eagerly seized upon, given greater point and misconstrued.[139]

In any event, there were considerable numbers of secular and religious clergy, officials of the congregations, and high-ranking members of the hierarchy in Rome who were at that time opposed to the Jesuits. Whether it was the Society's phenomenal growth, its success in establishing and staffing colleges and seminaries all over Europe and in the mission fields, or the Society's reluctance to modify its *ratio studiorum* in light of recent scientific developments, or its century-old opposition to Jansenism, the issue is still debated by scholars today. The existence of the opposition, however, is clear. And the problems in the mission fields, especially in China, simply added fuel to the fire. The fact that there were delays in the implementation of Clement XI's bull banning local rites and customs from the liturgy was blamed on the Jesuits. "In leading circles in Rome, in consequence, belief in the disobedience of the Chinese Jesuits had taken root so deeply as to be almost ineradicable."[140] (More will be said about this matter when dealing with the next two pontiffs, Clement XIII and Clement XIV.) Even during his last years as pontiff, Benedict continued to radiate energy and vitality. He was close to death on several occasions after 1756, and he finally succumbed in May 1758.

CLEMENT XIII, CLEMENT XIV, AND THE JESUITS

The conclave of 1758 witnessed the last use of the veto by one of the great powers in the eighteenth century. Although Cardinal Cavalchini was certainly the frontrunner, his advocacy of the beatification of Cardinal Bellarmine made him a target, and the French used their exclusive against him, making way for the election of Cardinal Carlo Rezzonico, the bishop of Padua. Throughout his papacy, Clement XIII (1758-69) was constantly confronted and tested by the Jesuit issue. The first of the fatal strikes against the Society occurred in Portugal through the efforts of the malevolent Marquis de Pombal, who became secretary of state under the weak and indolent king, Joseph I (1750-77). Pombal's relative, Cardinal Saldanha, had been appointed by Benedict XIV in the month before the pontiff's death to conduct an investigation regarding the conduct of the Jesuits in Portugal and their commercial ventures in the missions.[141] Without much of an investigation, Pombal issued an order in 1759 deporting the Jesuits and confiscating their assets in Portugal and in their mission territories. About 1,700 Jesuits were banished from their homeland, many of them dying in prisons, while most made their way to the Papal States as exiles. Four years later a similar fate befell the members of the Society in France, where there was considerable opposition to them already in Parlement. A failed commercial venture involving a superior of the order in the Antilles, Father Lavalette, forced the Society in France to take a stand on the question of indemnification for the losses involved. When the superiors in France decided that the order was not responsible for the repayment of the commercial losses, this sealed the fate of the Society in France. In 1762, almost 3,000 Jesuits were deported and the order's possessions and goods were confiscated by the government. To his credit, Pope Clement issued a bull defending the Society, but it was largely ignored.

> Clement XIII tried to befriend the order by issuing the bull, *Apostolicum pascendi munus* (1765), in which he renewed the papal approval, drew attention to the order's eminent services to the Church and denied the malicious charges against it.[142]

In 1767, Charles III of Spain issued a decree banning the Jesuits from Spain and the Spanish colonies due to alleged illegal commercial transactions which were never really investigated by the crown. This meant that over 4,000 members of the order were forced to find a home elsewhere. The pope protested, but his objections were ignored. The chaos that these deportations of thousands of Jesuits created can hardly be overemphasized. The impotence of the papacy in the face of these events could scarcely have been more evident. The German historian Kurt Aland notes:

> Clement was powerless in the face of these measures. He did impose an interdict on the countries which had dissolved the Jesuits, but that was only a meaningless gesture and led, naturally, to vehement attacks against the pope. For the nations were not satisfied with having driven the order out of their territory; they now demanded that it be totally abolished constitutionally, something justified to a certain extent by what had happened in their lands.[143]

Clement finally fell victim to the pressures placed on him by the Catholic kings. The elderly pontiff had a stroke in February 1769 from which he did not recover.

The selection of a replacement for Clement XIII centered around the question of the abolition of the Jesuits. France, Spain, and Austria were of one mind that no friend of the order would be elected. The conventual Franciscan, Lorenzo Ganganelli, who had been made a cardinal by Clement XIII in 1759, was chosen in May 1769.[144] Clement XIV (1769-74) did his best to forestall the suppression of the Society, but he was a weak man and afraid of offending any of the great powers, especially the Bourbons. The Spanish ambassador, Jose Moñino, proved to be the irresistible force, threatening that if the Jesuits were not suppressed, he would see to the expulsion of all the religious orders from Spain. Clement signed the brief of abolition in July 1773.

> Finally yielding to the incessant demands of the Bourbon courts and to prevent a schism which actually threatened, he issued the brief, *Dominus ac Redemptor*, on July 21, 1773, by which, in virtue of apostolic authority, he declared the Society of Jesus universally suppressed. While implying that the charges brought against the Society were false, the pope declared that under the circumstances, the Society was no longer able to produce the rich fruits for which it had been founded, and that it had become a source of constant discord in states and nations, and that true and lasting peace could not be restored to the Church so long as the Society existed.[145]

And so without a trial, without even an adequate explanation, the Society of Jesus was abolished, although it did survive for a time in Prussia and was never suppressed in Russia. The Society's general, Lorenzo Ricci, and a dozen or so leading Jesuits were shamelessly imprisoned in the Castel Sant' Angelo in Rome and left there to die. The treatment of the thousands of banished priests and brothers was inexplicably harsh. Some joined other congregations; some were imprisoned in Spain, Portugal, and elsewhere with no relief and no defense. Many found their way to the Papal States where there was in most cases little support for them. E.E.Y. Hales, an English historian, says regarding the action of Clement XIV:

> He showed a want of humanity in the way in which he carried out the suppression. And his attempts to treat defeat as though it were victory, on this occasion as in others, were naive and flippant.
>
> For defeat it was, the most serious the Church had suffered since Luther's revolt. The pope had been persuaded to suppress the Jesuits not because, as was claimed against the Templars, they had lost their virtue and become corrupt—there is no suggestion of this in the brief—but because certain of the governments demanded that he should do so since they found the Society inconvenient. He was simply yielding to pressure.[146]

One is inclined to agree with Hales when he says that Clement's action against the Society "was an act of appeasement, and in due course his successor would suffer in full measure for it."[147] Clement died in September 1774, a rather broken man who in his last months was overcome with depression and the fear of assassination. The pope's prestige had not been lower since the days of the Renaissance pontiffs before Trent.

PIUS VI (1775-99), PISTOIA (1786), AND NAPOLEON

The selection of Clement's successor was a tedious process lasting more than four months. The Jesuit issue was again a major concern because the great powers did not want the suppression reversed, and those cardinals who thought the action too harsh wanted to soften the ban. Cardinal Giovanni Braschi, who had been the private secretary of Benedict XIV and Clement XIV's treasurer, was elected, taking the name Pius VI. The new pontiff was very generous to his relatives, especially his nephew, Luigi Braschi, who became the Duke of Nemi, and Luigi's brother, who was created a cardinal. Since the Bourbons continued to pressure Pius to eliminate the Jesuits in Prussia and Russia, the pope succeeded in having Frederick the Great secularize the order in Prussia, but Catherine the Great insisted that they remain untouched in Russia.

After the death of Maria Theresa in Austria in 1780, her son, Joseph II (1780-90), pushed ahead with a vigorous program of state control over the Church. Joseph was committed to the principles of Febronianism which were formulated by an auxiliary bishop of Trier, Johann von Hontheim, who wrote a book entitled *On the State of the Church*, in 1763, employing the pseudonym,

Febronius. Hontheim's objective was to return Protestants to the fold. His program focused on the strengthening of the national churches and the de-emphasizing of the power of Rome. According to Hontheim, the early Church was grounded in episcopal rule, not papal supremacy, which developed out of the *False Decretals* of the ninth century. Hontheim reasoned:

> The church was never founded to be an absolute monarchy. That the pope is infallible is no article of faith. General councils are the ultimate government of the Catholic Church and should meet more frequently. . . . The Curia must be watched; princes must act to reform, though with the advice of bishops; excommunications need not be feared, and national churches or princes may rightly resist power when it is exercised without warrant.[148]

Although Hontheim's book was placed on the Index in 1764, "it became almost a textbook of political theory," in Austria.[149] For example, Joseph II required that all papal communications receive his approval before they could be published, and he insisted on nominating all the bishops of his realm. Further, he redrew the boundaries of all the dioceses and parishes, because many had become superfluous, and ordered that seminarians be educated in institutions run by the state. For these and other reasons, Pius VI decided to travel to Vienna to discuss these issues with the emperor.[150] Pius VI was feted in Austria for a month or so, returning to Rome in June 1782. The deliberations between pope and emperor were of no avail, for Joseph continued to dominate the church in Austria during his entire reign. Joseph's younger brother, Leopold, the duke of Tuscany, who was also deeply committed to Febronian principles, encouraged the bishops of Tuscany to hold a reform council at Pistoia in 1786. This synod, attended by over 200 clergy, espoused the Four Gallican Articles of 1682, and subscribed to a goodly number of Jansenist positions. In 1794, Pius VI condemned eighty-five propositions of the synod in the strongest possible terms. His bull, *Auctorem fidei*, was the last of the anti-Jansenist pronouncements in the tradition of *Unigenitus*.[151]

Leopold succeeded his brother as emperor in 1790. Although some of the more heavy-handed of the governmental regulations were softened in time, "Josephinism prevailed in Austria until the middle of the nineteenth century and exerted a strong influence in southwestern Germany."[152] The popes in the eighteenth century had very little to say in the selection of bishops in France, Spain, and the Austrian Empire. As a matter of fact, they did not normally enjoy the right of nominating bishops outside of Italy.[153]

It was during the pontificate of Pius VI that the clouds of revolution began to gather over France. In May 1789, King Louis XVI (1774-92) called the Estates General together at Versailles (for the first time since 1614) to address the financial plight of the country. Because France was on the brink of insolvency, the bankers refused to make any more loans to keep the country liquid. In June, the Estates General constituted itself as the National Constituent Assembly, and in July 1790 it enacted the Civil Constitution of the Clergy, which amounted to "a rearrangement, largely dictated by economic causes, of the temporal framework of the Church."[154] The king was compelled to promulgate the Civil Constitution in August 1790. This legislation completely reorganized diocesan (and parish) boundaries, reducing the number of dioceses from 134 to eighty-three. Bishops were to be elected by the laity and given their canonical investiture by the metropolitan. The pope was to be merely informed of the proceedings as an acknowledgment of his primacy. The Constituent Assembly dissolved the monasteries, nationalized the lands and the endowments of the Church, and elected to pay the clergy a salary. The salary scales were set by the Civil Constitution and, in effect, the bishops and the priests became state officials.

> The clear aim of the Constitution was to cut off the French church, for all practical purposes, from contact with Rome and to transform it into a self-contained national church. . . . Only a minority of the clergy accepted the Constitution, and for ten years the French church was split by the bitter conflict between the "constitutionals" and the "non-jurors" (i.e., those who out of loyalty to the papacy, refused to take the oath to the Civil Constitution).[155]

About one-third of the clergy took the oath, while the non-jurors among the bishops and the clergy (some thirty or forty thousand) for the most part emigrated to England, Italy, Germany, and elsewhere. Those who did take the oath formed the nucleus of the French constitutional church. Pius VI issued a condemnation of the Civil Constitution of the Clergy in March 1791, but his action had little effect, either on the French government or in the French church because his response came so late. The concordat of 1516 had been unilaterally revoked and the French church had been nationalized without any discussion with Rome.[156] By 1794 even the constitutional church was in financial difficulties because the government was no longer willing (or able) to pay the clerical salaries.

In 1795, a new experiment in constitutional government was launched with the establishment of the Directory which was to last four years. It was during this period that a young army officer named Napoleon Bonaparte rose to prominence. His victories against the Piedmontese army in the spring of 1796 and the legations (i.e., Ravenna, Ferrara, and Bologna) later in the year paved the way for his establishment of the Cisalpine Republic in Milan in May 1797. Italy was then within the grasp of Napoleon, but he did not pursue a military occupation of Rome at that time. Bonaparte set up his court just outside Milan, drawing up a constitution similar to the French constitution and appointing officials for his new republic. He remained there until November 1797. Although Pius VI was bitterly opposed to the new French rule in the North, Cardinal Barnaba Chiaramonti, the bishop of Imola and the future Pius VII, in his Christmas sermon in 1797 declared that the new democracy was not at all in opposition to the precepts of the gospel. "Do not believe," he said, "that the Catholic religion is against democracy."[157] As the new French version of democracy unfolded, however, with its excessive taxation, its confiscation of lands and personal property, sentiment in Italy turned against the French occupation. For example, in May 1798 the Cisalpine Republic, on the verge of insolvency, nationalized all the property of the church and ordered the dissolution of the monasteries. Because the government of Paris desired the establishment of a Roman republic, the assassination of a French general in Rome in December 1797 served as the occasion for the occupation of the Holy City by the French troops in February 1798. Pius VI, in his eighties at the time, was told that he would have three days to prepare himself to leave the city.

> So "Citizen Pope," with his half paralyzed legs, was trundled off, to suffer for eighteen months more and then to die in sordid circumstances at Valence while his books and his plate, and his sacred vessels were likewise carried away by the cartload.[158]

Cardinal Antonelli was left behind in Rome to carry on as best he could. The French occupation of Rome lasted until May 1799 when the Austrian forces operating in the north forced the French to withdraw from Rome. Bonaparte, however, defeated the Austrians at Marengo in 1800, restoring French control in northern Italy. Pius died in August 1799 at Valence in southeastern France after one of the stormiest pontificates since the Middle Ages. Roger Aubert, an eminent French ecclesiastical historian, says regarding Pius VI:

> Misfortune which pursued Pius VI in his later years has given rise to his idealization and has marked him as a martyr pope. There was a great difference, however, between the myth and the reality. The new pope was indeed pious and honest, and he demonstrated irreproachable and genuine courage in the face of adversity. But Pius was not a prepossessing personality. He was vain, worldly and proud of his handsome appearance. . . . He also revived nepotism once more and practiced it to a greater degree than any other pope during the eighteenth century.[159]

PIUS VII (1800-23)

The cardinals were generally in favor of accepting the Austrian Emperor Francis II's invitation to convene the conclave in Venice because they would be safer there than in Rome. Hence it was in the Benedictine monastery on the island of San Giorgio that the thirty-five cardinals (thirty of them Italians) gathered to select a successor to Pius VI. Cardinal Marius Mattei, the archbishop of Ferrara, was the choice of Austria, while those seeking to accommodate both France and Austria favored Cardinal Bellisomi. After a stalemate of more than three months, a compromise candidate, Cardinal Barnaba Chiaramonti, was elected. Chiaramonti had joined the Benedictines as a youth and became a professor of theology at Paris and then at Sant' Anselmo in Rome. He was open to new ideas which perhaps caused some hostility among his more traditional colleagues. He was appointed bishop of Tivoli in 1783, created a cardinal in 1785, and transferred to Imola where he demonstrated rather outstanding pastoral talents for fifteen years.[160] By the time the saintly, gracious Pius VII (1800-23) took possession of Rome, the political landscape had been transformed again. After Napoleon's victory at Marengo in April 1800, Austrian troops pulled out of central Italy and the Cisalpine region was again under French control. Bonaparte became the first consul of a new authoritarian Republic which replaced the unstable Directory in November 1799. "So great was the enthusiasm for Bonaparte's leadership that a national plebiscite produced a majority of 99.99 percent in favor of the new system."[161]

Both the pope and Bonaparte wanted a kind of regularization of Church-state relations which had been in complete disarray since 1790. The work on a new concordat was begun in November 1800 and was completed on July 15, 1801. It was Pius VII's Secretary of State, Cardinal Ercole Consalvi, who represented the pontiff in the final deliberations that summer. Regarding the new relationship between Rome and Paris, a number of principles were set forth in the new concordat:

> the right of the Holy See to a reorganization of the dioceses, and the right of bishops to a reorganization of the parishes, but in both cases with the prior agreement of the government; the appointment of bishops as under the Old Regime by the head of state, then canonical investment by the pope; appointment of parish priests by the bishops after agreement by the government; . . . the obligation of the government to pay appropriate salaries to bishops and parish priests as compensation for the nationalization of church lands, and finally, . . . the right of the faithful to make gifts to the Church.[162]

Although half the cardinals voted against the agreement, the pope declared his acceptance on August 15, 1801. Although Pius VII wanted Catholicism declared the official religion of France, the concordat stated only that it was the religion of the majority. On the occasion of the ratification of the concordat in Paris, Bonaparte added certain "police regulations," called the Organic Articles, which restored much of the state control over the Church.

They restored the *placet*, the right of government to prevent the publication of all bulls or briefs coming from Rome; banned nuncios and other representatives of Rome from exercising authority in the Church of France; . . . prevented bishops from establishing seminaries or chapters without the leave of government; required teachers at the seminaries to sign the Gallican Articles of 1682, which made general councils the masters of the pope. . . .[163]

Pius VII protested against the addition of the Organic Articles, but did not attempt to withdraw or abrogate the concordat which was to stand as the basis of Church–state relations in France until the Law of Separation in 1905. The removal of the independent financial resources of the French church amounted to a serious blow against Gallicanism because the clergy's only protection from government domination now consisted in its relationship with Rome. The financial subservience to the state agreed on by the concordat probably did more than anything else to weaken the Gallican spirit among considerable numbers of the French episcopate and clergy over the early decades of the nineteenth century. Ironically, because it was Napoleon's vision to strengthen the authority of the bishops who would be responsive to him, he substituted the local and nationalist traditions of the French church with an "administrative centralism," and thus actually set the scene for the weakening of the Gallicanism and episcopalism which was embedded in the nation's culture and unwittingly precipitated the rise of ultramontanism in France.[164]

Soon after Napoleon was declared emperor of the realm with hereditary title in May 1804, he let it be known that he wanted Pius VII to come to Paris to crown him. This created a serious dilemma for the pope inasmuch as his acceding to Bonaparte's wishes would alienate Austria that had secured the very peace which had enabled Pius to be elected in March 1800. Pius did decide to make the trip to Paris and then was treated shabbily by Napoleon while in France. After the coronation took place at Notre Dame in December 1804, Pius remained in Paris until April 1805 before returning to Rome. The pope's presence in France was very well received by the people, who responded to his public appearances with considerable enthusiasm.

The real significance, in the long run, of Pius VII's visit to Paris lay in these popular demonstrations. They represented the first flickering into flame of a new feeling about the papacy in France, a first open manifestation of a new ultramontane sentiment.[165]

Bonaparte left for Milan in April 1805 to be crowned king of Italy. His kingdom in Italy, however, only extended as far south as Ancona on the Adriatic. The Bourbons ruled Naples and Sicily and the Papal States lay inbetween. After the battle of Austerlitz in December 1805, Europe was largely under the sway of Bonaparte, because he had decisively defeated the Russian and Austrian armies in that crucial encounter. It was in 1806 that the emperor occupied the kingdom of Naples, proclaiming his brother, Joseph, king. In spite of the pope's entreaties, France occupied the Papal States in March 1807 and Rome in February 1808. Bonaparte then annexed the Papal States to the French Empire in May 1809. A contingent of French troops confronted the pope at the Quirinal palace and arrested him in June of 1809, carrying him off to Grenoble, and then, on Bonaparte's orders, back over the Alps to Savona on the Italian Riviera. All of the cardinals were taken to Paris save one, and the papal archives were transported there as well. Pius VII responded by excommunicating all "the robbers of Peter's patrimony," but did not explicitly refer to Bonaparte. The pope was confined at Savona until June 1812 when Napoleon had him moved to Fountainebleau, and then, six months later, back to Savona. After Pius was finally released in March 1814, he returned to Rome after an absence of five years. These years of house arrest were extremely trying for the pope because he had no curia and no officials to assist him in the government of the Church. By the end of 1809, Pius VII was clearly unable, and perhaps unwilling, to keep the machinery of government operating. As a result, the number of vacant dioceses multiplied all over Europe and elsewhere.

The years 1809 and 1810 were the absolute nadir for Pius VII and the point of highest exaltation for Napoleon. Ironically, however, as opposition mounted against Bonaparte during 1812, sympathy and support had been mounting for Pius VII throughout Europe. Napoleon's defeat at Leipzig in October 1813 at the hands of Russia, Prussia, and Austria marked the beginning of the end for the general. In March 1814, after the allied armies had occupied Paris, Napoleon abdicated, retreating to Elba. The historian Gordon Wright summarizes the cause of Napoleon's defeat:

> The crucial factor in Napoleon's defeat was the decision of Europe's monarchs to join forces, to suspend their jealous rivalries and cooperate for the duration of the war. Napoleon himself, by his ruthless and self-centered policies, had forged the iron ring of sovereigns that eventually choked and crushed his ambitions.[166]

Bonaparte surprised the allies in March 1815 by leaving Elba and taking control of France once again. However, the four powers (Austria, Prussia, Britain, and Russia) declared him an outlaw and pursued him until his final defeat at Waterloo in June 1815.

The Congress of Vienna—from September 1814 to November 1815—orchestrated the peace and reshaped the face of Europe largely through the efforts of the four powers. The Bourbon monarchy was restored in France under Louis XVIII, who was the creature of the allied powers rather than the choice of the French nation.[167] Austria, which had lost its holdings in Germany in the early 1800s, was given full control of northern Italy. In August 1806, the Austrian emperor, Francis II (1792-1806), decided to lay down his imperial crown and declare the end of the Holy Roman Empire. He henceforth bore the title of King Francis I of Austria (1806-35).[168] As a result of the Vienna deliberations, Prussia's acquisition of new territories along the Rhine and in eastern Europe was recognized, further confirming this nation's emergence as one of the principal players in nineteenth-century Europe. Ferdinand VII (1813-33) returned to govern Spain in March 1814, after the French had occupied it for about six years. The final act of the Vienna Congress was the restoration of the temporal power of the pope up to the River Po, including the legations (Ravenna, Ferrara, and Bologna). These territories were a mixed blessing for the papacy, for although they were the richest and most profitable sectors of the Papal States, they had become practically unmanageable for the Roman government. In the seventeen years of separation from the pope under French rule, they had become accustomed to a new way of life without clerical rule.

> The French had been hard taskmasters; they had taxed, conscripted and exploited; but they had brought into power, of a sort, Italian laymen at Bologna and Ferrara, at Ravenna and Rimini, at Forli and Imola and Cesena, who had never enjoyed any share in government before, and who would not now find it easy to hand it back to the clergy. The troubles of the next forty years in the Papal States mostly had their roots in that region. . . .[169]

Cardinal Consalvi, the pope's representative at Vienna, had been able to keep the Papal States mostly intact because the four great powers had been sensitive to the sufferings of the papacy at the hands of Napoleon. Consalvi's ideal was a Europe of strong monarchies which would be responsive to the pope in spiritual matters. He envisioned the Papal States as a theocracy wherein Europe's burgeoning aspirations toward democracy and liberalism would not be welcome. For a number of reasons, the Papal States were an anachronism. For example, the administration of government by clerics was really no longer a viable option after the French Revolution. Nonetheless, by an enactment of July 1816, four territories in the legations were to be ruled by cardinal legates and thirteen other regions were put under the control of bishop-delegates. This return to the old arrangement was not well received. A second problem for the papal territories was that there were no adequate resources to keep the peace internally. As Hales notes, "When the revolution struck in her own territories, in 1831-2, she [i.e., the papal government] had to call on the Austrians; when it struck in 1848, the French came to the rescue in the following year."[170]

Finally, throughout Italy, from north to south, there began to develop, especially in the 1820s and 1830s, a ground swell for national unification. More and more Italians were eager for the day when Italy would be one, with its own civilian political government like the rest of their European neighbors.[171]

Pius VII presided over the Church in the early years after the Congress of Vienna with considerable wisdom and a steady hand. He left most of the political issues inside and outside the Papal States to Cardinal Consalvi, who was much more open to the spirit of the times than the majority of the cardinals, who thought that the rise of liberalism and the revolutionary spirit across Europe were nothing more than recurrences of the *geist* of the Protestant Revolution. In spite of the opposition of the great powers, Pius VII revived the Jesuit order in 1814. During his last years, he did whatever he could through the efforts of Consalvi to create the most favorable conditions possible for the Church in Europe.

A revived pope saw all about him a devastated Church—empty sees, obsolete dioceses, closed monasteries, lost endowments, maimed chapters, few seminaries. The Church could only be built with the aid and consent of friendly governments.[172]

The negotiating of concordats and other lesser agreements was seen as the way to restore some of the Church's old prerogatives, but this inevitably meant the expansion of state controls over the selection of bishops and higher clergy, and the mutual recognition that the church lands which had been alienated during the French Revolution were lost forever. In return, there were in many cases written assurances of government salaries for a good share of the clergy, the freedom of bishops to communicate with Rome, and the right to reestablish seminaries and to provide other educational services.

LEO XII (1823-29) AND GREGORY XVI (1831-46)

With the death of Pius VII in August 1823, the conservative majority among the cardinals was intent on the removal of Cardinal Consalvi at any price. After Austria exercised its veto against one of the more inflexible zealots, Cardinal Severoli, the majority settled on Cardinal Annibale della Genga, who had spent most of his ecclesiastical career in diplomatic service for Pius VI and Pius VII, until he ran into trouble with the latter in 1814 over his failure to negotiate the return of Avignon to papal control. Leo XII proved himself to be a pontiff who was not up to the challenges and demands which the times had placed on him. Roger Aubert refers to him as "a somewhat pale figure who was not in control of events."[173] As a member of the zealots, the new pontiff was supposed to take a stand against Cardinal Consalvi's diplomatic efforts among the nations, but after a few years he decided to collaborate with the great powers as the best recourse against the movements of liberalism spreading throughout Europe. Leo's stringent policies in Rome, e.g., restricting the sale of alcohol and establishing a dress code for women, did not ingratiate him with the citizens of the Holy City. Furthermore, the situation in the Papal States within six to eight years after the Congress of Vienna had become desperate:

> After six more years of turmoil the Papal States became the home of foreign garrisons, because only foreign garrisons could secure the continued existence of the Papal States. This fateful predicament—the vocation to rule historic lands inalienable; the inability to rule effectively; the presence of Austrian and French soldiers and all that implied for political independence—conditioned the papacy of the nineteenth century.[174]

Aubert adds these rather sad comments regarding Pope Leo XII:

> Continually ill, the pope died on 10 February 1829, at a peak of unpopularity, despised by the Roman people, who did not think highly of his attempts at moral reform, looked down upon by liberals who called him a tyrant beholden to the Holy Alliance [i.e., Austria, Britain, Russia and Prussia], and unforgiven by the disappointed for his turning away from their party.[175]

Francesco Castiglione, who was nearly elected pope in 1823 and was favored by Pius VII to be his successor, was chosen by the cardinals after a five-week conclave in March 1829. Educated as a canon lawyer and having served as a bishop for a dozen or so years, he was brought to Rome by Pius VII in 1821. Castiglione, who called himself Pius VIII (1829-30), died after less than two years in the chair of Peter. Though he was not especially gifted as a politician, he did pursue the Cardinal Consalvi approach in dealing with the great powers. He took a rather liberal stand in approving of the transfer of power in France during the July 1830 revolution which deposed the autocratic Charles X (1824-30) and gave the crown to the king's cousin, the Duke of Orleans, Louis Philippe (1830-48). Pius VIII, who was ill during most of his short tenure as pope, died in November 1830.

It was during the fifty-day conclave that eventually elected Cardinal Bartolomeo Cappellari as Gregory XVI (1831-46) that the Italian revolution of 1831 began. The Carbonari (i.e., a political sect with liberal and nationalist leanings born in Calabria) operating in the legations used the occasion of the conclave in Rome to stage uprisings in Parma and Modena and to seize Bologna.

> By February 25 there was a provisional government at Bologna, to which not only the cities of the legations but almost all the cities of Umbria and

the Marches had given their adherence, and a declaration was issued that the temporal power of the pope was at an end.[176]

The rumblings in the North probably accelerated the cardinals' deliberations somewhat. They were aware that they had to elect someone who would be acceptable to the Austrians because it was they who would most likely be called on to put down the revolt in the legations. The Austrians were indeed called on and they did quell the uprising in March 1831, but this was only a very temporary solution. It became more and more obvious that the presence of the Austrian soldiers alone enabled the pope to continue his rule over the northern districts of his territories. Louis Philippe of France, desirous of challenging the Austrian presence in Italy, called for a conference in Rome to discuss the situation:

> At his insistence a conference met at Rome, and the major powers (including Austria) then advised the pope to liberalize his government so that another revolution would become less likely. One of their suggestions was to revive some of the old provincial liberties which used to exist in the Papal States. But the papacy did not seem grateful for the advice. . . .[177]

The presence of the Austrian troops at Bologna and the French garrison at Ancona until 1838 was a dramatic indication of the inability of the pope to control the Papal States without outside assistance. In spite of the fact that resentment and unrest continued to mount and fester, Gregory XVI lacked the vision to make the adjustments necessary to lessen the opposition. So long as changes in the political landscape of the Papal States—i.e., a greater degree of local autonomy and the removal of all or most of the clergy from the control of the civil government—were not made, the pope would have to depend totally on foreign troops and mercenaries to keep the peace.

Gregory XVI's background did not incline him to an openness to new developments. He became a Camaldolese monk in his teens, and taught for some time after his ordination. In 1799 he published a work entitled *The Triumph of the Holy See*, which took a strong position on papal infallibility and on the right of the popes to maintain their temporal power. Voices began to be raised attempting to justify the revolutionary movements that were gaining momentum throughout Europe, particularly in France. Félicité de Lamennais, a clergyman, and a small group of colleagues launched the publication, *L'Avenir*, in October 1830, which proclaimed the virtues of liberty, republican government, and the separation of Church and state as the wave of the future. An exception was made, of course, for the Papal States because *L'Avenir* defended the secular jurisdiction of the papacy over its territory. The overall political radicalism of the group was opposed by King Louis Philippe and the majority of the senior clergy of France. Lamennais and his group ceased publication of *L'Avenir* in November 1831 and made their way to Rome with the hope of gaining some acceptance of their ideas there. Gregory XVI ignored them while they were in Rome, but did respond in August 1832 with a rather vehement condemnation of many of Lamennais' positions in the encyclical, *Mirari vos*, although he did not mention Lamennais or *L'Avenir* by name.[178]

The anguish of the pope and his curia is reflected again and again in the text of *Mirari vos*. Gregory referred to the "storms of evil and toil" that afflicted him at the outset of his pontificate.[179] He made reference to "the insolent and factious men who endeavored to raise the standard of treason. . . . We see the destruction of public order, the fall of principalities and the overturning of all legitimate power approaching."[180] Gregory's views on freedom of speech and the press were unambiguous:

> Experience shows, even from earliest times, that cities renowned for wealth, dominion and glory perished as a result of this single evil, namely immoderate freedom of opinion, license of free speech and desire for novelty.
> . . . Here we must include that harmful and never sufficiently denounced freedom to publish any writings whatever and disseminate them to the people, which some dare to demand and promote with so great a clamor.[181]

Regarding the issue of the separation of Church and state, *Mirari vos* declared:

> Nor can we predict happier times for religion and government from the plans of those who desire vehemently to separate the Church from the state, and to break the mutual concord between temporal authority and the priesthood. It is certain that that concord which always was favorable and beneficial for the sacred and the civil order is feared by the shameless lovers of liberty.[182]

In June 1834, a shorter encyclical, *Singulari nos*, specifically targeted Lamennais, referring to him as a "wretched author" whose little book, *Words of a Believer*, Gregory condemned because "it contains false, calumnious and rash propositions which lead to anarchy."[183] Father Lamennais broke with the Church in November 1836. This siege mentality against the "democratic liberties" dogged Gregory XVI and Pius IX (1846-78) throughout their pontificates. It was only with Leo XIII (1878-1903) that this overriding political negativism began to disappear.

As a former head of the Congregation for the Propagation of the Faith, Pope Gregory did much to revive foreign missionary activity, and was greatly assisted in this endeavor by the various religious congregations, including the

Jesuit order which by 1840 or so had grown to more than 4,000 members. The mission activity extended to East and West, i.e., Africa, India, Indochina, China, the Philippines, the Americas, and elsewhere.[184] When Gregory died in June 1846, such needed reforms as allowing laymen to hold significant civil offices in the papal territories, or granting self-government to the municipalities, were not yet even seriously considered.

> Thus serious defects in management and the administration of justice not only continued but constantly grew worse. New inventions such as railroads and gas lights were not permitted in the Papal States. And all the while the indebtedness of the States increased. The curia paid no heed to the growing movement for national unity, while those who favored it were endeavoring in every possible way to realize the ideal of the Resorgimento.[185]

PIUS IX (1846-78)

Gregory's successor was Cardinal Mastai-Ferretti, who had been bishop of Imola for nearly sixteen years. Though the favorite candidate was Cardinal Raffaele Lambruschini, Pope Gregory's Secretary of State, Mastai was elected on the second day of the conclave. He was not very well known in Rome but was considered to be a moderate politically, and Cardinal Lambruschini had been too close to Austria to suit a number of the cardinals. Pius IX had earned a reputation as a moderate liberal during his days as bishop of Imola.

> Far from courting an easy popularity among the propertied classes, or the higher clergy, he continued to show, even after he had received the red hat [i.e., 1840], an independence and liberality of outlook which often cost him the friendship of the larger landowners in his diocese as well as that of senior government officials.[186]

Mastai was not a particularly learned bishop, but he did manifest at Imola a great pastoral heart and was widely respected for his generosity to the needy. He had the respect of the liberals in the region largely because he shared their dream of an Italy freed from the control of foreign powers. As pope he chose Cardinal Gizzi, the papal legate at Forli and the favorite of the liberal cardinals, as his Secretary of State. At the outset, Pius showed a great deal of kindness to Fr. Gioacchino Ventura, the very influential disciple of Lamennais.

Pius IX's moderate liberalism was not deeply rooted and, as a matter of fact, disappeared completely during the stirring events of 1848-49.[187] France was apparently the first neighboring country to be affected by the great wave of revolution which spread over Europe in 1848. The February revolution of 1848 precipitated Louis Philippe's abdication and the end of the Orleanist regime.

Since 1846, a severe economic crisis had created massive class conflicts and heavy unemployment in France and elsewhere. A provisional government set up a general election for Easter Sunday which drew a tremendous turnout, and the great majority of the seats in the new Constituent Assembly went to conservative or moderate candidates.[188] The new rather conservative Assembly made things worse by eliminating a number of public works programs and failing to be responsive to the mounting unemployment. The government's insensitivity resulted in a three-day civil war, referred to as the June Days, the bloodiest revolt since the Revolution. The Assembly set itself to the task of drafting a new constitution which featured a unicameral legislature and a president. In December 1848, the presidential election turned out to be a landslide victory for Louis Napoleon (1848-52), alleged to be the son of Napoleon Bonaparte's brother, Louis. After modifying the constitution in December 1851 and having it overwhelmingly ratified by a plebiscite, Louis Napoleon assumed the title of emperor, calling himself Napoleon III (1852-70).

The 1848 insurrections in Italy were propelled largely by the declaration of war on Austria issued by Charles Albert, the king of Piedmont-Sardinia in April 1848. It was widely expected by many liberals that Pius IX would cooperate somehow with Charles Albert in the fight to free the peninsula from Austrian control. But that was not to be. Although Pius had initiated some governmental reforms at the beginning of his pontificate, he never for a moment intended to transform the theocracy of the Papal States into a representative government, nor did he ever envision himself as the president of a unified Italy. The pope's liberal tendencies were wildly overestimated by those who were laboring for national unification. This became painfully clear to republicans and federalists alike when Pius delivered his famous allocution of April 29, 1848, wherein he discouraged the war against the Austrians and exhorted the Italians to remain at peace with their neighbors. The nationalists confronted the pope who was staying at the Quirinal palace "and demanded the convocation of a constituent assembly and a declaration of war on Austria."[189] Pius, on the advice of his new Secretary of State, Cardinal Giacomo Antonelli, fled the city, taking refuge in the Kingdom of Naples where he stayed for a year and a half, while Antonelli managed things in Rome. Both Pope Pius and Cardinal Antonelli were of the mind that keeping a tight rein on the Papal States through the continuation of an autocratic, clerical rule was the only way to secure the pope's independence. They did not waver in this conviction, although it proved to be hopelessly out-of-date, for the remainder of their lives.

In Rome, a Constituent Assembly was elected in January 1849, and in February it proclaimed itself a republic, with Giuseppi Mazzini occupying the principal leadership role. Responding to the pope's appeals for help, the neighboring states, especially France and Austria, drove out the republicans, allowing Pius to return to Rome in April 1850. "From 1849 to 1870 a garrison of

French troops remained in Rome to protect the pope. The northern legations were occupied by the Austrians until 1859."[190]

When Pius returned from his seventeen-month exile in the Kingdom of Naples, his mind and heart were set irrevocably against the goals of the Resorgimento. He would never waver again in his conviction that liberalism in all its forms was a product of the Revolution of 1789 and was to be condemned and resisted at all costs. From April 1850 to December of 1864 Pius issued some twenty or more letters, encyclicals, and allocutions against the multitude of errors of his day: e.g., naturalism, errors concerning the nature of the Church, and Church–state relations, which were then bundled together almost as indiscriminately as Pope Clement XI's *Unigenitus* against Jansenism in 1713. This document, the *Syllabus of Errors*, comprising eighty condemned propositions, was appended to his encyclical, *Quanta cura*, and promulgated on December 8, 1864. These two documents, when viewed together, represent a position almost diametrically opposed to Vatican II's, *The Church in the Modern World* and *The Declaration on Religious Freedom*. In *Quanta cura*, the pope reminded the bishops of the world of his many written attacks against "the chief errors of this most unhappy age," and then they were summarized again in this encyclical and in the accompanying *Syllabus*. The repeated attacks against freedom of religion and the doctrine of the separation of Church and state, the insistence on preferential treatment for the Catholic Church as the one true religion, and the absolute importance of preserving the temporal power of the papacy—these positions were all proclaimed as sacrosanct by Pio Nono. To present Vatican II's teachings as "developments" of the pronouncements of Pius IX is to push the limits of credulity a bit too far.[191]

Proposition eighty of the *Syllabus* was something of a recapitulation of all the errors condemned in 1864: "The Roman pontiff can and should reconcile and harmonize himself with progress, with liberalism and with recent civilization."[192] This was a stunning embarrassment, particularly for western bishops and churchmen because it cast a dark pall of disapproval on the positive developments that were occurring socially and politically in the nineteenth century. Also, proposition seventy-seven condemning religious tolerance when it was just becoming a reality in the western world, and seventy-nine which attacked freedom of speech, seemed to represent regressive positions which smacked of an age that had died in the 1700s. In January 1865, Bishop Felix Dupanloup, the bishop of Orleans, composed a commentary on the *Syllabus* which softened its harshness and its obtuse character. Dupanloup's pamphlet was widely circulated and became an unofficial commentary on the document.

Another one of Pius IX's overtures which backfired was his attempt to reopen discussions with the Orthodox churches. His lack of sensitivity to the distinctive character of the Orthodox communities is reminiscent of the actions of Cardinal Humbert vis-à-vis Michael Cerularius, and the stance of Pope Eugene IV at the Council of Florence. The efforts of the Congregation for the Propagation of the Faith to tie the Uniate churches more closely to Rome and to further Latinize them had an understandably negative effect on the larger eastern Orthodox bodies which were becoming increasingly more autocephalous with the breakup of the Ottoman Empire after 1850. Pius IX's bull of July 1867, *Reversurus*, although directed specifically at the Armenian Uniates, but by implication, at all the Uniate churches, intended to secure closer Roman control over all these communities.[193] At Vatican I, during the July 1870 voting on the constitution, *Pastor aeternus* (dealing with papal primacy of jurisdiction and papal infallibility), the Melchite, Syrian, and Chaldean Uniate patriarchs, along with several of their suffragans, who were afraid that this conciliar pronouncement would undermine the patriarchal constitution of the Eastern churches, left Rome before the final votes were taken. J. Hajjar notes in his treatment of Pius IX's unfortunate dealings with the Eastern churches: "In short, at the death of Pius IX, not only did the principal problems remain unsolved, but Eastern Catholicism was in distinct danger of losing confidence in its raison d'etre and its future."[194]

Another development which had been gaining momentum during the 1800s was the assertion of the pope's infallibility. As previously mentioned, Bartolomeo Cappellari (who became Gregory XVI) had written an influential treatise, *The Triumph of the Holy See*, in 1799, which forcefully advocated papal infallibility. Another important study entitled, *On the Pope*, published in 1819 by the French diplomat and philosopher, Joseph de Maistre, had an enormous effect in terms of popularizing the notion of the pope's infallibility outside the academic community in France and elsewhere. The Collegio Romano, which had been given back to the Jesuits by Leo XII in the 1820s, served as a base for the development of the theology of the papacy. The work of Giovanni Perrone, S. J. (d. 1876), and his colleagues, John Franzelin, S. J. (d. 1886), Carlo Passaglia, S. J. (d. 1887), Clemens Schrader, S. J. (d. 1875), and Joseph Kleutgen, S. J. (d. 1883), provided the foundations for the definitions of the primacy of papal jurisdiction and papal infallibility which were articulated in *Pastor aeternus* of Vatican I. (We shall deal with *Pastor aeternus* in the next chapter.)

Roger Aubert gives a rather succinct description of the limitations of Pius IX. First, he was a very emotional man who tended to follow the last advice given to him. Second, his philosophical and theological backgrounds were superficial, and this often led him to take regressive stands which were closed to new ideas. And finally, his closest advisors were even more insensitive to the social and political developments since 1789 than he was.[195] This having been said, Pio Nono's stately appearance and the fact that he was looked on as a martyr for all that he had to endure, tended to give rise to a cult. People came to Rome expressly to see the pope. Pictures of Pio Nono were to be found in countless homes throughout the Catholic world. The devotion to the person of the pope started with him (though some would say that it began with Pius VII). Klaus Schatz, a recent historian of the papacy, notes that Pius IX was a man whose charm, humor and spontaneous heartiness made him a very pleasant person to deal with. In any case, the phenomenon of "papal veneration" under Pius IX was something new, although it did have some precedents.[196]

SUMMARY

Although Pope Hadrian VI of Utrecht (1522-23) had accurately diagnosed the gravity of the situation in Rome during the early decades of the sixteenth century, he gravely underestimated the dimensions of the crisis in Germany in the 1520s. The unfortunate Clement VII (1523-34) was never able to come to grips with the prospect of an ecumenical council to engage in church reform because, according to some, he feared that his illegitimate birth and the allegedly simoniacal taint on his election as pope would be made an issue against him. It was Paul III who finally convoked the Council of Trent in 1545 to address the many problems of the age. Trent—in spite of frustrating delays and postponements—did in its three sessions go a very long way to confront the disciplinary abuses tearing the Church apart. It also articulated a whole series of doctrinal decrees which refined for Catholics many positions that had been ambiguous. Finally, the council solidified, perhaps once and for all, the monarchical status of the pope, so that in a sense the modern papacy could be said to have taken shape at Trent.

Although it took generations before the disciplinary enactments of the council were implemented everywhere, the curial offices in Rome, radically reformed by Pius V (1566-72), Gregory XIII (1572-85), and Sixtus V (1585-90), did spearhead most of the needed changes in discipline over time. The seventeenth and eighteenth centuries were not memorable ones for the Roman pontiffs, who fell under the control of the kings of Spain, France, and the Hapsburg Empire. Clement XI's imprecise bull, *Unigenitus* (1713), precipitated a heated discussion on the irreformable character of the popes' teaching authority which was not put to rest until Vatican I. Perhaps the most unfortunate papal action of the eighteenth century was the suppression of the Jesuits by Pope Clement XIV in 1773 which was brought about by unjustified political pressure from Portugal, Spain, and France. In the nineteenth century, Popes Gregory XVI and Pius IX were tragically determined to retain their hold on the Papal States, thus frustrating for decades the formation of a unified Italy which was yearning to join the European family of nations.

CHAPTER 8

The Installation
of the Absolutist Model

1869 to the Present

⌒

It was in December 1864 that Pius IX announced to the Roman cardinals his intention of calling an ecumenical council to remedy the many ills besetting the Church. Finding that the majority of them favored the idea, the pope sent a letter to some three dozen Latin bishops and several Uniate ordinaries, outlining the errors that he wanted condemned and emphasizing the need to define the notion of papal primacy. The pope also pointed to certain areas where church discipline should be reviewed and strengthened, and raised the long overdue issue of the reform of canon law. The majority of the bishops responded favorably, but a public announcement of the council was not made by Pio Nono until June 1867. In the winter of 1867-68, a commission of cardinals and consultors was appointed to prepare the topics and the schemata for deliberation. One of the consultors appointed at that time, Bishop-elect Karl Hefele of Rottenburg, was given the task of drawing up the rules of procedure for the conciliar sessions.[1] Hefele, who had taught church history at Tübingen before his appointment as bishop, had for a good number of years been writing a magisterial work on the councils of the Church, which he did not finish until a few years before his death in 1893. No one of his generation had a firmer grasp on the intricacies of the ecumenical councils than did Karl Hefele. According to the procedure drafted by him and approved by the commission, all cardinals and bishops were to be invited, along with the generals of the religious orders of men. Pius IX sent a letter of invitation to the bishops of the eastern Orthodox churches, but they refused to attend, as did the heads of the major Protestant denominations. This was not surprising given the pope's previous history with the Orthodox, his Latinizing efforts vis-à-vis the Uniates, and his overall lack of ecumenical sensitivity in both the East and the West.

Although the subject of papal infallibility had not been raised by the pope in his communications with the bishops, it had surfaced in Europe and elsewhere, and was widely discussed. In Germany, for example, fourteen of the

240

twenty bishops dispatched a letter to the pope in the fall of 1869 indicating that they felt that a definition of papal infallibility was "inopportune." The signatories included Bishop William Ketteler of Mainz, Hefele, and the archbishops of Munich and Cologne.[2] The French episcopate was divided into ultramontanes (e.g., Cardinal Donnet of Bordeaux and Bishop Pie of Poitiers) who desired the definition, and liberals who were opposed to it, such as Bishop Felix Dupanloup of Orleans who felt that such a definition was inopportune at that time. Bishop Maret, dean of the theology faculty at the Sorbonne, was the only French prelate who denied the personal infallibility of the pope.[3] The liberals were afraid that the definition would establish the papacy as an absolute monarchy once and for all. The English delegation, led by Cardinal Henry Manning of Westminster, was largely in the ultramontane camp, while the U.S. contingent was split between the ultramontanes (e.g., Archbishop Martin Spalding of Baltimore and Bishop Michael Heiss of La Crosse) and the inopportunists (e.g., Archbishop Peter Kenrick of St. Louis and Archbishop John Purcell of Cincinnati). A number of the U.S. bishops, however, e.g., James Gibbons of North Carolina and John McCloskey of New York, were not clearly on one side or the other at the outset of the council. The historian James Hennesey, S.J., evaluates the American delegation:

> Most of the American bishops during the council were conciliationists, willing to define the doctrine of [papal] infallibility but not using the word, or simply inopportunists, judging a definition for various reasons inexpedient. A dozen, mostly of French origin, were strong proponents; an equal number opposed the definition on historical and doctrinal grounds.[4]

Vatican I opened on December 8, 1869 with over 700 delegates in attendance, along with the pope. This amounted to about one-half of the bishops and dignitaries who had the right to attend. One of the first items of business for the general congregations which began to meet on December 10 was the election of the bishops who would be on the deputation *de fide* which was responsible for the preparation of the schemata to be presented to the council for deliberation. A small group of infallibilists, headed by Cardinal Manning and several others, managed to present a slate of twenty-four fathers—all of whom were infallibilists—for approval by the whole body. All twenty-four were elected without a single member of the opposition having been included on this most critical and influential committee. Dom Cuthbert Butler observes regarding the stacking of this deputation by the infallibilists:

> It was surely an error of judgment not to accord a considerable and influential minority, counting among its members a number of the foremost and most justly respected bishops of the Church, some represen-

tation, some vehicle for the expression of its views on the committee. The practical effect was that the minority became an opposition, exasperated by the sense that the majority was bent on overwhelming it by mere force of numbers, without giving it a fair hearing.[5]

At the third general congregation on December 20, 1869, the members of the deputation *de fide* were announced, and on December 28, deliberations began on the *Constitution on the Catholic Faith*, which after six days of discussion was sent back for a total reworking because its initial scope was too broad and not sufficiently focused on the problems of the day. Meanwhile a three-part schema on the Church had been distributed to the delegates: ten chapters on the Church itself, three chapters on the relationship between Church and state, and a final two chapters on the Roman pontiff, but no chapter on infallibility.[6] Cardinal Manning of Westminster, Bishop Ignaz Senestrey of Regensburg, and several others sent a letter to all the fathers asking that they subscribe to a petition requesting that the council define the infallibility of the pope. By the end of January there were about 480 who declared themselves in favor of the definition. Almost simultaneously, another petition was distributed urging that for various reasons the issue of infallibility not be defined. This second petition garnered about 140 signatures by the end of January. It was rather clear at that point that there was by no means a consensus on the matter, because there was a substantial minority (i.e., twenty percent or more) who did not want papal infallibility defined by the council. Most of the opposition came from countries where religious pluralism prevailed, such as Germany, eastern Europe, Hungary, and the United States, whereas the Italian, Spanish, and Spanish-American bishops were generally in favor of the definition. It should be noted that the Italian, Spanish, and Spanish-American prelates constituted about forty percent of the delegates present.[7] The eighty-one French delegates, however, were divided on the issue.

Between January 10 and March 18 (when the revised schema on the Catholic faith was ready for debate), the fathers discussed the reform of canon law, two schemata on the bishops, and a draft on the clergy, but all four of these documents were remanded to committee for extensive reworking. In the course of these discussions, there were frequent complaints about the growth of centralism and the loss of ordinary jurisdiction on the part of bishops both in the East and in the West.[8] Also, claims were made by the Uniate bishops that the Latin discipline was being applied more and more extensively to the eastern rite churches. After Bishop Audu, the patriarch of Babylon of the Chaldeans, had made that point very forcefully before a general congregation, he was summoned that evening to the pope's quarters and given a scolding.[9] Between February 22 and March 18 there was a break in the council sessions in order to remedy the acoustical problems in the south transept of St. Peter's basilica where the sessions were held, because it had been so difficult for the delegates to hear one another.

Debate resumed on the *Constitution on the Catholic Faith* on March 18. The preface enumerated the contemporary errors—rationalism, naturalism, pantheism, materialism, atheism—which were causing so many problems for the faith in the nineteenth century. Chapter one dealt with creation, which was identified as a free act of God wherein He manifested His perfection. The wonders of creation, which from the beginning of time, "brought into being from nothing the twofold created order, that is the spiritual and the bodily," were described as being continually governed by His providence.[10] In chapter two on revelation, although it is affirmed that men and women can come to know God "with certainty from the consideration of created things by the natural power of human reason," divine revelation was considered to be absolutely necessary; "the reason is that God directed human beings to a supernatural end, . . . a sharing of the good things of God that utterly surpass the understanding of the human mind."[11] The council defined faith in chapter three:

> This faith, which is the beginning of human salvation, the Catholic Church professes to be a supernatural virtue, by means of which, with the grace of God inspiring and assisting us, we believe to be true what He has revealed, not because we perceive its intrinsic truth by the natural light of reason, but because of the authority of God Himself, who makes the revelation and can neither deceive or be deceived.[12]

The final chapter on faith and reason analyzed "the twofold order of knowledge," one based on human reason and the other grounded in faith. The document warned that there can never be a true disparity between faith and reason, because the source of both kinds of knowledge is God.[13] Finally, the council went on record affirming that the Church is not in the business of hindering the development of the human sciences; "that in fact she assists and promotes them in many ways."[14] On April 24, 1870, the constitution, *Dei Filius*, was approved by the council fathers and the pope.

The next order of business was the discussion of the schema on the Church. Although a treatment of papal infallibility had not been included in the original draft, Pio Nono decided on March 1 to accede to the wishes of the majority of the fathers and a chapter on the subject was added. The pope's position prior to the beginning of the council was one of neutrality regarding this issue, but by February 1870 he very much wanted it included on the agenda.[15] As a matter of fact, Pius expressed the wish in April that papal primacy and infallibility be treated before any of the other topics in the lengthy draft on the Church. It seemed clear to most observers that if the tract on the Church with its fifteen chapters (plus the addition of a chapter on papal infallibility) were debated, one chapter after the other, the discussion of the papal prerogatives would not take place until at least the spring of 1871.[16] This was unacceptable to the infallibilist fathers and to Pio Nono. As a result, the majority of delegates, with Manning and Senestrey in the forefront, went into action.

> So they got up a petition, signed by nearly one hundred fathers, praying the Holy Father to order the schema on the Roman pontiff to be brought up at once. This he did, with immediate effect, so that on April 27 the deputation *de fide* got to work on the Roman pontiff, and at the general congregation of April 29 the presidents announced that the question of the Roman pontiff, his primacy and infallibility, would take precedence and come on forthwith.[17]

The revised schema was ready for deliberation on May 13, with the general discussion on the document lasting about fifteen days. The fathers who spoke were divided on the question of the opportuneness of the definition of the papal prerogatives (especially infallibility) at that time, while others were urging that the pope's role should be debated only after the theology of the Church had been dealt with amply. Because there was no time limit on the interventions, some of the fathers continued for as long as two hours or more, which must have tired the delegates inordinately because the repetitious character of the presentations must have worn down even the most patient among them. Most of the attention in this general discussion of the schema was directed to the question of the pope's infallibility because there was fairly broad agreement in the aula on the matter of papal primacy. On June 3, the general debate was terminated by the secretary of the council, Bishop Joseph Fessler of Austria, after the majority had expressed their desire to do so. Some eighty delegates—including three cardinals and many prominent bishops and archbishops—protested what seemed to them to have been an arbitrary action. Cuthbert Butler observes regarding the action of Fessler:

> The application of the closure—the only one—was one of the critical events of the council, the one which more than any other gave rise afterwards to criticisms and attacks outside on the validity of the acts of the council and of the definition of infallibility, on the ground that the closure was an unlawful suppression of the rightful liberty of speech.[18]

On June 6, 1870, the chapter on papal primacy began to be debated in the aula. Many of the bishops objected to the fact that there was no attention given to the episcopate and the other ministries in the Church. Nor was there any treatment of ecumenical councils in the document. Also, the description of the pope's jurisdiction over all of the dioceses of the Catholic world as "immediate" and "ordinary" prompted the objections that the local ordinaries were going to be seen as mere delegates and vicars of the pope. Some fathers such as Cardinal Rauscher of Vienna and Bishop Hefele of Rottenburg suggested that the pope's jurisdiction over individual dioceses be termed "extraordinary" to distinguish it from the ordinary and immediate power possessed by the local bishop by divine law. According to Butler, Bishop Dupanloup of Orleans urged that some limits "should be set on the usual exercise of the primacy," and the jurisdiction of patriarchs, metropolitans, and local bishops should be recognized.[19] The discussion of papal primacy closed on June 14, and on the following day the issue was joined on the question of papal infallibility. During the eleven days of debate, thirty-five of the delegates spoke in favor of the definition and twenty-two expressed reservations against it.[20] Cardinal Rauscher and quite a number of the minority advocated the formula of St. Antoninus who took part in the Council of Florence, and then served as bishop of Florence until his death in 1459. Antoninus' formula is articulated by Butler: "The pope, though, as an individual and acting by himself (*motu proprio*) can err in faith; nevertheless, using the council and seeking the help of the universal Church, God so ordaining, who said, 'I have prayed for thee,' he cannot err."[21]

Bishop Connolly of Halifax, Archbishop Landriot of Rheims, Bishop Ketteler of Mainz, Archbishop Ginoulhiac of Lyons, and others strenuously urged that Antoninus' phraseology be employed to contextualize the definition of papal infallibility. Debate was closed on July 4, allegedly due to the summer heat in Rome, although some sixty fathers—most of them inopportunists—were asked to forego their final interventions.

The deputation *de fide* then undertook to prepare the final text of the constitution, taking into account all the amendments and changes which had been submitted to them by the delegates in and after the public discussions. On July 11, Bishop Vincent Gasser of Austria delivered the deputation's definitive rendering of the decree before the council fathers. Papal infallibility was described as a personal gift belonging to the pontiff. It is separate from the infallibility enjoyed by the whole body of bishops joined with the pope. Although the cooperation and council of the Church are not ruled out, they are not required for the valid use of the papal prerogative. Further, the pope must speak *ex cathedra*, i.e., as supreme pastor and teacher of all Christians, and he must intend to teach a doctrine pertaining to faith or morals to be held by the whole Church. Finally, the object of papal infallibility extends only as far as the infallibility of the Church, and no further. The formula of St. Antoninus, "using the counsel and seeking the help of the universal Church," although its inclusion in the wording of the declaration would in all probability have secured unanimous consent for the definition, was ruled out by the deputation *de fide* because they felt it was too vague and uncertain in its application.[22] There is little doubt that if some reference had been added to the effect that what is defined *ex cathedra* is reflective of the faith of the whole Church, the response of the minority at the council would have been very different.

On Wednesday, July 13, a voting on the latest rendering of the constitution took place. The document, which bears the title, *Pastor aeternus*, consisted of a preface and four chapters:

Chapter 1. On the institution of the primacy of Peter
Chapter 2. On the permanence of the Petrine primacy
Chapter 3. On the power of the Petrine primacy
Chapter 4. On the infallibility of the pope

The trial vote on the constitution as a whole tallied as follows:

> In the preliminary balloting, 451 *placet* votes were cast, together with 88 *non placet* and 62 *placet juxta modum* votes. Hoping that the size of the opposition would provide a reconsideration, the minority made a final appeal to Pius IX in order to obtain the elimination of a controverted expression in the canon concerning papal primacy and the addition of a few words in the definition of the infallibility of the pope which would imply the close cooperation of the pope with the Church as a whole.[23]

Pio Nono was unwilling to take a stand against the majority, and hence the definitive text of the constitution was not amended to satisfy the minority. According to Aubert, during the final negotiations the pope repeatedly sided with the infallibilists.[24]

Prior to the final public session on Monday, July 18, the deputation *de fide* added another phrase to the declaration on papal infallibility which made the declaration even more unpalatable to the minority. The pope's infallible statements are to be considered irreformable "of themselves and not by the consent of the Church."[25] It is not clear how many of the minority fathers absented themselves from the solemn session on July 18 because they did not want to put themselves into the position of having to vote against their consciences or openly defying the pope by voting *non placet*. The number of those absenting themselves was probably in the neighborhood of sixty or seventy. Although the July 18 solemn voting had 533 *placets* and only two *non placets* for *Pastor aeternus*, this does not tell the whole story. There was probably a quarter of the delegates who opposed the wording of the definition of papal infallibility, and a far smaller but significant number who wanted a clarification concerning the nature of the pope's jurisdictional power over every diocese in the Catholic world. The latter group felt that describing this power as ordinary, episcopal, and immediate ran the risk of making the local bishops into mere delegates of the pope.

Chancellor Bismarck, who at that time was engaged in a bitter struggle with the Catholic Church in Germany, had indeed inferred from the acts of Vatican I that episcopal jurisdiction had been absorbed into papal jurisdiction, that the pope had effectively taken the place of each individual bishop. He asserted that the local bishops had become mere "tools" of the pope and, indeed, delegates of a foreign sovereign. The German episcopate responded in a famous declaration clarifying the relationship between the bishops and the papacy, insisting that the Roman pontiff is not the bishop of Cologne or Breslau or of any other diocese but Rome. Bishops, they said, pertain as much to the divine institution of the Church as does the pope, and nothing can change that. In March 1875, Pio Nono issued a brief to the German bishops affirming the accuracy of their declaration.[26]

Yves Congar notes that the absence of an adequate treatment of the episcopate—because Vatican I virtually collapsed after July 18—together with the strong and unambiguous assertions of papal power, introduced into post-Vatican I ecclesiology an imbalance which remains to some extent even after Vatican II.[27] Further, it is Congar's judgment that fully one-third of the fathers at Vatican I did not want the issue of papal primacy and infallibility treated apart from the inalienable prerogatives of the bishops. Such a treatment made the bishops look like simple delegates of the pope, as if the entire Catholic world were but one diocese which the pope effectively ruled, with of course the aid of the bishops.[28] After the council, the minority bishops had to reconcile themselves with the definition of papal inerrancy. This was the case in France, Austria, Hungary, and the United States, although such notables as Cardinal Schwartzenberg (Austria), Bishop Strossmayer (Croatia), and Archbishop Kenrick (United States) had their internal struggles before making their submission. In Germany, however, Bishop Hefele finally accepted the definition only some years after the council, hoping meanwhile that the conciliar deliberations would resume and contextualize the papal prerogatives which had already been defined.

The absence of moral unanimity among the council delegates immediately prior to the definition of July 18 represented quite a departure from the customary procedures followed in previous ecumenical councils. At Trent, for example, a nearly unanimous consensus was simply required before positions were defined. The failure of Vatican I to respond to the pleas of the minority— who represented twenty to twenty-five percent of the council—to include somehow a reference to the dependence on the witness of the Church as part of the formula in the definition of papal infallibility was, in the judgment of many, a crucial omission. Whether Professor Ignatius Döllinger of Munich and several other German university scholars would have refused their assent (and consequently incurred excommunication) if a formula similar to St. Antoninus' had been included in the wording of the definition will remain a mystery forever.

THE QUESTION OF PAPAL INFALLIBILITY

Compared with our position today, the general level of historical scholarship in the nineteenth century regarding papal primacy and infallibility was
quite inferior. One of the most influential nineteenth-century works was the
Universal History of the Catholic Church, in twenty-nine volumes, written by
René-Francois Rohrbacher, published in France in the 1840s. Although
Rohrbacher had little to say about papal inerrancy, his rendering of the history
of papal primacy in the first millennium was substantially inaccurate, and gave
rise to certain assumptions that are simply no longer sustainable.[29] Moreover,
according to Yves Congar, although Thomas Aquinas has often been represented as a star witness for the doctrine of papal infallibility, he never formally
expressed that opinion.

> St. Thomas does not ever expressly say that the pope, in his role of supreme
> interpreter of Christ's teaching, "non potest errare." Perhaps it is possible
> to deduce that from his teaching but the reasoning process has to be
> supplied by us. For it is not certain that St. Thomas would have said it, or,
> if he did, he might well have added a condition to the conclusion.[30]

Further, although his work has been contested by some, Brian Tierney says in
the conclusion of his highly regarded treatise, *Origins of Papal Infallibility*:

> The deepest objection that a Catholic can offer to the doctrine of papal
> infallibility is not that it exalts unduly the power of the pope, but that it
> grievously distorts the thinking of the most able Catholic scholars who
> have addressed themselves to these problems in modern times.
>   There is no convincing evidence that papal infallibility formed any part
> of the theological or canonical tradition of the Church before the
> thirteenth century; the doctrine was invented in the first place by a few
> dissident Franciscans because it suited their convenience to invent it;
> eventually, but only after much initial resistance, it was accepted by the
> papacy because it suited the convenience of the pope to accept it.
>   The doctrine of papal infallibility no longer serves anyone's conve-
> nience, least of all the pope's. The papacy adopted the doctrine out of
> weakness. Perhaps one day the Church will feel strong enough to
> renounce it.[31]

Whether one agrees with Congar's interpretation of St. Thomas' view of
papal inerrancy, or with Tierney's conclusion regarding the absence of data
substantiating the assertion of papal infallibility in the theological and canonical traditions up to the thirteenth century, their scholarly reservations should

at least give us pause, and open us to the desirability of pursuing the theological underpinnings of the pope's prerogatives much more thoroughly.

After July 18, 1870, a small contingent of Vatican I delegates—not many more than 100—remained in Rome discussing various aspects of church discipline. When the French garrison left Rome in early August, Italian troops invaded the area around the Holy City and occupied it on September 20. A month later, the pope formally suspended the activity of the council indefinitely. A little more than seven years after the suspension of Vatican I, Pius IX's thirty-two-year pontificate ended on February 8, 1878.

On the morning of February 8th Cardinal Pecci tapped the forehead of Pio Nono three times with the little silver hammer, calling him by his baptismal name, Joannes-Maria. There was no reply, and he turned to the cardinals present with the ritual words: "The pope is truly dead." By February 20th Pecci had been elected Pope Leo XIII.[32]

POPE LEO XIII (1878-1903)

Tradition has it that Leo XIII was favored by Pius IX to be his successor, although their world views were very different. Gioacchino Pecci had studied at the Roman seminary along with his brother, Giuseppi, who became a Jesuit. Gioacchino Pecci completed his theological and diplomatic training in Rome and was ordained in 1837. When he was thirty-three, he was dispatched on a diplomatic mission to Belgium which was not particularly successful. He was recalled to Rome and subsequently appointed bishop of Perugia in 1846. Pecci remained in Perugia until he was called to Rome by Pius IX in 1877. After Pius' death, the sixty-eight-year-old cardinal was elected pope in one of the shortest conclaves on record.

Unlike that of his predecessor, his mission was to reconcile the Church with the modern age. His many encyclicals over his twenty-five-year reign are, for the most part, a testimony to his efforts at reconciliation. Leo XIII had a fine mind, a superior education, and was a gifted writer. Although his first effort at diplomacy was not successful, he did develop superb political instincts which served him very well. He governed the world Church through a cadre of strong and reasonably effective nuncios, continuing the centralizing efforts of Pio Nono. One of his principal goals was the unification of all Christians, and to that end he reversed the counterproductive policies of his predecessor regarding the Orthodox and Uniate churches. His encyclical, *Orientalium dignitas*, of November 1894 served as a foundation for the renewal of relations between East and West for many years.[33] In the document, Leo advocated the importance of maintaining and encouraging the distinctiveness and uniqueness of eastern rites and discipline, and urged that the traditional prerogatives of the patriarchs be honored and respected by all. Although he desired to address the "Roman question," i.e., the settlement with the Kingdom of Italy after the confiscation of the Papal States by the Italian government, Leo was not content with the prospect of a modest little principality surrounding the Vatican. He referred to Rome and its environs as "la Roma nostra." Leo also spearheaded the Thomist revival through his 1879 encyclical, *Aeterni Patris*.[34] He opened the Vatican archives the same year and extended them to all scholars in 1883.

Leo's understanding of the Church and the role of the papacy is revealed in his notable encyclical, *Satis cognitum*, published in June 1896. After reaffirming the visible character of the Church against those who preferred to identify it as invisible, he referred to the Church as the mystical body of Christ: "So the mystical body of Christ is the true Church, only because its visible parts draw life and power from the supernatural gifts and other things whence spring their very nature and essence."[35]

His view of the unity of the Church went beyond a kind of confederation of a number of similar bodies:

> Jesus Christ did not, in point of fact, institute a Church to embrace several communities similar in nature, but in themselves distinct, and lacking those bonds which render the Church unique and indivisible after that manner in which in the symbol of faith we profess: "I believe in one Church."[36]

Only with this kind of unity will the Church be able to fulfil its mission which is to save the whole human race. Returning to the image of the body, Leo affirmed that separation from the body through heresy results in death. It is the magisterium that safeguards the unity of faith because the Scriptures by themselves are "subject to various and contradictory interpretations."[37] The teaching authority of the apostles was transmitted to the bishops, and it is this living and permanent magisterium that preserves the unity of faith. Those united in faith form a society which is "more perfect than any other."[38] As a true and perfect society, the Church requires a supreme authority whom Christ designated as Peter, who is the foundation and the chief shepherd of the flock.[39]

According to Leo, it is by divine right that Peter and his successors hold the supreme power in the Church, but theirs is not the only ruling authority. The bishops—who inherit their ordinary power from the apostles—also belong to the essential constitution of the Church.

> Although they do not receive plenary, or universal, or supreme authority, they are not to be looked [on] as vicars of the Roman pontiffs; because they exercise a power which is really their own, and are most truly called ordinary pastors of the peoples over whom they rule.[40]

The pontiff then proceeded to describe more fully the nature of papal jurisdiction over the whole Church.

> And as the bishops, each in his own district, command with real power not only individuals but the whole community, so the Roman pontiffs, whose jurisdiction extends to the whole Christian commonwealth, must have all its parts, even taken collectively, subject and obedient to his authority.[41]

This jurisdiction of the popes was not, according to Leo, an invention of the Vatican Council, but is "the venerable and constant belief of every age."[42] Quoting St. Thomas, he affirmed that there is nothing incongruous about the fact that both the pope and the local bishop hold equal authority over the same flock, because the pope's jurisdiction is supreme, universal, and independent, while the bishop's is limited and dependent.[43]

Satis cognitum provided the charter for the ecclesiology between Vatican I and Vatican II. The power of the local bishop was emphasized more than it was in Vatican I's *Pastor aeternus*, but the image of the bishop as a kind of substitute for the pope in the local church did not disappear. In the matter of the relationship between Church and state, Leo's views were close to those of his predecessor. In his encyclical *Immortale Dei* of November 1885, Leo built the case for the desirability of concordats so that issues of concern to both societies, e.g., marriage and the Christian education of youth, could be settled in an orderly manner. To address these mixed issues on a level playing field, the Church must be accorded status as "a supreme and legitimate power." In this regard, "all ought to hold that it is not without a singular disposition of God's providence that this power of the Church was provided with a civil sovereignty as the surest safeguard of her independence."[44]

Although the pontiff taught that "no one of the several forms of (civil) government is in itself condemned, inasmuch as none of these contains anything contrary to Catholic doctrine" (#361), he attacked the notion that government can or should be the expression of the will of the people (#24) or that power resides in the people (#35) who then choose their ruler. Public power comes from God, and does not reside "in the multitude" (#35).[45]

The ideal rapport between Church and state, according to Leo XIII, is realized when the state recognizes the privileged position of the Catholic Church vis-à-vis other religious bodies and gives it recognition as the one, true faith established by Christ. Then both perfect societies can address the matters of mixed jurisdiction and agree on a mutual set of policies for dealing with them. When, however, this more ideal relationship is not possible because the state has taken a neutral stand on religion, the Church must perforce settle for less but will continue to insist on its rights in those areas of mixed jurisdiction as best it can. Nevertheless, the ideal remains the former situation because it responds to the way things ought to be.[46] This theory of Church–state relations was the official teaching of the Church until Vatican II. As a matter of fact, Pope Leo felt the need to remind American Catholics that the relationship between Church and state prevailing in the United States—although it had brought forth some noteworthy results—was not to be viewed as the only way, or even the best way, for the Church and the civil government to relate to one another.[47]

During Leo XIII's twenty-five-year reign, respect for the papacy increased enormously throughout the world. His social and doctrinal encyclicals and his generally positive approach to the modern world enhanced the credibility of the papal office almost everywhere. Like his predecessor, he contributed significantly to the centralization of church government around the papacy. In spite of his advanced age, Leo remained, for the most part, vibrant and active up to the end of his long life. He died on July 20, 1903.

PIUS X (1903-14)

The conclave following Leo's death did not proceed quite as smoothly as the election of 1878. The favored candidate was Cardinal Mario Rampolla, who had been Pope Leo's Secretary of State since 1887. However, Rampolla—many of whose policies were not appreciated in Vienna—was vetoed by the Austrian representative. Since the majority of the cardinals favored a return to the more rigid policies of Pio Nono rather than the expansive diplomacy of Leo XIII, Giuseppe Sarto, the cardinal patriarch of Venice since 1893, was elected on August 4, 1903. The career of Pius X was of a pastoral character, having served as parish priest and chancellor in the diocese of Treviso until he was chosen bishop of Mantua in 1884. His record as bishop in Mantua and later in Venice was exemplary, for he widely promoted catechetical instruction, frequent Communion, and the expanded involvement of lay people in church activities of all sorts. As pope he worked towards a lessening of tensions between the Italian government and the Vatican, but showed little interest in other diplomatic ventures since he had made it clear at the outset that he intended to concentrate his attention on the Church's internal challenges. Although he was very bright, Roger Aubert says about Pius X: "He lacked a university education, which would have allowed him to be more receptive to the critical method in the crisis of modernism and to be more independent of the narrow-minded opinions of his informants. But everyone who had contact with him was astonished at his intelligence."[48]

Although Pius X was not fond of interacting with civil governments, his response to the enactment of the laws of separation of Church and state in France in 1905, abrogating unilaterally the concordat of 1801, revealed his mind concerning Church–state relations. According to the historian Gordon Wright,

By the separation laws that followed, all ties between Church and state were severed. Priests and bishops were taken off the state payroll; title to all Church property was transferred to the state; committees of Catholic laymen were to administer Church affairs in each parish.[49]

Pius' encyclical, *Vehementer nos*, of February 11, 1906, addressed to the clergy and people of France, laid out his view that the Church should in no way be separated from the state (#3). The state, as a matter of fact, has the duty to offer public worship to God, and must deal with those matters of common jurisdiction, e.g., marriage and the education of the young, only in collaboration with the Church. To do anything less "is to commit a great and pernicious error" (#3).[50] Although some of the things that Pius X said about the role of lay people in the Church must be weighed in light of what was happening in France at that time, they do reveal a state of mind that is quite opposed to the enactments of Vatican II.

> It follows that the Church is essentially an unequal society, that is, a society comprising two categories of persons, the pastors and the flock, those who occupy a rank in the different degrees of the hierarchy and the multitude of the faithful. So distinct are these categories that with the pastoral body only rests the necessary right and authority for promoting the end of the society and directing all its members to that end; the one duty of the multitude is to allow themselves to be led, and like a docile flock, to follow the pastors.[51]

THE MODERNIST CRISIS

The greatest challenge of Pius' pontificate was the modernist crisis which took shape in the latter years of the nineteenth century and came to term with the publication of Alfred Loisy's book, *The Gospel and the Church*, in 1902. Loisy wanted to correct the liberal Protestant position articulated by Adolf Harnack who maintained in his famous series of Berlin lectures entitled *What Is Christianity?* (1902), that the essence of Christianity consists largely in a sentiment, a filial confidence in God, the merciful Father, as revealed in Christ. Christology is not important in itself, nor is the Church which, as an institution, has no foundation in the gospel.[52] Alfred Loisy, who taught at the Institut Catholique in Paris from 1881 to 1893 when he was removed from his teaching position due to his progressive, liberal stands, insisted that Jesus identified himself as the Messiah whose fundamental message was the coming of God's kingdom. The Church, which was the inevitable outcome of Jesus' preaching on the kingdom, is in a constant state of evolution regarding its institutions, its creed, and its worship. This visible Church has had to adapt itself to the changing times.

> The identity of the Church . . . is not determined by permanent immobility of external forms, but by continuity of existence and consciousness of life through the perpetual transformations which are life's condition and manifestation.[53]

In 1903 Loisy wrote, *Concerning a Little Book*, which pushed the argument regarding the need to view dogmatic statements as subject to development and improvement from age to age beyond his position in *The Gospel and the Church*. In December 1903, five of Loisy's books were placed on the Index, and Loisy was excommunicated in March 1908. There were a number of other prominent figures in the modernist movement in France (Lucien Laberthonniere and Edouard Le Roy), England (Baron von Hügel and George Tyrrell), Germany (Herman Shell), the United States (Henry Poels), and even in Italy (Ernesto Buonaiuti). The movement is very difficult to define even to this day. Many of these scholars were operating in good faith in their attempt to apply the nineteenth-century discoveries in the areas of historical and biblical scholarship to their understanding of the Church and the gospel. Although some of them did push their historical and biblical criticism too far, the greater danger lay in the efforts on the part of other modernists (e.g., Edouard Le Roy) to locate the origin of the Church and of religion generally in the religious consciousness of the subject, thereby erasing the historical underpinnings of the Christian phenomenon.

That being said, the reaction on the part of Pius X and his curia to the movement called modernism was, in the estimate of many, more severe and indiscriminate than it should have been. Many well-intentioned scholars who were trying to update the teachings and the institutions of the Church were attacked, condemned without a hearing, robbed of their reputations, and in some cases, virtually destroyed. The zealots and the integralists who surrounded the pope fought to maintain the traditional biblical and doctrinal positions as they were. These prelates had no qualms about denouncing people as heretics with precious little evidence, and employing Star Chamber tactics to threaten, intimidate, and literally annihilate their targets.[54] Unfortunately, it would not be accurate to assume that Pius X was unaware of these sweeping inquisitorial procedures. Nor would it be fair to deny that he gave them his tacit approbation.[55]

The formal condemnation of modernism occurred in two stages. In July 1907, the decree *Lamentabili* was issued which consisted of sixty-five propositions from various authors (but largely from Loisy) that were labeled as errors in the areas of biblical interpretation, Christology, sacramental theology, ecclesiology, and the development of dogma. This was complemented by the encyclical *Pascendi*, which was promulgated in September 1907. According to the historian Alex Vidler,

> The encyclical, *Pascendi*, contains . . . an elaborate sytematization of the so-called "doctrines of the modernists." . . . The composition of a logically coherent system out of the heterogeneous materials provided in the writings of the modernists was undeniably a skillful undertaking; but if it was an attempt to give a just and accurate account of what the modernists had in fact taught, it must be pronounced a failure. They had all, it is true, in various ways desired some reform of the Church's teaching, but not one of them had desired the kind of system which the encyclical attributes to them.[56]

The purpose of *Pascendi*, according to Vidler,

> was to condemn every attempt to introduce a reform of the Church's teaching, and the method of *Pascendi* was recommended not by any desire to do justice to the modernists, but by its convenience. It was easier to canonize the scholastic system of philosophy and theology, when it appeared as the only alternative to an innovating system which was nothing less than "the synthesis of all heresies."[57]

In the final section of the encyclical entitled, *Remedies* (paragraphs 44 to 58), the pope commanded that the bishops eliminate from seminary faculties and from Catholic universities anyone "who in any way is found to be imbued with modernism"(#49). Such individuals should also be excluded from holy orders (#49). Ordinaries were directed to ban and eradicate the books of modernists (#51), even those that might have obtained an *imprimatur*. Further, diocesan watch committees were to be established (#55) so that these infectious errors could be rooted out. In this connection, no protections were outlined or envisioned for the accused. And thus the "anti-modernist inquisition," which damaged so many and stalled the growth of biblical, historical, and doctrinal scholarship for more than a generation, was launched.

In spite of these rather tragic developments in the modernist crisis, Pius X was in many respects a notable reform pope. His promotion of frequent Communion and the efforts he made to reform church music and to reorganize the seminaries were outstanding contributions, as was his inauguration of the codification of canon law under the aegis of Msgr. Peter Gasparri. Centralization of church government increased during Pius' reign through the efforts of Cardinal Gaetano De Lai, who strictly controlled the appointment of bishops as prefect of the Consistorial Congregation, and Cardinal Raphael Merry del Val, the Secretary of State, who fully shared Pius X's vision of the desirability of a highly centralized ecclesiastical government. As the war clouds were gathering over Europe, Pius X died on August 20, 1914. The venerable pontiff was canonized on May 29, 1954.

BENEDICT XV AND WORLD WAR I

The four-day conclave in which sixty cardinals took part resulted in the election of Giacomo Della Chiesa, who represented the return to the more open policies of Leo XIII.[58] Benedict XV (1914-22), an aristocratic Genoese, had attended the Capranica College in Rome for theology and received his diplomatic training at the Academia dei Nobili before entering the Vatican diplomatic service in 1882. He worked with Cardinal Rampolla at the Secretariate of State, and then as the second in command under Cardinal Merry del Val. Della Chiesa was named archbishop of Bologna in 1907 and was awarded the red hat in 1914. World War I broke out during the first months of his pontificate, and for four years it severely curtailed Benedict's activities. Although Peter Gasparri became his Secretary of State, the cardinal continued to direct the work of the Code Commission which had been established by Pius X in 1904. The new *Code of Canon Law* was promulgated by Benedict on May 27, 1917 and was to be effective on May 19, 1918. As the first complete collection of law for the Latin church, it paints a fairly accurate picture of the organizational design and the role of the papacy and the Roman curia at the outset of the twentieth century.

Canon 218 outlined the power of the pope over the whole Church in the wording of Vatican I's *Pastor aeternus*—full, supreme jurisdiction over faith, morals, and government, and over everyone everywhere. This jurisdiction was described as episcopal, ordinary, and immediate over all churches and church members, which resurfaced the post-Vatican I problem of total governmental overlap between the pope and the local bishop because the bishop's power is similarly defined (c. 329 #1), except that it is limited to a given diocese and dependent on the supreme pontiff. Even though the Code identified episcopal jurisdiction as "divinely instituted," and thus not simply delegated papal power, the manner in which the pope's jurisdiction was defined has made it more difficult to establish and maintain the integrity of a second layer of government within the Church, i.e., the distinct and inalienable episcopal shepherding function in the local churches. The local bishops have, since Vatican I, come to see themselves more and more as vicars and delegates of the pope, rather than as successors of the apostles in the governance of their respective churches. The prerogatives of the Roman pontiff have been so strongly emphasized in *Pastor aeternus* and in the 1917 Code that the divinely instituted second tier of shepherding within the Church has lost much of its distinctive identity and integrity. St. Cyprian of Carthage (d. 258) would, I fear, not have recognized his episcopal role as he understood it, nor would he have been able to identify with the understanding of the papal office as reflected in the 1917 Code. The same could be said, *mutatis mutandis*, of bishops in the succeeding centuries, even after the Council of Trent and, indeed, up to the French Revolution.

The Code's treatment of ecumenical councils (cc. 222-29) brought them firmly and squarely under the wing of the Roman pontiff in terms of the delegates to be invited, the issues to be deliberated, and the procedure to be followed throughout. This pattern was reflective of the Council of Trent and Vatican I, but certainly not of the councils of the first millennium, or even of a number of the ecumenical councils held in the West after 1100. The Code identified the cardinals as the pope's principal counselors and helpers in the administration of the universal Church (cc. 230-41), but left little of their traditional authority to primates and metropolitans in the Latin church (cc. 271-76). Further, the venerable institutions of plenary and provincial councils in the West (cc. 281-92) were made to look as though they were localized organs of papal government; the plenary gatherings were to be convoked and presided over by the pope's delegate (c. 281), and the acts and decrees of provincial synods were not to be promulgated until they were examined and approved by the Congregation of the Council in Rome (c. 291 #1). Klaus Schatz, the German ecclesiastical historian, observes:

> From a historical point of view it [i.e., the multi-leveled organizational pattern in the Church] was not achieved in the ancient Church by a movement directly from individual bishops' communities to the bishop of Rome. Instead it led by way of regional synods and Church provinces to the "principal churches" and finally to the patriarchates. The idea that the only theological entities are the individual bishop and the diocese on the one hand and the bishop of Rome and the universal Church on the other, while everything in between . . . is purely a set of administrative units that are created by canon law is a construct that does violence to history.[59]

This was nonetheless the shape of the Church and its organizational character as Benedict XV promulgated the *Code of Canon Law* on Pentecost Sunday of 1917. Just a few weeks before, he had made a positive contribution to the development of better rapport with the Uniate churches by establishing the Congregation for the Eastern Churches, which was to serve, with but a few exceptions, as the exclusive conduit between those communities and the Roman pontiff. World War I had indeed taken its toll on Benedict XV, for he died of pneumonia at the relatively young age of sixty-seven in January 1922.

PIUS XI (1922-39) AND THE LATERAN TREATY

There was a division at the following conclave between those cardinals who desired to return to the stricter policies of Pius X and those who wanted to pursue a more open approach after the pattern of Leo XIII and Benedict XV. Achille Ratti, the archbishop of Milan, was elected after the deadlock between Cardinal Gasparri and Cardinal Lafontaine of Venice could not be resolved since neither could achieve the two-thirds majority. Ratti, who was educated in Milan and then Rome, had taught for a few years at the seminary in Milan before joining the staff of the Ambrosian library in that city. After twenty-five years at the Ambrosian, he moved on to the Vatican library and became the prefect there in 1914. After spending three years as nuncio to Poland, he was appointed to the see of Milan in 1921. According to Hubert Jedin, Pius XI was probably the first scholarly pope since Benedict XIV.[60] His two closest aides were Cardinal Peter Gasparri and Cardinal Eugenio Pacelli. Ratti's reign was authoritarian, even autocratic, but he did shape the direction of the Church for the first half of the twentieth century. From the beginning of his pontificate, he had quietly resolved to solve the Roman question, and to that end he chose Gasparri as his Secretary of State. Negotiations began in earnest with the Italian government in August 1926, and an agreement was reached in February 1929. The famous Lateran treaty was signed by Benito Mussolini, the premier of Italy, and Cardinal Gasparri for the Vatican. The pope was recognized as the civil ruler of the tiny Vatican state (109 acres) and accorded all the rights that his political sovereignty required.

Pius XI was granted 1.750 billion lire in cash and bonds to compensate for the appropriation of papal property taken in the revolution of 1860. In turn, the pontiff recognized the territorial integrity of the Kingdom of Italy with Rome as its capital. The concordat, which was signed at the same time, acknowledged among other things the Church's holy days as state holidays (art. 11), committed the state to make up for the deficiencies in income from ecclesiastical benefices according to a predetermined schedule (art. 30), sanctioned the civil effects of ecclesiastical marriages, and determined that petitions of nullity were to be handled by the Church (art. 34). The document also sanctioned religious teaching in the elementary and secondary schools by teachers appointed by the appropriate ecclesiastical authorities (art. 36).[61] After the fall of the Fascist government, the Lateran agreements of 1929 were explicitly adopted by the Italian republican constitution of 1947.[62] The Lateran treaty, the concordat, and the financial settlement ended eighty years of bitter disputes and misunderstandings which kept popes from Pius IX to Pius XI at loggerheads with the Italian government. The pope and the Vatican were now able to enter into the twentieth century.

Pius XI's first encyclical, *Ubi arcano*, published in December 1922, announced the theme of his pontificate, "the peace of Christ in the reign of Christ." He outlined the evils besetting the post-World War I world (#7-19) and pointed to the need for a return to the "ideals and doctrines of Christ," which were "confided by Him to His Church."[63] It is the Church, he affirmed, that can bring peace and accord to mankind.

For He [Christ] bestowed on the Church the status and the constitution of a society which, by reason of the perfect ends which it is called upon to attain, must be held to be supreme in its own sphere; He also made her the depository and interpreter of His divine teachings, and, by consequence, the teacher and guide of every society whatsoever, not of course in the sense that she should abstract in the least from their authority, each in its own sphere supreme, but that she should really perfect their authority.[64]

Pius XI applauded the bishops of the world for their efforts in promoting the education and development of their clergy and laity, naming in particular the movement that went under the name of Catholic Action (#54), and applied to the laity, when acting in coordination with the bishops and priests, the universal priesthood designation of I Peter 2:9 (#58). One of Pius' more intriguing statements was his reference to the possibility of reassembling Vatican I,

which Pius IX, pontiff of our youth, had called but failed to see through except to the completion of a part, albeit the most important, of its work. We as leader of the chosen people must wait and pray for an unmistakable sign from the God of mercy and love of His holy will in this regard.[65]

Apparently this sign never came to him, although it is said that a reasonable amount of work had been initiated to that end during his pontificate.

Pius XI took a very negative stand against the ecumenical overtures which had blossomed in the twenties. In his encyclical *Mortalium animos*, of January 1928, he alluded to those striving to bring all Christians together to fight against the forces of irreligion as "pan-Christians" (#4). He understood that they were desirous of establishing a federation of many communities of Christians (#6), who would share some beliefs and disagree on other matters. According to these pan-Christians,

The Church itself, or of its nature, is divided into sections; that is to say, that it is made up of several churches or distinct communities, which still remain separate . . . that these all enjoy the same rights; and that the Church was one and unique from, at the most, the apostolic age until the first ecumenical councils.[66]

Pius served notice that he would have nothing to do with, much less preside over, their "motley assemblies" (#7 and 8). For him, "the union of Christians can only be promoted by promoting the return to the one true Church of Christ."[67] Toward the end of the encyclical, he climaxed his argument with an observation that was especially insulting to the Orthodox: "Did not the ancestors of those who are now entangled in the errors of Photius and the reformers, obey the bishop of Rome, the chief shepherd of souls?"[68]

In spite of the fact that in 1923 Pius XI had exhorted Catholics to study more carefully the history and customs of the East, and in September 1928 emphasized the need to study oriental affairs in major seminaries, he was not successful in reopening doors to the Orthodox churches.[69] But perhaps the most counterproductive of all his efforts vis-à-vis the Orthodox were the many Latinizing overtures directed against the Uniates.

> The subjection of Eastern communities in union with the Holy See to a flood of Latinizing influences naturally enough confirmed Orthodoxy in its radical opposition to everything represented by the form of "Eastern Catholicism" which went by the name of "Uniatism."[70]

This situation was not to change significantly until just before Vatican II. An issue related to this was the longstanding complaint by the Orthodox that they could not be expected to subscribe to the "amplifications of dogma" by the Latin church, e.g., the Vatican I definitions of papal infallibility and the pope's supreme power of jurisdiction over all the churches, "without being given an opportunity to share in a joint review of recent dogmatic definitions."[71]

In the tradition initiated by Pius IX and Leo XIII, Pius XI was a dedicated author of encyclicals. As a matter of fact, his scholarly background provided him with the resources to do more of his own writing than his predecessors had done. Perhaps his two most widely quoted works were *Casti connubii* (December 31, 1930) which served as the magna carta of the Church's teaching on Christian marriage and conjugal morality until Vatican II, and *Quadragesimo anno* (May 15, 1931), a summation of Leo XIII's teaching in *Rerum novarum* and a review of the church's social thinking since 1891.

In his masterful study, *Lay People in the Church*, Yves Congar emphasizes the importance of Pius XI's contribution to the development and growth of Catholic Action, which he defined as the participation of the laity in the hierarchical apostolate.[72] His active encouragement regarding the expansion of such organizations worldwide was one of the hallmarks of his pontificate. Without his efforts, Vatican II might not have been ready to address the apostolate of the laity and raise it to another level, as it did in *Apostolicam actuositatem* of November 1965.

In 1937 Pius XI issued a vigorous condemnation of Communism in his encyclical *Divini Redemptoris*, and in *Mit brennender sorge* (March 14, 1937) he unqualifiedly labeled Naziism as essentially anti-Christian. After a long and arduous reign, Pius XI died in February 1939, just months prior to the eruption of World War II in September 1939.

PIUS XII (1939-58)

Eugenio Pacelli seemed the logical choice to succeed Pius XI because the oncoming war called for a pope with superb diplomatic skills, as had been the case with Benedict XV at the onset of World War I. Besides, it was widely known that Pacelli was the choice of Pius XI. Pius XII was elected pope on his sixty-third birthday, March 2, 1939. He was born of a Roman family of lawyers and jurists and was educated at the Gregorian University and at the Apollinaris in Rome. Shortly after his ordination in 1899, he was appointed to the Secretariate of State where he worked until he was elected pope. His unusual talents of mind, prodigious energy, and extraordinary linguistic skills propelled his career as a diplomat. During most of the 1920s he worked in the German-speaking countries with considerable success. Pacelli then succeeded Cardinal Gasparri as Secretary of State in 1929. His vision of the papacy was a reflection of the highly monarchical portrait of the office found in Vatican I's *Pastor aeternus*. Actually, from the early years of his pontificate, he was inclined to bring more and more of the decision-making processes of the Vatican into his own hands. For example, when Cardinal Maglione, his Secretary of State, died rather suddenly, he assumed the direction of the office himself, and made Monsignors Montini and Tardini his deputy secretaries. Pius XII never appointed another Secretary of State. During the 1940s, much of the government of the Church was concentrated in the hands of the pontiff himself who was assisted by a coterie of Jesuits teaching in Rome: Augustine Bea, a biblicist; Francis Hürth, a moralist; Sebastian Tromp, a dogmatic theologian; Gustav Gundlach, a social philosopher; and Robert Leiber, a historian. The congregations and dicasteries of the Vatican became less involved in the key decisions and were relegated to the more routine and clerical tasks, which made them quite restless. The curial professionals therefore were not especially devoted to Pius XII. According to Roger Aubert, the pontiff had some rather revolutionary plans to reform the curia,

> which envisaged a more truly personal government in which new style cardinals, like so many *missi dominici*, would have been made responsible for the execution of the sovereign pontiff's orders by the national episcopates, thus restricting still further the role played by the successors of the apostles [i.e., the local bishops] in order to produce a monarchically governed Church.[73]

No pontiff was more committed to the teaching role of his ministry than Eugenio Pacelli. His encyclicals, radio messages, and allocutions filled volumes and dealt with every conceivable topic that bore a relationship to his understanding of the Church's mission. Although much of his energy was concentrated on the tragedies of the war until 1945, he issued the encyclical *Divino afflante Spiritu* in September 1943, which encouraged Catholic biblicists to apply the various methods of textual and form criticism to the original texts of the Bible. The encyclical prompted a veritable renaissance in biblical scholarship throughout the world. In November 1947, the pope's encyclical *Mediator*

Dei gave a similar emphasis to liturgical renewal, having stressed the importance of the participation of the laity in the liturgical rites. It was this encyclical more than anything else that prepared the way for Vatican II's important *Constitution on the Sacred Liturgy, Sacrosanctum Concilium*, of December 1963.

Pius' encyclical *Mystici Corporis* (June 29, 1943) brought into focus all the previous papal references to the Church as the Mystical Body of Christ and charted a new direction for the treatment of ecclesiology which for more than 100 years had been primarily juridical in tone.

> If we would define and describe this true Church of Jesus Christ as the One, Holy, Catholic, Apostolic Roman Church—we shall find nothing more noble, more sublime, or more divine than the expression "the Mystical Body of Jesus Christ"—an expression which springs from and is, as it were, the fair flowering of the repeated teaching of the Sacred Scriptures and the Holy Fathers.[74]

The question of membership in the Church was somewhat clarified in that the document distinguished between actual or full members (#22), i.e., those who are baptized, profess the true faith, and are not separated from the Body, and those who, although not members, have a certain relationship with the Mystical Body "by an unconscious desire and longing."[75] This distinction allowed theologians the opportunity to speculate as to who was in some way under the umbrella of the Church, until the issue of membership was addressed more fully in Vatican II's *Constitution on the Church* (#14) and in the *Decree on Ecumenism* (#3). In *Mystici Corporis*, Christ was identified as the invisible head of the Body, while the pope, his vicar, was identified as the visible head. And, indeed, one cannot accept Christ as head of the Church "while not adhering loyally to His vicar on earth."[76] Christ and all members are tied together by a mutual need: "as our Savior does not rule the Church in a visible manner, He wills to be helped by the members of His Body in carrying out the work of redemption."[77]

This joining together of Christ and the members is not merely a moral union, but a mystical union realized by the Spirit of God who "exists effectively in the whole and in each of its parts, and whose excellence is such that of itself it is vastly superior to whatever bonds of union may be found in a physical or moral body."[78] The juridical, institutional dimension of the Church was described by Pius XII as being the indispensable complement of the mystical union (#65). As such, the Church is the fullness of Christ, "the filling out and the complement of the Redeemer" (#77). Ecclesiologists after *Mystici Corporis* attempted to assimilate the theology of the encyclical into their treatises, but in most cases, the doctrine ended up as an appendage to the more traditional, juridical exposition of the Church.[79]

By 1950 it was becoming rather clear that Pius XII was losing some of his creativity, although his work load and his commitments remained as heavy as ever. He found himself depending more and more on that group of Jesuits from the Piazza Pilotta in Rome, and caution became the dominant theme of his policies. Something of that change is reflected in his encyclical *Humani generis*, of August 1950, and in his attack on the so-called "New Theology" coming out of France (e.g., De Lubac, Bouillard, Congar, Chenu, etc.) which was attempting to give theology a new face and a new vitality.[80] According to the pontiff, they were striving,

> to free dogma itself from terminology long established in the Church and from philosophical concepts held by Catholic teachers, to bring about a return in the explanation of Christian doctrine to the way of speaking used in the Holy Scripture and by the Fathers of the Church.[81]

The pontiff insisted that it was the "perennial philosophy" and the theology of St. Thomas that was to be used in the exposition of Catholic doctrine in the schools and in the seminaries (#29-32), and he warned Christian philosophers and theologians not to embrace "whatever novelty happens to be thought up from day to day."[82] The solemn definition of the dogma of the Assumption on November 1, 1950, although yearned for by many, raised again the objection of the Orthodox that the Latin church was amplifying Christian doctrine without consulting the eastern churches.[83] Moreover, there was only a modicum of interest shown at the Vatican regarding the efforts made by Catholics to respond somehow to the ecumenical developments sponsored by the World Council of Churches as they held their first assembly in Amsterdam in 1948, and their second world gathering at Evanston in 1954. The events of the post-World War II period were passing Pius XII by. His greatest days were behind him. But when his death was announced on October 9, 1958, the Catholic world became even more aware that it had lost the greatest pope of the first half of the twentieth century. Two comments by Cardinal Julius Döpfner, former archbishop of Munich, can serve as a summary of Pius XII's contribution:

> Anyone who once had the privilege of meeting him—even from a distance in one of the larger general audiences—could never forget the experience. But above all, he was esteemed and revered by the whole world, non-Catholic included, simply because he radiated the vigor and fulness of a great personality, and gave the world light, a new impulse and high ideals in many different spheres.[84]

His encyclical letters, addresses and other pronouncements on countless important questions opened the door to discussion and reform within the Church, or at least paved the way for future developments. Without the preparatory work of Pius XII, without his first steps to introduce reform, many of the measures at present under consideration by the council would be inconceivable.[85]

(N.B. These words of Cardinal Döpfner were delivered on March 8, 1964, in St. Michael's Church in Munich.)

JOHN XXIII (1958-63) AND VATICAN II

The conclave to elect Pius XII's successor opened on October 25, 1958, and the outcome was not as clear cut as the previous one in 1939. Pius had left the College of Cardinals seriously depleted, having held only two consistories during his pontificate, the first in 1946 and the last in 1953. As a result, there were only fifty-one papal electors, and nearly half of them were in their late seventies or older. Angelo Roncalli, the patriarch of Venice, was only one of a number deemed *papabili*, along with Cardinal Agaganian, the prefect of the Propagation of the Faith, Cardinal Lercaro of Bologna, and Cardinal Valeri, prefect of the Congregation of Religious. Roncalli was elected on October 28, on the eleventh ballot, at the age of seventy-seven. Pope John XXIII came from the simplest of surroundings, born the fourth of fourteen children of Battista and Marianna Roncalli in the town of Sotto il Monte near Bergamo. Angelo took his theological studies at the Apollinaris in Rome, received his doctorate in theology, and was ordained in Rome in 1904. After having served as a military chaplain in World War I, he worked in Rome for the Propagation of the Faith until he was appointed apostolic visitor to Bulgaria in 1925. Ten years later, he was appointed apostolic delegate in Turkey and Greece, and then made nuncio to France in 1944. Roncalli was appointed cardinal patriarch of Venice in 1953.

Pope John XXIII surprised the world on January 25, 1959, by announcing his intention to hold a diocesan synod in Rome and then an ecumenical council. There were a fair number of university theologians in Rome at that time who felt that the age of general councils was over, inasmuch as the definition of the papal prerogatives at Vatican I had rendered them superfluous. Although there had been some secret preparations for a council in 1948 under Pius XII, the project never materialized.[86] In June 1959, Cardinal Tardini, the Secretary of State, contacted the bishops of the world, the major superiors of religious orders and congregations, and the faculties of the Catholic universities for suggestions as to the topics to be considered. Ten preparatory commissions were appointed in June 1960 to draft the various schemata for discussion. In addition, a central commission was established to coordinate the drafts. The work of the commissions began in the fall of 1960 and was not completed until the summer of 1962. The sixty-nine schemata that were prepared largely reflected the thinking of the Roman curia and the Roman universities, and were not well received by the council delegates. As a result, an enormous amount of work had to be done during the council to revise, combine, and reshape the drafts before sixteen of them would be approved by the conciliar fathers during the four sessions.

On December 25, 1961, Pope John announced that the Second Vatican Council was to convene sometime in 1962. He felt "the urgency of our duty to call our sons together, to give the Church the possibility to contribute more efficaciously to the solutions of the problems of the modern age."[87] The opening date was set for October 11. At the first session, there were present over 2,500 delegates—and the average attendance over the four sessions ran between 2,100 and 2,300. On the opening day of the council, Pope John spoke of the Church's need "to bring herself up to date" where required and gain strength thereby so that she can face the future without fear.[88] "The greatest concern of the ecumenical council is this: that the sacred deposit of Christian doctrine should be guarded and taught more efficaciously."[89] The Church must look to the past, to "the sacred patrimony of truth received from the Fathers. . . . But at the same time she must ever look to the present, to the new conditions and new forms of life introduced into the modern world which have opened up new avenues to the Catholic apostolate."[90]

Then John observed that the traditional doctrines of the Church set forth in previous councils need not be repeated, but rather an attempt should be made to take a step forward, to speak the authentic doctrine, but in a way that would resonate in the minds of the faithful today.

> The substance of the ancient doctrine of the deposit of faith is one thing, and the way in which it is presented is another. And it is the latter that must be taken into great consideration with patience if necessary, everything being measured in the forms and proportions of a magisterium which is predominately pastoral in character.[91]

Thus the pontiff set the tone for a general council which would bring the Church up to date where necessary, and speak to the modern world the timeless message of the gospel and do so with a clearly pastoral voice.

The first session of Vatican II avoided the error of Vatican I in that the delegates refused to approve the suggested 160 candidates for the conciliar commissions which would bear the responsibility for revising and restructuring the schemata to be discussed. On the recommendation of Cardinal Lienart of Lille and Cardinal Frings of Cologne, the fathers agreed to wait for several days until they could draw up lists of their own candidates. Thus they avoided the mistake of the delegates at Vatican I who had had a deputation *de fide* foisted on them which was composed of all ultramontane bishops. Although no schema was approved during the first period of Vatican II in the fall of 1962, there were discussions on the document on the liturgy, the sources of revelation, the means of social communication, the eastern churches, and the schema on the Church. All of these were sent back for revisions during the interim between the sessions. Pope John XXIII was not to see the results of the work which he had initiated, for the aged pontiff died on June 3, 1963. His two wishes were that he be succeeded by his dear friend, Cardinal Montini, and that the council should continue. Both of his wishes came to pass.

PAUL VI (1963-78) AND THE RESUMPTION OF VATICAN II

The conclave that began on June 19 was not as clear-cut in terms of outcome as many have claimed. Among the eighty cardinals who took part, there was a solid block of conservatives who were not in favor of Cardinal Montini, and preferred instead either Cardinal Siri of Genoa or Cardinal Antoniutti, head of the Congregation of Religious. The progressives favored either Cardinal Lercaro of Bologna or Cardinal Montini. Apparently, it took six ballots before Montini was able to obtain the plurality needed to be elected pope.[92] There were some twenty to twenty-five cardinals—mostly Italian and mostly in the curia—who did not cast their final ballot for him, and this was a source of some anxiety for the future.[93] How would this block of opposition affect the council which had been interrupted by the death of Pope John? Pope Paul VI made it known on the day after his election that the council would be resumed, and he set the date of September 29, 1963, for the opening of the second session.

Giovanni Battista Montini was born of a middle-class family from Brescia in 1897. He studied canon law at the Gregorian after ordination, and then was enrolled at the Academia in Rome in preparation for a career in the diplomatic corps. From 1924 to 1954 he served in the Secretariat of State, and was appointed Pro-Secretary of State in 1952. Many were surprised that he did not receive the red hat in Pius XII's 1953 consistory, which seemed to rule him out as Pius' successor. In December 1954, Montini was appointed archbishop of Milan, succeeding Cardinal Schuster who had died in August of that year, and it was John XXIII who named him a cardinal in December 1958.

Pope Paul made it clear in his opening address to the second session of Vatican II that the schema on the Church was to take priority over all other business. He also startled many with his ecumenical gesture of asking forgiveness "from the brethren who should have felt themselves separated from us; for our part, we are prepared to forgive the wrongs which have been done to the Catholic Church."[94] The discussions on the revised document on the Church lasted throughout the month of October and featured a spirited debate on the subject of episcopal collegiality. Those who opposed the concept felt that it amounted to an attack against the pope's primacy of jurisdiction over the whole Church, while the proponents of collegiality argued that the biblical basis of the designation and the mission of the Twelve supported and required it. Deliberations on the schema on the pastoral office of bishops and on ecumenism took up most of November, and on December 4, the *Constitution on the Liturgy* and the *Decree on the Instruments of Social Communication* were formally adopted by the council and promulgated by Pope Paul. The leitmotif of the *Constitution on the Liturgy* was articulated in paragraph 14 of the document: "Mother Church earnestly desires that all the faithful be led to that full, conscious and active participation in liturgical celebrations which is demanded by the very nature of the liturgy."[95] To achieve this full and active participation, the use of the vernacular was encouraged, and it was up to the various national conferences of bishops to determine how much of the liturgy would be celebrated in the language of the place.[96]

Paul's closing speech at the end of the second session alluded to his intention to make a pilgrimage to the Holy Land where he was to meet with the Ecumenical Patriarch Athenagoras in January 1964. The encounters with Athenagoras in Jerusalem and Bethlehem had a tremendous symbolic impact, and gave a strong impetus to the ecumenical effort generally as well as to the final deliberations on ecumenism at the next session of the council.

Pope Paul opened the third session on September 14, 1964, with an admonition to complement the doctrine on the papacy with a full treatment of the nature and role of the episcopate. The schema *de ecclesia* had been thoroughly revamped in the interim on the basis of the four critical votes on collegiality which had been passed by a large majority of the council on October 30, 1963.[97] The new document was debated and voted on, part by part, and amended in many places from September 15 to 30. The revised schema on the pastoral office of bishops was also discussed and sent back for further revisions. However, the most heated interaction was precipitated by the schema on religious freedom which, at the last minute, was deferred until the fourth session. This caused great consternation among the proponents of the declaration, especially the Americans who considered this their special project.[98] At the final gathering of the third session, the *Constitution on the Church*, the *Decree on Ecumenism* and the *Decree on the Oriental Churches* were adopted with huge pluralities and promulgated on November 21, 1964. The third session had not accomplished all it wanted to accomplish, but its successes were considerable.

In the *Constitution on the Church*, the centerpiece of Vatican II, the fathers made a heroic effort to contextualize the papal prerogatives, that were so starkly articulated in 1870, within the college of bishops. Paragraph 22 of *Lumen gentium* draws a parallel between the Roman pontiff and Peter on the one hand and the bishops and the apostles on the other.

> The order of bishops is the successor of the college of the apostles in teaching authority and pastoral rule; or rather, in the episcopal order the

apostolic body continues without a break. Together with its head, the Roman pontiff, and never without this head, the episcopal order is the subject of supreme and full power over the universal Church.[99]

The constitution goes on to say that the supreme authority of the college is exercised in a solemn manner through an ecumenical council.[100] The bishops, as members of the episcopal college, are bound to exercise solicitude for the whole Church which "contributes immensely to the welfare of the universal Church."[101] Almost from the beginning, these local churches

> coalesced into several groups, organically united, which, preserving the unity of faith and the unique divine constitution of the universal Church, enjoy their own discipline, their own liturgical usage and their own theological and spiritual heritage.[102]

This variety of local churches is pointed to as "splendid evidence" of the catholicity of the Church. "In like manner the episcopal bodies of today are in a position to render a manifold and fruitful assistance, so that this collegiate sense may be put into practical application."[103]

In the treatment of the teaching role, Vatican I's pronouncement of papal infallibility is repeated, but the prerogative is related to the inerrancy of the Church.

> The infallibility promised the Church resides also in the body of bishops when that body exercises supreme teaching authority with the successor of Peter. To the resultant definitions the assent of the Church can never be wanting, on account of the activity of that same Holy Spirit, whereby the whole flock of Christ is preserved and progresses in unity of faith.[104]

The bishops who govern the local churches are ordinary and proper shepherds of their people. Although their shepherding power is regulated by the supreme authority of the Church, "The pastoral office of the habitual and daily care of their sheep is entrusted to them completely. Nor are they to be regarded as vicars of the Roman pontiff."[105]

The refreshing tone of the presentation of episcopal collegiality in paragraphs 21 to 27 is muted to a significant extent by the Prefatory Note attached to the *Constitution on the Church* by the theological commission at the direction of Pope Paul, who was probably making a concession to the curial cardinals who have fought the concept of episcopal collegiality at every turn from Vatican II to the present. The Note was to be considered as an authentic interpretation of the conciliar text. It clearly distinguishes the collegiality of the bishops from the unique powers of the apostles, and the relationship between the pope and the bishops is distanced from the relationship between Peter and the apostles. Further, the care of the universal Church is portrayed as the pope's proper responsibility which he can freely choose to exercise either individually or collegially at his own discretion.[106] Episcopal collegiality is characterized as almost nonexistent, except to the extent that the pope—on an ad hoc basis— calls it into action. This is not the way paragraphs 21 to 27 read, but episcopal collegiality has been consistently interpreted according to the Prefatory Note by the curial people since the promulgation of the document in 1964.

The *Decree on Ecumenism*, also promulgated at the end of the third session, is a truly remarkable document which not only stresses the need to work for unity among all Christians, but reveals a fresh approach to the ecclesial reality of the other Christian churches. Not only are non-Catholic Christians in good faith related to the Catholic Church in some way (*Mystici Corporis*), but the separated churches are recognized as having an ecclesial reality themselves.

> Moreover, some, even many, of the most significant elements or endow-ments which together go to build up and give life to the Church herself can exist outside the visible boundaries of the Catholic Church: the written word of God, the life of grace, faith, hope and charity, along with other interior gifts of the Holy Spirit and visible elements. All of these, which come from Christ and lead back to Him, belong by right to the one Church of Christ.
>
> It follows that these separated churches and communities, though we believe that they suffer from defects already mentioned [i.e., the lack of the fullness of the ecclesial gifts] have by no means been deprived of significance and importance in the mystery of salvation. For the Spirit of Christ has not refrained from using them as means of salvation which derive their efficacy from the very fullness of grace and truth entrusted to the Catholic Church.[107]

This represents a further clarification of the notion set forth in paragraph 8 of the *Constitution on the Church*, i.e., that the Catholic Church is part of, or subsists in, a larger corporate entity which is called the Church, or the Church of Christ.

> This Church, constituted and organized in the world as a society, subsists in the Catholic Church, which is governed by the successor of Peter and by the bishops in union with that successor, although many elements of sanctification and truth can be found outside of her visible structure.[108]

In the final document promulgated at the end of the third session, the *De-cree on the Oriental Churches*, the integrity of the eastern churches is especially emphasized. "For it is the mind of the Catholic Church that each individual church or rite retain its traditions whole and entire, while adjusting its way of life to the various needs of time and place."[109] Regarding the venerable institution of the patriarchate, Vatican II affirmed the following: "This sacred synod, therefore, decrees that their rights and privileges should be re-established in accord with the ancient traditions of each church and the decrees of the ecumenical councils."[110]

It is interesting to note in this connection the reaction of Bishop Kallistos Ware of the Greek Orthodox Church on the relationship between the Orthodox and Rome.

> The crucial issue between Orthodoxy and Rome is certainly the understanding of the papal ministry within the Church. We Orthodox cannot accept the definitions of the First Vatican Council, promulgated in 1870, concerning the infallibility and the supreme universal jurisdiction of the pope. These definitions were emphatically reaffirmed by the Second Vatican Council, but at the same time Vatican II placed the papal claims within a new context by insisting also on the collegiality of the bishops . . .
> We do not consider that, in the first ten centuries of the Church, the pope possessed direct and immediate power of jurisdiction in the Christian East, and so we find it impossible to grant such power to him today.[111]

The fourth and final session of Vatican II began on September 14, 1965. In his opening address to the assembled fathers, Paul VI announced his intention to establish a synod of bishops which was to be "a central ecclesiastical institution representing the total Catholic episcopate, by its nature perpetual, which would perform its duties for a time and when called upon."[112] This was viewed at the time with great optimism as a way of expressing, on an ongoing basis, the collegial relationship between the episcopate and the pope. The synod was to be a consultative rather than a deliberative body, but it was seen as an important beginning.

The volume of work to be completed in the final session was enormous. On October 28, five decrees were promulgated: the *Decree on the Pastoral Office of Bishops*, the *Decree on the Renewal of Religious Life*, the *Decree on Priestly Formation*, the *Declaration on the Non-Christian Religions*, and the *Declaration on Christian Education*. All of these had been worked and reworked in previous sessions and submitted to final voting in the early weeks of session four. Although much of the material on the *Pastoral Office of Bishops* had been set out before in previous conciliar documents, paragraph 8 enlarged the competence of local ordinaries regarding the issuance of dispensations from the common law. (This prerogative had already been expanded in a motu proprio, *Pastorale munus*, published by Paul VI on November 30, 1963.) Priests' councils and pastoral councils were recommended for all dioceses as a way of expanding the consultative and decision-making processes in the local churches.[113] And further, the document recommended the establishment of episcopal conferences in all national or regional churches:

This most sacred Synod considers it supremely opportune everywhere that bishops belonging to the same nation or region form an association to meet together at fixed times. Thus when the insights of prudence and experience have been shared and views exchanged, there will emerge a holy union of energies in the service of the common good of the churches.[114]

The decree provided for the possibility of regional or national legislation when enacted by two-thirds of the voting bishops, at least in those areas where the common law allows for such legislation, or when the pontiff permits it in special cases, as long as the decisions are reviewed by the Holy See before implementation.[115] A *motu proprio* of August 6, 1966, mandated the establishment of priests' councils and strongly recommended pastoral councils for each diocese. It also ordered the formation of episcopal conferences in every nation or region as soon as possible.[116]

On November 18, the hotly debated *Constitution on Divine Revelation* was finally ready for promulgation after the council decided to leave to the theological schools the liberty of defining in greater detail the relationship between Scripture and tradition. On the same day, the *Decree on the Laity* was promulgated with nearly unanimous approval. The role of the laity was described very differently from the portrait found in Pius X's *Vehementer nos* of 1906, where lay people were characterized as a docile flock whose role it was to be led around by their pastors. According to the *Decree on the Laity*,

They exercise a genuine apostolate by their activity on behalf of bringing the Gospel and holiness to men, and on behalf of penetrating and perfecting the temporal sphere of things through the spirit of the Gospel. . . . Since it is proper to the layman's state in life for him [her] to spend his [her] days in the midst of the world and of secular transactions, he [she] is called by God to burn with the spirit of Christ and to exercise his [her] apostolate in the world as a kind of leaven.[117]

The remaining three weeks of the fourth session witnessed the completion of the remaining four schemata which were approved by large margins and promulgated on December 7: the *Constitution on the Church in the Modern World*, the *Decree on the Missions*, the *Decree on the Priesthood*, and the *Declaration on Religious Freedom*. Hubert Jedin says about the *Constitution on the Church in the Modern World*: "It aimed to be a fundamental new definition of the relation of the Church to the world, and that meant to the spirit of the new epoch, from which it held itself aloof since a century earlier in the *Syllabus* [i.e., Pius IX, 1864]."[118]

It is somewhat disheartening to note that in the final report of the 1985 episcopal synod commemorating the twentieth anniversary of the closing of

Vatican II, a good deal of the freshness and optimism of the *Constitution on the Church in the Modern World* had disappeared, giving way to a heaviness and an overriding impression that conditions in the world and in the Church were less favorable than they were in the 1960s.

It is the *Declaration on Religious Freedom* that will long stand as the sterling example of doctrinal evolution in the Church. As John Courtney Murray, S.J., says in a short commentary on the declaration,

> The course of development between the *Syllabus of Errors* (1864) and *Dignitatis Humanae Personae* (1965) still remains to be explained by theologians. But the council formally sanctioned the validity of the development itself; and this was a doctrinal event of high importance for theological thought in many other areas.[119]

With regard to the relations between the Church and the state, Murray adds: "A long-standing ambiguity has finally been cleared up. The Church does not deal with the secular order in terms of a double standard—freedom for the Church when Catholics are a minority, privilege for the Church and intolerance for others when Catholics are a majority."[120]

The Second Vatican Council was closed on December 8, 1965. It stands as the outstanding ecclesial event of the twentieth century, much praised by many, often misread by not a few, and considered a tragedy by some. Ten years or so after the council, Roger Aubert asked whether it marked the end of the post-Tridentine era, and his answer was that it was too soon to say.[121] He felt that the restructuring of the Roman curia begun by Paul VI in August 1967 with his constitution, *Regimini Ecclesiae*, would be critical in bringing about this transformation. With the aid of a generation of hindsight I believe one can say that the Roman curia remains the same engine of Tridentinism it has been since the sixteenth century. Since Vatican II, departments and dicasteries have been restructured, combined, and some have been added. Procedures have been changed—some for good, some for ill. New people from various nations and cultures have taken their places beside the Italian regulars, but in the main, the more things changed, the more they remained the same.

PAUL VI'S THEME OF DIALOGUE MISFIRES
—HUMANAE VITAE

The theme of Paul's pontificate was articulated in his first encyclical, *Ecclesiam suam*, which was published in August 1964, just before the third session of Vatican II. Great emphasis was placed on the need to engage in dialogue with the modern world. First, the Church must "strive toward a clearer and deeper awareness of its mission in the world."[122] The Second Vatican Council, he said, will complete and complement the work of Vatican I, and Paul did not want to interfere in any way with that effort. However, he emphasized that dialogue with the various elements of contemporary society was critical to the fulfilment of the Church's role, for in this way, "the forms of thought and living" of our time can be corrected, ennobled, encouraged, and sanctified.[123] Paul adopted the word *aggiornamento* to characterize the aim and object of his pontificate. He asserted that the relationship that the Church is to establish with the world should be dialogical, "a dialogue of salvation."[124] This dialogue "is demanded by the pluralism of society, and by the maturity man has reached in this day and age."[125] Then he outlined the four types of dialogue in which the Church must engage:

1. the dialogue with mankind, i.e., the whole human race
2. the dialogue with all who worship the one, supreme God, i.e., the Jews, the Muslims, the Afro-Asiatic religions
3. the dialogue with all Christians
4. the dialogue with all Catholics

The pontiff concluded by celebrating the fact that this dialogue has already begun, noting that, "The Church today is more alive than ever before."[126] *Ecclesiam suam* was Paul's keynote address at the outset of his pontificate. Dialogue was to be the touchstone of his dealings with the world and with the various segments in the Church.

One controversial item which Paul VI withdrew from the council's agenda was the issue of the celibacy of priests. He promised the council fathers that he would deal with that matter himself, and this he did in his second encyclical, *On Priestly Celibacy*, dated June 24, 1967. After outlining with considerable thoroughness all the major objections to the retention of mandatory celibacy (#7-13), Paul declared that the venerable institution would be retained.[127] He set forth the traditional reasons for celibacy (#19-34) and summarized its history in the East and in the West (#28-44). He praised the guidelines which the council had formulated (#60-63) and stressed that those candidates who seem unfit should be weeded out as soon as possible (#64). The document dealt with priestly defections (which at that time were just beginning to mount), attributing them not to celibacy, but to the inadequacy of the selection process and to the lack of total consecration on the part of the departing priests (#83). The role of the bishop and the faithful to care for and pray for priests concluded the pontiff's treatment. Although he had promised the council delegates that it was his intention "to give new lustre and strength to priestly celibacy in the world of today" (#2), history has not borne that out. Also, the pope's commitment to dialogue as the most effective way to address challenges in today's world (even within the Church) was not applied in this case.

The second issue which had been removed from the council's agenda was the question of birth control and contraception. At the urging of Cardinal Suenens of Belgium, Pope John XXIII had appointed a commission to study that issue in March 1963. The commission, which met four times from October 1963 to June 1966, underwent considerable additions in personnel from one session to the next. From the initial group of six in 1963, the commission grew to about sixty in 1965, and in 1966, fifteen cardinals and bishops were added by Paul VI. The work of the commission was summarized in a report entitled *Responsible Parenthood* in late June 1966, and was approved by an overwhelming majority of the participants who agreed "that sexual activity makes sense only within the context of a chaste, permanent relationship of man and wife who are open to new life, but that does not mean that every conjugal act must be so open."[128] The majority report thus strongly advocated a change in the Church's position, and submitted its findings to the pope. However, the minority (no more than a half-dozen members), led by Cardinal Ottaviani, was to have its day in court, submitting to Pope Paul a minority report which ultimately prevailed. After a two-year delay, the pope's decision was handed down in the encyclical, *Humanae vitae*, of July 25, 1968. He referred to the work of the commission and added the following:

> The conclusions arrived at by the commission could not be considered by us as definitive and absolutely certain, dispensing us from examining personally this serious question. This was all the more necessary because, within the commission itself, there was not complete agreement concerning the moral norms to be proposed, and especially because certain approaches and criteria for a solution to the question had emerged which were at variance with the moral doctrine on marriage constantly taught by the magisterium of the Church.[129]

The papal decision at that point was predictable. Paul reiterated the position that "each and every marital act must of necessity retain its intrinsic relationship to the procreation of human life."[130] The encyclical condemned all direct abortion, even for therapeutic reasons, as a means of regulating the number of children, all direct sterilization, whether permanent or temporary, and finally, "any action which either before, at the moment of, or after intercourse, is specifically intended to prevent procreation—whether as an end or as a means."[131] The encyclical concluded with a plethora of pastoral directions urging married couples, among other things, to have frequent recourse to the sacrament of penance, and exhorting priests and bishops to exercise understanding and mercy when dealing with these penitents who were to be reminded never to "lose heart because of their weakness."[132]

Humanae vitae created an instantaneous fire storm of epic proportions throughout the Catholic world. Theologians such as Charles Curran, Philip Delhaye, Karl Rahner, S.J., Bernard Häring, C.Ss.R., and countless others raised their voices in protest. One episcopal conference after another reacted to the encyclical during the ensuing months, and the majority of them either significantly qualified its meaning (e.g., Austria, Belgium, Canada, and Holland) or issued responses that were capable of ambiguous interpretation (England, Italy, and the United States).[133] Five years after the publication of *Humanae vitae*, the moralist, Richard McCormick, S.J., concluded that the "very large body of dissent within the Church" was an indication that the papal teaching had not been received by the Church people.[134] Once again, Paul's unwillingness to accede to the conclusion of the papal commission, or to submit the issue to additional open dialogue prior to rendering his decision, seemed to be a violation of his rather solemn commitment to the dialogical process which he made in *Ecclesiam suam* at the outset of his papacy; and the result did not turn out well. The negative reactions of the Catholic world, bishops, priests, and laity, were almost too much for Paul to bear. *Humanae vitae* was the watershed of his pontificate. He never wrote another encyclical during the remaining ten years of his reign.

THE WORLD SYNOD OF BISHOPS

Probably the most ambitious and dramatic attempt on the part of Pope Paul to increase dialogue within the Church was his establishment of the synod of bishops which he announced at the beginning of the fourth session of Vatican II. The *motu proprio, Apostolica Sollicitudo* (September 15, 1965), which created the new body, referred to the need for dialogue between the pope and the bishops in order that they might more effectively fulfill the Church's mission.[135] The first of these gatherings met in Rome in the fall of 1967 for about four weeks. There was considerable optimism among the nearly 200 participants, but there were too many topics on the agenda which led many to believe that the synod was not well planned. One of the more important issues was the status of the revision of the 1917 *Code of Canon Law*. Cardinal Pericle Felici, president of the Code Revision Commission, outlined the ten norms that were to guide the commission in their work, and requested that they be approved by the synod. Among the ten were the following:

1. The bishops' power to dispense from the general laws of the Church was to be expanded (#4).
2. Greater application should be given to the principle of subsidiarity within the Church (#5).
3. The rights of the Church people were to be defined and safeguarded (#6).[136]

The delegates approved all ten working norms and were encouraged by the direction that the commission was apparently taking.

Another product of the 1967 synod was a document entitled *The Ministerial Priesthood*, which outlined some of the problems experienced by priests, attempted to set out a theology of the sacerdotal ministry in the Church, and issued directives regarding priestly activity, spirituality, and celibacy. Because the well-intentioned document did not add much to the teaching on the priesthood in Vatican II, its effects were limited.

The second synod (October 1969) was an extraordinary session which was called to deal with the question of collaboration between Rome and the episcopal conferences. The pope and the curia had been shocked and startled by the qualified responses of the various conferences to *Humanae vitae*. Although the delegates urged for more consultation between the curia and the conferences, Paul reserved that matter to himself. Some changes were made regarding the workings of episcopal synods for the future, but generally the gathering was not a successful experience either for the bishops or for Pope Paul.

In late September 1971, the third session of the bishop's synod opened in Rome to discuss two topics: the priestly ministry and justice in the world. Again, the agenda was too ambitious for a meeting that was to last little more than a month, but it did produce a valuable document, *Justice in the World* (November 30, 1971), which was a wide-ranging piece pointing up the many instances of economic injustice in the world. Education of all sorts was underlined as one of the most effective remedies for these inequities, as well as the need to distribute economic resources more fairly throughout the globe.[137] In connection with the second topic, the priestly office, a good number of delegates wanted to discuss the ordination of married men as a way of solving the critical priest shortage in many areas, but Paul removed that topic from consideration. Once again, the pope's commitment to dialogue with his bishops within the context of the world synod was passed over.

In the fall of 1974 the topic of the bishops' synod was evangelization, which proved to be too broad and extensive for such a relatively short session. In addition, the discussions were needlessly mired in all sorts of procedural tangles, and as a result, no document was drafted articulating the findings of the meeting except a brief statement on human rights. The task of formulating the message of the synod was left to Pope Paul, who described the situation thus:

> When the synod had concluded its meetings, the fathers decided to place the results of their deliberations in the hands of the pastor of the universal Church in a spirit of simplicity and confidence, saying that they looked to the Roman pontiff to provide a new stimulus which would introduce the Church, now more thoroughly imbued with the strength and power of Pentecost, into a new and more fruitful era of evangelization.[138]

Paul's exhortation, *Evangelization in the Modern World* (December 8, 1975), took the deliberations of the synod as a point of departure for a lengthy presentation which adds little to Vatican II's *Constitution on the Church in the Modern World* and the *Decree on the Church's Missionary Activity*.[139] This procedure of allowing the pope to publish the final results of the synod, rather than the synod itself publishing its own position paper at the end of its deliberations, established a pattern which has been more or less followed ever since the 1974 convocation. The effect has been unfortunate in that the fruits of the discussions have often been lost—swept up into papal exhortations written much later which have frequently skirted some of the more valuable and relevant deliberations and conclusions of the synodal delegates over the years. Once again, Paul's commitment to dialogue with his brother bishops in the context of the world synod fell short of the mark.

Paul's final episcopal synod was held in October 1977 on the subject of catechesis, which flowed rather naturally out of the 1974 discussion of evangelization. Although there was much talk during the meetings about a new catechism for the universal Church, there was not much consensus as to what kind of catechism was desired. "In the end, the 1977 synod made no recommendation regarding a catechism."[140]

> In his closing address to the bishops, the pope commented on several of the synod's recommendations. He took comfort in the emphasis that the assembly put on "systematic catechesis" because "the orderly study of the Christian mystery is what distinguishes catechesis itself from all other forms of presentation of the word of God." He also endorsed the synod's insistence on the need for "some fundamental formulas which will make it possible to express more easily, in a suitable and accurate way, the truths of the faith and of Christian moral doctrine."[141]

Paul VI was working on the apostolic exhortation dealing with the issues raised by the synod when he died in August 1978. The task was completed by John Paul II in October 1979.[142]

In spite of the fact that many of Pope Paul's efforts at dialogue were not particularly successful, his overtures in the direction of the eastern Orthodox will long be remembered. Not only did he do the unusual by announcing his election to the heads of the eastern churches in June 1963, but, as mentioned above, he traveled to Jerusalem in January 1964 to meet with Athenagoras II, the ecumenical patriarch. This was the first visit ever of a bishop of Rome to the Holy Land. Through Paul's efforts, on the second-to-last day of Vatican II (December 7, 1965), the mutual excommunications of 1054 were erased forever in Istanbul and in Rome. The pontiff visited Athenagoras in Turkey in July 1967, and invited the patriarch as a guest to Rome that following October. In the bull *Anno ineunte*, which Paul sent to Athenagoras in July 1967, he referred to the church in Rome and the church in Constantinople as "sister" churches:

We have lived this life of sister churches for centuries, celebrating together the ecumenical councils which defended the deposit of faith against any alteration. Now, after a long period of division and mutual incomprehension, the Lord has allowed us to rediscover ourselves as sister churches, despite the obstacles with which we have been confronted. In the light of Christ, we see how urgent is the need to transcend these obstacles, so that we can bring to its fullness and perfection the communion existing between us which is already so rich.[143]

Paul's pontificate was especially difficult. The council was an event that changed almost everything, and it was his nearly impossible task to guide the "bark of Peter" into the new post-conciliar era. We witness in his fifteen years as pope the collision of the *aggiornamento*, initiated by Pope John and espoused by Paul, with the *semper idem* mentality (i.e., always the same) of the Roman curia. By the end of Paul's life, the curial traditionalists had again assumed the dominant position.

The conclave of August 1978 was one of the shortest in recent history, for Albino Luciani, the patriarch of Venice, was chosen on the fourth ballot on August 26. He was something of a surprise choice, but was probably the only electable Italian since there were at least three recognized blocks of cardinals holding out for their respective candidates (i.e., Cardinal Benelli of Florence, Cardinal Siri of Genoa, and Cardinal Pignedoli of the Roman curia). Although something of a traditionalist in doctrine, John Paul I seemed to have many of the personal qualities of John XXIII.

He announced that he was dispensing with the traditional pomp of the papal coronation and the gestatorial chair. He declared that he wished to be known as "pastor" of the church, rather than pontiff. He was universally dubbed the "smiling pope." Seldom had a papacy begun with such popular appeal.[144]

On the thirty-third day after his election—on September 29, 1978—Pope John Paul I died suddenly of a heart attack at the age of sixty-six. We can only speculate as to what kind of "pastor of the Church" he might have been, or where this "smiling pope" would have taken us.

THE ELECTION OF KAROL WOJTYLA

The second conclave of 1978 began with a much more somber tone on October 14, with 111 cardinals present. The prominent Italians were Cardinals Benelli, Siri, Ugo Poletti, chairman of the Italian bishops' conference, and Pericle Felici of the Roman curia. By the end of balloting on October 15, it was evident that there was a hopeless logjam among the Italian prelates, and on the eighth ballot, Cardinal Karol Wojtyla of Kraków was elected—the first non-Italian pope since Hadrian VI (1522-23). Wojtyla was reasonably well known and appreciated in Rome due to his rather traditionalist views expressed during Vatican II and at the bishops' synods. Also, Paul VI had chosen him to preach the Lenten retreat for the pope in 1976.[145] Although Pope John Paul II (1978-) spoke nine times in the aula during Vatican II, it is difficult to discern much concerning his theology of the Church.[146] Apparently he did not have strong feelings about episcopal collegiality, but he did make his views heard on the question of religious liberty and on the *Pastoral Constitution on the Church in the Modern World*.

Perhaps the best window into his views on the council can be found in his book *Sources of Renewal*, published in 1972, to introduce Polish Catholics to the conciliar deliberations. Peter Hebblethwaite comments,

> The council appears as wholly content-less, as though what was said does not matter compared with the mere fact of meeting. Again, the council is presented as though it were a private spiritual experience of bishops, as though it had not aroused expectations amongst almost everyone in the Church. . . . Thus, while theologians in the West were, as they used to say, "exploring the new insights of Vatican II," Cardinal Karol Wojtyla was telling Poles that the council had been an intense spiritual experience.[147]

In the conclusion of the work, Cardinal Wojtyla reminded the readers that his aim was not to explain how the council's teachings were to be put into practice in terms of concrete methods and institutions. These did not constitute for him the essence of Vatican II as a pastoral council. The primary theme was the renewal of faith. "The council outlined the type of faith which corresponds to the life of the modern Christian and the implementation of the council consists first and foremost in enriching that faith."[148]

Because little was said about the significance of episcopal collegiality or the desirability of establishing priest senates or parish councils at the local level, one could judge that for the cardinal, the structural reforms called for by Vatican II were not really that important. It is certain that his emphasis—which was that shared by most of the prelates of the Roman curia—was noted in the Vatican.

One of the changes that occurred rather quickly under the new pontiff was the acceleration of proceedings against theologians who were deemed to have deviated from the path of orthodoxy. Fr. Hans Küng, the dogmatic theologian from Tübingen who had been under scrutiny during the sixties and the seventies for his teachings on ecclesiology, papal infallibility, and Christology, received a notification from the Office of the Doctrine of the Faith in December 1979 that he could no longer be considered a Catholic theologian and hence had to be removed from his post. Because of his successes at Tübingen, the university created a new chair of ecumenical theology for him, and Küng has remained in that position up to the present. In 1968, the same congregation initiated an action against Fr. Edward Schillebeeckx, O.P., of the University of Nijmegen, whom they suspected of heresy due to his notion of revelation. Although this process was dismissed without incident, he was summoned again in 1976 to answer questions regarding his recently published work on Christology. This dispute dragged on into 1980 when he received a letter from Cardinal Seper, the Prefect of the Congregation for the Doctrine of the Faith, indicating that there were still some unresolved issues, but there was no closure. The Dominican's book on the ministry in 1980 precipitated another inquiry which lasted for some six years over the question of a nonordained person celebrating the Eucharist in very extreme circumstances. Schillebeeckx was notified that he should be more attentive to the teachings of the Church in this area. In 1985, Fr. Charles Curran of the Catholic University in Washington was informed by the Doctrine of the Faith Office that because of his dissent in certain areas of sexual morality, he could no longer be considered a Catholic theologian.[149] Curran fought the decision because he and many others were convinced that it was unjust since he was being disqualified simply on the basis of his respectful dissent in an area of reformable church teaching.[150]

In September 1984, the Brazilian Franciscan Leonardo Boff was ordered to respond to an inquiry regarding his book, *The Church, Charism and Power* (1981). In spite of the intercession of the Brazilian cardinals, Lorscheider and Arns, on his behalf, Boff was informed in writing that because of the dangers to sound doctrine regarding the notion of the Church, he was to be silenced for a year. Boff submitted to the restriction placed on him, but he eventually left the ministry in 1992. Possibly the saddest and most depressing of all the stories of doctrinal trials was the process against Fr. Bernard Häring, the Redemptorist moralist, over certain of his views on sexual morality and medical ethics. The doctrinal proceeding which was initiated in 1975, dragged on into 1979 and at the time of his death in 1998 was still unresolved. Although Pope John Paul II was quite possibly not directly and overtly involved in any of these processes, of which the above examples are only among the most notable; that they reflect on the character of his papacy cannot be denied. No one would claim that the Roman curia has no right to correct and even admonish theologians who are speaking and writing against accepted and irreformable positions of the Church. However, it is the inquisitorial manner in which these proceedings are so often carried out that remains a source of embarrassment and scandal within and outside the Church.[151]

THE 1983 *CODE OF CANON LAW*

The new 1983 *Code of Canon Law* has been portrayed by Pope John Paul II as a final step in the completion of the work of Vatican II. Its arrangement was structured according to the design of the recent council.[152] After the general statutes outlining the nature of ecclesiastical law, the rights and obligations of the people of God are set forth, followed by the canons on the teaching office, and then the sanctifying office of the Church. The next group of canons deal with ecclesiastical temporalities, followed by church sanctions or penalties and, finally, procedures. Much of the legislation has been revised in the light of the Vatican II decrees. The Church is seen as a communion of particular or local churches (c. 368) rather than as a single global entity. The pope and the college of bishops are identified as successors of Peter and the college of apostles (c. 330), and the power of the Roman pontiff over the local churches is described in a much less abrasive fashion than in *Pastor aeternus* of Vatican I (c. 333, #1). The treatment of ecumenical councils (cc. 337-41), although located under the rubric of the college of bishops, seems to lack the emphasis which this crucial institution deserves, given the critical role that universal councils have played over the centuries. Canons 342-48, which deal with the World Synod of Bishops established by Paul VI, describe it as a permanent institution, but outline its role a bit too restrictively so that its growth and development as a universal collegial instrument seems bound to be stunted. Conferences of bishops for each nation or region are mandated (cc. 447-59). They are to prepare their own statutory framework, but their power to enact decrees for the whole regional church is extremely limited (c. 455). Here especially, the principle of subsidiarity, which was established as one of the controlling norms for code revision in 1967, was all but ignored. Also, "the requirement that decrees of the conference be reviewed by the Holy See could be seen as an unnecessary centralization."[153]

Given the current level of suspicion regarding participative government and the application of the principle of subsidiarity in the Church, the 1983 Code deserves a good deal of praise. It can be considered as a largely positive contribution of Pope John Paul II's pontificate. In light of the present Vatican trend—which maximizes the authority at the center, acknowledges the subordinated reality of the local churches or dioceses, and minimizes the importance of any governmental institution inbetween—the 1983 Code offers a vision of the Church wherein decision making could be more widely distributed, allowing the intermediary levels to play a greater part in Church governance.[154] Unfortunately, however, the current trend features a very highly concentrated and overreaching papal authority which prefers to deal with the particular churches (i.e., the dioceses) on an individual basis because they are thus more easily controlled. This pattern surely flies in the face of the marvelous description of regional collegiality found in paragraph 23 of the *Constitution on the Church*.

> By divine Providence it has come about that various churches established in diverse places by the apostles and their successors have in the course of time coalesced into several groups organically united, which, preserving

the unity of faith and the unique divine constitution of the Church, enjoy their own discipline, their own liturgical usage, and their own theological and spiritual heritage.[155]

Then several lines later the constitution goes on to say:

This variety of local churches with one common aspiration is particularly splendid evidence of the catholicity of the undivided church. In like manner the episcopal bodies of today are in a position to render a manifold and fruitful assistance, so that this collegiate sense may be put into practical application.[156]

This regional expression of the Church's catholicity will never find verification unless the principle of subsidiarity is more widely applied, allowing these national and regional bodies to become what they could be.

JOHN PAUL II AND THE BISHOPS' SYNOD

One can learn a great deal about the character of John Paul II's pontificate by taking a brief glance at the first three bishops' synods that were convened by him. His first general synod, which opened in September 1980, dealt with the role of the Christian family. It was Archbishop John Quinn of San Francisco who, as president of the U.S. episcopal conference, declared that *Humanae vitae*'s ban on birth control was clearly not working. Catholic couples were in general not responding favorably to the encyclical's teaching, and Catholic priests were only infrequently applying it in their ministry.[157] At the end of the synod, the pope reaffirmed the validity of *Humanae vitae* and also reemphasized the discipline of not admitting divorced and remarried Catholics (without a previous declaration of nullity) to communion.[158] John Paul's apostolic exhortation on the Christian family, issued one year after the close of the synod, restated the traditional stands against contraception, divorce and remarriage, and the role of the Christian family in the modern world.[159]

The 1983 synod, which met throughout October, focused on the issue of the Church's penitential discipline. Ample evidence was provided by the delegates that the sacrament of penance was in crisis almost everywhere, and that more attention should be given to the practice of communal penance because auricular confession had been in precipitous decline in terms of use and frequency.[160] The pope's closing address (October 29, 1983) and his post-synodal exhortation (December 2, 1984) summarizing the labor of the synod simply referred—in response to petitions for the wider use of communal penance—to canons 961 and 962 of the 1983 Code. These canons do nothing more than repeat the longstanding and carefully circumscribed practice regarding general absolution which has been taught for generations. This refusal to adapt the practice of penance to the needs of the time prompted Cardinal Lorscheider of Brazil to point to the 1983 synod as something of a disappointment.[161]

In January 1985 the pope surprised the Catholic world by announcing that it was his intent to convoke an extraordinary session of the world synod in November of that year in honor of the twentieth anniversary of the closing of Vatican II. The purpose was to assess the results of the recent council and the degree to which it had been faithfully implemented thus far throughout the world. The two-week session, which opened on November 25, involved the presidents of the national and regional conferences and a great number of the officials of the Roman curia. Cardinal Godfried Daneels of Brussels provided the fathers with a rather extensive overview of the topics submitted for consideration by the various hierarchies prior to the gathering.[162] Almost from the outset the delegates were divided into several language groups to discuss the principal issues outlined in Daneels' presentation. It was the German group (animated to a great extent by Cardinal Ratzinger) whose summation apparently had the greatest impact on the formulation of the synod's final report.[163] Compared with the principal documents of Vatican II, the concluding report had a chilling effect. The optimism and enthusiasm of 1962-65 were gone. It was felt that the council had not been as well received in the "first world" as had been expected. Among the affluent nations, "a certain blindness to spiritual realities has set in." Perhaps, the document opined, there has been too much emphasis on structural change and not enough on spirituality and on the Church as mystery. The report expressed reservations regarding the application of the principle of collegiality, which has its maximum expression in an ecumenical council, but perhaps is not directly operative in the synod of bishops or in episcopal conferences. As a matter of fact, it was suggested that the "theological status" of the episcopal conferences be studied, especially with regard to their "doctrinal authority."[164] Then, as a final gesture, the report stated the following: "It is recommended that a study be made to examine whether the principle of subsidiarity in use in human society can be applied to the Church and to what degree and in what sense an application can and should be made."[165]

After so much had been said and written about the application of subsidiarity to the organization of the Church since Pius XII's statement of 1946, this suggestion to start all over again was indeed disconcerting. Pope John Paul II's synods of 1980, 1983, and 1985 established a pattern which has not been deviated from significantly in his three subsequent synods of 1987 on the mission of the laity, 1990 on priestly formation, and 1994 on the consecrated life of religious. Moreover, it is very likely that any subsequent episcopal synods in this pontificate will follow the same procedure.

THE NEW CATECHISM

One of the *desideranda* lifted up by the 1985 synod was the formulation of a universal catechism which would counteract the undesirable "pluriformity" in doctrinal expression which had surfaced since Vatican II. The *Catechism of the Catholic Church* appeared in 1992. The English edition (published in 1994) is a massive 803-page document which outlines the articles of the creed (13-276), the sacraments (277-420), human destiny and the commandments (412-611), and prayer (613-680).[166] Norbert Greinacher of the Catholic theological faculty at Tübingen comments regarding the *Catechism*:

> The *World Catechism* represented a further attempt on the part of the Roman curia to restore the pre-conciliar identity. Without observing either the letter or the spirit of the Second Vatican Council, leaving aside the various continents and ignoring the results of theological scholarship, an attempt is made here to define in detail what Catholic faith and morality is: a vain attempt![167]

Avery Dulles, S.J., in his 1994 review of the books published to that point on the *New Catechism*, while expressing himself in favor of the document, did reflect some of the objections raised in a symposium on the early English edition of the *Catechism* in the spring of 1993. He relates some of the objections:

> Is the ecclesiology too triumphalistic and complacent? Does the concentration on Catholic doctrine give the impression that there are no other forms of Christianity? Does the Catechism convey a "super sessionist" view in which Judaism appears obsolete since the time of Christ? Does the use of the ten commandments as a structuring principle force morality into a legalistic mode? . . . Does the catechism tend to restrict the pluralism of styles and cultures within the Catholic Church?[168]

The *Catechism* of 1992 will go down in history as the first official catechism issued by the Catholic Church since Pius V in 1566, and it will be known as the catechism of John Paul II.

JOHN PAUL II AND THE MORALISTS

With the publication of his long anticipated encyclical on moral theology, *Veritatis splendor*, in August 1993, the pope attacked those moralists who advocate proportionalism, i.e., those who attempt to evaluate human conduct from a perspective wider than an appraisal of the physical act alone. Richard McBrien of Notre Dame notes,

The pope misreads proportionalist thinkers when he insists that they reject the notion of intrinsically evil acts. What the proportionalists deny is not the very notion of an intrinsically evil act, but the supposition that an act can be intrinsically evil independently of other factors. Killing another human being is not intrinsically evil, but the direct killing of an innocent person is. It is called murder. . . . Thus for the proportionalist it is never enough to look at the physical act alone. One must take a look at all the factors that enter into the act and, therefore, into a determination of its moral quality.[169]

According to the proportionalist theologians (e.g., Richard McCormick, S.J., Joseph Fuchs, S.J., Charles Curran, Bernard Häring, C.Ss.R., etc.), it is the human act in its fullness (with concrete circumstances and foreseeable results) that is the one object of decision. According to Pope John Paul II, for example, any artificial means for regulating birth is intrinsically evil and sinful, without exception. The proportionalists, on the other hand, argue that a contraceptive act has to be weighed in the context of the whole loving relationship between husband and wife. Are they fulfilling their obligations regarding their Christian marital union and Christian parenthood in their total relationship? Bernard Häring's reaction to *Veritatis splendor* is worth repeating here:

[A]lmost all real splendor is lost when it becomes evident that the whole document is directed above all towards one goal: to endorse total assent and submission to all utterances of the pope, and above all on one crucial point: that the use of any artificial means for regulating births is intrinsically evil and sinful, without exception, even in circumstances where contraception would be a lesser evil.[170]

Richard McCormick draws the following conclusions concerning the pope's encyclical:

For me, *Veritatis splendor* is a symbol of a notion of the Church—of the Church as a pyramid where truth and authority flow uniquely from the pinnacle. Vatican II adopted the concentric model wherein the reflections of all must flow from the periphery to the center if the wisdom resident in the Church is to be reflected persuasively and prophetically to the world. That this is not the case with *Veritatis splendor* seems clear.[171]

THE ORDINATION OF WOMEN

Perhaps an even more striking instance of this pyramidal mentality wherein "truth and authority flow uniquely from the pinnacle" is the case of the apostolic letter, *Ordinatio sacerdotalis*, issued by John Paul II on May 22, 1994. In this document, the pope wished to close the question of the admissibility of women to priestly ordination. Leaning heavily on a 1977 declaration of the Doctrine of the Faith Congregation which he said was approved and ordered to be published by Pope Paul VI, John Paul made the following declaration:

> Although the teaching that priestly ordination is to be reserved to men alone has been preserved by the constant and universal tradition of the church and uniformly taught by the magisterium in its most recent documents, at the present time in some places it is nonetheless considered still open to debate, or the Church's judgment that women are not to be admitted to ordination is considered to have a merely disciplinary force...
>
> Wherefore, in order that all doubt may be removed regarding a matter of great importance, a matter which pertains to the Church's divine constitution itself, in virtue of my ministry of confirming the brethren (cf. Lk 22:32) I declare that the Church has no authority whatsoever to confer priestly ordination on women and that this judgment is to be definitively held by all the Church's faithful.[172]

In spite of the fact that the Pontifical Biblical Commission, in response to a request from the Doctrinal Congregation, had issued in 1976 a unanimous judgment that "the New Testament does not by itself alone permit us to settle in a clear way once and for all the problem of the possible access of women to the priesthood,"[173] the Doctrine of the Faith office issued in 1977 the declaration, *Inter insigniores*, which stated that the Church, in fidelity to the example of the Lord, does not consider itself authorized to admit women to priestly ordination.[174]

Judging from the reaction throughout the Catholic world to John Paul II's letter of 1994, it can be said that there was still a considerable amount of discussion in the journals during the next several years on the question of the priestly ordination of women. However, the apostolic letter, *Ad tuendam fidem*, given by the pope on May 18, 1998, seems to close the door on any further public debate or discussion of this issue, inasmuch as the prohibition has been judged by the pontiff (in *Ordinatio sacerdotalis*) as a truth "to be definitively held by all the Church's faithful."

THE SELECTION OF BISHOPS

There is yet a final matter regarding John Paul's conduct of the papacy which should be briefly explored. Seldom in the long history of the papal office has there been as systematic and controlled a program governing the selection of bishops worldwide. In his first twenty years as pontiff, John Paul II appointed roughly 2,700 bishops, and that means that during that period almost three-quarters of the active world episcopate was chosen on his terms. In addition to the canonical norms (canon 378 of the 1983 Code), a set of "hidden criteria" has been in operation almost from the outset of his papacy. According to a document revealed a few years ago, there is a rather detailed litmus test which is applied to episcopal candidates, especially with regard to their theological orthodoxy. Their views must be in complete accord with John Paul regarding sexual ethics in general and the teaching of *Humanae vitae* in particular, the issue of the priestly ordination of women, the retention of priestly celibacy, and generally, they must manifest complete fidelity and obedience to the Holy Father, the Apostolic See, and the hierarchy. Further, each candidate must evidence faithfulness to true church tradition and commitment to Vatican II and the renewal that followed it, *according to papal instructions.*[175] A deviation or lapse into more progressive or innovative ideas in any of these areas would apparently disqualify a candidate at the outset. It is very doubtful that such demands regarding a whole gamut of a candidate's theological positions—except for the last seven or eight years of Pius X's pontificate—have ever been made before. A potential selectee who has been seen to blink on any of these issues (by those invited to fill out a questionnaire on his behalf) would no doubt be ruled out of the running.

It does not take a great deal of imagination to envision the effect that the demand for rigid theological uniformity has had and is having on the local churches placed in the care of these men. The reports of unrest and frustration experienced by priests and laity in Austria, Holland, Belgium, France, Germany, Brazil (and elsewhere in Central and South America), Africa, and the United States over the past ten to fifteen years cannot but be related at least in part to the reactionary stance of Pope John Paul II's bishops. The pope's view of Vatican II, revealed so clearly in his *Sources of Renewal*, published in 1972 when he was cardinal archbishop of Kraków, must be judged as a rather restrictive interpretation of that epic-making event.[176] Many, if not most of the participants at Vatican II, and countless clergy and laity since, saw and continue to see a stronger call for *aggiornamento* and a challenge to institutional reform in the conciliar documents than do the Holy Father and the great majority of the prelates of the Roman curia.

JOHN PAUL II'S SPECIAL APOSTOLATE

Although a number of the institutional reforms advocated by Vatican II have not evolved as some had envisioned a generation ago, it is hoped that these issues will resurface at some future date. It must be said that no one pope can possibly address all the *desideranda* articulated by the recent council. One must not forget the notable contributions that John Paul II has made and is making to the Church and to the world. His emphasis from the outset has been on personal renewal and the deepening of faith. These were the themes of his *Sources of Renewal,* and he refocused on the same issues in his *Crossing the Threshold of Hope* in 1994.[177] The pontiff's inaugural encyclical of 1979, *Redemptor hominis,* set the stage for his subsequent exhortations and letters.[178] He returned again and again to the notion that human freedom and human dignity can only be fully achieved within the context of the saving grace of Christ.

Avery Dulles, S.J., has employed the word "prophetic" to describe the program and approach of John Paul II:

> A prophet is someone who speaks out of a strong conviction and with a sense of vocation. John Paul II evidently sees himself and the church as divinely commissioned to be advocates of authentic humanity. The prophet speaks with a certain sense of urgency. . . . He is conscious of speaking to a world that is in the throes of a crisis – a crisis of dehumanization. Like most prophets, he sees that he is faced with enormous opposition and that he is perhaps a lonely voice.[179]

The pope's prophetic impulse can be observed especially in his moral and ethical teachings. There are certain traditionally held values, e.g., in the realm of sexual morality, which he clearly and unambiguously insists on in the midst of what he sees as a rising tide of moral relativism.[180] One can discern a prophetic tone in many of his pronouncements, for he is utterly convinced that he is speaking these values to the Church and to the world for God. It is the persistence of his ethical message that makes him a moral beacon in the world. Also, it is this prophetic charism that might explain to some degree his consistent effort to surround himself with an episcopate that speaks with one voice, particularly in the areas of marital ethics, sexual morality, priestly celibacy, and the ordination of women.

John Paul II has over his long tenure made an unremitting effort to visit, speak with and be present to men, women, and children everywhere, of all nationalities and cultures. His background and talents have equipped him well. His sense of the dramatic, his genuine love of people, and his mastery of many languages have made him a spokesman to the world. Year after year he has traveled literally to the four corners of the earth. In this regard he has vastly expanded the overtures of Paul VI in rendering the papacy present and visible everywhere. There is no question but that he has thereby given to the papal role a distinctive stamp, and expanded the pope's personal involvement in the worldwide mission of the Church.

Finally, John Paul II's election as the first non-Italian pope since Hadrian VI (1522-23) could very well open up a whole new range of options for papal elections in the future. Having broken the chain of Italian pontiffs, and then having reigned as pope for such a long period, he could well have put a more universal cast on the papal office, thereby expanding the number of viable candidates for the future and contributing in another way to the universality of the Church.

Epilogue

Looking Back and Looking Forward

⁓

The five New Testament models of church organization analyzed at the outset of this book do not give the impression of a uniformly structured group of Christian communities. When the Vatican II document on the Church, *Lumen gentium*, presumed to reconcile these various strains into a uniform understanding of ministry with which the various New Testament writers are assumed to agree, the constitution seems to have gone beyond the evidence. Moreover, the Vatican II assertion that the monarchical bishops are the direct descendants of the apostles in the churches is simply not borne out in much of the New Testament data. As a matter of fact, apart from the bond of *communio* linking the various churches together, the New Testament evidence points to a pluriformity and a diversity, rather than a uniformity of church structure and organization.

A study of the period after the death of the apostles (ca. 70-75 A.D.) to the middle of the second century indicates that there was apparently no monarchical bishop in Rome until 140-150 A.D. An eastern scholar named Hegesippus, while staying in Rome in the third quarter of the second century, either presumed to construct a list of Roman bishops going back to St. Peter, or found such a list devised by someone else and included it in his memoirs. It was Pope Victor I (189-98) who seems to have been the first Roman bishop to assume the right to dictate policy beyond his original zone of influence in the Italian peninsula; and it was Pope Stephen I (254-57), in the controversy over the issue of rebaptism, who was apparently the first Roman pontiff to ground his assertion of authority over distant Christian churches in Christ's promise to Peter in Matthew 16:18-19.

With Popes Damasus (366-84) and Siricius (384-99), the influence of the Roman pontiff expanded dramatically, and was given a discernible shape during the important reign of Leo I (440-61). In central and southern Italy, the pope had always been the sole metropolitan bishop, while in the remainder of the West, especially after the fall of Carthage in 439, he came to assert a certain "primacy of jurisdiction" which he normally exercised through the metropolitans of the various provinces. In the East, however, the situation was quite different. There he was coping with the patriarchs of Constantinople, Antioch,

Alexandria, and Jerusalem who recognized that the bishop of Rome possessed a certain primacy of honor, but not a primacy of jurisdiction over them. Although Leo I's doctrinal contribution to the Council of Chalcedon (451) represented a high point in papal influence in the East, the oriental churches were still unwilling to concede to him anything more than a primacy of honor over the whole of Christendom. After Chalcedon, doctrinal differences regarding the nature and person of Jesus Christ, particularly in the East, precipitated lasting divisions between Monophysites and Chalcedonians. Attempts by the Roman emperors to bring the factions together were unsuccessful, and occasioned the tragic doctrinal compromises of Pope Vigilius (537-55) in the "Three Chapters" affair, which in turn divided the West for several generations. Much of the work of Leo I and several of his predecessors to strengthen Rome's position vis-à-vis the churches of the West was at least temporarily undone by Vigilius' vacillation and weakness.

Although Pope Gregory I (590-604) exercised considerable jurisdictional authority throughout almost all of Italy, his control over the churches in Gaul was quite limited, while the churches in Spain, north Africa, the Balkans, and Dalmatia were largely on their own. Regarding the churches in the East, the pontiff's many letters to the oriental communities reveal that he viewed the five patriarchs as the regional heads of Christendom, with no one of them exercising a universal or controlling jurisdiction over the others. As the Roman (or Byzantine) emperors became less and less active in the West, the eighth-century popes gravitated into the sphere of the burgeoning Frankish kingdom, thus imperiling the longstanding bond between Byzantium and Rome. In the mid-eighth century, the duchies of Rome, Perugia, and to some extent, Ravenna had come together as the Papal States, and the pope thus became a political player in the newly forming political arena of Europe. To secure protection from belligerent neighbors such as the Lombards, the popes allied themselves with the Frankish kings, especially Charlemagne and his descendants. As the Carolingians became more and more politically inept in the ninth century, the popes (e.g., Nicholas I and John VIII) claimed for themselves more and more power, spiritual and temporal, over the churches. Such expanded claims, however, were never really accepted or acknowledged in the East. The ninth-century popes had lost the ability which Pope Gregory I had employed so effectively in keeping the East and the West together. By 1000 A.D. or thereabouts, the papacy and the eastern churches were moving apart.

The Roman see was rescued from its scandalous tenth-century doldrums by the Saxon kings of Germany who installed a series of German popes, beginning in 1046. Leo IX (1049-54) began the line of reform pontiffs which included Gregory VII (1073-85) and Urban II (1088-99). Just after Leo IX's death, on the occasion of the excommunication of Patriarch Michael Cerularius of Constantinople in July 1054, eastern and western Christendom embarked on a period of formal separation which has never been healed. For a variety of reasons, the papacy must be considered as one of the principal agents, if not the principal agent, of this most tragic division. The papal office, originally destined to be the source of unity among all the churches, had become a major cause of dissonance. Furthermore, in the West, the centralization of church decision making in the papal curia—which accelerated dramatically around the time of Eugene III (1145-53)—was to a great extent the result of the flood of court cases of all sorts which were dispatched to Rome for settlement. The papal curia was simply consumed with judicial business, which precipitated a marked increase of staffing in Rome, and ever expanding financial demands. To subsidize this centralization, control over the conferral of ecclesiastical benefices especially throughout the West was increasingly asserted by the popes from the second half of the twelfth century on. It was not uncommon for Roman clerical officials to hold title to several of these offices (e.g., bishoprics, parishes, canonries) in distant locations, receiving the major part of the revenues, and leaving only a fraction behind for the delegated cleric who managed the office for the absentee prelate.

Such a situation proved to be gravely damaging and disruptive to pastoral care everywhere. In this regard, things were clearly out of hand by 1300, with no relief in sight for a couple of centuries. Although some centralization was indeed beneficial because it brought about certain needed reforms and rendered a number of ecclesiastical procedures uniform throughout the West, by 1250 or so the centralizing tendency had become counterproductive. By the time of Innocent IV (1243-54), the papacy was in a state of decline. The glorious days of Innocent III (1198-1216) were over, and trouble loomed ahead.

The early years of the fourteenth century witnessed the awesome conflict between Boniface VIII (1294-1303) and Philip IV of France over the pope's claim to temporal power over kings. Innocent III and Innocent IV had made similar claims in the previous century, but the assertions of Boniface resulted in his utter humiliation at Anagni (1303). The papacy moved to France with Clement V (1305-14) and remained there for nearly seventy years, settling at Avignon in 1309. The Council of Vienne (1311-12) was orchestrated by King Philip IV and resulted in no real reforms, but only the rather shameful and unjustified extermination of the Knights Templar. John XXII (1316-34), the second Avignon pope, reserved the conferral of more and more ecclesiastical benefices worldwide to himself, and markedly increased the tax burdens throughout Christendom. Clement VI (1342-52) made the papal court the most lavish in Europe and thereby weighed down the remaining Avignon popes with an enormous burden of debt. This simply escalated the need for additional reservations and taxes on dioceses, religious houses, parishes, and clergy everywhere, precipitating additional dissent and unrest. Under Boniface VIII, the papal court consisted of some 300 clerics, and by 1350 or so, the staffs (including the cardinals' households) had exploded to almost 1,500.

It was during the reign of Innocent VI (1352-62) that Italy was pacified, thereby opening up the possibility of the pope's return to Rome. Gregory XI (1370-78) did return to Rome in 1377, but his death in 1378 occasioned the election—within a six-month period—of two concurrently reigning popes, Urban VI (Rome) and Clement VII (who returned to Avignon). This divided Europe into two allegiances. Nations, dioceses, even parishes and monasteries were divided. A good many dioceses had two bishops, one committed to Urban and the other to Clement—and each proclaiming the other a heretic. In 1409, cardinals from both allegiances, who could bear the chaos no longer, gathered in Pisa to settle the deplorable situation. They made an effort to depose the two sitting popes and elected a new pontiff, Alexander V (1409-10), who was soon succeeded by John XXIII (1410-15). The actions at Pisa were not universally accepted by the churches, and now there were three popes who claimed to be the only true pontiff. Emperor Sigismund of Germany was largely responsible for the convocation of the Council of Constance (1414-18) which finally settled the issue by deposing the Pisan and Avignonese popes, and allowing the Roman pope to resign. Martin V was elected in council in 1417, and together with Eugene IV (1431-47), his successor, managed to dampen and frustrate the moderate conciliarist movement which had provided the very rationale for Constance. The reconstituted monarchical papacy settled into one of its darkest periods during the second half of the fifteenth century, with nepotism, provincial political preoccupations, and a notoriously luxurious court reducing the image of the papacy to that of a local Renaissance potentate. The revolt of the sixteenth century was now inevitable.

The scandals and political intrigues of the Renaissance popes from Sixtus IV (1471-84) to Clement VII (1523-34) severely damaged the image and the influence of the papacy worldwide. It was Paul III—something of a Renaissance man himself—who finally convoked a reform council at Trent in 1545. The religious revolt instigated by Martin Luther in 1517 had not been taken seriously by Rome or dealt with adequately; as a result, a very large portion of northern and central Europe cut itself off from Rome, beginning in the sixteenth century. Trent (1545-63) addressed the doctrinal differences between Rome and the Reformers, and also attempted to legislate appropriate reform measures which had been urgently called for since the twelfth century (e.g., the prohibition of pluralism and absenteeism, the elimination of excessive papal taxation, the establishment of a suitable system of education for the clergy, etc.). Implementation of these sorely needed reforms came rather slowly over the next one hundred or two hundred years, but eventually the gravest abuses were remedied throughout most of the Church.

In retrospect, the Protestant Revolt was not only inevitable but indispensable for the initiation of the badly needed and long overdue reforms within the Catholic Church. As was the case regarding the division between eastern and western Christendom commencing in the eleventh century, the Roman pontiffs must accept a large amount, if not the lion's share, of the responsibility for the split between Protestants and Catholics. The Petrine office, which was designed to be the source of unity among the believers in Christ, had actually become a principal agent of division and hence a sign of contradiction. After a half century of strong, reform-minded popes following the Council of Trent, the papacy in the sixteen and seventeen hundreds became rather subservient to the kings of France, Spain, and the Hapsburg Empire. Clement XI's carelessly drafted bull, *Unigenitus* (1713), versus Quesnel, raised the issue of the value of the pope's teaching authority which did not resolve itself until Vatican I (1869-70), while the weakness of Clement XIII and Clement XIV, in the face of pressures from Portugal, Spain, and France, occasioned the unjustified suppression of the Jesuits in 1773. The deepest tragedy in the nineteenth century was the dogged effort of Gregory XVI and Pius IX to hold on, at any cost, to the temporal power over the Papal States, thus frustrating and delaying Italy's attempts to become one nation among the European family of nations. Finally, Pius IX's ominous *Syllabus of Errors* (1864) left many inside and outside the Church wondering whether the papacy would ever make peace with the modern world.

In December 1864, Pius IX announced his intention of calling an ecumenical council to confront the many errors of the age and address, once and for all, the issue of papal primacy. There were mixed reactions to the announcement, especially regarding the related issue of papal infallibility. A good many bishops from countries with Catholic and Protestant populations were of the mind that a definition of the pope's infallibility would be inopportune. Vatican I, which opened in December 1869, was from the outset controlled by the ultramontanists (i.e., those prelates who were bent on maximizing the prerogatives of the pope) who managed, with the help of Pio Nono, to address the questions of the pope's ruling and teaching power prior to a discussion of the schema on the Church. Perhaps as many as a quarter of the 700 or so delegates from all over the Catholic world were not in favor of dealing with papal prerogatives before a general consideration of the Church's constitution, especially the teaching and shepherding missions of the college of bishops. The ultramontanists, however, had their way and orchestrated a very strong definition of papal jurisdictional supremacy and papal infallibility which could have been much more acceptable to the rather sizeable minority (twenty to twenty-five percent) with some very modest qualifications in both cases. Since these adjustments were not acceptable either to the majority of delegates or to Pius IX, the Vatican I definitions left the Church with an extremely papalist tilt, in regard to both the shepherding and the teaching functions of the Church.

Pius IX's rather negative views regarding progress and nineteenth-century society were countered to a considerable extent by his successor, Leo XIII (1878-1903) who reflected, especially in his many encyclicals, a more amenable view of contemporary society. The saintly Pius X (1903-14) narrowed the vision again, especially in his bitter struggle with the modernists who, in the main,

were simply attempting to assimilate nineteenth-century historical and biblical scholarship into the Catholic understanding of the Bible and theology.
Pius XI (1922-39) was able to settle the vexing "Roman question" in the Lateran
treaty of 1929 so that the Church could put that painful issue aside once and
for all and enter the twentieth century. It was Pius XII (1939-58) who steered
the Church through the troubled waters of World War II. His was a very
gracious but extremely monarchical regime, although his encyclicals did open
the doors to a renaissance in biblical and liturgical studies, as well as new directions in ecclesiology. These developments came to term in the outstanding
event of the twentieth century, the Second Vatican Council, which was convoked and animated by the singular genius of Pope John XXIII (1958-63),
although he died after the first session. *Aggiornamento* remained the order of
the day under Pope Paul VI (1963-78) until *Humanae vitae* (1968), which
became the watershed of his pontificate. Although it was Paul who brought
the World Synod of Bishops into being, his five synods suffered frequently
from inadequate planning, a lack of focus, and a refusal on his part to allow
dialogue on some of the more crucial questions besetting the Church of his
day. In spite of his solemn pledge to conduct his pontificate dialogically (see
his inaugural encyclical, *Ecclesiam suam*, of August 1964), dialogue broke down
with *Humanae vitae* and in a good many of the sessions of the World Synod of
Bishops over which he presided. John Paul II (1978-) brought a warm and
open demeanor to the papacy, but a mind that was not particularly open to
institutional innovation. His smile is engaging indeed, but his heart is not
especially attuned to some of the new directions which have their ground in
the Vatican II documents. It is the Holy Father, the Roman curialists, the
great majority of the roughly 2,700 bishops appointed by the current pontiff—
along with the conservative bishops consecrated before 1978—who are in full
control of the Church's agenda. However, there are countless Catholics—clergy,
religious, and laity the world over—who remain committed (perhaps more
than their hierarchy) to work toward the institutional *aggiornamento* which the
recent council envisioned.

What of the future? Will those who are dedicated to institutional innovation and *aggiornamento* be overcome, as were the proponents of change after
the Council of Constance (1414-18)? Out of frustration will they become
radicalized like the conciliarists in the 1420s and the 1430s? It is rather unlikely that those opposed to more extensive institutional change will lose control in the Roman curia or in the world episcopate any time soon. Roger Aubert's
observation ten years after Vatican II that the end of Tridentinism depends to
a great extent on the radical reform of the Roman curia still pertains today.[1]
This kind of change has not occurred, nor is such a reform feasible in the
forseeable future.

It is important to keep in mind that there is in the Vatican II decrees an admixture of the new and the old. In the words of George Lindbeck, a Protestant observer at the council:

Its documents are often compromises between stale and tired ways of thinking and fresh and vital ones. Sometimes they are even deliberately ambiguous; the only way to rally a consensus from bishops of all parties was to clothe the new in old language (or the old in new language) so that what was said would at least be tolerable, if not satisfying, to both conservatives and progressives.[2]

Lindbeck then addressed the question as to which would prevail, the old or the new:

My own view . . . is that because the council is part of a dynamic, ongoing process, it is the new theological emphases which are likely to be the most significant as a basis and guide for further developments. As a matter of fact, the majority of the most active drafters and interpreters of the documents understood them as favoring the fresh approaches.[3]

So far, one would have to judge that the "new emphases" are not prevailing over the older currents of thought, at least in the areas of structural reform. Those paragraphs of the conciliar documents which look forward to a more locally and regionally governed Church—a Church where decision making would be more broadly based as it was in the early centuries—represent the hopes of those Catholics who identify themselves with what Lindbeck refers to as the "fresh approaches." So while those of the more centrist persuasion freely quote sentences and paragraphs from the enactments of Vatican II, the proponents of a wider and deeper institutional *aggiornamento* can cite other conciliar passages with equal justification.

It must be noted that as the world is moving toward more participative government and a wider sharing in the decision-making process on the part of ever greater numbers, the Catholic Church is currently, in many ways, more of an absolute monarchy—with more stringent controls maintained at the center—than ever before in its long history.

Even John Paul II in his 1995 encyclical, *Ut unum sint*, has admitted that the current structure and exercise of the papal role is an obstacle to Christian reunion, and he has acknowledged his responsibility to give the office a new shape and "a new situation."[4]

Will this happen? Will the awesome power of the pope and his curia be redistributed, allowing the principle of subsidiarity to be applied in a more meaningful way in the Church? It is not easy to be overly optimistic in this regard. There are also those who feel that the current highly monarchical exercise of the papal role is indeed an obstacle even to the growth and vitality of faith and communion within the Church. The charismatic structure of the Church would seem to provide a base for a wider distribution of decision making, especially in regard to issues like the selection of bishops and the regional organization of various apostolic endeavors. There are ample precedents for these developments in the first millennium of the Church's life.

These suggestions are put forward in response to Pope John Paul II's prayer in the presence of the Ecumenical Patriarch, Dimitrios I, on December 6, 1987, and repeated in the papal encyclical, *Ut unum sint*:

> . . . *I insistently pray the Holy Spirit to shine his light upon us, enlightening all the Pastors and theologians of our Churches, that all may seek— together, of course—the forms in which this [papal] ministry may accomplish a service of love recognized by all concerned.*[5]

Appendices

I. The Role of the Papacy in the Twenty-one Ecumenical Councils

In these brief summaries, the considerable variations in the role of the popes in the conduct of the general councils is emphasized, especially in the first eight councils compared with the last thirteen.

Nicaea I—325

Because of the unrest and confusion caused throughout the East by the teaching of the Alexandrian priest, Arius, who was claiming that the Son, the Logos, was created by the Father and did not always exist, Emperor Constantine (324-337) convoked a general council to address this and a number of other doctrinal and disciplinary issues which were then in dispute in the East. Pope Sylvester (314-35) did not attend but was represented by Bishop Ossius of Cordova and two presbyters. The council apparently opened in June of 325 and lasted some weeks. Constantine was present at the opening session, but seemingly did not direct the deliberations of the synod. It is not known who presided over the sessions, which were held in the imperial summer residence in Nicaea, but it was probably one of the eastern archbishops. No official acts of the meetings have been preserved. Nicaea I published a creed which proclaimed the Son to be of the same substance (*omoousios*) with the Father, although no attempt was made to explain this unbiblical term. It is quite possible that it was contributed by Bishop Ossius, the papal representative, although there is no evidence that Pope Sylvester provided any theological input into the deliberations. The pope did not convoke the council nor did he attend, and it is unlikely that his representative presided over the sessions.

Constantinople I—381

After Theodosius (379-95) succeeded Valens as emperor in the East, he convoked—along with Gratian, the emperor in the West—a general council to reemphasize the creed of Nicaea in the hope that this would bring all the churches together in terms of doctrine. This council, attended by about 150 eastern prelates, reaffirmed the creed of Nicaea and asserted the full divinity of the Holy Spirit which had been denied by a group called the Pneumatomachians. Although the council's doctrinal statements have been lost, the disciplinary canons have survived. The third disciplinary canon, which designated the see of Constantinople as second only to Rome in dignity and honor, was not well received in Rome, and hence the disciplinary decrees were never given formal papal approval. Aside from the fact that the acts of the local Roman synod held in 378—dealing with the equal dignity of Father, Son, and Holy Spirit—had been dispatched to the East, there does not seem to have been any participation on the part of Pope Damasus I (366-84) in Constantinople I, which was presided over by eastern bishops.

Ephesus—431

The third ecumenical council was summoned by the two emperors, Theodosius II (408-50) and Valentinian III (425-55), at the behest of Nestorius, the patriarch of Constantinople. Nestorius had been condemned for his alleged views concerning the divinity and humanity of Christ by a local Roman synod in 430, and he appealed to Theodosius for another hearing. Before the Roman delegates and a number of the eastern bishops (led by the patriarch of Antioch) had arrived at Ephesus, Cyril, the patriarch of Alexandria, opened the proceedings, summoned Nestorius (who failed to appear), and had the gathered bishops pass judgment on Nestorius' writings. Their condemnation was later ratified by the three Roman delegates once they had joined the deliberations. However, the patriarch of Antioch and the bishops accompanying him refused to join Cyril's council and set up their own. The position condemned by the council headed by Cyril declared that there are not two distinct persons in Christ, one human and one divine, but only one person, i.e., that of the Word. (Whether Nestorius did indeed hold this condemned doctrine is still debated by theologians today.) The title *Theotokos* (i.e., mother of God) applied to Mary was vigorously defended by Cyril and those with him. The decrees of the so-called Cyrilline council were subsequently approved by the newly elected Pope Sixtus III in 432. The participation of Pope Celestine I (422-32) in the council of 431 was limited to the presence of his three delegates who arrived after the condemnation of Nestorius had been decreed.

Chalcedon—451

Emperor Marcian (450-57) convoked a general council which met at Chalcedon in 451 to address the Christological debates precipitated by the teachings of the monk Eutyches of Constantinople. Pope Leo I (440-61) had recently sent a letter to Flavian, the patriarch of Constantinople (446-49), outlining his views on the question of the one personhood and the two natures in Christ, and was of the mind that the eastern bishops should sign on to his *Tome to Flavian*. The pope felt that it was a clear and satisfactory articulation of the orthodox position. Although Leo was opposed to the convocation of the council because he thought that the Christological issues had been settled, he sent five delegates, three of whom presided over the conciliar deliberations. Leo's *Tome to Flavian*—along with the writings of Cyril of Alexandria (d. 444)—did play a significant role in the formulations of the doctrinal decrees of Chalcedon which defined that there are two natures and one person in Christ. Historians consider that Leo's *Tome to Flavian* and its influence on the conciliar fathers in 451 constituted the high point of the doctrinal prestige of the papacy in the East. Leo belatedly ratified the council's doctrinal decrees in 453. However, one of the disciplinary enactments, canon 28, declared that Constantinople as the new Rome should have equal prerogatives with the old Rome and be elevated to her level in ecclesiastical affairs, taking second place after her. This canon neither Leo nor any of his successors could ratify because, in Rome's judgment, it ran counter to the venerable Council of Nicaea and the most ancient traditions. Pope Leo's victory in the doctrinal arena was frustrated by the set-back he suffered through canon 28.

Constantinople II—553

For decades Emperor Justinian (527-65) had attempted to reconcile the Monophysites with the adherents of Chalcedon. He was finally persuaded that the only solution lay in the condemnation of several works of three theologians considered by the Monophysites to be their archenemies: Theodore of Mopsuestia (d. 428) and two others. The emperor felt that this action should eliminate the Monophysites' objection to the doctrine of Chalcedon once and for all. Pope Vigilius (537-55) was hesitant about being a party to the condemnation because most of the western church opposed it. Nevertheless, he did advise the emperor to convoke a general council on the matter. Justinian summoned the council which convened in May 553. Although Vigilius was not in attendance, the overwhelming majority of the 160 bishops present were from the East and favored the condemnation. The writings of the three theologians were therefore condemned, but Vigilius—whom the emperor had meanwhile put under house arrest in Constantinople—withheld his consent for about six months before approving the acts of the council and the condemnation of Theodore and the two others. The pope was then released, and he died in Syracuse on his way back to Rome. Constantinople II is an example of Caesaropapism at its worst because Justinian simply commandeered the pope and the eastern prelates to do his bidding in order to achieve the goal of political unity. Most of the churches in the West severed relations with Rome over Vigilius' condemnation of Theodore and the others. Opposition to the papal condemnation ran high in the West for many years.

Constantinople III—680-81

The divisions resulting from the Chalcedonian definition of 451 simply would not go away. Hybrid theories like Monoenergism (one energy or principle of action in Christ) and Monotheletism (one will in Christ) became popular in the East in the seventh century. Pope Honorius I (625-38) apparently went along with the Monothelete position in a letter which he sent to the patriarch of Constantinopole, Sergius. In an effort to bring the warring sides together again, Emperor Heraclius (610-41) produced a document of union called the *Ecthesis* in which he quoted the pope as favoring Monotheletism. Pope Martin I (649-55) promptly condemned the *Ecthesis* along with Patriarch Sergius and his two Monothelete successors, but did not hurl any thunderbolts against Emperor Heraclius, his successor Constans II (641-68), or Pope Honorius. After Constans' assassination in 668, he was succeeded by his son, Constantine IV (668-85), who was interested for political reasons in making peace with the pope. Hence the young emperor called a general synod to settle the issue of Monoenergism and Monotheletism once and for all. Thus the sixth ecumenical council, Constantinople III, convened in the imperial palace in the fall of 680 under the presidency of the emperor. Attendance was quite sparse because of the fact that Egypt, Africa, Palestine, Syria, and most of Asia Minor were overrun by the Muslims. The council fathers proclaimed two wills and two natural principles of action in Christ in the presence of the papal legates. The acts of the synod were sent to Pope Leo II (682-83) who approved them and ordered them to be signed by all the bishops in the West. Constantine IV promulgated the decrees in all parts of the empire by imperial edict.

Nicaea II—787

The iconoclast struggle reached its peak during the reign of Emperor Constantine V (741-75). His successor, Emperor Leo IV (775-80), was a more moderate man who continued to enforce the prohibitions against those favoring icon veneration, but not with the rigor of his predecessor. After Leo's premature death, his ten-year-old son, Constantine VI (780-97), became co-emperor with his mother, Irene, who gradually changed the longstanding policies against icon veneration. Empress Irene arranged for the general synod (Nicaea II) which was attended by more than 250 prelates, including the legates of Pope Hadrian (772-95). The council fathers defined the desirability of venerating the icons and sacred images of Jesus, Mary, and the saints, and also enacted a number of disciplinary decrees. Pope Hadrian accepted the acts of Nicaea II although he never acknowledged his acceptance to Patriarch Tarasius who presided over the council, because Irene failed to restore a sizeable share of papal lands which had been confiscated by Emperor Leo III (717-41). Nicaea II was the last council to be recognized as ecumenical by the eastern churches.

Constantinople IV—869-70

At the outset of the pontificate of Hadrian II (867-72), the Byzantine emperor, Michael III, was deposed and murdered by a confidant, Basil the Macedonian, who proceeded to proclaim himself Basil I (867-86). The new emperor banished the reigning patriarch of Constantinople, Photius (then something of a *persona non grata* at the papal court), and reopened relations with Rome. Basil requested that the pope call a general council to settle a number of issues rising out of the removal of Photius. A council was held from October 869 to February 870 in the presence of the papal delegates who presided at the sessions. Photius was condemned because it was agreed that he had unjustly deposed his predecessor, Patriarch Ignatius, and therefore had become patriarch illegally. The validity of Constantinople IV was subsequently disputed by Pope John VIII (872-82) due to its unjust actions against Photius and also because the synod's acts had not been signed by Pope Hadrian II. Upon the death of Patriarch Ignatius in 877, Photius succeeded him as patriarch. The acts of Constantinople IV are not found in any Byzantine collections and, as a matter of fact, this council was not considered as ecumenical in the West until a couple of centuries later.

NOTE: Although we frequently see the twenty-one ecumenical councils grouped together in chronological order—stressing their similarities—those held after 1000 are very different from the general councils of the first millennium. These earlier synods were all held in Byzantine territory and, except for the papal legates, there were very few if any western representatives present. The first eight councils were invariably convoked by the Byzantine emperors, and the agendas (responding largely to eastern crises) were not really set in Rome but in the East. The sessions were usually presided over by eastern prelates and the acts were ordinarily promulgated by the emperor who dispatched them throughout the Roman world, East and West. In Rome the popes confirmed most of the conciliar enactments *post factum* and, on occasion, either ignored or objected to others. It is fair to say that the ecumenical synods of the first 1,000 years were conducted in the main by the emperors and eastern prelates, with the eastern bishops and theologians the principal contributors.

Beginning with Lateran I (1123) the situation is very different indeed. All of the general councils since 1123 (except perhaps for Constance, 1414-18) were summoned by the pope, who issued the invitations, controlled the agendas, presided over the sessions either personally or through his delegates, and assumed full responsibility for the promulgation and execution of conciliar acts and decrees. For reasons that will be reviewed in Appendix II, the papacy became more and more a western power and a major player in the politics of the West. The parameters of the Christian *oikoumene* were contracting as the Christian West lost meaningful contact with the Christian East.

Lateran I—1123

The first of the western general councils was held at the Lateran in Rome in the spring of 1123. Although there were apparently no representatives from the eastern churches, about 300 western bishops, abbots, and religious took part under the leadership of Pope Callistus II (1119-24). Disciplinary reform constituted the main agenda of the gathering. Twenty-two canons were promulgated on a whole range of subjects from prohibitions against simony and clerical concubinage to the subordination of religious to the local bishops in the pastoral care of the faithful. Norms were established for the elections of bishops, and the prohibition of marriage for priests, deacons, subdeacons, and monks was restated. A number of scholars have called into question the ecumenical character of Lateran I because it differed so much from the earlier councils and was very similar to other western synods that were held in the eleventh and twelfth centuries. Lateran I's ecumenical character was confirmed by the later tradition of the western Church.

Lateran II—1139

After the death of the antipope, Anacletus II, in 1138, Pope Innocent II (1130-43) was able to return to Rome from France, where he had been staying because Anacletus' family had held control of the Holy City. One of Innocent's priorities on his return to Rome was the calling of the Second Lateran Council which met in April 1139. Under the presidency of the pope, the thirty canons, which were enacted by the roughly 500 prelates present dealt with many of the same matters that were treated in Lateran I. Also, the practice of revenues from ecclesiastical benefices going to lay people such as kings and princes was condemned, as was the practice of usury. The same doubts have been raised about the ecumenicity of Lateran II as were raised concerning Lateran I.

Lateran III—1179

Under the inspiration and direction of the first of the great lawyer popes, Alexander III (1159-81), 300 delegates assembled at the Lateran—all Latins but one—in March 1179. The council produced twenty-seven reform canons which clearly bear the stamp of Alexander himself. The statutes deal with such matters as papal elections (which henceforth required a two-thirds vote of the cardinals), episcopal ordinations and visitations, clerical concubinage, pluralism in the holding of ecclesiastical offices, and arrangements for the education of the clergy. Canon 27 established sanctions against opposition groups on the margins of the Church, especially the Cathars in France. The Cathars, the Waldensians, and others—although in many ways distinct from one another—were all searching for a return to the simplicity of life reflected in the Gospels because they opposed the growing wealth and power of the organized Church. Compared with Lateran I and II, Lateran III was more representative of the typical council of the Middle Ages presided over by the pope.

Lateran IV—1215

Innocent III (1198-1216) let it be known that this was to be a reform council touching many aspects of the Church's life and affecting all of the faithful. Accordingly he announced it as an ecumenical council. In November 1215, 400 cardinals, archbishops, and bishops, along with hundreds of other prelates, religious superiors, and even civil authorities, came together at the Lateran. The invitees represented the widest crosscut ever to be gathered together for a general synod. However, no Greeks were present, save for the patriarch of the Maronites and a delegate of the patriarch of Alexandria. The seventy decrees of the council, which were for the most part prepared beforehand, clearly reflected the mind and the priorities of Pope Innocent. In all probability they were simply read out and adopted, not debated at the sessions. Western heretical movements were condemned and penalties were threatened. Greek Christians, especially the clergy, were ordered to conform to the dictates of their mother, the Roman Church—thus revealing the West's growing insensitivity to the eastern churches. The remaining decrees dealt with western disciplinary matters, e.g., the reform of clerical morals, episcopal elections, the administration of benefices, the elimination of pluralism among unscrupulous officeholders, the exacting of taxes, canonical trials, matrimony, tithes, simony, and the requirement of annual confession and communion for all the faithful. The legislative program of Lateran IV was extremely thorough and well structured. Had the decrees been implemented more consistently, an effective plan of reform could have been launched, and perhaps the history of the Church in the West would have taken a different turn.

Lyons I—1245

The struggle between Pope Innocent IV (1243-54) and Frederick II of Germany occasioned the pope's flight from Rome to Lyons, France, where the pontiff wasted no time in summoning a general council. About 150 bishops, other religious, and secular officials convened in Lyons in June 1245. Almost all of the participants were Italian, English, French, or Spanish, because Frederick kept most of the German prelates away. Innocent engineered the council to depose Emperor Frederick, much to the chagrin of the delegates who felt that such action was without precedent. Apart from a good number of canons regarding the conduct of ecclesiastical trials, prohibitions against usury, a condemnation of the Tartars (who were menacing eastern Europe at the time), and a plea to come to the aid of beleaguered Constantinople, there were no reform canons passed nor was there any action taken against the heretical sects then active in Europe. The reform movement which had animated the four Lateran councils seemed to have died. In sum, Pope Innocent IV can be said to have used the council to wage his war against Emperor Frederick.

Lyons II—1274

Pope Gregory X (1271-76) called a general council which was to meet at Lyons in 1274. Ecclesiastical reform, union with the Byzantines, and aid for the embattled Holy Land were set forth by the pontiff as the principal topics for discussion. There were about 300 bishops, sixty abbots, and a good many theologians in attendance, as well as representatives of the rulers of Aragon, France, Germany, England, and Sicily. Greek representatives and a delegation of the Turks were also present. Efforts made to effect a reunion with the Greeks were for the most part motivated by political considerations, because the Byzantine emperor, Michael VIII, desperately needed the pope's assistance to ward off the threats of Charles of Anjou, the king of Sicily, who had designs on the domination of the entire Mediterranean. Emperor Michael was ready to agree to almost anything, including an acknowledgment of the primacy of the pope, to secure that assistance. However, his clergy and people back home were of another mind entirely. They simply refused to go along with the concessions which the emperor had made. Without an effective union with the Greeks, the question of a crusade to assist the Holy Land receded into the background. The reform of the Church—the first item on Gregory's agenda—was the one that received the least attention. A new set of regulations governing papal elections was promulgated, and the strong prohibitions of Lateran III and IV against the holding of a plurality of offices with the care of souls attached were rendered ineffective by canon 18. Pope Gregory's dream of a genuine reform council to address the many needs of the Church was never fulfilled.

Vienne—1311-12

It is quite likely that King Philip IV of France had been urging Pope Clement V (1305-14) to call an ecumenical council from the day of his pontifical coronation in November 1305. Philip wanted to see the late Pope Boniface VIII (1294-1303) tried posthumously for his alleged "crimes," and all of Boniface's measures against France annulled. The monarch also wanted the Knights Templar to be examined because of the "scandalous character" of their lives. Philip's vendetta against the Templars was probably due to his desire to appropriate their considerable lands and wealth in France because the king was perennially in serious financial straits. Pope Clement, a timid and rather sickly man, was clearly no match for the crafty and ruthless Philip. After postponing the inevitable for several years, the pope summoned a general council to be held in Vienne in October 1311. Only 231 ecclesiastics (i.e., cardinals, bishops, abbots, and priors) were invited. As the conciliar debate on the fate of the Templars was proceeding rather slowly, King Philip lost patience and arranged for the condemnation of the order with Clement, who probably secured in return the king's consent at least to delay any action against the late Pope Boniface. Clement ordered the suppression of the Knights Templar in March 1312 with the approval of the sitting council. There was little time to address the crying needs of church reform—the excessive centralization of decision making into the papal curia, the overpowering burden of papal taxation, the scandal of pluralism, and the ever expanding papal control over the conferral of benefices (often to absentee prelates). There seemed to be time only to condemn and suppress the

Templars who, in the judgment of the majority of historians today, were largely inno-cent of the charges brought against them. Vienne stands as a tragic example of a gen-eral council which was convened, conducted, and closed under extreme political pres-sure. Although certain rather mild reform enactments were published after Clement's death (April 1314), it is difficult to determine which of these were concilar decrees and which were late pronouncements of Clement.

Constance—1414-18

In 1414 there was deep confusion in the Christian world as to who was the true pope (see Appendix III). There were three claimants: John XXIII of the Pisan line, Gregory XII of the Roman line, and Benedict XIII of the Avignonese line. The only way in which this division could be healed was through a convocation of a general council. King Sigismund of Germany took the initiative and persuaded John XXIII (who had the allegiance of most of Germany) to call a council which gathered at Constance in November 1414. During 1415 the members in attendance grew so dra-matically that Constance could justifiably be called the greatest ecclesiastical congress of the Middle Ages. The peace and reform of the Church could only be achieved through the reunion of all three allegiances under one pontiff. In spite of the fact that the Pisan line at that time represented for perhaps a great number of churches the true succes-sion, the resignation of all three claimants and the election of a new pontiff by the cardinals seemed to be the only way to bring about a definitive end to the conflict. In April 1415 the conciliar fathers issued a decree, *Haec sancta synodus*, which simply ar-ticulated what had to happen. Since it was impossible to determine who was the true pope, these three either had to resign or be deposed so that a new pontiff could be elected. The council had to assume the sovereign power over the three claimants in order to break the deadlock. In this, and presumably in any similar situation, the gen-eral council was the body that represented the universal Church which needed and demanded a solution to the impasse. The three claimants were either deposed or re-signed so that the way was cleared for the election of a new pope. Before proceeding with the election, however, an enactment of October 1417 set forth a schedule for regular convocations of general councils for the future. The plan was to settle eventually on the calling of a synod every ten years for the purpose of "rooting out evils and culti-vating the Lord's patrimony." In November 1417, Martin V (1417-31) was elected pope by the fifty-three cardinals present at the council. Seven reform decrees were promulgated in the name of the new pontiff in March 1418. It must be added that these dealt with only a fraction of the issues pinpointed by the conciliar fathers for immediate attention just prior to the election of Pope Martin. The council adjourned in April 1418. The constitutional issues raised at Constance for the ongoing life of the Church have not as yet been fully explored. Mainly because of the two decrees on the relationship between the pope and the general council (*Haec sancta synodus* and *Frequens*), Constance was not widely accepted for a considerable period as an ecumenical council.

Basel, Ferrara, Florence—1431-45

According to the decree, *Frequens*, enacted at Constance in 1417, the next general council was to be held at Pavia in northern Italy in 1423. Even the change of location to

Siena for reasons of security failed to arouse sufficient interest among the bishops and delegates, and therefore Pope Martin V canceled the sessions with the promise that the next synod would be held seven years hence according to *Frequens*. Before his death in February 1431, Martin reluctantly summoned the Council of Basel. Eugene IV (1431-47), his successor, who was even more leery of conciliar activity than Pope Martin, attempted to dissolve the synod at Basel before it got under way. However, in 1433 he did eventually reconcile himself with the synodal proceedings. Undoubtedly the uncooperative attitude and the manifest reluctance of Martin V and Eugene IV had done much since 1418 to sour and embitter the conciliarists. In any event, the moderate conciliar position which prevailed at Constance almost immediately gave way at Basel to the more radical variety which identified the sitting council almost from the beginning as the normal, regular, juridical sovereign power in the Church. As the months progressed, participation at the council shifted from the higher to the lower clergy, so that by 1438, university and junior clergy comprised more than fifty percent of the delegates. Because the power to vote at Basel was never limited to bishops and major religious superiors, as time went on the synodal decisions were made principally by the lower clergy. After several years of discussions the council reached an agreement with the Hussites from Bohemia over their grievances which had not been addressed at Constance. The delegates also legislated against clerical concubinage, excessive papal taxation, and attempted to abolish a goodly number of papal reservations of benefices. After 1437 the council became more and more radical and thus lost even more of its support from bishops and princes throughout Europe. In January 1438, Eugene IV transferred the council to Ferrara, and then to Florence in January 1439. Papal control of the deliberations was thus asserted in order that a reunion with the Greek churches might be more effectively pursued. At this time the Byzantines were again in dire need of military assistance from the West because the Ottoman Turks were threatening to take over what was left of Byzantium. The emperor, John VIII, was willing to discuss dogmatic concessions if they would open the way to western military assistance against the Turks. Through the efforts of Pope Eugene, the emperor, and the patriarch of Constantinople, rather sweeping dogmatic agreements were reached, even concerning the primacy of the pope. The decree of union with the Greeks (1439) did not prove to be acceptable to the Byzantine people or to the majority of their clergy. Agreements with the Armenians, the Copts, and several eastern churches apparently concluded the work of the council. It must be said that in the estimate of most historians of the eastern churches, these decrees of union did not have much tangible effect.

Lateran V—1512-17

Even after 1450 the desire to hold an ecumenical council ran high in Europe. The cardinals, who had much to lose from a reform synod, expressed the wish for one every time they entered a conclave to elect a new pope during the second half of the sixteenth century. At the heart of this movement lay the almost universal conviction that the renewal of the Church could not happen except through an ecumenical council. Most theologians and canonists of the period saw general councils as a necessary, indispensable counterpoint to papal sovereignty. The Roman pontiffs after 1450, however, rather consistently opposed the idea of a council because they feared a curtailment of their authority and a diminution of their prerogatives. Pope Julius II (1503-13) finally called a council at the Lateran in 1512, which was concluded by his successor, Leo X (1513-21), in 1517. Lateran V was never well attended by bishops and prelates outside of Italy, which has raised doubts as to whether the sessions were indeed ecumenical. After issuing a dogmatic declaration on the immortality of the human soul, such matters as the reform of the Roman curia and the curtailment of the practice of nepotism in the conferral of ecclesiastical offices were addressed, but there was no will to confront these challenges effectively. The decrees were characterized by timidity, and hence nothing really came of them. Lateran V did not honestly and courageously confront the needs of the Church for thoroughgoing reform in head and members.

Trent—1545-63

It took Paul III (1534-49) more than eight years to convene the reform council for which the entire Catholic world was waiting. The first period of Trent (December 13, 1545 to June 2, 1547) issued its initial declaration on the nature of divine revelation in April 1546, and then concentrated for some months on the questions of original sin and justification to differentiate Catholic teaching on the subjects from the positions of Luther and the Reformers. On March 3, 1547, the delegates published their treatment of the sacraments in general and the sacraments of baptism and confirmation, declaring that all seven of the sacraments were directly instituted by Christ. Along with the dogmatic pronouncements, the council fathers produced a number of disciplinary norms such as those governing the Church's preaching and teaching functions and the obligation of residence for bishops and pastoral clergy. The longstanding abuse of pluralism was confronted more forcefully than ever before, and the obligation of bishops to engage in regular parish visitations was strongly emphasized. Due to the alleged threat of typhus at Trent, the council was transferred to Bologna on March 11, 1547, but the number of delegates who reassembled at Bologna was so small that continued discussion and deliberation proved to be impractical by June of that year. Hence, Paul III formally suspended synodal activity in February 1548.

Paul's successor, Julius III (1550-55), was anxious to reassemble the Council of Trent and he did so in the fall of 1551. The Eucharist, penance, and extreme unction were explained to correct the Reformers, especially Luther, who held that there were strictly speaking only two sacraments, baptism and the Lord's Supper. The disciplinary enactments expanded the authority of the local bishops over their clergy, including the religious clergy. In April 1552 the council was suspended again due to the hostilities between Maurice of Saxony, who was aided by the French, and Charles V of the German Empire. The intermission this time was to last almost ten years.

The third and final period of Trent was initiated by Pope Pius IV (1559-65) in January 1562 with 109 voting delegates in attendance—a much more auspicious beginning than the inaugural gathering in December 1545. The question of episcopal residence was raised again because the absenteeism of bishops for long periods had done untold damage to the pastoral life of many dioceses. How much control did the pope have over the question? Was episcopal residence a matter of divine law (from which the pope could not dispense) or of human law? The issue was remanded to the pope who never resolved the question. The reform decree of July 1562 increased the power of local bishops over the opening and closing of parishes, and reaffirmed that no one was to be ordained without a benefice (i.e., a stable source of support). In September 1562, the Sacrifice of the Mass was taken up for definition, at which time it was asserted that it was not advantageous to celebrate Mass everywhere in the vernacular. (Liturgies in Latin were viewed as abuses by the Reformers.) A lengthy set of reform decrees was drafted in July 1563, outlining in considerable detail the discipline of the clergy. There were regulations regarding ordinations, the duty of residence, and expanded directives for the establishment of seminaries for the education of the clergy. At the same time, the council's doctrine on the ministerial priesthood was defined. The second last session of Trent (November 11, 1563) witnessed the declaration of the sacramental nature of marriage and its indissolubility, while the final gathering on December 3 and 4, 1563, issued brief dogmatic statements on the existence of purgatory and on the merits of appealing to the intercession of the saints. On June 30, 1564, Pope Pius IV formally promulgated the acts of Trent and the long awaited reform council was history. Much of the synod's unfinished business was left in the hands of the Roman pontiff. In retrospect it can be affirmed that the monarchical dimension of the papal role was unambiguously reasserted during the eighteen years of the conciliar period so that, in a sense, the modern papacy could be said to have taken shape out of the Council of Trent.

Vatican I—1869-70

Pius IX (1846-78) announced to the Roman cardinals in December 1864 his intention of calling an ecumenical council to remedy the many ills besetting the nineteenth-century Church. After months of preparation, Vatican II opened on December 8, 1869 with over 700 delegates in attendance, along with the pope. Although the question of discussing papal infallibility was not initially on the agenda, it was on the minds of most of the delegates from the opening day. A small but well-organized group of bishops (referred to as infallibilists), led by Cardinal Manning of England, urged the pope to have the infallibility question placed on the agenda because a majority of the fathers was in favor of a discussion of the subject. The first document or schema considered by the council was the *Constitution on the Catholic Faith* dealing with creation, revelation, and the relationship between faith and reason. After more than a month of discussion, this schema was approved by the delegates and the pope on April 24, 1870. The next topic to be discussed was the schema on the Church. It seemed clear to most observers that if the tract on the Church with its fifteen chapters (plus the addition of a chapter on papal infallibility) were debated one chapter after another, the discussion of the papal prerogatives would not take place until at least the spring of 1871. This was unacceptable to the infallibilist fathers and to Pius IX. Accordingly, a new schema was quickly prepared on the question of the Roman pontiff, his primacy of jurisdiction, and his infallibility, which was introduced for debate on May 13. The delegates were divided on the opportuneness of defining papal primacy and especially papal infallibility at that time, particularly before the theology of the Church had been fully deliberated by the council. On June 6 debate began on the chapter on papal primacy, and on June 14, the discussion was brought to a peremptory close. During the nine days of debate, thirty-five delegates spoke in favor of the definition and twenty-two expressed reservations against it. On June 15 the issue was joined on papal infallibility and this debate was terminated on July 4. On July 11, the definitive rendering of the schema on the papal prerogatives was placed before the council, and on July 13, a trial vote was held in which 451 delegates voted for the schema without any qualification, while 88 voted against it and 62 gave only qualified approval. This meant that twenty-five percent of the voting fathers wanted changes in the document. Since Pius IX was unable to take a stand against the majority, the definitive text was not amended to satisfy the minority. The final balloting took place on July 18, with 533 voting in favor and only two voting against the constitution, *Pastor aeternus*. The failure of Vatican I to respond to the pleas of the minority—who represented twenty to twenty-five percent of the council—to include somehow a reference to the dependence on the witness of the Church as part of the formula in the definition of papal infallibility was, in the judgment of many, a crucial omission. Although most of the delegates left Rome after the solemn session of July 18, Pius XI did not suspend the council until October 1870—after Italian troops invaded the area around the Holy City.

Vatican II—1962-65

Pope John XXIII (1958-63) surprised the world on January 25, 1959, by announcing his intention to summon an ecumenical council. There were quite a few university theologians in Rome at the time who felt that the age of ecumenical councils was over, inasmuch as the definition of the papal prerogatives at Vatican I had rendered them superfluous. Although there had been some secret preparations for a council in 1948 under Pius XII (1939-58), the project never materialized. After two years of work (1960-62) the preparatory commissions put together sixty-nine schemata which reflected the thinking of the curia and the Roman universities. On October 11, 1962, Vatican II opened with over 2,500 delegates present. Pope John's desire was to have the deliberations bring the message of the Gospel "up to date" so that it would resonate more convincingly in the minds of the faithful. In contrast to the rather regressive schemata prepared by the curial people, the pastoral and forward-looking direction of the discussions set the tone in the first session during the fall of 1962, although no documents were approved by the body at that time. Pope Paul VI (1963-78), who succeeded John XXIII, opened the second session in September 1963. Deliberations in the fall of 1963 centered principally on the nature of the Church and its structure, the role of the bishops, and the relations that should prevail between the Catholic Church and the other religious bodies in the world. On December 4, the *Constitution on the Liturgy*—which advocated full, conscious, and active participation on the part of all and encouraged the use of the vernacular languages in liturgical actions—won formal approval. It was the *Constitution on the Church* that became the centerpiece of the third session which met in the fall of 1964. In the document on the Church the delegates made a concerted effort to contextualize the papal prerogatives, that had been so starkly articulated at Vatican I, within the college of bishops. Although the 1870 pronouncement of papal infallibility is repeated, the prerogative is related to the inerrancy of the Church. The refreshing tone of the presentation of episcopal collegiality in paragraphs 21 to 27 is muted to a significant degree by the *Prefatory Note* attached to the document by the theological commission at the direction of Pope Paul. At the end of the third session, the fathers promulgated the *Decree on Ecumenism* which reveals a dramatically new approach to the ecclesial reality of the other Christian churches.

The fourth and final session of Vatican II began on September 14, 1965. Paul VI opened the proceedings by announcing that he was establishing a Synod of Bishops which was to be a central ecclesiastical institution representing the whole Catholic episcopate as an expression of the collegiality of the body of bishops in union with the pope. No fewer than twelve decrees were published in the final session which completed the task of redefining the role of the bishops, priests, religious, and the laity for the Church of the future. New institutions came into being to enhance dialogue at every level, such as episcopal conferences, priests' councils, and pastoral councils, in the belief that by working together, discussing together, sharing the gifts of the Spirit with each other, the Church might become more vibrant and outgoing, and thus be rendered more effective in its mission to contribute to the transformation of the world into the Kingdom of God. Vatican II, which closed on December 8, 1965, stands as the preeminent ecclesial event of the twentieth century, and calls us now to open our eyes, ears, and hearts to heed its message.

II. The Stages in the Separation
of the Eastern Churches from Rome

Although the Roman Empire reached from Britain to the Tigris and Euphrates in the fourth century, there were vast differences in terms of cultural development and affluence between the East and the West. When Constantine transferred the seat of imperial government to Constantinople (324-30), the political balance in terms of influence and prestige had clearly shifted to the East. In spite of the fact that Rome did what it could to claim its previous status as capital of the world, by the second half of the fourth century it had been surpassed by Constantinople. The third disciplinary canon enacted at Constantinople I (381) which designated Constantinople as second only to Rome in dignity and honor was never accepted by Rome because, among other things, it disregarded the ancient ecclesiastical traditions of Jerusalem, Antioch, and Alexandria. The Council of Chalcedon (451) declared in its canon 28 that Constantinople as the new Rome should have equal prerogatives with the old Rome and be elevated to her level in ecclesiastical affairs, taking second place to her, but this was absolutely unacceptable to Pope Leo I (440-61) and his successors.

It is during the pontificate of Gregory I (590-604) that we can catch an exceptionally clear glimpse of the way in which the pope could exercise his influence throughout the Christian world. His many letters reflect the varied approaches that he employed in dealing with the churches in the West (e.g., Africa, Gaul, Italy) as compared with those in the East. Although there were variations in the exercise of his jurisdiction relating to the western bishops, his many letters to the patriarchs of Constantinople, Antioch, Alexandria, and Jerusalem disclose a rather different tone. It seems that he saw the five patriarchs, including himself, as the regional heads of the Church, with no one of the patriarchs exercising an overriding jurisdiction over the others. With just a couple of exceptions, Gregory never addressed any of the patriarchs in any other than a fraternal manner. He was not exercising jurisdiction, but rather solicitude toward the eastern leaders. His dealings with the East were successful in that through his constant communication, Gregory kept the *communio* alive and active throughout the Christian world. He was in a true sense the leader of the *communio* and that is the way in which he envisioned and exercised his role as patriarch of Rome.

This gift of Gregory's was not shared by many of his successors in the seventh and eighth centuries for one reason or another. The doctrinal fights between East and West over Monotheletism, and later over the cult of icons—along with the military crises in Byzantium caused by the Muslims—widened the gulf between Rome and Constantinople. When Popes Gregory II (715-31) and Gregory III (731-41) were having serious trouble with the hostile Lombards in Italy, the Byzantine emperor was either unable or unwilling to help, and that was when Rome turned to Gaul for assistance. It was these two Gregorys who were largely responsible for easing the papal domain out of the Byzantine Empire. Within a little more than 100 years—by the time of Popes Nicholas I (858-67), Hadrian II (867-72), and John VIII (872-82)—Rome had lost its capacity to deal creatively and effectively with Constantinople and with the East generally. These pontiffs were now asserting supreme jurisdiction over the entire Christian world, and this was a claim that neither the emperor, the patriarch of Constantinople, nor the eastern Christians could accept. Granted that it would be almost 200 years before the final split between the East and West, it was obvious that after Popes Nicholas I, Hadrian II, and John VIII, neither Rome nor Constantinople was any longer capable of comprehending the other.

Although the relations between Rome and Constantinople had been worsening since the ninth century, the tragic separation took place on the occasion of the fateful encounter between the papal envoy, Cardinal Humbert, and Michael Cerularius, the patriarch of Constantinople, in the summer of 1054. For a number of years, Greek Christians in southern Italy had been forced to follow the Latin rite. Patriarch Cerularius responded by requiring that Latin churches in Constantinople adhere to Greek practices, and when they refused, he forced them in 1052 to close their doors. Cerularius wrote to Pope Leo IX (1049-54), requesting that an attempt be made to settle the dispute. Leo dispatched Cardinal Humbert and other delegates to Constantinople to open negotiations. After Humbert learned that the emperor was not especially inclined to support his patriarch in this matter, the cardinal laid down a bull of excommunication against Cerularius and his supporters on the high altar of the Hagia Sophia in July 1054. Cerularius, of course, responded in kind by excommunicating the papal legates. These actions were not seen as events culminating in the final and complete separation between Rome and the East until some years later. Since 1054, however, the western and the eastern churches have gone their separate ways.

In spite of the efforts made at the Council of Lyons II (1274) and at Basel, Ferrara, Florence (1431-41) to bring the East and West together again, these negotiations failed for several reasons. Rome had lost something of its ability to dialogue and compromise with the East, while the Byzantine delegates were moved to reconcile for largely political rather than theological motives. The result was that the Greek faithful and clergy at home repudiated the accords.

Over the centuries a number of oriental churches or segments thereof have made their way back to communion with Rome. These bodies have been called Uniate or eastern Catholic churches, whereas the communities that have not returned to communion with Rome are termed Orthodox churches. Although total membership of the Uniate bodies has traditionally amounted to no more than ten to fifteen percent of the estimated enrollment of the Orthodox churches, the manner in which Rome has treated the Uniates has been watched very closely by the Orthodox, century after century. For example, when Pius IX (1846-78) sent letters of invitation to the bishops of the eastern Orthodox churches to attend the deliberations of Vatican I, they refused to be present. That was not surprising given the pope's previous history with the Orthodox, and especially his Latinizing efforts with regard to the Uniates, which the Orthodox have always deeply resented. Pope Leo XIII (1878-1903) opened some doors to the East with his 1894 encyclical, *Orientalium dignitas*, which was to serve as a foundation for the renewal of relations between Rome and the East. In spite of the efforts of Pope Pius XI (1922-39) to advance relations with the Orthodox churches by emphasizing the need to study oriental affairs, especially in major seminaries, his many Latinizing overtures against the Uniates continued to alienate Orthodox Christians. It was not until the publication of the *Decree on the Oriental Churches* (1964) by Vatican II that some of the critical misunderstandings regarding the Orthodox were addressed. Such issues as the importance of preserving the venerable traditions of each oriental rite and the restoration of the prestige and privileges of the patriarchs according to "the ancient traditions of each church and the decrees of the ecumenical councils," were asserted in unambiguous terms. However, the essential element of the division between East and West remains. That is, because the Orthodox do not believe that in the first ten centuries of the Church the pope possessed direct and immediate powers of jurisdiction over the Christian East, they find it impossible to grant such authority to the Roman pontiff today.

III. A Clarification of the Two (and Eventually Three) Papal Lines Leading up to the Council of Constance: 1414-18

Pope Gregory XI (1370-78) returned to Rome on January 17, 1377, bringing to a close the papal sojourn at Avignon which had lasted some sixty-eight years. Although he was only fifty years old, his delicate health succumbed to the Roman climate and he died in March 1378. Since the consistory following Gregory's death was unable to decide on one of the current cardinals, it eventually settled on the archbishop of Bari, who became Urban VI (1378-89). In spite of the fact that the election seems to have been initially accepted as valid by the cardinals, within a matter of months Urban's erratic, insulting, and high-handed behavior led the cardinals (eventually all of them) to leave Rome and reside at Anagni, southeast of Rome. (We will take up their story below.) Urban VI died in Rome and was succeeded by Boniface IX (1389-1404), who was one of the cardinals appointed by Urban after all those who had elected him had abandoned his court. In October 1404, Boniface died in Rome, and the cardinals in the Holy City chose Innocent VII to succeed him. Within two years, Innocent died and was replaced by a Venetian cardinal, who identified himself as Gregory XII (1406-15). These four prelates from 1378 to the Council of Constance (1414-18) constituted *the Roman line*:
- Urban VI—1378-89
- Boniface IX—1389-1404
- Innocent VII—1404-06
- Gregory XII—1406-15

Returning to the summer of 1378, the cardinals who parted company with Urban VI proceeded to elect Robert of Geneva as their pontiff in September 1378 after they had declared that the election of Urban was null and void. Robert, who took the name Clement VII (1378-94), left Anagni for Avignon in May 1381 because he was unable to take possession of Rome. In September 1394, Clement died and was succeeded by Benedict XIII (1394-1423), who lived for almost thirty years convinced that he was the true pope. *The Avignonese line* of papal claimants was as follows:
- Clement VII—1378-94
- Benedict XIII—1394-1417

In 1409, Gregory in Rome and Benedict in Avignon were the protagonists—each insisting that he was the true pope. Italy, England, most of the German Empire, Hungary, and the Nordic countries were at that time pledged to Gregory, while France, Savoy, Scotland, Aragon, and Castile were allied with Benedict. Religious orders and many dioceses were split down the middle, with some houses and parishes adhering to Gregory and others to Benedict. With tensions mounting for a decade or more to bring to a conclusion this tragic impasse, twenty-four cardinals and several hundred major prelates met in council at Pisa in March 1409. After more than two months of hearings and discussions, the council declared that both popes were notorious schismatics and obdurate heretics. Obedience was therefore withdrawn from both claimants, and the Roman see was declared vacant. The cardinals of both allegiances proceeded to elect a new pope, the archbishop of Milan, who became Alexander V (1409-10). When Alexander died in May 1410, he was followed by John XXIII (1410-15). Although most church historians today hold that Pisa was not a true ecumenical council and hence the depositions and the new papal election were meaningless, this position was not apparently shared by a considerable number of ecclesiastics at that time. *The Pisan line* of prelates from 1409 until Constance was as follows:

- Alexander V—1409-10
- John XXIII—1410-15

In 1414, just prior to the convocation of the Council of Constance, John XXIII (Pisa) seems to have had the largest allegiance because France, England, and several Italian and German states were behind him. Apparently, Gregory XII (Rome) was in a considerably weaker position after the Council of Pisa, but Benedict XIII (Avignon) with his followers on the Iberian peninsula and in southern France was still a force to be reckoned with. It was King Sigismund of Germany who took the initiative and persuaded John XXIII to summon the Council of Constance which opened on November 5, 1414. In spite of the fact that the Council of Pisa was widely acknowledged at that time as valid and that the Pisan line of popes represented for perhaps a large number of Christians the true succession, the resignation of all three popes and the election of a new pontiff by the cardinals of all three allegiances seemed to be the only way to bring about a definitive end to the conflict. (For a summary of the events of the Council of Constance, see Appendix I.)

IV. The Papacy and the Protestant Revolt

There has been long-standing debate among a number of Catholic scholars as to whether the Protestant Reformation was inevitable, or if it could have been avoided from within. In the following paragraphs the points made by those who hold the "inevitability position" will be summarized briefly, allowing readers to render their own judgment on the matter. The facts of the case are aligned under four headings.

Papal Claims

Although the assertions concerning the extent of papal prerogatives began to mount from the ninth century on, these did not of themselves generate widespread alienation and unrest within the Church. Rather, it was what the popes did on the basis of these claims in later years that generated the growing frustration among bishops, clergy, religious, and faithful throughout the Christian world. It was Nicholas I (858-67), Hadrian II (867-72), and John VIII (872-82) whose claims served as a foundation in the West for the expansion of papal authority. Although these three pontiffs brought the ideology into focus, they could not execute their aspirations because the ninth-century popes were simply not in a position to do that, given their political situation. They did what they could, however, to weaken notably the traditional power and authority of the metropolitan bishops in the West. Two centuries later, Pope Gregory VII (1073-85) in his *Dictatus Papae* of 1075 left an outline of an expanded view of papal authority which he was not able to act on fully due to the tenor of the times. But a little more than 100 years later, Pope Innocent III (1198-1216) was indeed able to assert a good many of these sweeping prerogatives because in his day the papacy was truly the focal point of Europe. Although the prestige of the popes had declined by the time of Boniface VIII (1294-1303), the claims asserted since the 1150s had generated precedents which remained in force.

Papal Centralization

The factors contributing to the centralization of ecclesiastical decision making within the papal curia were largely twofold: the ongoing expansion of the activity of the papal courts and offices, and the reservation of the conferral of more and more benefices and endowments to the Roman pontiff. The judicial business, which was decried by St. Bernard already in 1150 or thereabouts as a tragic distraction deflecting the pope from his primary spiritual responsibilities, continued to grow over the next 200 years or more into a dizzying maze of courts and dicasteries, officers and clerks. The pontifical court at Avignon (1309-77) had become a lawyer's paradise, teeming with job hunters of all sorts who were seeking to better themselves with whatever benefices and endowments they might acquire.

The evolution of papal reservations of offices and benefices of every variety seems to have started with Pope Innocent II (1130-43). The first general reservations (i.e., over certain classes of benefices and endowments) began with Clement IV (1265-68). Boniface VIII (1294-1303) and Clement V (1305-14) added further categories of reserved benefices to the papal list, and John XXII (1316-34) codified the previous enactments. It was Blessed Urban V (1362-70) and Gregory XI (1370-78) who extended papal reservations to include every major benefice and a considerable number of minor benefices of note in western Christendom. The elective process, respected and cherished by the early Church, was simply disappearing. The rights and responsibilities of the bishops and the local church communities to select their own ecclesiastical officials were ebbing away. Whole layers of ecclesial government—sacred from subapostolic times—had been for all practical purposes emasculated.

The other side of this tragedy was that a great many of these papal provisions were granted so that prelates in the pontifical curia, as well as other clerics who were papal favorites for one reason or another, could acquire more substantial revenues thereby. The papal officials or other favored clergymen would take a major share of the revenue accruing to their benefices and leave the remainder for clerical substitutes who would bear the responsibility of fulfilling the obligations of the offices which often had pastoral duties attached. This damaging situation affecting all of western Christendom was prohibited by Lateran Council III (1179) and many subsequent canons until Trent, but the problem continued to grow and fester until it was finally resolved by the gradual and painful implementation of the decrees of the Council of Trent (1545-63). There is no doubt that some centralization of dispensations, privileges, and judicial decision making was advantageous for the maintenance of Church unity and uniformity of discipline, but it has to be said that the popes simply did not know when to stop.

Papal Taxation

All of this unceasingly expanding activity was expensive and the popes—especially during their Avignon sojourn (1309-77)—were not able to draw from the Papal States nearly the same levels of revenue available to them at previous times. Hence the need for increasing the other sources of revenue. The logical first targets were the benefices and endowments conferred by the Holy See. The fees which were to be paid on the occasion of the nomination, confirmation, or translation of bishops or abbots were originally voluntary, but with Boniface VIII they became actual assessments. These fees could amount to a sizeable fraction of the appraised value of the benefice or endowment conferred. In addition, there were substantial tariffs for any services rendered by the papal curia as well as those to be paid at the time of a prelate's regular *ad limina* visits. Then there were papal taxes exacted in the beneficiary's own country. Furthermore, the annates were revenues demanded from the new beneficiaries appointed by the pope out of the first year's income. By Gregory XI's time (1370-78), almost all bishops and abbots had to pay the annates which then amounted to a notable share of the first year's revenue. And finally, since the time of Innocent III there were tithes or taxes imposed for the support of the Crusades or other extraordinary expenses, and these usually amounted to ten percent of the estimated value of the beneficiary's property.

Perhaps the grizzliest aspect of the papal financial system was the collection process. There were thirty-one collectories in Christendom, fifteen of them in France. Each financial district had a certain number of treasury agents whose task it was to collect the revenues due and to dispatch the funds to Avignon. The chief collectors had to return to Avignon to make a detailed account of their activities every two years. These principal collectors had awesome authority, including the power to excommunicate delinquents for nonpayment. It is not particularly difficult to imagine how these heavy tax burdens and the odious collection procedures caused a mountain of aggravation and resentment everywhere.

Papal Life Style

Around 1200, roughly twenty percent of the land in western Europe was owned by ecclesiastical institutions. All of these income-producing assets were subject to tithes which were levied on occasion by the popes to cover extraordinary costs, such as the Crusades. The Cathars, the Waldensians, and others were active in southern France, northern Italy, Germany, and Spain in the thirteenth century, protesting vigorously against the growing wealth of the Church. As a matter of fact, after 1250 or thereabouts, resentment against all forms of taxation by the popes was running high everywhere in western Europe. Prior to Pope Boniface VIII (1294-1303), the pontifical curia employed about 200 officials, and by 1340 the number had swelled to more than 500. These officials, especially the major prelates, hired servants and often supported relatives and family so that the numbers to be sustained out of the central ecclesiastical coffers were increasing almost geometrically. The widespread practice of nepotism on the part of the popes and cardinals caused a further drain on resources and created an ever greater demand for more and more revenue. The papal court at Avignon (1309-77) devoured huge sums of money. New palaces, offices, and other residences were built in a town with a population of 5,000-6,000 in 1300 which grew close to 30,000 by 1370. It is said that the court of Clement VI (1342-52) was the most lavish in all of Europe, supporting in addition to all the clerics and their retinue, flocks of painters, sculptors, poets, and such like. Clement was quoted as saying that his predecessors really did not know how to live as popes. After his reign, the last three Avignonese pontiffs were simply buried under Clement VI's debts.

After Avignon came the Great Western Schism when two and eventually three papal claimants were vying with one another for respect and support throughout Christendom. (See Appendix III.) It is hardly possible to overstate the damage wrought in the western Church throughout that forty-year period. The Council of Constance brought about the restoration of the monarchical papacy under Martin V (1417-31) and Eugene IV (1431-47), who were succeeded by the so-called Renaissance popes. Sixtus IV (1471-84), a Renaissance man par excellence, was an avid nepotist who presided over an expensive court populated with artists and humanists of every sort. To support all of these ventures, including the masterful job he did in the reconstruction of large sections of Rome, new curial posts had to be invented and sold to the highest bidders. At this time the granting of indulgences became more widespread, and this brought additional monies into the papal treasury. The elections of Innocent VIII (1484-92) and Alexander VI (1492-1503) were undoubtedly tainted with bribery and simony, and both of them were notorious nepotists. It is difficult from our vantage point to comprehend how Alexander VI could have been elected to the supreme pontificate, given the fact that he had sired no fewer than six illegitimate offspring prior to 1492. The saga of this Borgia pope and his family is the stuff out of which romance novels are written. Alexander's successor, Julius II (1503-13), was truly more a field general than a pope, and Clement VII (1523-34) throughout his papacy feared to convoke a reform council largely because he was an illegitimate son of one of the Medicis. It was Paul III (1534-49), something of a Renaissance man himself, who finally turned the tide and called together the reform Council of Trent in 1545.

Given these events and conditions, the readers can decide for themselves whether the Church in the sixteenth century could have reformed itself, or required a massive impulse, i.e., the Protestant Revolution, from the outside in order to ignite the fires of restoration.

Glossary of Terms

ad limina visits. Regular visits that local ordinaries are required to make to the Holy See and to the pope to report on the conditions of their dioceses. Gregory VII (1073-85) established the practice which became a general obligation under Gregory IX (1227-41).

Americanism. A late nineteenth-century development in the United States influenced by Father Hecker (1819-88), the founder of the Paulist Fathers. The movement, which pointed to the American relationship between Church and state as something of an ideal, was censured by Rome in 1899.

annates. Revenues collected by the pope from the holders of new papally appointed offices out of the first year's income of the benefices.

antipope. A person invalidly elected to the papal office because the office is already occupied by one who was duly elected.

Arianism. A heresy fostered by Arius (ca. 250-ca. 336), a priest from Alexandria. His teaching, which was condemned at Nicaea I in 325, maintained that the Son of God did not exist from eternity and hence was not divine but only the first among creatures.

Avignon papacy. From 1309 to 1377 the popes resided at Avignon in southern France because of the hostile conditions which prevailed at that time in central Italy. The majority of these seven pontiffs became famous (or infamous) because of their excessive taxing and centralizing policies and their elaborate court.

benefice, ecclesiastical. A church office which carries certain responsibilities and the right to a regular income. The Vatican II *Decree on the Ministry and Life of Priests* advocated the reform of the benefice system. According to the provisions of canon 281 of the 1983 *Code of Canon Law*, the remuneration of office holders is now to be arranged in a different manner.

bishop, suffragan. A bishop who is in some respects responsible to the ordinary of a larger see.

Byzantine Christianity. The mode of Christian discipline and worship which originated in and around Constantinople and expanded its influence after 400 into many of the eastern churches.

Caesaropapism. The excessive interference in ecclesiastical matters on the part of the Roman emperors and, later, on the part of a number of European monarchs.

canon law. The legislation of the Catholic Church which dates back to the earliest councils and papal decrees. This legislation was organized notably by Gratian in ca. 1140, although there had been a number of previous, less influential compilations. The **Code of Canon Law** was promulgated in 1917 and went into effect in 1918. This was the first codification of the whole Western church legislation. The 1917 *Code* was revised in 1983. The word **canon** is the term which has been used from

321

antiquity to refer to each individual ecclesiastical statute.

cathedral chapter. A body of clerics usually appointed by the local bishops. The task of the chapter is to recite the divine office in common regularly in the cathedral church and, on occasion, to advise the bishop regarding certain matters of diocesan policy. The individual members of the chapter are called **canons.**

causae majores. Cases which are to be submitted to Rome for settlement. It was Innocent I (401-17) who ordered that all significant disputes, such as conflicts between metropolitans, be dispatched to Rome for adjudication.

College of Cardinals. A select group of prelates who serve as a consultative body for the popes, and who, since the time of Nicholas II (1058-61), have been the electors of the popes. From earliest times there were three levels: the cardinal bishops, the cardinal priests, and the cardinal deacons. The responsibilities of the cardinals changed rather dramatically after the reorganization of the curia under Sixtus V (1585-90).

collegiality. The thesis that maintains that the bishops in communion with the pope and with one another share the responsibility for the governance and the teaching role of the entire Church. The concept was revived and clarified at Vatican II in *Lumen gentium*, paragraphs 22 and 23.

conciliarism. A theological position popularized in the fourteenth and fifteenth centuries, which maintained that the authority of an ecumenical council (including the pope) was superior to the pope alone in matters of faith and in questions impacting the well-being of the whole Church (**moderate conciliarism**). The **radical conciliarists,** who controlled a good share of the Council of Basel-Ferrara-Florence (1431-45), actually attempted to set up a central ecclesiastical government apart from the pope.

conclave. The gathering of cardinals to elect a new pope after the death of the previous Roman pontiff.

concordat. A formal legal agreement between the Holy See and a sovereign state, which makes arrangements for dealing with issues of common concern to both entities. Concordats became popular after the Council of Constance (1414-18) and continue to be used to this day.

consistory. An official meeting between the cardinals and the pope to settle important church matters. This venerable institution, dating back to the early centuries, has been used less and less since the establishment of the Roman congregations after the Council of Trent (1545-63).

Crusades. A series of wars waged by the Christian West to recover possession of the Holy Land which had been occupied by the Muslims. The five Crusades extended over the period from 1095-1270.

Decree of Gratian. A general compilation of ecclesiastical legislation which had accumulated up to 1140. Gratian, a Camaldolese monk from Bologna, put together this massive unofficial collection of papal and conciliar decrees and canons which served as the base for subsequent development of canon law. The **decretists** were the commentators on Gratian's *Decree*.

decretal, papal. An official letter dispatched by a pope to give a response to a dogmatic or disciplinary question raised by a particular ecclesiastical person or entity. The more significant of these letters issued after ca. 1140 were gathered together in a series of collections which served, along with the *Decree of Gratian*, as the source of canonical legislation until the 1917 *Code of Canon Law*. The **decretalists** were the canonists who wrote commentaries on the various compilations of decretals.

Dictatus Papae. A list of twenty-seven propositions found in Gregory VII's register for March 1075. These statements reveal the mind of Gregory regarding the extent of papal prerogatives, and probably represent an outline of a canonical collection which was to be compiled in his lifetime, but never was.

diocesan synod. According to canon 460 of the 1983 *Code of Canon Law*, this is a group of selected priests and other Christian faithful who gather with the local bishop to discuss and settle on policies that affect the well-being of the entire diocesan community.

dispensation. The relaxation of a law in a particular case.

divided sovereignty. A theory of constitutional government which distributes the supreme ruling and teaching authority in the Church between the pope alone and the ecumenical council (including the pope). In Vatican I (1870) the declaration of universal papal sovereignty rendered this thesis somewhat obsolete.

Donation of Constantine. A significant medieval document confected in Rome, probably in the mid-eighth century, which masqueraded as the work of Constantine I who supposedly set forth in writing a series of permanent gifts and conveyances to Pope Sylvester and his successors ca. 315-325.

Donatism. A schism that arose in the early fourth century in northern Africa. It denied the validity of sacraments administered by unworthy ministers. The Donatists insisted on the rebaptism of Christians who fell back into sinful ways.

ecumenical council. The supreme deliberative assembly within the Church involving the pope, the bishops of the world, and the other major prelates. There have been twenty-one such gatherings, beginning with the Council of Nicaea in 325. The most recent ecumenical council was Vatican II (1962-65).

episcopal conference. A body of the bishops of a given nation or territory who gather together at fixed times to promote the greater good of the Church in their area. The *Decree on the Bishops* of Vatican II recommended the establishment of such bodies throughout the Church, and a subsequent decree of 1966 mandated their establishment.

exarch. The official delegate or representative of the Byzantine emperor in certain significant areas of the empire, such as Ravenna.

excommunication. Exclusion from access to the sacraments and the exercise of full rights in the Church.

False Decretals. A collection of conciliar enactments, papal letters, and decretals, probably confected around 850 in northern France and falsely attributed to Isidore Mercator. Although the *Pseudo-Isidorian Decretals* were not the only forged collections produced at this time in the Gallo-Frankish North, they came to have the greatest influence over the centuries.

Febronianism. A theory of Church–state relations named after the coadjutor bishop of Trier, Johann von Hontheim (1701-90), who published under the title of "Febronius." This theory denied papal jurisdiction on most issues outside of the metropolitan area of Rome.

Gallicanism. This position, enunciated in 1682 in France, affirmed two basic tenets. First, the civil monarch remains supreme in temporal matters, and the popes cannot directly or indirectly interfere with the relationships between the ruler and his subjects. Second, although the pope possesses universal jurisdiction over all the churches, his decrees relating to faith and morals must be confirmed by the consent of the Church in order to be irreformable. This theological position was set aside by the enactments of Vatican I (1870).

Gnosticism. A heretical religious movement affecting the teachings of the Church from at least the second century on. The heart of gnostic belief consisted in the claim that those gifted with the gnosis possessed a privileged knowledge concerning God and human salvation from secret revelations which were never communicated to Christians in general.

Great Western Schism. The division that took place in the Church in 1378 when two popes were chosen in separate elections by the cardinals, thus initiating a Roman and an Avignonese line of pontiffs. An effort was made in 1409 to conclude the schism, but unfortunately it resulted in the establishment of a third (Pisan) line of popes. These three papal lines disputed one another's authenticity until the Council of Constance (1414-18), when the successors of each line either resigned or were deposed. This opened the way for the election of a new pope, Martin V, in 1417.

heresy. Wilful and persistent refusal to profess certain orthodox doctrines of faith.

iconoclasm. A movement in the Byzantine church which forbade the use of any religious images or **icons** in Christian worship. The Council of Nicaea II (787) restored the use of images and their veneration.

indulgence. The remittance of temporal punishment due to sin that has already been forgiven. The commerce in indulgences in the sixteenth century contributed largely to the onset of the Protestant Revolt.

Inquisition. An ecclesiastical tribunal for searching out and punishing heretics. The Inquisition began in the twelfth century, and after 1232 was especially identified with the Dominican friars. The techniques that were employed bordered in many cases on flagrant injustice and unbridled cruelty. In 1542, Paul III established the Holy Office as the final court of appeal in all heresy trials.

interdict. An ecclesiastical penalty frequently employed in the Middle Ages, according to which all liturgical services, some of the sacraments, and other sacred rites were forbidden. For example, local interdicts affecting all of England and all of France were imposed for considerable periods of time by Innocent III (1198-1216). Personal interdicts (those just affecting certain individuals) are still treated in the 1983 *Code of Canon Law*.

Jansenism. A religious movement which stressed very strict morals and had a pessimistic view concerning the human situation. It originated with Cornelius Jansen (1585-1638) whose posthumous study, *Augustinus* (1640), served as the base of later developments. Several statements from the book were officially condemned on three separate occasions in the seventeenth century. Probably because of the papal condemnations, Jansenism moved into the antipapalist camp, emphasizing the authority of the local bishops.

Josephinism. A policy on the part of Emperor Joseph II of Austria (1765-90) which asserted the sovereignty of the state in church affairs. He suppressed religious orders not involved in charitable functions and took full control over church property and the conferring of church benefices.

jurisdiction. The power to rule and govern in the Church. It is present in its fullness according to Vatican I (DS 3055) in the Roman pontiff (**primacy of jurisdiction**), and is possessed in limited degrees by the ordinaries.

lay investiture. The practice of lay lords appointing individual clerics as pastors, abbots, bishops, etc., in their territories. Since this practice struck at the very root of the Church's mission, it was opposed by a number of popes in the eleventh and early twelfth centuries. The final solution reached at the Council of Worms (1122), involved the conferral of the spiritual power by the appropriate ecclesiastical authority, while any temporal power accruing to the officeholder was conferred by the appropriate prince or king.

liberalism. A political and religious mind-set which grew out of the Enlightenment of the eighteenth century. It tended, in political affairs, to stress the constitutional safeguarding of basic human liberties and the establishment of democratic governments. In the religious realm, besides defending the expansion of human rights, it espoused new theological and biblical ideas and approaches which were occasionally opposed to the old orthodox positions.

local ordinary. The bishop who is in charge of a local diocese.

magisterium. The formal teaching power of the Church which according to Vatican I (DS 3074) is possessed in its fullness by the Roman pontiff and shared in a limited way by all of the ordinaries.

metropolitan. The local bishop (usually an archbishop) of a major see who currently possesses some limited jurisdiction over a number of lesser dioceses in the same region. From the middle of the eleventh century, the powers of the metropolitan have steadily declined. Whereas in the first millennium of the Church's life this function was extremely critical for regional governance, it has been reduced over the years to a largely ceremonial prerogative.

modalism. An early heresy which denied that Father, Son, and Holy Spirit are distinct persons, but were instead merely three manifestations of the one God. One of the more notable modalists was Sabellius who taught in the third century.

modernism. A theological and biblical movement originating in the latter half of the nineteenth century which attempted to apply the most recent discoveries in the areas of historical and biblical scholarship to the contemporary understanding of the Church and the gospels. Although some of these scholars may have pushed their historical and biblical criticism too far, the greater danger lay in the efforts on the part of other modernists (e.g., E. Le Roy) to locate the origin of the Church and of religion generally in the religious consciousness of the subject, thereby erasing the historical underpinnings of Christianity. Modernism was condemned by Pius X in July 1907.

monarchical bishop. The prelate who has sole responsibility for the governance of a diocese. In the earliest centuries many dioceses (e.g., the diocese of Rome) were ruled by a college of presbyters or priests. (Rome apparently did not have a monarchical bishop until ca. 140-150.)

Monophysitism. The heretical position that grew out of a refusal to accept the teaching of the Council of Chalcedon (451) that in Christ there are two natures—divine and human—in one person (DS 300-303). The Monophysites maintained that there was only one nature in Christ which was either divine or a blend of the divine and human. This heresy, perhaps the most damaging in the post-Constantinian Church, resulted in a massive schism in the East which has never been healed. **Monoenergism,** a seventh-century hybrid of Monophysitism, held that there was only "one energy" in Christ, while **Monotheletism,** also a seventh-century development, affirmed only "one will" in Christ. Both of these heresies were condemned by Constantinople III in 680-81 (DS 553-557).

nepotism. The practice of conferring offices and benefices on relatives. This was an extremely common practice in the Middle Ages for both popes and bishops. In spite of repeated condemnations of the practice, it really did not die out until a century or more after the Council of Trent (1545-63).

Oikoumene. A Greek term used to signify the entire inhabited world.

Orthodox churches. The churches that have separated for doctrinal and/or governmental reasons from the see of Rome. These schisms, which began as early as the fourth century, created a large group of independent Christian communities that have throughout history maintained their independence from the pope. The two most prominent of these bodies are the Russian Orthodox and the Greek Orthodox churches.

papal bull. A solemn papal letter written in the most formal style and employed for transactions of major importance.

papal curia. A collective term for all the congregations, offices, and courts that assist the pope in carrying out the business of the Holy See.

papal encyclical. An official letter usually addressed to the bishops of the world (or to the whole Catholic population) which the pope utilizes in the exercise of his ordinary teaching function. Encyclicals became popular in the nineteenth century and have been used frequently by the pontiffs since Pius IX (1846-78).

papal infallibility. A much discussed prerogative which preserves papal teaching on matters of faith and morals from any error whenever the pope intends to define solemnly some truth of faith or morals **ex cathedra** (i.e., to be held true by the whole Church). This prerogative was widely discussed in the late Middle Ages, and the debate resurfaced in the eighteenth century. The formal statement of Vatican I in 1870 (DS 3074) identified this prerogative as a defined doctrine.

papal judges-delegate. Judges in various parts of Christendom appointed by the Roman pontiff to hear and decide cases submitted for adjudication to the Roman courts. The practice of employing judges-delegate expanded dramatically under Alexander III (1159-81) and remained popular until Trent (1545-63). Through these judges the pope augmented his judicial outreach enormously and reduced thereby the workload of the Roman courts. As a result of this practice, the local jurisdictions, i.e., the metropolitan and diocesan courts, were notably reduced in importance.

papal nuncios, papal legates. Official representatives of the Roman pontiff sent to various nations to further the work of the Holy See in those areas. They establish liaisons with the secular governments and serve as conduits of information between their respective territories and Rome. Although they were used from the earliest times, the employment of nuncios and papal legates expanded dramatically after the Council of Trent (1545-63), because they were the most important agents for the implementation of the Tridentine decrees and directives of Trent.

papal provision. The papal practice of appointing individuals to offices and benefices. Beginning with the pontificate of Innocent IV (1243-54), the popes notably expanded their sphere of influence in the making of such appointments throughout Christendom until the abuse was curbed at Trent (1545-63). This practice resulted in the reduction of the rightful prerogatives of local ordinaries everywhere.

papal rescript. The official response on the part of the pope to a question, usually of law or discipline, submitted to Rome by an ecclesiastical entity. The instrument *per se* settled only the particular dispute presented to the pope, but often became normative in an entire province or nation.

papal reservations. The papal practice of asserting control over certain classes of benefices and endowments, thereby depriving the local ecclesiastical officials of that right. The first general reservations began with Clement IV (1265-68) and were greatly amplified under Boniface VIII (1294-1303) and Clement V (1305-14). The Avignon popes Urban V (1362-70) and Gregory XI (1370-78) extended papal reservations to include every major benefice and a considerable number of minor benefices of note in western Christendom. In spite of several papal and conciliar efforts to curb the practice, it was not effectively controlled until after the implementation of the Council of Trent (1545-63). The principal objective of the popes in the expansion of reservations was to provide sources of revenue from the benefices to the rising number of curial officials.

Papal States. The territory in central Italy (and for a time, a small section of southern France) governed by the pope. Papal sovereignty over the Italian lands was formally recognized by Charlemagne (768-814). From the eighth to the nineteenth century, the territory expanded and contracted according to the political fortunes of the pontiffs. In the nineteenth century, the existence of the Papal States constituted a major obstacle to the unification of Italy, greatly desired by the majority of Italians. Although the Papal States were taken over by the Italian forces (1860-70), the so-called "Roman Question" was not settled until the Lateran Treaty between Italy and the Vatican in 1929. This treaty established Vatican City as a tiny independent state and provided financial compensation to the popes for the properties that had been taken from their possession.

patriarch. The head of one of the five major jurisdictional areas in the post-Constantinian Church. The organizational structure of the early Church grew, as it were, from bottom up, with the ordinaries of Rome, Alexandria, Antioch, Jerusalem, and Constantinople becoming the chief liturgical, disciplinary, and to some extent, doctrinal authorities in their respective regions. The pope in Rome was acknowledged by the others as having a primacy of honor, but probably not a primacy of jurisdiction. With the separation of the eastern and western churches in the eleventh century, each of the eastern patriarchs became fully independent, but eventually Antioch, Alexandria, and Jerusalem gravitated into the sphere of influence of the **ecumenical patriarch** of Constantinople, the head of the Byzantine church.

pentarchy. The coordinated rule of the five great patriarchs over all of Christendom, which had grown up in the early centuries of the Church. Although it was not formally proposed as an ecclesiological system until the eighth and ninth centuries by eastern scholars, the pentarchical arrangement was implicit in the conduct of the second, third, fourth, and fifth ecumenical councils (381-553).

plenitudo potestatis. A description of full papal power which was popularized by St. Bernard (d. 1153). It became the favorite designation of Innocent III (1198-1216) to dramatize the extent of papal power.

pluralism. The practice of conferring more than one ecclesiastical benefice on a given subject. This abuse, especially with regard to pastoral benefices, was prohibited by canon 13 of Lateran III (1179) and by many subsequent canons over the years. Unfortunately the practice did not go away but continued to become more and more widespread as a means of providing ample income for the ever growing number of officials in the papal curia. The papal official would take a major share of the revenue accruing to the benefices, and leave the remainder for substitutes who bore the responsibility for fulfilling the obligations of the offices. This pastorally damaging situation was finally remedied through the gradual implementation of the Council of Trent (1545-63).

presbyters. The officials in the early Church who were responsible for the conduct of the pastoral offices in the primitive communities. For the first four or five generations after Christ, some local churches, including Rome, were governed by a college of such officials who were in some instances called **presbyter-bishops.** For example, Rome apparently did not have a monarchical bishop until 140-150, whereas Antioch enjoyed a single head from ca. 100.

primatial see. The most influential diocese in a given province or country. For example, St. Cyprian (d. 258) was the primate of the see of Carthage, the most prominent diocese in north Africa.

provincial and plenary councils. The gathering of all the bishops (at least the ordinaries) of a given ecclesiastical province or, in the case of **plenary councils,** of a given region or nation.

Roman congregations. The most important administrative offices of papal government. The congregations were given their modern shape in 1588 by Sixtus V (1585-90) who created fifteen permanent organizations, each office having a distinct and complementary set of responsibilities. There were several adaptations in the structure and competencies over the centuries, with the last major reorganization accomplished by Paul VI from 1965-69.

schism. The separation of one believer or group of believers from the other members of the Church. The reason for the division can be doctrinal or disciplinary. The two most damaging schisms were those between the Catholic West and the Orthodox East in the eleventh century, and between Protestants and Catholics in the sixteenth century.

Secretary of State. The papal official who traditionally had responsibility for the relations between the Holy See and civil governments. Since the reorganization of the curia by Paul VI (1963-78), this office is charged with the task of assisting the pope in his dealings with the universal Church and with the other departments of the curia.

simony. The sale or purchase of a church office or a sacrament. This was a persistent problem in Rome and elsewhere during the Middle Ages. One of the early medieval popes to wage war against the practice was Leo IX (1049-54).

subordinationism. Any doctrine that makes the Son inferior to the Father, or the Holy Spirit inferior to both Father and Son. Arius (condemned at Nicaea, 325) made the Son inferior to the Father, while the Pneumatomachians (condemned at Constantinople I in 381) taught that the Holy Spirit was inferior both to the Father and to the Son.

subsidiarity, principle of. The norm that asserts that what can be accomplished effectively by a lower level of government should not be assumed by a higher level. Pius XI first proposed the principle in *Quadragesimo anno* (1931), and it was established as one of the controlling norms for the revision of the *Code of Canon Law* in 1967.

ultramontanism. A somewhat derogatory term to describe those prelates and theologians wishing to maximize the prerogatives of the pope. At Vatican I (1869-70) they vigorously negotiated for the definition of papal infallibility.

Uniate churches. The term applied to those eastern Christian schismatic communities which at various times over the centuries returned to full communion with the Roman pontiff.

World Synod of Bishops. A body created by Paul VI in September 1965 to promote a higher level of ongoing dialogue between the Roman pontiff and the bishops, in order that pope and bishops might more effectively fulfill the Church's mission in the world. The first of these gatherings met in Rome in the fall of 1967.

Notes

1. The Models of Church in the New Testament

N.B. Biblical quotations are taken from *The Catholic Study Bible*, Donald Senior general ed. (New York: Oxford University Press, 1990).

1. Gerd Theissen, *Sociology of Early Palestinian Christianity*, trans. John Bowden (Philadelphia: Fortress Press, 1978), 7.

2. Ibid., 52.

3. Wayne A. Meeks, *The First Urban Christians* (New Haven: Yale University Press, 1983), 17.

4. Ibid., 28.

5. Ibid., 26.

6. Ramsay MacMullen, *Roman Social Relations 50 B.C. to A.D. 284* (New Haven: Yale University Press, 1974), 57.

7. Hans von Campenhausen, *Ecclesiastical Authority and Spiritual Power in the Church of the First Three Centuries*, trans. J.A. Baker (Stanford: Stanford University Press, 1969), 79.

8. Raymond E. Brown and John P. Meier, *Antioch and Rome* (New York: Paulist Press, 1983), 56.

9. Jack Dean Kingsbury, *Matthew: Structure, Christology, Kingdom*, 2d ed. (Minneapolis: Fortress Press, 1986), 94.

10. Raymond E. Brown, *The Community of the Beloved Disciple* (New York: Paulist Press, 1979), 33.

11. Ibid., 102.

12. Ibid., 86-91.

13. Ibid., 151-8.

14. David L. Bartlett, *Ministry in the New Testament* (Minneapolis: Fortress Press, 1993), 113-4.

15. Brown, *Community of the Beloved Disciple,* 161-2.

16. Campenhausen, 118.

17. Raymond E. Brown, *The Churches the Apostles Left Behind* (New York: Paulist Press, 1984), 146.

18. Ibid., 148.

19. Bartlett, 5-6.

20. James D. G. Dunn, *Unity and Diversity in the New Testament,* 2d ed. (Philadelphia: Trinity Press International, 1990), 122.

21. Ibid., 121.

22. Ernst Käsemann, *Essays on New Testament Themes*, trans. W.J. Montague (London: SCM Press, 1964), 103.

23. Dunn, 122.

2. Developments from *I Clement* to Pope Stephen I

1. Johannes Quasten, *Patrology*, Vol. 1 (Westminster, MD: Christian Classics, Inc., 1990), 49-50.

2. *The Apostolic Fathers*, 2d ed., trans. J.B. Lightfoot and J.R. Harmer, ed. Michael W. Holmes (Grand Rapids: Baker Book House, 1989), 55 (47,6).

3. Berthold Altaner, *Patrology*, trans. Hilda C. Graef (New York: Herder and Herder, 1960), 100-101.

4. *The Apostolic Fathers*, 52-53 (44, 1-3).

5. Hans von Campenhausen, *Ecclesiastical Authority and Spiritual Power in the Church of the First Three Centuries*, trans. J. A. Baker (Stanford: Stanford University Press, 1969), 91.

6. Raymond E. Brown and John P. Meier, *Antioch and Rome* (New York: Paulist Press, 1983), 204, n. 433.

7. Eusebius, *The History of the Church*, trans. G.A. Williamson (New York: Dorset Press, 1965), 145 (3,36,3).

8. *The Apostolic Fathers*, 102 (*To the Romans*, intro.).

9. Ibid., 103 (Romans 4,3).

10. Herbert A. Musurillo, *The Fathers of the Primitive Church* (New York: The New American Library, 1966), 88.

11. Justin, *Dialogue*, Chapter 2, in *The Ante-Nicene Fathers*, Vol. 1, ed. A. Roberts and J. Donaldson (Reprint, Grand Rapids: Eerdmans, 1989), 195.

12. Ibid., *The First Apology*, Chapter 67, 186.

13. Justin, *Dialogue*, Chapter 82, 240.

14. Ibid., Chapter 134, 267.

15. Eusebius, 181 (4,22,1).

16. Irenaeus, *Against Heresies*, Book III, Chapter 3,1, *The Ante-Nicene Fathers*, Vol. 1, ed. A. Roberts and J. Donaldson (Reprint, Grand Rapids: Eerdmans, 1989), 415.

17. Henry Chadwick, *The Early Church* (New York: Dorset Press, 1986), 81.

18. Quasten, 303.

19. Irenaeus, *Against Heresies*, Book III, Chapter 3,2,415-416.

20. Ibid., Chapter 3,3,416.

21. Karl Baus, *From the Apostolic Community to Constantine, History of the Church*, Vol. 1, ed. H. Jedin and J. Dolan (Tunbridge Wells: Burns and Oates, 1980), 356-357.

22. Eusebius, 232 (5,24,8).

23. G. Alberigo et al., *Decrees of the Ecumenical Councils*, Vol. 1, English ed., N. Tanner (Washington, DC: Georgetown University Press, 1990), 19.

24. Hippolytus of Rome, *The Apostolic Tradition*, 2d ed., ed. G. Dix, Reissue, H. Chadwick (Ridgefield, CT: Morehouse Publishing, 1992), xx-xxi.

25. Ibid., xxvii*.

26. Ibid., 2-12.

27. Ibid., 13-14.

28. Ibid., 15-18.

29. Ibid., 30-43.

30. Cyprian, *The Letters of St. Cyprian of Carthage*, Vol. 3, trans. G. W. Clarke, *Ancient Christian Writers*, no. 46, ed. J. Quasten et al. (New York: Newman Press, 1986), 121 (Epistle 66, 8.3).

31. Cyprian, *The Letters of St. Cyprian of Carthage*, Vol. 4, trans. G.W. Clarke, *Ancient Christian Writers*, no. 47, ed. W. Burghardt and T. Lawler (New York: Newman Press, 1989), 54 (Epistle 72, 3.2).

32. Cyprian, *The Letters of St. Cyprian of Carthage*, Vol. 1, trans. by G.W. Clarke, *Ancient*

Christian Writers, no. 43, ed. J. Quasten et al. (New York: Newman Press, 1984), 89 (Epistle 14,4).

33. Cyprian, *Letters*, Vol. 4, 23 (Epistle 67, 4.1).

34. Ibid., 24 (Epistle 67, 5.1).

35. Cyprian, *Letters*, Vol. 3, 45-46 (Epistle 55, 21.1).

36. Cyprian, *Letters*, Vol. 4, 81 (Epistle 75, 6.1). Note: This letter, although included in the letters of Cyprian, was sent to him by Bishop Fermilian of Caesarea.

37. Cyprian, *The Unity of the Catholic Church*, trans. M. Bévenot, *Ancient Christian Writers*, no. 25, ed. J. Quasten and J. Plumpe (New York: Newman Press, 1956), Chap. 5, 47-48.

38. Cyprian, *Letters*, Vol. 4, 29-30 (Epistle 68, 3.2).

39. Ibid., 70 (Epistle 74, 1.2).

40. Ibid., 88-89 (Epistle 75, 17.1).

41. Ibid., 93 (Epistle 75, 25.1).

42. Cyprian, *The Unity of the Catholic Church*, Chap. 4,46.

43. Ibid., Chap. 4,46. See J. Bévenot's comments, 6-8.

3. The Expansion of the Papal Office

1. Eusebius, *The History of the Church*, trans. G.A. Williamson (New York: Dorset Press, 1965), 291 (7,7,1).

2. H. Denzinger and A. Schönmetzer, *Enchiridion Symbolorum*, 32nd ed. (Freiburg: Herder, 1963), 112-115.

3. *The Ante-Nicene Fathers*, Vol. 12, ed. A. Roberts and J. Donaldson (New York: Charles Scribner's Sons, 1926), 365-366.

4. W.H.C. Frend, *The Rise of Christianity* (Philadelphia: Fortress Press, 1984), 401.

5. Ramsay MacMullen, *Christianizing the Roman Empire A.D. 100-400* (New Haven: Yale University Press, 1984), 32.

6. A.H.M. Jones, *The Later Roman Empire 284-602*, Vol. 2 (1964; Reprint, Baltimore: Johns Hopkins University Press, 1990), 1040.

7. Eusebius, 282 (6,43).

8. Karl Baus, *History of the Church*, Vol. 1, ed. H. Jedin and J. Dolan (Tunbridge Wells: Burns and Oates, 1980), 398.

9. Eusebius, 330 (8, 2).

10. Ibid., 354 (8, 17, 5).

11. Walter Ullmann, *A Short History of the Papacy in the Middle Ages* (1972; New York: Methuen and Co., 1982), 4-5.

12. Geoffrey Barraclough, *The Medieval Papacy* (New York: W.W. Norton and Co., 1968), 17.

13. Ibid., 18.

14. Henri Marrou, *The First Six Hundred Years*, Vol. 1 of *The Christian Centuries* (New York: Paulist Press, 1964), 249-251.

15. Hamilton Hess, *The Canons at the Council of Sardica A.D. 343* (Oxford: Clarendon Press, 1958), 5.

16. *Nicene and Post-Nicene Fathers*, Vol. 14, ed. P. Schaff and H. Wace (Reprint, Grand Rapids: Eerdmans, 1991), 417.

17. Marrou, 260.

18. Giuseppe Alberigo et al., *Decrees of the Ecumenical Councils*, Vol. 1 (Washington, DC: Georgetown University Press, 1990), 22.

19. Ibid., *32.

20. MacMullen, 49.

21. Ibid., 53 (statement in quotes from the historian Sozomen).

22. Jones, *The Later Roman Empire 284-602*, Vol. 2, 910.

23. MacMullen, 83.

24. Ibid.

25. Marrou, 226.

26. Robert Markus, *The End of Ancient Christianity* (Cambridge: Cambridge University Press, 1990), 27-28.

27. Ibid., 32-33.

28. Marrou, 327.

29. *The Book of Pontiffs (Liber Pontificalis)*, trans. Raymond Davis (Liverpool: Liverpool University Press, 1989), 14-26.

30. Jones, 904.

31. Karl Baus, *The History of the Church*, Vol. 2, ed. H. Jedin and J. Dolan (London: Burns and Oates, 1980), 45-46.

32. Jones, *The Later Roman Empire 284-602*, Vol. 2, 887.

33. *Nicene and Post-Nicene Fathers*, Vol. 14, Canons 23 and 28, 453, 456.

34. *Documents of the Christian Church*, 2d ed., ed. Henry Bettenson (London: Oxford University Press, 1963), 22-23.

35. Yves Congar, *After Nine Hundred Years* (New York: Fordham University Press, 1959), 63.

36. Ibid., 69.

37. Ibid.

38. *Nicene and Post-Nicene Fathers*, Vol. 12, ed. P. Schaff and H. Wace (Reprint, Grand Rapids: Eerdmans, 1989), 117.

39. Trevor Jalland, *The Life and Times of St. Leo the Great* (New York: Macmillan, 1941), 105.

40. Ibid., 104, note 43.

41. *Nicene and Post-Nicene Fathers*, Vol. 12, Letter 12, 16.

42. Jalland, 112.

43. *Nicene and Post-Nicene Fathers*, Vol. 12, Letter 10, 8-12.

44. Ibid., Letter 108, 79.

45. Ibid., Letter 108, 80-81.

46. Ibid., Letter 14, 16.

47. Ibid., 18-19.

48. Alberigo et al., *85.

49. Ibid., *100.

50. A.H.M. Jones, *The Later Roman Empire 284-602*, Vol. 1 (1964; Reprint, Baltimore: Johns Hopkins, 1990), 220-221.

51. *Documents of the Christian Church*, 91.

52. Jones, *The Later Roman Empire 284-602*, Vol. 1, 244.

53. Ibid., 247.

54. Aloysius K. Ziegler, "Pope Gelasius and His Teaching on the Relation of Church and State," *Catholic Historical Review*, 27, 4 (1942): 430.

55. Brian Tierney, *The Crisis of Church and State 1050-1300* (1964; Reprint, Toronto: University of Toronto Press, 1990), 13-14.

56. Ziegler, 435.

57. A.S. McGrade, "Two Fifth-Century Conceptions of Papal Primacy," *Studies in Medieval and Renaissance History*, 7 (1970): 21.

58. Ibid., 29.

59. Jeffrey Richards, *The Popes and the Papacy in the Early Middle Ages 476-752* (London: Routledge and Kegan Paul, 1979), 129-130.

60. Ibid., 130.

61. *The Book of Pontiffs*, 56.

62. Berthold Altaner, *Patrology*, trans. Hilda C. Graef (New York: Herder and Herder, 1960), 371.

63. *The Book of Pontiffs*, 59.

64. Richards, 159.

65. *The Book of Pontiffs*, 60.

66. Ibid., 61.

67. Richards, 167.

4. The Pope Turns to the West

1. *The Book of Pontiffs, (Liber Pontificalis)*, trans. Raymond Davis (Liverpool: Liverpool University Press, 1989), 61.

2. Henri Marrou, *The First Six Hundred Years. The Christian Centuries*, Vol. 1 (New York: Paulist Press, 1964), 438-9.

3. Jeffrey Richards, *Consul of God* (London: Routledge and Kegan Paul, 1980), 140.

4. Ibid.

5. *Nicene and Post-Nicene Fathers*, Vol. 12, ed. P. Schaff and H. Wace (Reprint, Grand Rapids: Eerdmans, 1989), Book 1, Letter 1, 73. Hereafter cited in text by Bk. number and Ep. number.

6. Richards, 176.

7. Ibid., 177.

8. *Nicene and Post-Nicene Fathers*, Vol. 12, Book 3, Letter 49, 135.

9. Richards, 200.

10. John Meyendorff, *Imperial Unity and Christian Divisions* (Crestwood, NY: St. Vladimir's Seminary Press, 1989), 322.

11. Ibid.

12. Ibid., 322-3.

13. *Nicene and Post-Nicene Fathers*, Vol. 12, Book 5, Letter 53, 183.

14. Ibid.

15. *Nicene and Post-Nicene Fathers*, Vol. 12, Book 5, Letter 54, 184.

16. *Nicene and Post-Nicene Fathers*, Vol. 12, Book 1, Letter 25, 81.

17. *Nicene and Post-Nicene Fathers*, Vol. 12, Book 5, Letter 18, 166.

18. *Nicene and Post-Nicene Fathers*, Vol. 12, Book 5, Letter 43, 179.

19. Ibid.

20. *Nicene and Post-Nicene Fathers*, Vol. 12, Book 7, Letter 40, 229.

21. Berthold Altaner, *Patrology*, trans. Hilda C. Graef (New York: Herder and Herder, 1960), 562.

22. George Ostrogorsky, *History of the Byzantine State*, trans. Joan Hussey (1952; New Brunswick: Rutgers University Press, 1969), 80.

23. Ibid., 92.

24. Meyendorff, 337.

25. Ibid., 352-3.

26. H.G. Beck, *The History of the Church*, Vol. 2, ed. H. Jedin and J. Dolan (London: Burns and Oates, 1980), 458.

27. Meyendorff, 367.

28. Ibid.

29. Ibid., 370.

30. Guiseppe Alberigo et al., *Decrees of the Ecumenical Councils*, Vol. 1 (Washington, DC: Georgetown University Press, 1990), 123.

31. Ibid., 128.

32. Ibid., 125.

33. Meyendorff, 372-3.

34. Ostrogorsky, 139.

35. *The Book of Pontiffs*, 90-91.

36. Ibid., 91.

37. Thomas F.X. Noble, *The Republic of St. Peter* (Philadelphia: University of Pennsylvania Press, 1984), 23.

38. Ostrogorsky, 160.

39. Ibid., 161.

40. *The Lives of the Eighth-Century Popes* (*Liber Pontificalis*), trans. R. Davis (Liverpool: Liverpool University Press, 1992), 11.

41. Ibid., 20.

42. Walter Ullmann, *A Short History of the Papacy in the Middle Ages* (1972; Reprint, New York: Methuen & Co., 1982), 72.

43. Noble, 44.

44. Ibid., 46.

45. Geoffrey Barraclough, *The Medieval Papacy* (New York: W. W. Norton and Co., 1968), 40.

46. Noble, 44.

47. Ibid., 51.

48. Barraclough, 40.

49. *Documents of the Christian Church*, 2d ed., ed. H. Bettenson (London: Oxford University Press, 1963), 100-1.

50. Noble, 135-7.

51. *The Lives of the Eighth-Century Popes*, 60-65.

52. Ibid., 63.

53. Noble, 86.

54. Ibid., 87-88.

55. *The Lives of the Eighth-Century Popes*, 99.

56. Noble, 117.

57. Ibid., 138.

58. Jeffrey Richards, *The Popes and the Papacy in the Early Middle Ages 476-752* (London: Routledge and Kegan Paul, 1979), 270.

59. Noble, 188.

60. Ibid.

61. Ostrogorsky, 177-8.

62. Alberigo et al., 136.

63. Barraclough, 52.

64. Noble, 200.

65. Ostrogorsky, 185-6.

66. Meyendorff, 331-2.

67. Ibid., 327.

68. Ibid.

69. Yves Congar, *L'Église de saint Augustin à l'époque moderne* (Paris: Les éditions du Cerf, 1970), 79.

70. Ibid.

71. *The Lives of the Eighth-Century Popes*, 99.

72. Ibid., 233.

73. Noble, 204.

74. Barraclough, 60-1.

75. Yves Congar, *Ecclésiologie du haut moyen age* (Paris: Les éditions du Cerf, 1968), 137.

76. Ibid., 169.

77. Ibid., 164.

78. Yves Congar, "Reception as an Ecclesiastical Reality," *Concilium*, Vol. 77 (New York: Herder and Herder, 1972), 45.

79. Congar, *Ecclésiologie du haut moyen age*, 175.

80. Eugen Ewig, *The History of the Church*, Vol. 3, ed. H. Jedin and J. Dolan (New York: Crossroad, 1989), 167.

81. Ullmann, 99-100. For a more expanded treatment, see Walter Ullmann, *The Growth of Papal Government in the Middle Ages* (1955; 3d ed., Northampton: John Dickens and Co., 1970), 180-189.

82. Ibid., 100.

83. Ibid., 101.

84. J.M. Wallace-Hadrill, *The Frankish Church* (Oxford: Clarendon Press, 1983), 276.

85. Congar, *Ecclésiologie du haut moyen age*, 189.

86. Ibid., 208.

87. Ibid., 209.

88. Ibid., 211.

89. Ibid., 215.

90. *Documents of the Christian Church*, 95.

91. Ibid., 96.

92. Ostrogorsky, 225-6.

93. Congar, *Ecclésiologie du haut moyen age*, 218-20.

94. Walter Ullmann, *The Growth of Papal Government in the Middle Ages* (1955; 3d ed., Northampton: John Dickens and Co., 1970), 209-10.

95. Ostrogorsky, 232.

96. Alberigo et al., 163.

97. Ibid., 166-86.

98. Ibid., 157.

99. Congar, *Ecclésiologie du haut moyen age*, 235. Especially note 14.

100. Ullmann, *The Growth of Papal Government in the Middle Ages*, 224.

101. Ewig, 154.

102. Ludwig Hertling, *A History of the Catholic Church*, trans. A. G. Biggs (London: Peter Owen, Limited, 1958), 184. For a fuller and more current view of the information available on the tenth-century popes, see J.N.D. Kelly, *The Oxford Dictionary of Popes* (1986; Reprint, Oxford: Oxford University Press, 1989), 117-38.

5. The Rise of the Medieval Papacy

1. Geoffrey Barraclough, *The Origins of Modern Germany* (New York: W. W. Norton and Co., 1984), 44.

2. Ibid., 33.

3. Yves Congar, *L´Église de saint Augustin á l´ époque moderne* (Paris: les éditions du Cerf, 1970), 66.

4. Walter Ullmann, *A Short History of the Papacy in the Middle Ages* (1972; Reprint, New York: Methuen and Co., 1982), 127.

5. Colin Morris, *The Papal Monarchy. The Western Church from 1050 to 1250* (Oxford: Clarendon Press, 1989), 86.

6. Ibid.

7. Barraclough, *The Origins of Modern Germany*, 104.

8. R. W. Southern, *Western Society and the Church in the Middle Ages* (New York: Viking Penguin, Inc., 1970), 100.

9. Friedrich Kempf, *History of the Church*, Vol. 3, ed. H. Jedin and J. Dolan (New York: Crossroad, 1987), 353.

10. Ibid.

11. Timothy Ware, *The Orthodox Church* (1963; New edition, New York: Penguin Books, 1993), 57-58.

12. George Ostrogorsky, *History of the Byzantine State*, trans. Joan Hussey (1952; Reprint, New Brunswick: Rutgers University Press, 1969), 336; Ware, 58.

13. Ostrogorsky, 337.

14. Ware, 59.

15. Brian Tierney, *The Crisis of Church and State 1050-1300* (1964; Reprint, Toronto: University of Toronto Press, 1990), 24.

16. Ibid., 24-25.

17. Ibid., 42.

18. Ibid.

19. Morris, 93.

20. Ibid., 95.

21. Tierney, 45.

22. I. S. Robinson, "Pope Gregory VII (1073-85)," *The Journal of Ecclesiastical History*, 36, 3 (July 1985): 439; Geoffrey Barraclough, *The Medieval Papacy* (New York: W.W. Norton and Co., 1968), 89.

23. Morris, 114.

24. Ibid., 113.

25. Kempf, 368.

26. Ibid., 373.

27. Tierney, 49-50.

28. Morris, 117.

29. Tierney, 66.

30. Morris, 120.

31. Tierney, 55.

32. *The Correspondence of Pope Gregory VII*, translated with introduction by Ephraim Emerton (1932; Reprint, New York: Columbia University Press, 1990), xvi.

33. Ibid., 133.

34. Ibid., 51-2.

35. Ibid., 64-5.

36. Ibid., 166-7.

37. Ibid., 167.

38. Ibid., 169-71.

39. Kempf, 373.

40. Alexander Murray, "Pope Gregory VII and His Letters," *Traditio*, 22 (1966): 165.

41. Morris, 121-2.

42. Stephen Kuttner, "Cardinals: The History of a Canonical Concept," *Traditio*, 3 (1945): 172-3.

43. Ibid., 174.

44. Geoffrey Barraclough, *The Medieval Papacy* (New York: W.W. Norton and Co., 1968), 95-6.

45. Ibid., 95.

46. Morris, 125-6.

47. Tierney, 85.

48. *Church and State through the Centuries*, trans. and ed. S. Ehler and J. Morrall (New York: Biblio and Tannen, 1967), 48.

49. Ibid., 49.

50. Giuseppe Alberigo et al., *Decrees of the Ecumenical Councils*, Vol. 1 (Washington, DC: Georgetown University Press, 1990), 187.

51. Ibid., 187.

52. Southern, *Western Society and the Church in the Middle Ages*, 107-8.

53. Morris, 184.

54. Bernard of Clairvaux, *Five Books on Consideration*, trans. J. Anderson and E. Kennan (Kalamazoo, MI: Cistercian Publications, 1976), 5.

55. Ibid., 8.

56. Morris, 186.

57. Alberigo et al., 195.

58. Southern, *Western Society and the Church in the Middle Ages*, 115-17.

59. Bernard of Clairvaux, 14.

60. Ibid., 89-93.

61. Ibid., 97-8.

62. Ibid., 29.

63. Morris, 192-3.

64. Ibid., 195.

65. Southern, *Western Society and the Church in the Middle Ages*, 132.

66. Alberigo et al., 206.

67. Ibid., 207.

68. Ibid., 218.

69. Ullmann, 199-200.

70. Morris, 200.

71. A. L. Poole, *From Domesday Book to Magna Carta 1087-1216*, 2d ed. (Oxford: Oxford University Press, 1955), 219.

72. Adrian Morey, *Bartholomew of Exeter* (Cambridge: Cambridge University Press, 1937), 60-74.

73. Ibid., 50.

74. Ibid., 47-54.

75. Morris, 388.

76. Ibid., 224-6.

77. Ibid., 225.

78. H. Wolter, *The History of the Church*, Vol. 4, ed. H. Jedin and J. Dolan (New York: Crossroad, 1986), 82.

79. Barraclough, *The Origins of Modern Germany*, 204.

80. Bernard of Clairvaux, 67-8.

81. *Selected Letters of Pope Innocent III*, ed. C. R. Cheney and W. H. Semple (London:

Thomas Nelson and Sons, 1953), x.

82. Helene Tillmann, *Pope Innocent III*, trans. W. Sax (1954; Reprint, Amsterdam: North Holland Publishing, 1980), 22.

83. Ibid., 23.

84. Ibid., 24.

85. Ibid., 25.

86. Ibid., 26.

87. *Selected Letters of Pope Innocent III*, xiv-v.

88. Christopher Cheney, *Pope Innocent III and England* (Stuttgart: Anton Hiersemann, 1976), 97.

89. Tillmann, 60.

90. Morris, 436.

91. Tillmann, 210.

92. Barraclough, *The Medieval Papacy*, 114.

93. Ibid., 115.

94. J. M. Hussey, *The Orthodox Church in the Byzantine Empire* (Oxford: Clarendon Press, 1986), Chapter 7, 184-219.

95. Alberigo et al., 236.

96. Cheney, 43.

97. Ibid., 44.

98. Ibid., 46.

99. Alberigo et al., 228.

100. Ibid.

101. Tillmann, 318-9.

102. Wolter, 81.

103. Southern, *Western Society and the Church in the Middle Ages*, 252-60.

104. Ibid., 285.

105. Morris, 454.

106. Tierney, 140.

107. Ibid.

108. Ullmann, 257.

109. Ibid., 258.

110. J. N. D. Kelly, *The Oxford Dictionary of Popes* (1986; Reprint, Oxford: Oxford University Press, 1989), 191.

111. Wolter, 225.

112. Morris, 485.

113. Wolter, 211.

114. Ibid., 214.

115. Ibid.

116. Ibid., 215.

117. Ullmann, 253.

118. Alberigo et al., 273.

119. Ibid., 274.

120. Ibid., 283.

121. Tierney, 145-6.

122. *Sources for the History of Medieval Europe*, ed. Brian Pullan (Oxford: Basil Blackwell, 1971), 218.

123. Ullmann, 261.

124. Barraclough, *The Medieval Papacy*, 118.

125. Morris, 547.

126. Ibid., 549.

127. R. W. Southern, *Robert Grosseteste*, 2d ed. (Oxford: Clarendon Press, 1992), 278.

128. Ibid., 279-80.

129. Ibid., 290.

130. Morris, 558.

131. J. Lynch, "The History of Centralization: Papal Reservations," *The Once and Future Church*, ed. James A. Coriden (New York: Alba House, 1971), 97.

132. Wolter, 203.

133. Alberigo et al., 304.

134. Ibid., 305.

135. Wolter, 206-7.

136. Alberigo et al., 323.

137. Barraclough, *The Medieval Papacy*, 136-8.

138. Wolter, 235.

139. Ibid., 234. (N. B. Charles of Anjou was the brother of King Louis IX of France, 1226-70.)

140. Ibid., 267.

141. Barraclough, *The Medieval Papacy*, 124.

6. The Worldly Papacy

1. T.S.R. Boase, *Boniface VIII* (London: Constable and Co., 1933), 15.

2. Ibid., 17.

3. Brien Tierney, *The Crisis of Church and State 1050-1300* (1964; Reprint, Toronto: University of Toronto Press, 1990), 177.

4. *Documents of the Christian Church*, 2d ed., ed. H. Bettenson (London: Oxford University Press, 1963), 113-114.

5. See the bull *Etsi de statu* in Tierney, *The Crisis of Church and State*, 178-9.

6. See the bull *Ausculta fili*, in Tierney, *The Crisis of Church and State*, 186.

7. Jean Rivière, "Boniface's Theological Conservatism," *Philip the Fair and Boniface VIII*, 2d ed., ed. Charles Wood (New York: Holt, Rinehart, and Winston, 1971), 60.

8. Ibid.

9. Ibid., 61.

10. Tierney, *Crisis of Church and State*, 189.

11. Ibid.

12. Boase, 92.

13. Ibid., 99.

14. Ibid.

15. Yves Renouard, *The Avignon Papacy*, trans. Denis Bethell (New York: Barnes and Noble, 1994), 83.

16. Boase, 106.

17. Ibid., 377-8.

18. K. A. Fink, *History of the Church*, Vol. 4, ed. H. Jedin and J. Dolan (New York: Crossroad, 1986), 292. Benedict was not a Roman. He was born in Treviso, north of Venice.

19. G. Mollat, *The Popes at Avignon*, trans. Janet Love (London: Thomas Nelson and Sons Ltd., 1963), 6.

20. Fink, 298.

21. Ibid., 296-7.

22. Mollat, 230-1.

23. Ibid., xiv.

24. Ibid.

25. Guiseppe Alberigo et al., *Decrees of the Ecumenical Councils*, Vol. 1 (Washington, DC: Georgetown University Press, 1990), 333.

26. Ibid., 334.

27. Ibid., *341-*342.

28. Mollat, 241.

29. Alberigo et al., 335.

30. Mollat, 245.

31. Ibid., 335.

32. Ibid., 8.

33. Fink, 307.

34. Geoffrey Barraclough, *The Medieval Papacy*, (New York: W.W. Norton and Co., 1968), 147-8.

35. Mollat, 16.

36. E. Iserloh, *History of the Church*, Vol. 4, ed. H. Jedin and J. Dolan (New York: Crossroad, 1986), 372-3. N.B. In November 1331, Pope John precipitated another theological dispute when he taught that the souls of the just do not enjoy the beatific vision until after the Last Judgment, nor do the damned reside in hell until that time. Shortly thereafter he stated that he was speaking only as a "private theologian." On the day before he died (December 3, 1330), he partially recanted his position in the presence of the cardinals.

37. Renouard, 128.

38. Mollat, 24.

39. Fink, 314-5.

40. Walter Ullmann, *A Short History of the Papacy in the Middle Ages* (1972; Reprint, New York: Methuen and Co., 1982), 240-1.

41. Ibid., 245.

42. Mollat, 34.

43. Mollat, 35.

44. Fink, 316-8.

45. Mollat, 37.

46. Fink, 324.

47. Mollat, 38.

48. Renouard, 86-7. N. B. Based on his premises, Renouard's totals seem somewhat inflated. However, the 3,000 number does correspond with other projections found elsewhere.

49. Fink, 323-4.

50. Mollat, 44.

51. Ibid., 45.

52. Renouard, 52-3.

53. Fink, 326.

54. Mollat, 56.

55. Ibid.

56. Renouard, 59.

57. Ibid., 60.

58. Ibid., 99.

59. N. B. In March 1870, the Church declared him "Blessed."

60. Mollat, 63.

61. Ibid., 316.

62. Ibid., 310-18; Renouard, 116-22.

63. Renouard, 93.

64. Ibid., 117.

65. Mollat, 341.

66. Ibid., 322-3.

67. Ibid., 321-2.

68. Fink, 343-4.

69. Mollat, 331.

70. Fink, 344.

71. Ibid., 402.

72. Walter Ullmann, *The Origins of the Great Schism* (London: Burns Oates and Washbourne Ltd., 1948), 29.

73. Ibid., 52.

74. Ibid., 54.

75. Ibid., 9-43; Fink, 401-6.

76. Fink, 402.

77. Ullmann, *The Origins of the Great Schism*, 96-7.

78. Ibid., 96.

79. Fink, 418.

80. Ibid.

81. Ibid., 422.

82. See J. Gill, "The Fifth Session of the Council of Constance," *The Heythrop Journal*, 5, 2 (April 1964): 131-2; Ullmann, *The Origins of the Great Schism*, 172.

83. Fink, 423.

84. Brian Tierney, *Foundations of the Conciliar Theory* (Cambridge: University Press, 1955), 3.

85. Ibid., 53.

86. Ibid., 55.

87. Ullmann, *The Origins of the Great Schism*, 177.

88. Ibid., 179.

89. Ibid., 181.

90. Tierney, *Foundations of the Conciliar Theory*, 102.

91. Ibid., 141-2.

92. Ibid., 105.

93. Iserloh, 366-7.

94. Marsilius of Padua, *Defensor Pacis*, trans. and introduction Alan Gewirth (Toronto: University of Toronto Press, 1992), xxvii.

95. Ibid., 302.

96. Fink, 451.

97. Alberigo et al., *405.

98. Fink, 451-2.

99. Alberigo et al., 407.

100. Ibid., *409.

101. Antony Black, *Council and Commune: The conciliar movement and the fifteenth-century heritage* (London: Burns and Oates, 1979), 8.

102. Fink, 454.

103. Alberigo et al., *408.

104. Ibid., *420; *435.

105. Ibid., *439.

106. Ibid.

107. Ibid., *438-9.

108. Ibid., *444.

109. Fink, 466.

110. Alberigo et al., 403.

111. Fink, 466.

112. Brian Tierney, "Hermeneutics and History: The Problem of *Haec Sancta*," reprinted in *Church Law and Constitutional Thought in the Middle Ages* (London: Variorum Reprints, 1979), 361.

113. Ibid., 360.

114. Ibid., 366.

115. Brian Tierney, "Divided Sovereignty at Constance: A Problem of Medieval and Early Modern Political Theory," reprinted in *Church Law and Constitutional Thought in the Middle Ages*, 244.

116. Tierney, "Hermeneutics and History," 369.

117. Tierney, "Divided Sovereignty at Constance," 242.

118. Barraclough, 172.

119. Fink, 471.

120. Ibid., 473.

121. Black, 30-1.

122. Ibid., 33.

123. Ibid., 29.

124. Ibid., 32-3.

125. Alberigo et al., *456.

126. Fink, 476.

127. Alberigo et al., *473.

128. Black, 41.

129. Fink, 475-6.

130. Alberigo et al., *533.

131. Black, 47.

132. Fink, 481.

133. George Ostrogorsky, *History of the Byzantine State*, trans. Joan Hussey (1952; Reprint, New Brunswick: Rutgers University Press, 1969), 563.

134. Ibid.

135. Alberigo et al., *528.

136. Ibid., *559.

137. Ibid., *591, note 1.

138. Fink, 482.

139. *Church and State through the Centuries*, trans. and ed. Ehler and Morrall (New York: Biblio and Tannen, 1967), 112-21.

140. Fink, 485.

141. Ibid., 487.

142. Margaret Aston, *The Fifteenth Century: The Prospect of Europe* (New York: W. W. Norton and Co., 1979), 31.

143. Andrew Wheatcroft, *The Ottomans* (New York: Viking, 1993), 23.

144. Ibid., 24.

145. Ullmann, *A Short History of the Papacy in the Middle Ages*, 314.

146. Fink, 536.

147. *Church and State through the Centuries*, 132-3.

148. Fink, 543.

149. Ullmann, *A Short History of the Papacy in the Middle Ages*, 317.

150. Fink, 547.

151. Ibid.

152. Ullmann, *A Short History of the Papacy in the Middle Ages*, 322.

153. Fink, 548.

154. Ibid., 549.

155. Joseph Lortz, *The Reformation. A Problem for Today*, trans. John Dwyer (Westminster, MD: Newman Press, 1964), 167.

156. Fink, 556-7.

157. Hubert Jedin, *A History of the Council of Trent*, Vol. 1, trans. Ernest Graf (London: Thomas Nelson and Sons Ltd., 1957), 92.

158. Fink, 559.

159. Jedin, 94-5.

160. Ibid., 95.

161. Ibid.

162. Ibid.

163. John Bartlett, ed. *Familiar Quotations*, 13th ed. (Boston: Little, Brown and Co., 1955), 335a, note 1.

164. Tierney, "Divided Sovereignty at Constance," 244.

165. Alberigo, 593.

166. Ibid.

167. Ibid., *618.

7. The Evolution of Papal Absolutism

1. Francesco Guicciardini, *The History of Italy*, ed. and trans. Sidney Alexander (Princeton: Princeton University Press, 1984), 361-2.

2. Giuseppe Alberigo et al., *Decrees of the Ecumenical Councils*, Vol. 1, (Washington, DC: Georgetown University Press, 1990), 593; K.A. Fink, *History of the Church*, Vol. 4, ed. H. Jedin and J. Dolan (New York: Crossroad, 1986), 564.

3. Heiko A. Oberman, *Luther* (New Haven: Yale University Press, 1989), 187.

4. Joseph Lortz, *How the Reformation Came*, trans. Otto M. Knab (New York: Herder and Herder, 1964), 95.

5. Ludwig Hertling, *A History of the Catholic Church*, trans. A.G. Biggs (London: Peter Owen Limited, 1958), 350.

6. A.G. Dickens, *The Counter Reformation* (New York: W.W. Norton, 1968), 95-6.

7. Erwin Iserloh, *History of the Church*, Vol. 5, ed. H. Jedin and J. Dolan (New York: Crossroad, 1990), 241.

8. John C. Olin, *Catholic Reform from Cardinal Ximenes to the Council of Trent 1495-1563* (New York: Fordham University Press, 1990), 64-79.

9. Oberman, 14.

10. Ibid., 22.

11. Ibid., 38.

12. Ibid., 39.

13. Ibid., 203.

14. Leon Cristiani, *The Revolt against the Church*, trans. R.F. Trevett, *The Twentieth Century Encyclopedia of Catholicism*, Vol. 78, ed. Henri Daniel-Rops (New York: Hawthorn Books, 1962), 68.

15. Bernhard Lohse, *Martin Luther, An Introduction to His Life and Work*, trans. Robert

C. Schultz (Philadelphia: Fortress Press, 1986), 50.

16. Ibid., 69.

17. Ibid., 36.

18. Iserloh, 295.

19. Ibid., 278.

20. Hubert Jedin, *History of the Church*, Vol. 5, ed. H. Jedin and J. Dolan (New York: Crossroad, 1990), 457.

21. A. Michel, "Concile de Trent," *Dictionnaire de Theologie Catholique*, Vol. 15 (Paris: Librairie Letouzey et Ane, 1947), Part 1, col. 1416.

22. Ibid., col. 1432.

23. Alberigo et al., *663.

24. Ibid., *664.

25. Ibid., *667.

26. Paul Althaus, *The Theology of Martin Luther*, trans. Robert C. Schultz (Philadelphia: Fortress Press, 1966), 153.

27. Ibid., 227.

28. Alberigo et al., *673.

29. Michel, Part 1, col. 1438.

30. Alberigo et al., *682-3.

31. Ibid., *687.

32. Ibid.

33. Ibid., *688.

34. Ibid., *689.

35. Jedin, 473.

36. Ibid., 475.

37. Alberigo et al., *693.

38. Ibid., *695.

39. Althaus, 346.

40. Alberigo et al., *712.

41. Leon Cristiani, *L'Église à l'époque du concile de Trente*, *Histoire de Église*, Vol. 17, ed. A. Fliche and V. Martin (Paris: Bloud and Gay, 1948), 114.

42. Jedin, 483.

43. Ibid., 485.

44. Iserloh, 298.

45. Ibid., 299.

46. Jedin, 489.

47. Ibid., 490.

48. Michel, Part 1, col. 1456.

49. Alberigo et al., *726-7.

50. Cristiani, *The Revolt against the Church*, 126.

51. Alberigo et al., *728-31.

52. Ibid., *731.

53. Ibid., *733.

54. Ibid., *734-5.

55. Ibid., *741.

56. Jedin, 493-4.

57. Alberigo et al., *743.

58. Ibid., *749-50.

59. Ibid., *750.

60. Ibid., *751.

61. Ibid., *760.

62. Ibid., *784.

63. Ibid., *795.

64. Ibid., *796-7

65. Ibid., *797.

66. Ibid., *798.

67. Ibid.

68. Dickens, 109.

69. Ibid., 129.

70. Ibid., 133.

71. Lortz, 110-11.

72. Geoffrey Barraclough, *The Medieval Papacy* (New York: W.W. Norton and Co., 1968), 135.

73. Ibid., 138.

74. Owen Chadwick, *The Reformation* (New York: Viking Penguin, 1986), 108.

75. Ibid., 109.

76. Jedin, 522-3.

77. Ibid., 531.

78. Chadwick, *The Reformation*, 154-5.

79. Ibid., 167.

80. Michel, Part 1, cols. 1488-89.

81. Ibid., 1490.

82. Ibid.

83. Ibid., 1491.

84. Ibid., 1492-3.

85. Jedin, 500.

86. Berard L. Marthaler, *The Catechism Yesterday and Today* (Collegeville, MN: The Liturgical Press, 1995), 36.

87. Jedin, 517.

88. Dickens, 135.

89. Jedin, 504.

90. Ibid.

91. Marcel Pacault, *L' Epoque Moderne*, Tome 15, Vol. 1, *Histoire du Droit et des Institutions de l' Eglise en Occident*, ed. G. Le Bras and J. Gaudemet (Paris: Editions Cujas, 1976), 195.

92. Ibid., 200.

93. H. Outram Evennett, *The Spirit of the Counter-Reformation* (Notre Dame: University of Notre Dame Press, 1986), 119.

94. Jedin, 504.

95. Dickens, 143.

96. Jedin, 506.

97. Ibid., 508. Urban VII (1590); Gregory XIV (1590-91); Innocent IX (1591).

98. Henri Rondet, *The Grace of Christ*, ed. and trans. Tad W. Guzie (Westminster, MD: Newman Press, 1966), 310-11.

99. Ibid., 320.

100. Ibid.

101. Jedin, 542-3.

102. Rondet, 326.

103. Jedin, 545. (That is, since the Christological controversies of the first millennium.)

104. Cristiani, *The Revolt against the Church*, 132.

105. Evennett, 122-3.

106. Hertling, 440-1.

107. Kurt Aland, *A History of Christianity*, Vol. 2, trans. James L. Schaaf (Philadelphia: Fortress Press, 1986), 208-19.

108. Rondet, 344-5.

109. Louis Cognet, *History of the Church*, Vol. 6, ed. H. Jedin and J. Dolan (New York: Crossroad, 1989), 41.

110. Jedin, 631.

111. Ibid., 628.

112. H. Denzinger and A. Schönmetzer, *Enchiridion Symbolorum*, 32nd ed. (Frieburg: Herder, 1963), 2021-65.

113. Hertling, 444.

114. Denzinger and Schönmetzer, 2101-67.

115. Burkhart Schneider, *History of the Church*, Vol. 6, ed. H. Jedin and J. Dolan (New York: Crossroad, 1989), 123.

116. *Documents of the Christian Church*, 2d ed., ed. H. Bettenson (London: Oxford University Press, 1963), 270-1.

117. Oliver Bernier, *Louis XIV, A Royal Life* (New York: Doubleday, 1987), 214-5.

118. Ibid., 232.

119. Schneider, 118.

120. Denzinger and Schönmetzer, 2301-32.

121. Schneider, 128.

122. Bernier, 267.

123. Owen Chadwick, *The Popes and European Revolution* (Oxford: Clarendon Press, 1981), 274-5.

124. Rondet, 350-1.

125. Ibid., 351.

126. See the interesting study by Jacques Gres-Gayer, "The *Unigenitus* of Clement XI: A Fresh Look at the Issues," *Theological Studies* (June 1988): 259-82.

127. Chadwick, *The Popes and European Revolution*, 282.

128. Cognet, 381-2.

129. Chadwick, *The Popes and European Revolution*, 284.

130. Ibid., 288.

131. Charles Lefebvre and L. Chevailler, *L' Epoque Moderne*, Tome 15, Vol. 1, *Histoire du Droit et des Institutions de l' Eglise en Occident*, ed. G. Le Bras and J. Gaudemet (Paris: Editions Cujas, 1976), 123.

132. Ibid., 125.

133. Chadwick, *The Popes and European Revolution*, 76.

134. Schneider, 568.

135. Ludwig Pastor, *The History of the Popes from the Close of the Middle Ages*, Vol. 35, *Benedict XIV*, trans. E.F. Peeler (St. Louis: B. Herder, 1961), 297.

136. Ibid., 358.

137. Ibid., 379.

138. Ibid., 383.

139. Ibid., 381-2.

140. Ibid., 442.

141. Schneider, 571.

142. K. Bihlmeyer and H. Tüchle, *Church History*, Vol. 3, trans. V. Mills and F. Muller (Westminster, MD: Newman Press, 1966), 268.

143. Aland, 296.

144. Schneider, 578.

145. Bihlmeyer and Tüchle, 269-70.

146. E.E.Y. Hales, *Revolution and Papacy 1769-1846* (Garden City, NY: Hanover House, 1960), 43.

147. Ibid., 44.

148. Chadwick, *The Popes and European Revolution*, 408.

149. Ibid., 409.

150. Ibid., 417.

151. Ibid., 572.

152. Bihlmeyer and Tüchle, 283-4.

153. Hales, *Revolution and Papacy 1769-1846*, 69.

154. *Church and State Through the Centuries*, trans. and ed. S. Ehler and J. Morrall (New York: Biblio and Tannen, 1967), 237.

155. Ibid., 238.

156. Hales, *Revolution and Papacy 1769-1846*, 88.

157. Chadwick, *The Popes and European Revolution*, 456.

158. Hales, *Revolution and Papacy 1769-1846*, 115.

159. Roger Aubert, *History of the Church*, Vol. 7, ed. H. Jedin and J. Dolan (New York: Crossroad, 1989), 9.

160. Ibid., 52-3.

161. Gordon Wright, *France in Modern Times*, 5th ed. (New York: W.W. Norton, 1995), 65.

162. Aubert, *History of the Church*, Vol. 7, 57.

163. Chadwick, *The Popes and European Revolution*, 490.

164. Aubert, *History of the Church*, Vol. 7, 59.

165. Hales, *Revolution and Papacy 1769-1846*, 171.

166. Wright, 78.

167. Ibid., 93.

168. Chadwick, *The Popes and European Revolution*, 503-4.

169. Hales, *Revolution and Papacy 1769-1846*, 235.

170. Ibid., 243-4.

171. Aland, 310.

172. Chadwick, *The Popes and European Revolution*, 540-1.

173. Aubert, *History of the Church*, Vol. 7, 95.

174. Chadwick, *The Popes and European Revolution*, 570.

175. Aubert, *History of the Church*, Vol. 7, 98.

176. Hales, *Revolution and Papacy 1769-1846*, 265.

177. Denis Mack Smith, *The Making of Italy 1796-1866* (Reissue, New York: Holmes and Meier, 1988), 64.

178. Aubert, *History of the Church*, Vol. 7, 286.

179. *Papal Encyclicals*, Vol. 1, 1740-1878, ed. Claudia Carlen Ihm (Ann Arbor, MI: The Pierian Press, 1990), 235(1).

180. Ibid., 236 (5).

181. Ibid., 238 (14,15).

182. Ibid., 239 (20).

183. Ibid., 250 (6).

184. Aubert, *History of the Church*, Vol. 7, 204.

185. Bihlmeyer and Tüchle, 320.

186. E.E.Y. Hales, *Pio Nono* (New York: P.J. Kenedy and Sons, 1954), 33.

187. Aubert, *History of the Church*, Vol. 8, 59.

188. Wright, 127.

189. Aubert, *History of the Church*, Vol. 8, 62.

190. Bihlmeyer and Tüchle, 322.

191. See Brian Tierney, *Origins of Papal Infallibility 1150-1350* (Leiden: E.J. Brill, 1972), 273-81.

192. Hales, *Pio Nono*, 258.

193. J. Hajjar, "The Eastern Churches," *The Church in a Secularized Society*, Roger Aubert with P.E. Crunican, John Tracy Ellis et al., *The Christian Centuries*, Vol. 5 (New York: Paulist Press, 1978), 455.

194. Ibid., 461-2.

195. Roger Aubert et al., *The Church in a Secularized Society: The Christian Centuries*, Vol. 5 (New York: Paulist Press, 1978), 4.

196. Klaus Schatz, *Papal Primacy*, trans. J. Otto and L. Maloney (Collegeville, MN: The Liturgical Press, 1996), 154.

8. The Installation of the Absolutist Model

1. Dom C. Butler, *The Vatican Council, 1869-70*, ed. Christopher Butler (Westminster, MD: Newman Press, 1962), 71-2.

2. Ibid., 92.

3. E. Amann, "Concile du Vatican," *Dictionnaire de Theologie Catholique*, Vol. 15 (Paris: Librarie Letouzey et Ané, 1947), Part 2, col. 2562.

4. J. Hennesey, S.J., "Catholicism in an American Environment," *Theological Studies*, (Dec. 1989):674.

5. Butler, 145.

6. Yves Congar, *L'Èglise de saint Augustin á l'époque moderne* (Paris: Les éditions du Cerf, 1970), 441.

7. Amann, 2549.

8. Butler, 192-4.

9. Ibid., 195.

10. Guiseppe Alberigo et al., *Decrees of the Ecumenical Councils*, Vol. 2 (Washington, DC: Georgetown University Press, 1990), *805-6.

11. Ibid., *806.

12. Ibid., *807.

13. Ibid., *808.

14. Ibid., *809

15. Butler, 294-5.

16. Roger Aubert, *History of the Church*, Vol. 8, ed. H. Jedin and J. Dolan (New York: Crossroad, 1989), 327.

17. Butler, 298-9.

18. Ibid., 315.

19. Ibid., 338.

20. Ibid., 362.

21. Ibid., 352.

22. Ibid., 397.

23. Aubert, *History of the Church*, Vol. 8, 329.

24. Ibid., 329 (#39).

25. Alberigo et al., *816.

26. H. Küng, *The Council, Reform and Reunion* (New York: Sheed and Ward, 1961), 193-201.

27. Congar, *L' Eglise de saint Augustin á l' époque moderne*, 442.

28. Ibid., 443.

29. R. Costigan, S.J., *Rohrbacher and the Ecclesiology of Ultramontanism* (Rome: Universitá Gregoriana Editrice, 1980), 157-68.

30. Yves Congar, "Saint Thomas and the Infallibility of the Papal Magisterium," *The Thomist* (1974): 102.

31. Brian Tierney, *Origins of Papal Infallibility 1150-1350* (Leiden: E. J. Brill, 1972), 280-81. See the review by Alfons Stickler, *Catholic Historical Review* (1974): 427-41, and Tierney's response, *Catholic Historical Review* (1975): 265-79.

32. E.E.Y. Hales, *Pio Nono* (New York: P. J. Kenedy and Sons, 1954), 330.

33. J. Hajjar, *The Christian Centuries*, Vol. 5, ed. R. Aubert et al. (New York: Paulist Press, 1978), 468.

34. O. Köhler, *History of the Church*, Vol. 9, ed. H. Jedin and J. Dolan (New York: Crossroad, 1989), 24-25.

35. *Papal Encyclicals*, Vol. 2, 1878-1903, ed. Claudia Carlen Ihm (Ann Arbor, MI: The Pierian Press, 1990), 388 (#3).

36. Ibid., 389 (#4).

37. Ibid., 391 (#7).

38. Ibid., 396 (#10).

39. Ibid., 398 (#12).

40. Ibid., 400 (#14).

41. Ibid., 402 (#15).

42. Ibid.

43. Ibid., 403 (#15).

44. Ibid., 110 (#12).

45. Ibid., 112 (#24); 114-15 (#35).

46. Ibid., 115 (#35, 36).

47. *Documents of American Catholic History*, Vol. 2, ed. John Tracy Ellis (Wilmington, DE: Michael Glazier, 1987), 537-47.

48. Roger Aubert, *History of the Church*, Vol. 9, ed. H. Jedin and J. Dolan (New York: Crossroad, 1989), 385.

49. Gordon Wright, *France in Modern Times*, 5th ed. (New York: W. W. Norton, 1995), 250.

50. *Papal Encyclicals*, Vol. 3, 1903-37, 46 (#3).

51. Ibid., 47-8 (#8).

52. A. von Harnack, *What Is Christianity?* trans. T.B. Saunders (Philadelphia: Fortress Press, 1986), xv-xviii.

53. A. Loisy, *The Gospel and the Church*, ed. B.B. Scott (Philadelphia: Fortress Press, 1976), 171.

54. Aubert, *History of the Church*, Vol. 9, 468.

55. Ibid., 470.

56. Alec Vidler, *The Modernist Movement in the Roman Church* (Cambridge: Cambridge University Press, 1934), 217-18.

57. Ibid., 218.

58. Benedict XV's first encyclical, *Ad beatissimi apostolorum*, of November 1914 attempted to soften the harshness of the anti-modernist attacks of his predecessor's regime.

59. Klaus Schatz, *Papal Primacy*, trans. J. Otto and L. Maloney (Collegeville, MN: The Liturgical Press, 1996), 180.

60. Hubert Jedin, *History of the Church*, Vol. 10, ed. H. Jedin and J. Dolan (New York: Crossroad, 1989), 25.

61. *Church and State through the Centuries*, ed. S. Ehler and J. Morrall (New York: Biblio and Tannen, 1967), 382-407.

62. Ibid., 385.

63. *Papal Encyclicals*, Vol. 3, 1903-37, 233 (#41).

64. Ibid., 234 (#48).

65. Ibid., 235 (#51).

66. Ibid., 315 (#7).

67. Ibid., 317 (#10).

68. Ibid., 317-18 (#11).

69. Hajjar, 503.

70. Ibid., 508.

71. Ibid., 483.

72. Yves Congar, *Lay People in the Church*, trans. D. Attwater (Westminster, MD: Newman Press, 1967), 362.

73. Roger Aubert, *The Church in a Secularized Society. The Christian Centuries*, Vol. 5 (New York: Paulist Press, 1978), 567.

74. *Papal Encyclicals*, Vol. 4, 1939-1958, 39-40 (#13).

75. Ibid., 58 (#103).

76. Ibid., 45 (#41).

77. Ibid., 45 (#44).

78. Ibid., 49 (#62).

79. For example, see J. Salaverri, S.J., in the *Summa Sacrae Theologiae*, Vol. 1 (Madrid: Biblioteca de Autores Christianos, 1950), 497-925.

80. See H. de Lubac's *At the Service of the Church* (San Francisco: Communio Books, 1993), 60-96; and T. O'Meara's "Raid on the Dominicans," *America* (Feb. 5, 1994): 8-16.

81. *Papal Encylicals*, Vol. 4, 1939-1958, 177 (#14).

82. Ibid., 180 (#30).

83. Hajjar, 517.

84. Julius Döpfner, *The Questioning Church* (Montreal: Palm Publishers, 1964), 2.

85. Ibid., 3-4.

86. Aubert, *The Christian Centuries*, Vol. 5, 625.

87. *The Documents of Vatican II*. gen. ed. W. M. Abbott (New York: Herder and Herder, 1966), 705.

88. Ibid., 712.

89. Ibid., 713.

90. Ibid., 714.

91. Ibid., 715.

92. Peter Hebblethwaite, *Paul VI, the First Modern Pope* (New York: Paulist Press, 1993), 329.

93. Ibid., 331.

94. Jedin, 117.

95. *The Documents of Vatican II*, 144.

96. Ibid., 150 (#36, #3).

97. Hebblethwaite, *Paul VI*, 357.

98. Ibid., 400-01.

99. *The Documents of Vatican II*, 43.

100. Ibid., 44 (#22).

101. Ibid., 45 (#23).

102. Ibid., 46 (#23).

103. Ibid.

104. Ibid., 46 (#25).

105. Ibid., 52 (#27).

106. Ibid., 98-101.

107. Ibid., 345-6 (#3).

108. Ibid., 23 (#8).

109. Ibid., 374 (#2).

110. Ibid., 378 (#9).

111. Timothy Ware, *The Orthodox Church* (1963; New Edition, New York: Penguin Books, 1993), 315-16.

112. *The Documents of Vatican II*, 721.

113. Ibid., 416 (#27).

114. Ibid., 425 (#37).

115. Ibid., 425-6 (#38, 4).

116. Paul VI, *Norms for Implementation of Four Council Decrees. Ecclesiae sanctae*, August 8, 1966 (Washington DC: National Catholic Welfare Conference, 1966), 26 (#41,1); 15-16 (#16).

117. *The Documents of Vatican II*, 491-2 (#2).

118. Jedin, 145.

119. *The Documents of Vatican II*, 673.

120. Ibid.

121. Aubert, *The Christian Centuries*, Vol. 5, 637.

122. *Papal Encyclicals*, Vol. 5, 1958-78, 138 (#18).

123. Ibid., 144 (#42).

124. Ibid., 151 (#75).

125. Ibid., 152 (#78).

126. Ibid., 159 (#117).

127. *Vatican Council II*, Vol. 2, gen. ed. A. Flannery (Northport, NY: Costello Publishing Co., 1982), 285-317.

128. Robert McClory, *Turning Point* (New York: Crossroad, 1995), 113-14.

129. *Papal Encyclicals*, Vol. 5, 1958-1978, 224 (#26).

130. Ibid., 226 (#11).

131. Ibid., 226-27 (#14).

132. Ibid., 232 (#29).

133. McClory, 145.

134. Richard McCormick, "The Silence Since *Humanae Vitae*," *America* (July 21, 1973): 31.

135. *The Documents of Vatican II*, 720-4.

136. *Code of Canon Law, Latin-English Edition* (Washington, DC: Canon Law Society of America, 1984), XXI.

137. *Vatican Council II*, 695-710.

138. Ibid., 711-12.

139. Ibid., 711-61.

140. Berard Marthaler, *The Catechism Yesterday and Today* (Collegeville, MN: The

Liturgical Press, 1995), 135.

141. Ibid.

142. *Vatican Council II*, 762-814.

143. Yves Congar, *Diversity and Communion* (Mystic, CT: Twenty-Third Publications, 1985), 88.

144. John Cornwell, *A Thief in the Night* (London: Viking, 1989), 9.

145. C. Bernstein and M. Politi, *His Holiness* (New York: Doubleday, 1996), 162.

146. Peter Hebblethwaite, *Synod Extraordinary* (New York: Doubleday, 1986), 16.

147. Ibid., 22-23.

148. Karol Wojtyla (John Paul II), *Sources of Renewal*, trans. Wm. Collins Sons & Co. (San Francisco: Harper and Row, 1980), 420.

149. Bernard Häring, "The Curran Case," *The Church in Anguish*, ed. Hans Küng and Leonard Swidler (San Francisco: Harper and Row, 1987), 245.

150. Ibid., 246.

151. Bernard Häring, *My Witness for the Church* (New York: Paulist Press, 1992), 184.

152. James Coriden, "Highlights of the Revised Code," *The Jurist* (1984): 28-29.

153. Francis Morrisey, "Is the New Code an Improvement for the Law of the Church?" *Concilium*, #185, ed. J. Provost and K. Walf (Edinburgh: T. and T. Clark Ltd., 1986), 40.

154. See P. Huizing, "The Central Legal System and Autonomous Churches," *Concilium*, #185, ed. J. Provost and K. Walf (Edinburgh: T. and T. Clark Ltd., 1986), 23-27; P. Huizing, "Subsidiarity," *Concilium*, #188, ed. G. Alberigo and J. Provost (Edinburgh: T. and T. Clark Ltd., 1986), 118-23.

155. *The Documents of Vatican II*, 46.

156. Ibid.

157. "Contretemps over Contraception," *Time* (Oct. 13, 1980): 74.

158. John Paul II, "The Pope's Closing Synod Homily," *Origins*, 10, 21 (Nov. 6, 1980): 327-8.

159. *Vatican Council II*, 815-98.

160. Aloisio Lorscheider, "Evaluating Synods Themselves," *Origins*, 20, 19 (Oct. 18, 1990): 309.

161. Ibid., 309.

162. Godfried Danneels, "Cardinal Daneels: An Overview," *Origins*, 15, 26 (December 12, 1985): 427-9.

163. "Synod of Bishops: The Final Report," *Origins*, 15, 27 (Dec. 19, 1985): 444-50.

164. John Paul II's *motu proprio* of July 23, 1998, on the theological and juridical nature of episcopal conferences gives a rather restrictive interpretation to the institution of regional episcopal collegiality which was such a critical part of the fabric of the Church in the early centuries. Paragraph 23 of Vatican II's *Lumen gentium* seems to reflect a rather different spirit.

165. Ibid., 449. See Pius XII's Allocution of Feb. 20, 1946, *Acta Apostolicae Sedis* (April 1, 1946), 144-5.

166. *Catechism of the Catholic Church* (Mahwah, NJ: Paulist Press, 1994).

167. Norbert Greinacher, "Catholic Identity in the Third Epoch of Church History," *Catholic Identity. Concilium 1994/1995*, ed. J. Provost and K. Walf (London: SCM Books, 1994), 10.

168. Avery Dulles, S. J., "Books on the New Catechism," *America* (October 22, 1994):22.

169. Richard P. McBrien, "Teaching the Truth," *The Christian Century* (October 20, 1993): 1005.

170. Quoted in Richard A. McCormick's "Some Early Reactions to *Veritatis Splendor*,"

Theological Studies, 55, 3 (September 1994): 489.

171. Ibid., 505-6.

172. John Paul II, *Ordinatio Sacerdotalis*, #4, Apostolic Letter, *National Catholic Reporter* (June 17, 1994): 7.

173. Pontifical Biblical Commission. "Can Women Be Priests?" *Origins*, 6, 6 (July 1, 1976): 96.

174. Congregation for the Doctrine of the Faith, "Vatican Declaration: Women in the Ministerial Priesthood," *Origins*, 6, 33 (Feb. 3, 1977): 522. It should be noted that the same congregation—about eighteen months after the publication of John Paul II's *Ordinatio sacerdotalis*—issued a statement affirming that "the doctrine excluding the ordination of women to the priesthood pertains to the deposit of faith and that it has been infallibly taught by the universal and ordinary magisterium." See Francis Sullivan's comments in *America*, December 9, 1995, 5-6. Father Sullivan stated that it is not clear how the congregation came to the conclusion that this exclusion of women pertains to the deposit of faith, and then he added the following:

The statement of the C.D.F. to this effect is not infallible, because, even published with papal approval, it remains the statement of the congregation, to which the Pope cannot communicate his prerogative of infallibility (6).

However, John Paul II's *Ad tuendam fidem* does seem to make a firm case for the irreformability of *Ordinatio sacerdotalis*. It is for the theologians to determine if and to what extent *Ad tuendam fidem* enlarges the infallible teaching prerogative of the Roman pontiff over the presentation of the subject in chapter 4 of the dogmatic constitution, *Pastor aeternus* of Vatican I (D.S. 3065-75), and in #25 of Vatican II's *Lumen gentium*.

175. Peter Hebblethwaite, " 'Secret' Criteria Set Bishops' Appointments," *National Catholic Reporter* (Feb. 4, 1994): 14. N.B. Italics mine.

176. Peter Hebblethwaite, *Synod Extraordinary*, 21-25.

177. John Paul II, *Crossing the Threshold of Hope* (New York: Alfred A. Knopf, 1994).

178. John Paul II, *Redeemer of Man*, Encyclical Letter, March 4, 1979 (Washington, DC: U.S. Catholic Conference, 1979).

179. Avery Dulles, S.J., "The Prophetic Humanism of John Paul II," *America* (Oct. 23, 1993):7.

180. John Paul II, *The Splendor of Truth*, Encyclical Letter, August 6, 1993 (Washington, DC: U.S. Catholic Conference, 1993), 112-16.

Epilogue

1. Roger Aubert et al., *The Church in a Secularized Society. The Christian Centuries*, Vol. 5 (New York: Paulist Press, 1978), 637.

2. George A. Lindbeck, *The Future of Roman Catholic Theology* (Philadelphia: Fortress Press, 1969), 3.

3. Ibid., 4.

4. John Paul II, *That They May Be One*, Encyclical Letter, May 25, 1995 (Washington, DC: U. S. Catholic Conference, 1995), 106.

5. Ibid., 107.

Bibliography

Aland, Kurt. *A History of Christianity*. Vol. II. Translated by James L. Schaaf. Philadelphia: Fortress Press, 1986.

Alberigo, G., et al. *Decrees of the Ecumenical Councils*. Vols. I and II. Nicea I—Vatican II. English editor, N. Tanner. Washington, DC: Georgetown University Press, 1990.

Alberigo, Guiseppe, and A. Weiler, editors. *Election and Consensus in the Church*. Concilium Series, Vol. 77. New York: Herder and Herder, 1972.

Altaner, Berthold. *Patrology*. Translated by Hilda C. Graef. New York: Herder and Herder, 1960.

Althaus, Paul. *The Theology of Martin Luther*. Translated by Robert C. Schultz. Philadelphia: Fortress Press, 1966.

Amann, E. "Concile du Vatican." *Dictionnaire de Theologie Catholique*. Vol. XV. Paris: Librarie Letouzey et Ane, 1947.

The Ante-Nicene Fathers. Vol. I. Edited by A. Roberts and J. Donaldson. American Reprint of Edinburgh Edition. Grand Rapids: Eerdmans, 1989.

The Ante-Nicene Fathers. Vol. VII. Edited by A. Roberts and J. Donaldson. New York: Charles Scribner's Sons, 1926.

The Apostolic Fathers. 2d ed. Translated by J. B. Lightfoot and J. R. Harmer. Edited and revised by Michael W. Holmes. Grand Rapids: Baker Book House, 1989.

Aston, Margaret. *The Fifteenth Century: The Prospect of Europe*. New York: W. W. Norton and Co., 1979.

Aubert, Roger. *History of the Church*. Vol. VIII. Edited by H. Jedin and J. Dolan. New York: Crossroad, 1989.

Aubert, Roger, et al. *The Church in a Secularized Society*. The Christian Centuries. Vol. V. New York: Paulist Press, 1978.

Barraclough, Geoffrey. *The Medieval Papacy*. New York: W.W. Norton and Co., 1968.

———. *The Origins of Modern Germany*. New York: W. W. Norton and Co., 1984.

Bartlett, David L. *Ministry in the New Testament*. Minneapolis: Fortress Press, 1993.

Bartlett, John, editor. *Familiar Quotations*. 13th ed. Boston: Little, Brown and Co., 1955.

Baus, Karl. *From the Apostolic Community to Constantine*. History of the Church. Vol. I. Edited by H. Jedin and J. Dolan. Tunbridge Wells: Burns and Oates, 1980.

Bernard of Clairvaux. *Five Books on Consideration*. Translated by J. Anderson and E. Kennan. Kalamazoo, MI: Cistercian Publications, 1976.

Bernier, Olivier. *Louis XIV. A Royal Life*. New York: Doubleday, 1987.

Bernstein, Carl, and Marco Politi. *His Holiness*. New York: Doubleday, 1996.

Bihlmeyer, K., and H. Tüchle. *Church History*. Vol III. Translated by V. Mills and F. Muller. Westminster, MD: Newman Press, 1966.

Black, Anthony. *Council and Commune. The conciliar movement and the fifteenth-century heritage.* London: Burns and Oates, 1979.

Boase, T. S. R. *Boniface VIII.* London: Constable and Co. Ltd., 1933.

The Book of Pontiffs (Liber Pontificalis). Translated by Raymond Davis. Liverpool: Liverpool University Press, 1989.

Brown, Raymond E. *The Churches the Apostles Left Behind.* New York: Paulist Press, 1984.

———. *The Community of the Beloved Disciple.* New York: Paulist Press, 1979.

Brown, Raymond E., and John P. Meier. *Antioch and Rome.* New York: Paulist Press, 1983.

Butler, Dom C. *The Vatican Council 1869-70.* Edited by Christopher Butler. Westminster, MD: Newman Press, 1962.

Campenhausen, Hans von. *Ecclesiastical Authority and Spiritual Power in the Church of the First Three Centuries.* Translated by J. A. Baker. Stanford: Stanford University Press, 1969.

Catechism of the Catholic Church. Mahwah, NJ: Paulist Press, 1994.

The Catholic Study Bible. General editor, Donald Senior. New York: Oxford University Press, 1990.

Chadwick, Henry. *The Early Church.* New York: Dorset Press, 1986.

Chadwick, Owen. *The Popes and European Revolution.* Oxford: Clarendon Press, 1981.

———. *The Reformation.* New York: Viking Penguin, 1986.

Cheney, Christopher. *Pope Innocent III and England.* Stuttgart: Anton Hiersemann, 1976.

Church and State through the Centuries. Translated and edited by S. Ehler and J. Morrall. New York: Biblio and Tannen, 1967.

Code of Canon Law, Latin-English Edition. Washington, DC: Canon Law Society of America, 1984.

Congar, Yves. *After Nine Hundred Years.* New York: Fordham University Press, 1959.

———. *Diversity and Communion.* Mystic, CT: Twenty-Third Publications, 1985.

———. *L'Ecclésiologie du haut moyen age.* Paris: Les éditions du Cerf, 1968.

———. *L'Église de saint Augustin á l'époque moderne.* Paris: Les éditions du Cerf, 1970.

———. *Lay People in the Church.* Translated by D. Attwater. Westminster, MD: Newman Press, 1967.

———. "Reception as an Ecclesiastical Reality." *Concilium,* Vol. 77. New York: Herder and Herder, 1972.

———. "Saint Thomas and the Infallibility of the Papal Magisterium." *The Thomist* (1974): 102.

Congregation for the Doctrine of the Faith. "Vatican Declaration: Women in the Ministerial Priesthood." *Origins* 6, 33 (February 3, 1977): 517-531.

"Contretemps over Contraception." *Time* (October 13, 1980): 74.

Coriden, James. "Highlights of the Revised Code." *The Jurist* (1984): 28-29.

Cornwell, John. *A Thief in the Night.* London: Viking, 1989.

The Correspondence of Pope Gregory VII. Translated with Introduction by Ephraim Emerton, 1932. Reprint, New York: Columbia University Press, 1990.

Costigan, S. J., Richard F. *Rohrbacher and the Ecclesiology of Ultramontanism.* Rome: Universitá Gregoriana Editrice, 1980.

Cristiani, Léon. *L'Église à l'époque du concile de Trente.* Vol. XVII, *Histoire de l'Église.*

Edited by A. Fliche and V. Martin. Paris: Bloud and Gay, 1948.

————. *The Revolt against the Church.* Translated by R. F. Trevett. Vol. 78, *The Twentieth Century Encyclopedia of Catholicism.* Edited by Henri Daniel-Rops. New York: Hawthorn Books, 1962.

Cyprian of Carthage. *The Letters of St. Cyprian of Carthage.* Vol. I. Translated by G. W. Clarke. *Ancient Christian Writers.* No. 43. Edited by J. Quasten et al. New York: Newman Press, 1984.

————. *The Letters of St. Cyprian of Carthage.* Vol. III. Translated by G. W. Clarke. *Ancient Christian Writers.* No. 46. Edited by J. Quasten et al. New York: Newman Press, 1986.

————. *The Letters of St. Cyprian of Carthage.* Vol. IV. Translated by G. W. Clarke. *Ancient Christian Writers.* No. 47. Edited by W. Burghardt and T. Lawler. New York: Newman Press, 1989.

————. *The Unity of the Catholic Church.* Translated by M. Bévenot. *Ancient Christian Writers.* No. 25. Edited by J. Quasten and J. Plumpe. New York: Newman Press, 1956.

Daniélou, J., and H. Marrou. *The First Six Hundred Years. The Christian Centuries.* Vol. I. New York: Paulist Press, 1964.

Danneels, Cardinal Godfried. "Cardinal Danneels: An Overview." *Origins* 15, 26 (December 12, 1985): 427-429.

Denzinger, H., and A. Schönmetzer. *Enchiridion Symbolorum.* 32nd ed. Freiburg: Herder, 1963.

Dickens, A. G. *The Counter Reformation.* New York: W. W. Norton, 1968.

Documents of American Catholic History. Vol. II. Edited by John Tracy Ellis. Wilmington, DE: Michael Glazier, 1987.

Documents of the Christian Church. 2d ed. Edited by Henry Bettenson. London: Oxford University Press, 1963.

The Documents of Vatican II. General editor, W. M. Abbott. New York: Herder and Herder, 1966.

Döpfner, Julius. *The Questioning Church.* Montreal: Palm Publishers, 1964.

Dulles, Avery. "Books on the New Catechism." *America* (October 22, 1994): 21-22.

————. "The Prophetic Humanism of John Paul II." *America* (October 23, 1993):7.

Dunn, James D. G. *Unity and Diversity in the New Testament.* 2d ed. Philadelphia: Trinity Press International, 1990.

Eusebius. *The History of the Church.* Translated by G. A. Williamson. New York: Dorset Press, 1965.

Evennett, H. Outram. *The Spirit of the Counter-Reformation.* Notre Dame: University of Notre Dame Press, 1986.

Frend, W. H. C. *The Rise of Christianity.* Philadelphia: Fortress Press, 1984.

Gill, Joseph. *The Council of Florence.* Cambridge: Cambridge University Press, 1959.

————. "The Fifth Session of the Council of Constance." *The Heythrop Journal* 5, 2 (April 1964): 131-143.

Greinacher, Norbert. "Catholic Identity in the Third Epoch of Church History." *Catholic Identity. Concilium 1994/1995.* Editors, J. Provost and K. Walf. London: SCM Books, 1994.

Gres-Gayer, Jacques. "The *Unigenitus* of Clement XI: A Fresh Look at the Issues." *Theological Studies* (June 1988): 259-282.

Guicciardini, Francesco. *The History of Italy*. Edited and translated by Sidney Alexander. Princeton: Princeton University Press, 1984.

Hajjar, J. *The Christian Centuries*. Vol V. Edited by Roger Aubert et al. New York: Paulist Press, 1978.

Hales, E. E. Y. *Pio Nono*. New York: P. J. Kenedy and Sons, 1954.

———. *Revolution and Papacy 1769-1846*. Garden City, NY: Hanover House, 1960.

Häring, Bernard. "The Curran Case." *The Church in Anguish*. Editors, Hans Küng and Leonard Swidler. San Francisco: Harper and Row, 1987.

———. *My Witness for the Church*. New York: Paulist Press, 1992.

Harnack, Adolf von. *What Is Christianity?* Translated by T. B. Saunders. Philadelphia: Fortress Press, 1986.

Hebblethwaite, Peter. *Paul VI, the First Modern Pope*. New York: Paulist Press, 1993.

———. " 'Secret' Criteria Set Bishops' Appointments." *National Catholic Reporter* (February 4, 1994): 14.

———. *Synod Extraordinary*. New York: Doubleday, 1986.

Hennesey, S. J., "Catholicism in an American Environment." *Theological Studies* (Dec. 1989): 674.

Hertling, Ludwig. *A History of the Catholic Church*. Translated by A. G. Biggs. London: Peter Owen Limited, 1958.

Hess, Hamilton. *The Canons of the Council of Sardica A.D. 343*. Oxford: Clarendon Press, 1958.

Hippolytus of Rome. *The Apostolic Tradition*. 2d ed. Edited by G. Dix. Reissued by H. Chadwick. Ridgefield, CT: Morehouse Publishing, 1992.

Hussey, J. M. *The Orthodox Church in the Byzantine Empire*. Oxford: Clarendon Press, 1986.

Jalland, Trevor. *The Life and Times of St. Leo the Great*. New York: Macmillan, 1941.

Jedin, Hubert. *A History of the Council of Trent*. Vol. I. Translated by Ernest Graf. London: Thomas Nelson and Sons Ltd., 1957.

Jedin, H., and J. Dolan, editors. *History of the Church*. Vols. I-X. New York: Crossroad, 1980-1989.

John Paul II. *Ad Tuendam Fidem*. Apostolic Letter. *Origins* 28, 8 (July 16, 1998): 113-16.

———. *Crossing the Threshold of Hope*. Translation by Alfred A. Knopf, Inc. New York: Alfred A. Knopf, 1994.

———. *On Catholic Universities*. Apostolic Constitution, August 15, 1990. Washington, DC: U.S. Catholic Conference, 1990.

———. *Ordinatio Sacerdotalis*, #4. Apostolic Letter. *National Catholic Reporter* (June 17, 1994): 7.

———. "The Pope's Closing Synod Homily." *Origins* 10, 21 (November 6, 1980): 325-29.

———. *Redeemer of Man*. Encyclical Letter. March 4, 1979. Washington, DC: U.S. Catholic Conference, 1979.

———. *Sources of Renewal*. Translated by Wm. Collins Sons & Co. Ltd. San Francisco: Harper and Row, 1980.

———. *The Splendor of Truth*. Encyclical Letter. August 6, 1993. Washington DC: U.S. Catholic Conference, 1993.

———. *The Theological and Juridical Nature of Episcopal Conferences*. Apostolic Letter. *Origins* 28, 9 (July 30, 1998): 152-58.

————. *That They May Be One*. Encyclical Letter. May 25, 1995. Washington, DC: U. S. Catholic Conference, 1995.

Jones, A. H. M. *The Later Roman Empire 284-602*. Vols. I and II. 1964; Reprints, Baltimore: Johns Hopkins University Press, 1990.

Käsemann, Ernst. *Essays on New Testament Themes*. Translated by W. J. Montague. London: SCM Press, 1964.

Kelly, J. N. D. *The Oxford Dictionary of Popes*. 1986; Reprint, Oxford: Oxford University Press, 1989.

Kingsbury, Jack Dean. *Matthew: Structure, Christology, Kingdom*. Minneapolis: Fortress Press, 1975.

Küng, Hans. *The Council, Reform and Reunion*. New York: Sheed and Ward, 1961.

Kuttner, Stephen. "Cardinals: The History of a Canonical Concept." *Traditio* 3 (1945): 129-214.

Lefebvre, C., M. Pacault, and L. Chevailler. *L' Epoque Moderne*. Tome XV. Vol. I, *Histoire du Droit et des Institutions de l' Eglise en Occident*. Edited by G. LeBras and J. Gaudemet. Paris: Editions Cujas, 1976.

Lindbeck, George A. *The Future of Roman Catholic Theology*. Philadelphia: Fortress Press, 1969.

The Lives of the Eighth-Century Popes (Liber Pontificalis). Translated by Raymond Davis. Liverpool: Liverpool University Press, 1992.

Lohse, Bernhard. *Martin Luther, An Introduction to His Life and Work*. Translated by Robert C. Schultz. Philadelphia: Fortress Press, 1986.

Loisy, Alfred. *The Gospel and the Church*. Edited by Bernard B. Scott. Philadelphia: Fortress Press, 1976.

Lorscheider, Cardinal A. "Evaluating Synods Themselves." *Origins* 20, 19 (October 18, 1990): 308-310.

Lortz, Joseph. *How the Reformation Came*. Translated by Otto M. Knab. New York: Herder and Herder, 1964.

————. *The Reformation. A Problem for Today*. Translated by John Dwyer. Westminster, MD: Newman Press, 1964.

MacMullen, Ramsay. *Christianizing the Roman Empire A.D. 100-400*. New Haven: Yale University Press, 1984.

————. *Roman Social Relations 50 B. C. to A.D. 284*. New Haven: Yale University Press, 1974.

Markus, Robert. *The End of Ancient Christianity*. Cambridge: Cambridge University Press, 1990.

Marsilius of Padua. *Defensor Pacis*. Translation and Introduction by Alan Gewirth. Toronto: University of Toronto Press, 1992.

Marthaler, Berard L. *The Catechism Yesterday and Today*. Collegeville, MN: The Liturgical Press, 1995.

McBrien, Richard P. "Teaching the Truth." *The Christian Century* (October 20, 1993): 1004-5.

McClory, Robert. *Turning Point*. New York: Crossroad, 1995.

McCormick, Richard A. "The Silence Since *Humanae Vitae*." *America* (July 21, 1973): 31.

————. "Some Early Reactions to *Veritatis Splendor*." *Theological Studies* 55, 3 (September 1994): 481-506.

McGrade, A. S. "Two Fifth-Century Conceptions of Papal Primacy." *Studies in Medieval and Renaissance History* 7 (1970): 3-45.

Meeks, Wayne A. *The First Urban Christians*. New Haven: Yale University Press, 1983.

Meyendorff, John. *Imperial Unity and Christian Divisions*. Crestwood, NY: St. Vladimir's Seminary Press, 1989.

Michel, A. "Concile de Trent." *Dictionnaire de Theologie Catholique*. Vol. XV. Paris: Librairie Letouzey et Ane, 1947.

Mollat, G. *The Popes at Avignon 1305-1378*. Translated from ninth French edition by Janet Love. London: Thomas Nelson and Sons Ltd., 1963.

Morey, Adrian. *Bartholomew of Exeter*. Cambridge: Cambridge University Press, 1937.

Morris, Colin. *The Papal Monarchy. The Western Church from 1050 to 1250*. Oxford: Clarendon Press, 1989.

Morrisey, Francis. "Is the New Code an Improvement for the Law of the Church?" *Concilium*. #185. Editors, J. Provost and K. Walf. Edinburgh: T. and T. Clark Ltd., 1986.

Murray, Alexander. "Pope Gregory VII and His Letters." *Traditio* 22 (1966): 149-201.

Musurillo, Herbert A. *The Fathers of the Primitive Church*. New York: The New American Library, 1966.

Nicene and Post-Nicene Fathers. Vol. XII. Edited by P. Schaff and H. Wace. Reprint, Grand Rapids: Eerdmans, 1989.

Nicene and Post-Nicene Fathers. Vol. XIV. Edited by P. Schaff and H. Wace. Reprint, Grand Rapids: Eerdmans, 1991.

Noble, Thomas F. X. *The Republic of St. Peter*. Philadelphia: University of Pennsylvania Press, 1984.

Oberman, Heiko A. *Luther*. New Haven: Yale University Press, 1989.

Olin, John C. *Catholic Reform from Cardinal Ximenes to the Council of Trent 1495-1563*. New York: Fordham University Press, 1990.

The Once and Future Church. Edited by James A. Coriden. New York: Alba House, 1971.

Ostrogorsky, George. *History of the Byzantine State*. Translated by Joan Hussey. 1952; Reprint, New Brunswick: Rutgers University Press, 1969.

Papal Encyclicals. Vols. I-V. 1740-1978. Edited by Claudia Carlen Ihm. Ann Arbor, MI: The Pierian Press, 1990.

Pastor, Ludwig. *The History of the Popes from the Close of the Middle Ages*. Vol. XXXV, *Benedict XIV*. Translated by E. F. Peeler. St. Louis: B. Herder, 1961.

Paul VI. *Norms for Implementation of Four Council Decrees. Ecclesiae Sanctae*. August 8, 1966. Washington, DC: National Catholic Welfare Conference, 1966.

Pontifical Biblical Commission. "Can Women Be Priests?" *Origins* 6, 6 (July 1, 1976): 92-96.

Poole, A. L. *From Domesday Book to Magna Carta 1087-1216*. 2d ed. Oxford: Oxford University Press, 1955.

Quasten, Johannes. *Patrology*. Vol. I. Westminster, MD: Christian Classics, Inc., 1990.

Renouard, Yves. *The Avignon Papacy*. Translated by Denis Bethell. New York: Barnes and Noble, 1994.

Richards, Jeffrey. *Consul of God*. London: Routledge and Kegan Paul, 1980.

———. *The Popes and the Papacy in the Early Middle Ages 476-752*. London: Routledge and Kegan Paul, 1979.

Robinson, I. S. "Pope Gregory VII (1073-1085)." *The Journal of Ecclesiastical History* 36, 3(July 1985): 439-477.

Rondet, Henri. *The Grace of Christ.* Edited and translated by Tad W. Guzie. Westminster, MD: Newman Press, 1966.

Schatz, Klaus. *Papal Primacy.* Translated by J. Otto and L. Maloney. Collegeville, MN: The Liturgical Press, 1996.

Selected Letters of Pope Innocent III. Edited by C. R. Cheney and W. H. Semple. London: Thomas Nelson and Sons, 1953.

Smith, Denis Mack. *The Making of Italy 1796-1866.* Reissue, New York: Holmes and Meier, 1988.

Sources for the History of Medieval Europe. Edited by Brian Pullan. Oxford: Basil Blackwell, 1971.

Southern, R. W. *Robert Grosseteste.* 2d ed. Oxford: Clarendon Press, 1992.

———. *Western Society and the Church in the Middle Ages.* New York: Viking Penguin Inc., 1970.

"Synod of Bishops: The Final Report." *Origins* 15, 27 (December 19, 1985): 444-450.

Theissen, Gerd. *Sociology of Early Palestinian Christianity.* Translated by John Bowden. Philadelphia: Fortress Press, 1978.

Tierney, Brian. *Church Law and Constitutional Thought in the Middle Ages.* London: Variorum Reprints, 1979.

———. *The Crisis of Church and State 1050-1300.* 1964. Reprint, Toronto: University of Toronto Press, 1990.

———. *Foundations of the Conciliar Theory.* Cambridge: Cambridge University Press, 1955.

———. *Origins of Papal Infallibility 1150-1350.* Leiden: E. J. Brill, 1972.

Tillmann, Helene. *Pope Innocent III.* Translated by W. Sax. 1954. Reprint, Amsterdam: North Holland Publishing Co., 1980.

Ullmann, Walter. *The Growth of Papal Government in the Middle Ages.* 1955. 3d ed., Northampton: John Dickens and Co., 1970.

———. *The Origins of the Great Schism.* London: Burns Oates and Washbourne Ltd., 1948.

———. *A Short History of the Papacy in the Middle Ages.* 1972. Reprint, New York: Methuen and Co., 1982.

Vatican Council II. Vol. II. General editor, Austin Flannery. Northport, NY: Costello Publishing Co., 1982.

Vidler, Alec C. *The Modernist Movement in the Roman Church.* Cambridge: Cambridge University Press, 1934.

Wallace-Hadrill, J. M. *The Frankish Church.* Oxford: Clarendon Press, 1983.

Ware, Timothy. *The Orthodox Church.* 1963. New edition, New York: Penguin Books, 1993.

Wheatcroft, Andrew. *The Ottomans.* New York: Viking, 1993.

Wood, Charles T., editor. *Philip the Fair and Boniface VIII.* 2d ed. New York: Holt, Rinehart and Winston, 1971.

Wright, Gordon. *France in Modern Times.* 5th ed. New York: W. W. Norton, 1995.

Ziegler, Aloysius K. "Pope Gelasius and His Teaching on the Relation of Church and State." *Catholic Historical Review* 27, 4 (1942): 412-437.

Index